**Life-Span Developmental
Psychology**

METHODOLOGICAL ISSUES

CONTRIBUTORS

DONALD M. BAER

PAUL B. BALTES

P. M. BENTLER

RAYMOND B. CATTELL

LUTZ H. ECKENSBERGER

L. R. GOULET

ECKHARD H. HESS

FRANK H. HOOPER

JOHN R. NESSELROADE

JUM C. NUNNALLY

WILLIS F. OVERTON

SLOBODAN B. PETROVICH

HAYNE W. REESE

KLAUS F. RIEGEL

TODD R. RISLEY

K. WARNER SCHAIE

EDWIN P. WILLEMS

MONTROSE M. WOLF

LIFE-SPAN DEVELOPMENTAL PSYCHOLOGY

METHODOLOGICAL ISSUES

Edited by

JOHN R. NESSELROADE and HAYNE W. REESE

Department of Psychology
West Virginia University
Morgantown, West Virginia

   1973

ACADEMIC PRESS   New York   San Francisco   London

A Subsidiary of Harcourt Brace Jovanovich, Publishers

ACADEMIC PRESS, INC.
111 Fifth Avenue, New York, New York 10003

United Kingdom Edition published by
ACADEMIC PRESS, INC. (LONDON) LTD.
24/28 Oval Road, London NW1

LIBRARY OF CONGRESS CATALOG CARD NUMBER: 72-77362

PRINTED IN THE UNITED STATES OF AMERICA

Contents

v

4. Models of Development: Methodological Implications

Willis F. Overton and Hayne W. Reese

5. Research Strategies and Measurement Methods for Investigating Human Development

Jum C. Nunnally

6. Unraveling Maturational and Learning Development by the Comparative MAVA and Structured Learning Approaches

Raymond B. Cattell

List of Contributors

Numbers in parentheses indicate the pages on which the authors' contributions begin.

DONALD M. BAER (187), Department of Human Development, University of Kansas, Lawrence, Kansas

PAUL B. BALTES* (219), Department of Psychology, West Virginia University, Morgantown, West Virginia

P. M. BENTLER (145), Department of Psychology, University of California, Los Angeles, California

RAYMOND B. CATTELL (111), Laboratory of Personality Analysis, Psychology Building, Champaign, Illinois

LUTZ H. ECKENSBERGER (43), Psychologisches Institut der Universität des Saarlandes, Germany

L. R. GOULET (281), Department of Educational Psychology, University of Illinois at Urbana-Champaign, Urbana-Champaign, Illinois

ECKHARD H. HESS (25), Department of Psychology, The University of Chicago, Chicago, Illinois

FRANK H. HOOPER (299), Department of Home Management and Family Living, University of Wisconsin, Madison, Wisconsin

*Present address: College of Human Development, The Pennsylvania State University, University Park, Pennsylvania.

ix

JOHN R. NESSELROADE* (219), Department of Psychology, West Virginia University, Morgantown, West Virginia

JUM C. NUNNALLY (87), Department of Psychology, Vanderbilt University, Nashville, Tennessee

WILLIS F. OVERTON† (65), Department of Psychology, State University of New York at Buffalo, Buffalo, New York

SLOBODAN B. PETROVICH‡ (25), Department of Psychology, The University of Chicago, Chicago, Illinois

HAYNE W. REESE (65), Department of Psychology, West Virginia University, Morgantown, West Virginia

KLAUS F. RIEGEL (1), Department of Psychology, University of Michigan, Ann Arbor, Michigan

TODD R. RISLEY (177), Department of Human Development, University of Kansas, Lawrence, Kansas

K. WARNER SCHAIE (253), Department of Psychology, West Virginia University, Morgantown, West Virginia

EDWIN P. WILLEMS (197), Department of Psychology, University of Houston, Houston, Texas

MONTROSE M. WOLF (177), Department of Human Development, University of Kansas, Lawrence, Kansas

*Present Address: College of Human Development, The Pennsylvania State University, University Park, Pennsylvania.

†Present address: Department of Psychology, Temple University, Philadelphia, Pennsylvania.

‡Present address: Department of Psychology, University of Maryland, Baltimore, Maryland.

Preface

During the past three years, a series of conferences held at West Virginia University has focused on the general topic of Life-Span Developmental Psychology. The second conference, held in 1971 and reported in this volume, provided a forum for the discussion of a variety of methodological issues related to the study of developmental processes over the life-span.

The principal objectives of the Life-Span Conference have been not only to explicate, by successive approximation, the range of empirical phenomena with which a life-span developmental psychology should be concerned, but also to explore issues about theory, measurement, design, and data analysis which bear upon it. Although the situation is changing, a sufficiently large cadre of "true" life-span developmentalists does not exist to permit mounting such a conference wholly from their ranks. Consequently, our strategy was to invite several participants who, by their research activities, showed interest in related aspects of developmental psychology, and to challenge them to identify, formulate, and discuss critical methodological issues as, in their perception, they pertained to a life-span approach.

Augmenting the schedule of conference participants by researchers not ostensibly committed to a life-span orientation was not only necessary but may be seen as a virtue to the extent that the various perspectives and interests each offers serve to sharpen and refine the meaning of Life-Span Developmental Psychology. Until time renders possible a judgment based on hindsight you, the reader, must evaluate the success of the venture.

Acknowledgments

The editors gratefully acknowledge the cooperation and assistance of all those who helped to make the second Life-Span Conference a reality. Ray Koppelman, Provost for Research and Graduate Affairs, and K. Warner Schaie, Chairman of the Department of Psychology, arranged the necessary financial support. Graduate students in our program, whom the conference was designed to benefit directly, assumed many of the responsibilities related to playing host and discharged them admirably. They include William Arnold, Thomas Bartsch, William Birkhill, Barbara Buech, John Burke, Dana Cable, Nicholas Cavoti, Joseph Fitzgerald, Edward Forbes, Wanda Franz, John Friel, Carol Furry, Frances Hoyer, William Hoyer, Erich Labouvie, Gisela Labouvie, Anne Nardi, Diane Papalia, Leighton Stamps, and Richard Swanson.

Life-Span Developmental Psychology

METHODOLOGICAL ISSUES

Developmental Psychology and Society: Some Historical and Ethical Considerations

KLAUS F. RIEGEL

UNIVERSITY OF MICHIGAN
ANN ARBOR, MICHIGAN

Ethical issues, as commonly conceived, concern the individual's actions toward other individuals. Thus, the guidelines prepared by the American Psychological Association (1963) provide standards on professional interactions. By and large, they disregard the scientist's responsibility toward the society within which his discipline has emerged. The second ethical consideration concerns this connection and impels the scientist to be engaged in or, at least, to be conscious of social actions. In the following paper, attention will be directed exclusively toward the latter issue.

I. Social, Political, and Economic Bases of the Developmental Sciences

A. Historical Node Points in the Conception of Man

> . . . for what everyone wanted was denied by everyone else, and
> what resulted was what no one had wanted
>
> —FRIEDRICH ENGELS

1. Psychological Interpretations

Our concern with the history of civilization and, especially, our atempts to answer the question of whether a non-Western developmental psychology, for instance, a black psychology is possible, might be compared with the attempts of psychoanalysts. Inquiries into the distant past of our society are similar to their attempts at discovering points of choice and/or catastrophe in the life of an individual (Wyatt, 1963). The psychoanalyst essentially restricts his efforts to the discovery of these points; it is left to the patient to reconstruct his life in a new and "healthier" fashion. Similarly, our historical inquiries aim at uncovering points in time at which crucial choices were made. We can trace the history back to these points, but any distinct groups, such as minority groups, would have to construct their own new interpretation of life, a new philosophy of man and his development.

A great many writers have expressed similar viewpoints. In his theory of human development, Erikson (1968) distinguishes various binary choice points which lead to either trust or distrust, initiative or guilt, identity or identity confusion, etc. Erikson extended his interpretations to cultural developments, for instance, by relating the identity choice to the historical period of the Reformation and by demonstrating this interpretation through an analysis of the *Young Man Luther* (1958). It is tempting to suggest that minority groups within the Western civilization are faced with similar identity problems. Thus, like an individual, perhaps they need to go back to such points in history in order to find their identity and aim at its conceptual description.

In contrast to Erikson, Jung's work (Jacobi, 1962) has focused more strongly upon universal features of civilization. By looking at art, symbolism, customs, and social conventions across developmental and historical stages, he searched for those forms and expressions common to all men. Jung (unlike his teacher, Freud) emphasized the constructive aspects in the therapeutic process. It is not enough, he maintained, to rediscover and identify the choice points of the past, but it is necessary to construct new perspectives, a new philosophy of life. This should not be left to the patient; the therapist should be of active assistance.

In his *Comparative Psychology of Mental Development*, Werner (1926) drew parallels between the development of children and that of so-called primitive societies. Thus, he revived the recapitulation hypothesis of evolutionary theory and extended it to psychological and social conditions, claiming that children undergo developmental sequences similar to those that characterize historical progression. Psychopathological conditions are regarded as regressions to or fixations upon early developmental levels. With much support from cultural anthropologists, Werner restricted his interpretations to noncognitive behavior. In comparison, Piaget in his studies of *Genetic Epistemology* (1950) claimed that in the development of intellectual and logical operations as well, children recapitulate the steps through which societies had to pass in order to attain the knowledge of modern civilization.

We do not intend to draw upon these recapitulation models in order to specify different conceptualizations of man and his development. However, historical studies make us aware of critical node points at which alternative models of interpretation were still existent but, afterward, were repressed for the sake and success of the dominant civilization.

2. Pre-Grecian Civilizations

In a recent presentation, Smith (1970) delineated modes of psychological conceptualization which characterize the civilizations preceding the Greco–Roman period. While the latter has been described by an ontological dualism between being and becoming and modern Western civilization by the epistemological dualism between mind and body, the ancient civilizations of Sumer, Babylon, Assyria, or Egypt emphasized distinctly different dimensions and dichotomies (Moscati, 1957). The corresponding philosophies of the universe, life, and man need not concern us in detail, but it is of interest to analyze how these conceptions were overcome or repressed through the emergence of the Greco–Roman civilization.

During the early periods of this civilization, we find an array of different world views with which the Greeks became acquainted. This confrontation has been emphasized by several scholars. Nestle (1940) considered the entire development of Greek civilization as a struggle between *mythos* and *logos*, between the forces of darkness and light and—as elaborated by Nietzsche (1872) and Benedict (1934)—between the Dionysian and Appollonian ideals. During the history of the Greek civilization, the latter and thus rational thought attained dominance and the "alien" ecstatic forces of emotionality were successfully controlled and repressed.

Early in Greek history, the term "barbarian" denoted nothing else than "the other," i.e., a person of non-Greek origin. However, it soon came to indicate an uncivilized, alien, inferior person. This change characterizes the effort among ancient Greeks to facilitate their own cultural identity by downgrading persons and groups with different languages, habits, customs, and conceptions of man. Since many of these so-called barbarians had attained a much higher level of civilization than the Greeks of the Homeric period, their attempts appear highly artificial. The Greeks at that period were the "barbarians," indeed.

For similar reasons, romantic and idealized interpretations of Greek civilization have dominated modern historical views since the Renaissance and, especially, since the classicism of Winkelmann, Herder, and Goethe. Consequently, the Greek civilization appears as an elevated historical period initiated by a distinct historical break. Only recent research and interpretations have revealed the heritage from pre-Greek civilizations, especially from Persia, Mycenae, and Egypt.

It has been documented, for instance, that even such distinct and typically Greek innovations as the mathematics of Thales, Pythagoras, and Euclid had their origin in earlier civilizations. Pythagoras gained his insights while working as a surveyor in Egypt, and it is likely that the theorem named after him was already known in his host country.

It is not my intent to downgrade the astounding intellectual achievements of the Greeks. What I would rather like to note are the strenuous efforts within this civilization and on the part of sympathetic historians to maximize its distinctiveness and to neglect the transitions. At the beginning, alternatives were readily available; as the civilization advanced, these choices were successfully suppressed. If we look for alternative models of man and his development, we might have to go back to these early periods of a civilization at which different views coexisted. The pre-Greek period represents the first node point to be considered if we were to develop a non-Western developmental psychology.

3. Scholastic Period

At about 400 AD, the Greco–Roman civilization had collapsed and the Middle Ages had begun. Judean–Christian ideology penetrated into the areas around the Mediterranean and those north of it, i.e., the areas that were to become the basis of modern Western civilization. The intellectual life during this period aimed toward a consolidation of religious ideas and an absorption of the sociopolitical remains of the Roman empire. These developments led to the foundation of dogmatic theology and to the establishment of the administrative organization of the Christian church. At the same time, a slow revival of commerce and trade occurred, spreading from the northern shore of the Mediterranean toward the central parts of Europe. Here, between 700 and 800, a political consolidation took place leading to the formation of the Carolingian empire (Ducket, 1962; Hay, 1964).

Preceding these developments by about 150 years, an upsurge occurred in the southern area dominated by Semitic civilization (i.e., in the Arabian peninsula) conquering both politically and intellectually the whole Near East and, within less than a century, sweeping through northwestern Africa and the Iberian peninsula deep into France. The rapid advance of Islam brought about important intellectual conflicts representing a second historical node point in the modern conception of man.

At the time of the conquest and, especially, during the reign of Charlemagne, the spread of Semitic civilization was by no means regarded as a threat. As persuasively documented by Pirenne (1939), deep admiration existed for the more advanced civilization represented by the Arabs. Material and intellectual exchanges were sought and diplomatic relations were maintained. This beneficial competition was soon destroyed, however, through the continuing theological and philosophical attempts toward an identification of a Christian-Western civilization. Intolerance and degradation began to take the place of intellectual exchanges. The Moslem civilization was increasingly seen as alien, inferior and, in the derived sense, as "barbaric" or, as it was now to be called, "heretic."

Scholasticism, in attempting to consolidate Greek philosophy with Christian religion, represents the culmination of this development. Although the knowledge of Greek philosophy was transmitted through the Arabs, increasingly, this assistance was downgraded and the competing Semitic civilization, represented by Islam, was sharply rejected.

Scholasticism provided the "blueprint" for modern Western civilization in which the major philosophical and scientific trends were already implicitly represented. Comparable to the present-day actions within the Communist party of the Soviet Union, it marked off the acceptable boundaries within the Christian world. From this time onward, philosophy, sciences, and the arts had to operate within the confines of these conceptualizations or, if not, they were persecuted as heretical.

The dogmatic constraints imposed by scholasticism faced serious challenges during the liberating movements of the Renaissance. Even though stimulated by the rediscovery of Greco–Roman civilization, Renaissance philosophers such as Giordano Bruno and Thomas Campanella, as well as Francis Bacon, rejected the tradition of Greek philosophy which, by that time, had been thoroughly distorted and rigidified. Renaissance philosophy, therefore, regarded it as its main task to rejuvenate man's thinking by throwing off ancient philosophical constraints. That they succeeded in abandoning the scholastic dogmatizations of classical philosophy is well documented by the sudden burst of intellectual advances during the following historical periods, but ultimately, the Greco–Roman tradition in its purified form was not only retained but gained greater influence than ever before.

4. Conclusions

A first node point in the history of the conception of man occurred at the end of the period prior to the Greco–Roman civilization. We know least about these developments, but from the little that we do know, we comprehend the attempts to downgrade influences outside Greece and originating within the older civilizations of the Near East. These rejections served to establish the identity of the Greco–Roman civilization, a tradition which laid the foundation of our modern conception of man. In order to gain a fuller understanding of man and his development, however, we might have to return to these earlier, alternative interpretations.

A historical node point of greater impact occurred at the end of the prescholastic period of the late Middle Ages. Originally, the influence of the outside civilization, represented by Islam, was regarded as highly beneficial. In the search for an identity within the Western civilization, these connections were soon denounced, however, by the secular and spiritual leaders of the Christian church. Among these leaders, the Scholastics represent the most important intellectual group explicating the "blueprint" of modern Western civilization.

A more dramatic challenge yet is being provided by the philosophy and dogmatism which emerged in the Soviet Union. While we shall return to this issue at a later occasion, we draw attention next to the postscholastic developments in Central Europe, which, again, led to the differentiation of competing conceptions of man and his development.

B. Open and Closed Developmental Systems in Western Sciences

> One of the chief values of existential–phenomenological thought is the reemphasis of the **unity** between man and world. This is in direct opposition to the Cartesian model, upon which most of nineteenth century thought is based, which stressed the absolute dichotomy between man and world.
>
> —AMEDEO GIORGI

Qualitative growth models imply a progression in leaps and are sensitive to multigenerational and multicultural differences. They were developed in continental Europe with its mercantilistic economic systems. Quantitative growth models imply a continuous progression toward an abstract achievement ideal. They were developed in the capitalistic countries, especially England and the United States, with their emphasis on free trade, competition, and entrepreneurism. In the past, we have outlined these models (Riegel, 1972b) and have shown the dependency of their development upon social, political, and economic conditions (Riegel, 1972a).

Related to though not identical with this comparison is the distinction between open and closed developmental systems.[1] In the past, developmental psychology, being dominated by the notion of continuous growth, has shown a preference for open developmental systems. According to such an interpretation, growth consists in the acquisition of bits and pieces of information, habits, or experiences which are being accumulated in a subject's repertoire, making him increasingly more able. If, at a given time, certain problems cannot be resolved, the *individual will have to acquire more information so that he finally may succeed.* In contrast to the notion of unlimited expansion, a closed developmental system is characterized by the principle that *everything that grows, grows at the expense of something else.* Such a model assumes limits in basic capacities. Development consists in an increasingly finer organization and, perhaps, in systematic restruc-

---

[1]The distinction between open and closed biological and psychological systems has been introduced by Bertalanffy (1960). In contrast to his physical models, we will emphasize changes in internal organization of these systems. This distinction as well as the one between quantitative and qualitative changes, has been comprehensively discussed in an excellent chapter by Reese and Overton (1970).

turing of information, habits, and experiences, but not in a ceaseless addition of new materials.

(a) Our distinction of open and closed developmental systems has a wide range of applications. Some of the most dramatic comparisons are those of political, economic, and administrative operations. Here, the concept of open systems has become singularly associated with the development of the modern industrialized world. Both West and East, Democrats and Republicans subscribe wholeheartedly and completely to the social and economic philosophy of ceaseless expansions. Whenever problems arise, such as a business slump, a high rate of unemployment, a trade deficit, an instability of international exchange rates etc., the single, overall solution proposed consists in accelerating production and increasing spending, but rarely in reorganizations. Undoubtedly,there are variations between different camps; the Democrats willingly subscribe to Keynes and deficit spending, whereas the Republicans are more reluctant and aim for a balanced budget; the farmers care less about the unemployed; the urbanites favor increases in welfare subsidies. However, in spite of any specific and often forceful disagreements, the belief in the open system is not questioned. In contrast, closed systems are seen as backward, as unable to produce solutions, and, generally, as representing the antithesis of growth. As Looft (1971) has put it so ably, our decisions and thinking are dominated by the "psychology of more, more, more."

Underdeveloped, rural societies are frequently cited as counterexamples to open social and economic systems. Typically, members of such communities have been engaged in the same activities for countless generations. Changes in these activities are often viewed by the participants with suspicion and, if possible, prevented. It would be inappropriate, however, to limit the description of closed systems to underdeveloped societies. There are numerous other communities which, though stable in the size of their population or in the area occupied, have shown considerable growth through internal reorganization, better utilization of their resources, and more efficient planning. Most of the former city states in central Europe as well as in the eastern Mediterranean are cases in point. Today, the smaller European countries such as Sweden, the Netherlands, and Switzerland serve as outstanding examples, having increased their productivity and the quality of their products, education, and welfare to a degree much higher than that of the most advanced expansionist nations.

The differences between open and closed social systems are also revealed by administrative policies. For example, the uncritical support of continuous land annexation in communal development has been challenged by the policy of zero growth aiming toward improvements of internal organization, such as traffic, transportation, schooling, housing, and recreational facilities. Similarly, in the evaluations of our large professional and scientific organizations, we have become cognizant of the strains caused by our commitment to an open system. For example, we have realized that the disarray of such organizations as the American Psychological Association can result in nothing but its substitution by smaller, structurally more efficient (and aesthetically more pleasing) organizations. The same fate might befall large universities and colleges which, by committing themselves to ceaseless expansion, have sacrificed organizational efficiency and the quality of higher education. On the basis of these experiences, it is reasonable to reconsider the underlying administrative philosophy of such organizations and formulate alternate ways of conceptualization and operation.

(b) In regard to psychological functioning, open systems consider development as a ceaseless expansion, produced by the addition of bits and pieces of information, habits, or experiences. The more material an individual has accumulated, the brighter, more knowledgeable and successful he is thought to be. A good example of a closed developmental system is the interpretation of Piaget's developmental theory by McLaughlin (1963). This author described the four major developmental periods of Piaget as successive enlargements of the child's ability to operate with classes. During the sensori-motor period, the child attends to one concept only and does not discriminate along any dimension or attribute. During the period of preoperational intelligence, the child handles two concepts along one dimension, such as red versus nonred. During the period of concrete operational intelligence, the child succeeds in double classifications of four concepts along two dimensions, and during the period of formal operational intelligence he performs triple classifications of eight concepts. Thus the child apprehends and operates with the same material in successively more differentiated and structurally more complex ways. At the beginning, he lacks discrimination; at the end he makes succinct differentiations and performs complex operations and judgments.

While McLaughlin's interpretation might be accommodated within a closed developmental system, Piaget's own theory requires modifications. To Piaget, the intellectual operations of a child during successive periods of development are characterized by distinctly different logics that are only partially embedded in one another. Development does not merely consist in the discrimination along an additional dimension, but in the appearance of new types of operations. Thus, at each period, the child acquires a unique logic which he continues to improve until, suddenly, he shifts toward a more complex form of operation. Piaget's theory, therefore, represents an open system which, during long-term development, incorporates different closed systems, i.e., a system that accumulates information but also changes its internal organization (see Van den Daele, 1969).

(c) Piaget's theory of cognitive development resembles the theory of scientific growth proposed by Kuhn (1962). Kuhn distinguished between paradigmatic and normal sciences. The former provide new perspectives and interpretations of data either already available or collected in view of the proposed paradigms. Different scientific paradigms may coexist, such as the wave theory and the particle theory of light. They shift the attention to new scientific aspects or to those disregarded in the past. Like Piaget's theory of cognitive development, Kuhn's interpretation proposes an accumulation of information within paradigms, a process which he compares with the solving of a jigsaw puzzle. Major progress in sciences is brought about, however, by shifts from one paradigm to another.

Kuhn's interpretation of the history of sciences, like Piaget's theory of cognitive development, suggests a synthesis between closed and open developmental systems. "Pure" cases of the latter have traditionally dominated interpretations of the history of sciences. Progress was seen as a ceaseless accumulation of information, leading to ever-increasing "factual" knowledge, thereby stripping "nature" of its secrets. Such an interpretation is compatible with utopian views of political and cultural history as expressed in both democratic and socialistic theories. A "pure" interpretation of political and cultural history in terms of a closed system, on the other hand, has been proposed by Spengler (1918–1922). According to his view, a civilization starts with a basic theme which through artistic, philosophical, and scientific advances is explicated in successive steps until, toward the end, it deteriorates through overdifferentiation. Even though such an interpretation, when adopted to describe the history of philosophy or sciences (as well as for the description of individual development), is one-sided, it provides a challenging alternative to the traditional view of history in which events follow events and persons follow persons without any explicit origin or goals.

C. Dialectic Interactionism in Soviet Psychology

> *The important thing is not to grasp the laws behind the objective world, but to make use of these objective laws and employ them to actively change the world.*
>
> —MAO TSE-TUNG

In Section A, we described historical node points in the conception of man. In Section B, we compared two major models of development predominant in modern Western behavioral and social sciences. This section represents a further historical extension which ought to be of interest for at least two reasons: (1) It attempts to synthesize the two developmental models previously described; and (2) it represents a node point in the conception of man which we are experiencing in its very own emergence and, thus, concerns future actions rather than biases of the past. For this reason, the issues to be raised are intimately tied to the major theme of this chapter, i.e., to the ethical problems in the interactions between individual and society.

The two models of growth which we have described conceive of development as either an accumulation of external information by an essentially passive organism or as the spontaneous emergence of new modes of operation for which the environment merely provides information as necessary material in order to enable the organism to make his own selections. Soviet psychology incorporates both these viewpoints and, thus, overcomes the dualistic conception outlined by Reese and Overton (1970). In this synthesis, new operations represent the internalization of external structures, such as language, but these operations also represent the outcome of internal structural processes. Both the material basis within and the material basis outside of the organism represent origins of interaction processes through which activity and consciousness emerge.

The trends in Soviet philosophy and sciences are comparable to those which led to the consolidation of Greek philosophy with Christian thoughts and beliefs. Much as the Scholastics incorporated Aristotelian philosophy but warded off the influences of the Skeptics, Epicureans, and Stoics, so does Soviet ideology incorporate the dialectic philosophy of Hegel but rejects his idealism and Mach's positivism. Whereas the church and the scholastics repressed the Islamic influences (although Arab scholars were the main transmitter of knowledge from the Greco–Roman period to the late medieval world), Soviet philosophers and scientists seem to remain free of such external "threat" and, therefore, are directing additional defenses against Western philosophy whose traditions they, nevertheless, cultivate and transcend.

1. The Beginning of Soviet Psychology

Among the few surveys of Soviet psychology, the treatise of Payne (1968) on S. L. Rubinstein seems by far most sensitive toward the intrinsic dynamic of Soviet sciences. According to Payne, the post-Revolutionary history of Russian psychology can be subdivided into the Mechanistic Period (1917–1930), the Dialectic Period (1930–1950), and the period of Synthesis (after 1950).

(a) The period immediately after the Russian Revolution saw the elimination of the existing teaching and research traditions which were following Western, especially German, introspective psychology and philosophical idealism. This development was terminated at the time of the First All-Russian Psychological Congress in 1923 and through the appointment of Kornilov as Director of the Moscow Psychological Institute in 1924. At the same time, Pavlov and, especially, Bekhterev established themselves firmly. By considering behavior as a biosocial phenomenon, they denied any distinct place to psychology. This view was opposed by Kornilov as mechanistic and reductionistic and for failing to consider the dialectic roots of communism according to which the objective and subjective have to be brought into an organic synthesis.

During the ensuing controversy between the mechanistic materialists (who considered all changes as quantitative and reducible to biological contingencies) and the dialectic materialists (who insisted on Hegel's notion of "dialectic leaps" through which qualitative transformations were achieved) the latter received strong support through the posthumous publication of Lenin's "Philosophical Notebook" (1929) and through the efforts of Deborin. Although the latter gained a clear victory over the mechanistic materialists, he was soon criticized for adopting Hegel's idealistic dialectics without sufficient consideration for the materialistic reformulation by Marx and Engels. Nevertheless, dialectics, stripped of its idealistic features, continued to win out over mechanistics, as confirmed at the First All-Union Conference for Human Behavior in 1930.

(b) The period from 1930 to 1950 was characterized by intensive criticisms and reevaluations. Of greatest consequence was the purge of the educational movement known as Pedology.

According to a decree by the Central Committee of the Communist Party in 1936, this movement (especially connected with the work of Blonskii) had undermined the responsibility of the teacher and developed a laissez-faire if not a negative attitude toward so-called backward children. The use of psychological tests had been accepted for the categorization of these children who, then, were kept in their "backward" states by assigning them to special schools in which "bad habits" became even harder to correct. Individual differences were either related to inherited biological factors or to the social environment. The proponents of the former view, the "biologists," came under sharp attack for preserving the aims of the bourgeois classes instead of emphasizing the duty of the educators toward active modification of the child's development. Instead of accepting the child's development as predetermined, the participatory role of the teacher as a representative of the historical–cultural conditions of the society became the dominant theme not only for education, but also for behavioral and social sciences in general.

Although criticized for his support of the bifurcation into hereditary and environment, Vygotskii (1962), the most prominent "sociologist," was credited with directing full attention to the normative effects of the sociocultural factors. This interpretation was consonant with the dialectic materialism of Marx, Engels, and Lenin, especially since Vygotskii emphasized the historical impact of these factors (1929). Consciousness, according to this interpretation, emerges through historical evolutions which, in turn, originate from a material basis through human labor.

The victory of dialectics was greatly enhanced by Vygotskii. After his early death, his arguments were carried forward by his associates and students, especially Leont'ev and Luria. Partially because of the disruptions of the war, there was no major confrontation during the late 1930s and the 1940s, and it did not become apparent until the late 1950s how thoroughly Vygotskii's interpretations had introduced the dialectic materialism of the "classics" into psychology. When consolidated with Pavlov's interpretations of the "first and second signaling systems," a theory could emerge in full conformity with the goals of the Communistic ideology. This synthesis has been most clearly elaborated in the system of psychology proposed by S. L. Rubinstein.

(c) The third major period in the history of Soviet psychology was initiated by the Pavlov Conference in 1950. This meeting was dominated by physiologists and medical researchers, with psychologists in a small minority and on the defensive throughout. The conference had the declared purpose of firmly establishing Pavlov's legacy and, primarily, consisted in proclamations of allegiance coupled with self-criticisms of those who had failed to appreciate his contributions in the past. Stated more positively, the conference by rejecting psychophysical parallelism of Western thinking, adopted dialectic interactionism. Such an interactionism had been made possible through the development of Pavlov's theory of the "second signaling system" and, thus, the conference accepted and promoted this change in interpretation with its far-reaching consequences.

According to Pavlov, "conditioned and unconditioned reflexes realize the connection of the organism with its environment and are directed towards the maintenance of a state of equilibrium between the systems of the organism and external conditions [Payne, 1968, p. 14]." The activity involved in the formation of this connection is called "higher nervous activity" in distinction from "lower nervous activity" which serves to integrate the different parts of the organism. The stimuli from the environment, signaling the objects necessary for the organism's survival, represent the "first signaling system," which is common to men and animals. Through his culture and history, man has developed, however, a second system which "does not directly signalize [sic] reality but rather the data of the first signaling system [Payne, 1968, p. 14]." The second signaling system allows for a much higher degree of abstraction and for an expansion of activities resulting in the cultural–historical achievements of society.

Pavlov's extension of his early theory of conditioning thus paved the way for a consolidation of the dialectic materialism of Marx, Engels, and Lenin with the mechanistic materialism of Pavlov's earlier work. This possibility was realized and accepted by the participants of the Pavlov Conference. One of the most penetrating proponents of this development was S. L. Rubinstein.

2. The Psychology of S. L. Rubinstein

Rubinstein's synthesis tries to overcome the mind–body dualism which has remained unbridgeable in Western thought and had led to development of several different "psychologies." On the one hand, the introspectionists focused exclusively upon consciousness. However, because of its absolute subjective character, consciousness has remained unattainable for scientific description. The methodologically powerful movement of behaviorism (being intrinsically weak in its epistemological basis) did not fare any better. According to Rubinstein, behaviorism represents "vulgar mechanism" and a mere denial or inverse of introspectionism.

(a) Rubinstein's synthesis emphasizes the unity of consciousness and behavior. The terms do not denote separate systems, nor is the former all internal and the latter external, but both interpenetrate each other. Consciousness is not a passive contemplative state, but an activity; behavior is not merely a movement, but is directed by internal organization. On the one hand, activity objectifies the inner-subjective world; on the other hand, the objective world is reflected in and by the subject. This distinction is very similar to Piaget's comparison of accomodation (of the subject to the object) and assimilation (of the object to the subject). Both processes are interdependent leading to adaptation of the subject. Rubinstein refers to Marx: "By acting on the external world and changing it, he, at the same time, changes his own nature [Marx, 1954, p. 177]."

For Rubinstein, the study of the ontogenesis of consciousness is not conceivable without the study of phylogenesis. Piaget likewise emphasized both genetic and individual epistemology; development in neither case consists in the continuous accumulation of information, but progresses in qualitative leaps. At the beginning, development of organisms is determined for Rubinstein by the laws of biological evolution. At higher levels of phylogenesis, however, development becomes codetermined by the laws of sociohistorical evolution. In particular, man, through his activities and labor, transforms his environment and creates new conditions for individual development. As stated by Payne (1968), man "creates himself by his own labor—by transforming nature to transform himself [p. 90]."

When focusing upon the ontogenesis, the individual's development consists in the acquisition of human culture through his own activities. In rejecting pedology, Rubinstein insisted that this process has to be supplemented by the activity of the society. In other words, it is insufficient merely to point out the sociohistorical conditions of the culture; if necessary, society also has the duty of imposing these conditions upon the growing organism. The activities have to permeate in both directions: from the individual to the culture and from the culture to the individual. Knowledge is acquired through the individual's activities, but the activities of the society are of equal importance. Knowledge is social in nature.

(b) In the preceding paragraph, we emphasized the dialectic interactions between the individual and sociohistorical conditions. These conditions are codetermined by a second system of interactions, i.e., those between psychic states and higher nervous activities. Rubinstein did not elaborate these interactions at length, but referred to the work of Pavlov and his followers. With this renewed emphasis on the biological, material basis, Rubinstein completed his synthesis. In the words of Payne (1968),

> The relation of the psychic to the material world is fundamentally two-fold: to the inner matter of the brain (this relation constitutes the psychic in the quality of higher nervous activity) and to the outer matter of the external world in which relationship the psychic

takes on the quality of ideal and subjective. The first quality Rubinstein calls the *ontological* aspect of the psychic; the second he calls *gnoseological* or theory-of-knowledge aspect [p. 98].

Rubinstein supported Lenin's dialectic notion of *reflection*, i.e., of the "mirroring" of external reality in consciousness. Thus, he reinterpreted Pavlov's notion of reflexes, which in the view of most scholars (especially, the "vulgar mechanists" of American behaviorism) represent *reactions*, i.e., external responses of an organism to external stimuli. In contrast, Rubinstein emphasized reflexes as basic relational units which, though triggered by external stimuli, are also being modified by the responses produced, or rather through the ongoing activity of the organism. This mutual relationship is explicated in Lenin's theory by adding the concept of *refraction* to that of *reflection*. "Not only does Action A . . . change the nature of B but the inner characteristics of B change or refract the action of A. The inner characteristics of the object acted upon behave like a prism through which the action of the agent is refracted [Payne, 1968, p. 103]."

(c) The seriousness with which the notion of dialectic interactions penetrates all of Rubinstein's thinking is most clearly revealed by the concept of "constitutive relationism" which he adopted from Hegel and Lenin. Lenin (1929) emphasized that: "Every concrete thing, every concrete something, stands in multifarious and often contradictory relations to everything else: ergo it is itself and some other [p. 124]." In Payne's (1968) formulation, ". . . every phenomenon or thing is determined and constituted by its relation to all the other phenomena of reality [p. 99]." Consequently, psychic states have a plurality of structure. There are several intrinsic structures, relating higher nervous activities to the brain, and several extrinsic structures, relating these psychic activities to the external reality. The emphasis upon structure implies that relations are both logically and genetically prior to the elements which they connect; our experiences are always contextual, and meaning, for instance, is prior to words (Riegel, 1970a, b).[2]

Rubinstein's interpretations imply nothing more than a reformulation of the mind–body problem. Traditionally, the solution of this problem has been sought by determining the nature of both the mind and the body, and then contemplating their interdependence. For Rubinstein, the solution has to proceed in the reverse order. The relationship determines how we conceive of the mind and the body. As we have seen, the psychic is determined by the dual relationship to outer and inner matter. However, matter also appears in this dual relationship. For

[2]Strong support for such an interpretation is given by Piaget in his recent book on structuralism (1970b).

instance, a crystal is determined by its inner atomic structure as well as by its relationships to the external, material conditions. Thus, the boundaries between mind and matter become fluid. Similar to Leibniz, "the material world has traits which are, in some faint way, similar to consciousness and which provide the premises for its natural evolution. The psychic is therefore one link in the chain of properties of the material world [Payne, 1968, p. 106]."

The two anchoring conditions of the internal and external material reality characterize the new dualism of Soviet philosophy. Since both represent processes rather than fixed entities (such as the mind and body), they relate to the contrast between ontogenetic and phylogenetic changes. Psychic activities emerge through the interaction of both. Thus, mind and body collapse upon the intersection of these two interaction processes. At the same time, psychic activities are relegated to a secondary position. Their study has to be founded upon that of internal biochemical processes as well as upon that of external sociocultural processes. Psychology without these foundations is fictitious.

3. Conclusions

Rubinstein's synthesis reformulates on a relational basis, and thereby overcomes, the old mind–body dualism of Descartes. With the exception of the latter himself, who described an interactionistic interpretation on a somewhat superficial level (by placing the locus of interaction in the pineal gland), Western philosophy and psychology either adopted parallelism or materialistic and idealistic reductionism (Jessor, 1958). These Western approaches placed all their emphasis on the separate descriptions of these two entities; they studied their relative contributions in terms of the biogenetic and environmental influences upon development, but by splitting them apart at the beginning, they precluded the possibility of bringing them together again.

This split also characterizes the two major Western branches of developmental psychology which, at a different occasion (Riegel, 1972a), we have called its "capitalistic" and "mercantilistic" modes. Only recently have attempts been made, notably by Piaget (1970b) and by Chomsky (1968), to emphasize interaction processes rather than parallel descriptions. Both these scholars have restricted their discussions to mental states. Thus,they have created a neomentalism and have failed to emphasise the interaction of the growing organism with the sociohistorical contingencies. Rubinstein, by reviving the early interpretations of Vygotskii but, most important, by taking the "classics" seriously (i.e., Marx, Engels, and Lenin), has provided a synthesis which leads to new perspectives in social and psychological philosophy. In agreement with Piaget and Chomsky, the individual is no longer seen as a passive recipient of external information, but in contrast to Piaget and Chomsky, the notion of activity is not restricted to the individual alone.

II. Phenomenal, Logical, and Existential
Bases of Sciences and Knowledge

> *All scientists are participant–observers in their own systems . . . .*
> *Hence the system changes as it is studied and **because** it is studied.*
> *There can be no myth of an unchanging universe with the scientist*
> *acquiring abstract knowledge about it.*
>
> —KENNETH E. BOULDING

Psychological operations have been categorized into those that focus upon motor-productive, sensory-perceptual, and symbolic-structural processes. Recently, this distinction has been emphasised in Bruner's (1964) description of *enactive*, *iconic*, and *symbolic* modes of representation. By enactive representation, Bruner means

> . . . a mode of representing past events through appropriate motor response. We cannot, for example, give an adequate description of familiar sidewalks or floors over which we habitually walk, nor do we have much of an image of what they are like. Yet we get about them without tripping even looking much. . . . Iconic representation summarizes events by the selective organization of percepts and of images, by the spatial, temporal, and qualitative structures of the perceptual field and their transformed images. . . . Finally, a symbol system represents things by design features that include remoteness and arbitrariness. A word neither points directly to its referent here and now, nor does it resemble it as a picture. . . . The other property of language that is crucial is its productiveness in combination, far beyond what can be done with images or acts [p. 2].

In this section, we will use this distinction in a quite different sense from Bruner's, namely to characterize and evaluate the state of knowledge and science. Generally, in Western thinking, the criterion for knowledge and science has been a sensory-perceptual one, or, as we shall call it, *iconic*; the "truth" of a scientific statement is evaluated by the degree to which it corresponds to sensory data, regardless of whether these are of a common-sense type or are attainable only under complex observational conditions. Since even the simplest statement implies a structure of logic and grammar, the iconic criterion blends into that on the *symbolic* level. Here, in conjunction with sensory-perceptual information, an isomorphism is sought between the structure of the observed phenomena and that of their formal description. While Western scientists and philosophers have emphasized the second criterion through the elaboration of mathematical formalism and the first through empirical research, they have hardly ever considered *enactive* representation as a criterion for knowledge and science i.e., they have disregarded the effects of particular scientific contributions upon science as well as upon society.

In contrast to the truth criterion adopted, the scientific methodology has often been of the opposite type. Developmental psychology, for example, has preferred to study enacted, "objectified" changes in a proactive manner, e.g., in verbal or psychomotor skills; the truth criterion, however, has been of the iconic type. History, in contrast, has been restricted to the study of iconic changes in a retrospective manner. While there seems to be concurence in the study of history between the truth criterion and the method of approach (in that both are of the iconic type), experienced historical changes affect us enactively. This issue has neither been studied nor has it been emphasized as a criterion of historical knowledge (see, however, Lynd, 1971).

Although most of the problems raised cannot be brought to a satisfactory conclusion, it seems obvious enough that both disciplines, developmental psychology and history, would benefit greatly if they were to supplement their own approach by adopting the research strategy of the other discipline. This would be especially desirable since changes in the individual and those in the society are intimately confounded. The adoption of the alternate strategies would lead to a phenomenological retrospective developmental psychology and to an "objectified" proactive, nomothetic history. The latter would be able to utilize the methodologies and formal theories of developmental psychology; it would become a developmental sociology (Riegel, 1969). The former would be forced to appreciate more forcefully the individual's unique experiences in developmental progression as well as the mutual dependency of the changes in the individual and those of society, i.e., the implications for social actions and responsibility.

1. Iconic Evaluations

Western philosophy has methodically abandoned a realism which assumes nothing less than the existence of a physical world with its substances and movements. Locke rejected the notion that our impressions of hardness, color, warmth, etc. directly represent the physical world—they rather represent the interpretations of the observer. Nevertheless, Locke did not question the existence of the physical world which, in his opinion, causes our sensations and impressions.

The subjective contributions of the observer were more strongly emphasized by Hume and the positivists of the late 19th century, especially by Mach. Consequently, it became necessary to explain how different observers, on the basis of their subjective experiences, could, nevertheless, agree on the quality of these experiences, e.g., could agree to denote some experiences as red, warm, hard, etc. The positivists, especially Poincaré, proposed that such agreements are the results of conventions and, thus, they emphasized the importance of sociocultural contingencies. Unlike the materialists, they regarded these contingencies as arbitrary inventions without a physical basis. By declaring that sensations, perceptions, and cognitions are the only information available to us and that statements about the existence of a real physical world are metaphysical speculations, the positivists found themselves, surprisingly, in the company of the phenomenologists (who did not share their elementaristic zeal, however), as well as the rationalists such as Descartes who, after all, maintained that all our knowledge comes from the mind and is in our mind (downgrading, of course, reliance on sensory data).

All of the philosophers mentioned share a commitment to cognitive judgments. The criteria for truth lie exclusively in rational decisions, regardless of whether knowledge is gained from a sensory basis or through thinking alone. For Locke, the truth criterion is external and either lies in the primary qualities of the real world or is based upon the linguistic agreements of the community. For Hume and Mach, these conventions remain the sole criterion. For Descartes, the truth criterion is internal and, ultimately, consists in rational self-observations, even though, like Locke, he did not take this idea to its radical conclusion, but reintroduced sensory data, through the mediation of God, from the real, mechanistic world.

The positivists of the late 19th century, especially Poincaré and Avenarius, realized that it would be insufficient to reach agreements on labels for subjective experiences, but that knowledge and sciences also depend upon the logical, syntactic organization of the labeled impressions and interpretations. Earlier, these structures were thought of as intrinsically given and, subsequently, as universally true and immediately apparent to the observer. Kant, for instance, insisted upon the universality of Euclidean space and, therefore, upon the indisputable status of traditional geometry and algebra. The positivists, however, regarded the choice of logical and syntactic structures as arbitrary and dependent upon social conventions as well as upon their utility in providing economical though comprehensive descriptions for a particular field of investigation. With this shift, they supported an increased flexibility in the development and application of formal systems to empirical research. In physics, for instance, they justified the shift from the Euclidean geometry to those of Lobachevski or Riemann. In the behavioral and social sciences, they promoted the utilization of a great variety of mathematical and logical models.

2. Enactive Evaluations

Among the epistemologists, Marx was one of the first who, by denying the arbitrary character of social and linguistic conditions, emphasized the noncognitive basis of knowledge and sciences. The material conditions force man to activity; through his labor he produces a world which, in turn, imposes changes upon him. The internal and external material conditions are realized only through the actions which thus become part of the criterion for truth and knowledge. Instead of asking how one can gain distinct and firm knowledge, the question now becomes how one's actions change the world (and knowledge) and how the changed world affects the individual.

The shift from iconic to enactive truth criteria is not only characteristic for the Marxism of the 19th century, but also for existentialism as initiated by Schopenhauer, Kierkegaard, Nietzsche, and others. In contrast to the material deterministic foundation of Marx's philosophy, this movement aims toward non-scientific or antiscientific interpretations and, for this reason, is of lesser interest in the present context. The emphasis on an action criterion for knowledge has gained momentum in the Western world through the realization of political injustice and social irrelevance of some of our scientific efforts. Among several contemporary proponents ranging from Heisenberg (1952) to Boulding (1967) and Merleau-Ponty (1963), Amedeo Giorgi (1969) has written a thoughtful analysis of the socioepistemological problems from a phenomenological–existentialistic point of view. Klaus Holzkamp (1970) has provided action-related interpretations of knowledge and sciences through his critical review of the more conservative theories.

The behavioral sciences, in their attempt to reach the standards of the natural sciences, have made extraordinary efforts to improve their methodological bases and the formalism of their theories. This has led to a disregard for the relevance of psychological investigations. So long as a study was based on a firm methodological foundation—it was argued—any type of investigation would add at least some small bits of information to the growing repertoire of psychological knowledge and thus, ultimately, would contribute to the advancement of science and society. This attitude has produced the enormous and rapidly increasing number of research reports by which the progress and status of a science has been evaluated. Little or no attention was given to the question of the usefulness of the material. The criterion of social relevance remained overshadowed by the request for methodological rigor and abstract formalism.

To the philosophical realist, the goal of sciences was to detect the "laws of nature." Any social or political considerations would only sidetrack the scientist in this task and thus were not only inappropriate, but positively harmful to his efforts. Even more so to the rationalists, social relevance of science was of little concern; truth was found through contemplative introspections and, ultimately, was guaranteed through the intervention of God. With the advent of the positivists, social factors gained importance as a basis for scientific knowledge. Subsequently, societies with different languages and social conventions might not only produce different types of sciences, but also arrive at different scientific "laws." Thus, these philosophers emphasized the social determination of the sciences, but still paid little or no attention to the problem of how scientific activities would, in turn, influence the conditions of the society. Scientific efforts were seen as passive reflections of external though culturally dependent conditions. The active normative character of scientific efforts was not yet emphasized.

Much as Piaget and Vygotskii provided us with new interpretations of children's development, so do we need new perspectives of the growth and the direction of knowledge and science. In contrast to the behaviorists, Piaget maintained that intellectual development does not consist merely in the passive accumulation of data from the environment, but the individual participates actively in a search and exploration process. For Piaget, the environment still represents little else than a source for material from which the individual selects according to his wishes and level of intellectual competence. Vygotskii and Rubinstein, however, emphasized also the active role of the environment in developmental processes.

For Piaget, a scientist actively imposes modes of interpretations upon environmental data. For Rubinstein, these modes not only represent possible ways of interrelating scientific phenomena, but also signify the wider social context into which they are to be embedded. Thus, the scientist needs to ascend a hierarchy of interpretations, each successive level representing a wider context and emphasizing more strongly the social significance of observations and interpretations. As he proceeds, the scientist has to ask himself what effect any of his interpretations will have upon the society of which his science is a part. It is not only his task to provide interpretations of his scientific observations, but also to determine how society and the changes in the society brought about will influence individuals' future activities and well being.

Scientific activities consist in more than the recording of so-called facts. They involve a weighting for social significance. These evaluations are not left to the reviewer and the critic, but each scientist is, from the beginning, expected to consider his activities in regard to modifications which they produce (Lynd, 1971). Universal criteria for scientific activities are, of course, hard to provide. These criteria will vary from society to society. Thus, the criteria developed by a socialistic society will differ from those of a capitalistic society (see Stalin, 1951). What we can attempt, however, is to compare different conceptualizations of man and his development on a cultural, historical basis. In this way, we may clarify some of the issues in the determination of criteria for social relevance in scientific activities.

3. Alternative Conceptions of Man and His Development

In summary, we may contrast four major viewpoints of man and his development. The first regards both the environment and the organism as essentially passive. Such theorizing is based upon the sensationalism, associationism, and mechanism of British philosophy as initiated by Locke. Combinations of events in the environment which happen to occur in the presence of a subject are imprinted into his mind. On the basis of the contiguity of these stimuli, their frequency, recency, etc., the mind of the individual, originally a black box or *tabula rasa*, is being built up. Modern proponents of such interpretations can be found among the behaviorists and students of verbal learning.

The educational philosophy implied in the first model has hardly ever been rigorously applied. Even the most rigid trainer, sticking firmly to drill, memorization, and rehearsal, chooses his material and reinforcements selectively and, thus, determines actively the direction of the learning process. In a more general sense, however, this model represents the status quo behind which the teachers and administrators of our public educational systems try to hide. All too often, their main concern seems to be to stay out of discordant situations, be they simple quarrels among two or three first graders or racial or political strifes which tear apart the whole nation. By maintaining that these conflicts have to be worked out between the individuals themselves or within the groups, these teachers fail to see that their evasion, nevertheless, implies a decisive choice, which generally lends the upper hand to the physically rather than intellectually more forceful individual and to the dominant power group.[3]

The second type of theory retains the notion of a passive environment, but introduces the individual as an active agent. Such viewpoints were very common among the Greeks and were reintroduced into philosophy through Leibniz's monadology. Monads change their internal state from passivity and trance to activity and consciousness, but do not compound to form complex percepts. The theory of cognitive development by Piaget and of language and mind by Chomsky are the most outstanding examples of the modern revival of such an activity model. Both regard the environmental stimulation as a necessary prerequisite for development; neither of them spells out and emphasizes, however, its influence in detail. Evironmental stimulation functions like surrounding material contingencies from which the organism makes his spontaneous selections. If there were no such contingencies, he could not make his selections; development is, however, internally initiated and directed.

In recent years, there has been a growing and understandable interest in applying Piaget to education (Aebli, 1951; Bruner, 1966; Furth, 1970). By putting ''activity'' back where it belongs, namely into the organism, Piaget has profoundly changed our conception of man and his development. As pointedly emphasized by Hans Aebli (1951), the application of Piaget's ideas of education has, however, serious limitations. For example, let us consider intellectual prog-

---

[3]The educational attitude prevailing in the public school system contrasts sharply with the 19th century elitism which in spite of Bergen-Belsen and Buchenwald, continues to dominate the educational philosophy of the so-called institutions of higher learning. Here, we engage in systematic efforts to make the best better (or at least more arrogant) by providing supportive fellowships to them rather than to disadvantaged students who never in their lives had the opportunity of working under such favorable conditions and who, with little aid, might show true improvements because, after all, they have further to go and more gains to make.

ression. As long as a child attends to one form of thought, e.g., at the preoperational level, there is no point in training him for more advanced, i.e., concrete, operations; he would not yet be able to comprehend and apply them. Once a child has attained the level of concrete operations, there is no need any longer for providing such training; he is now competent to perform these operations anyway.

Undoubtedly, such a laissez-faire attitude is more characteristic for the Summerhill school program (Neill, 1960) than for Piaget, and our statements overemphasize the limitations of his theory. They also indicate the similarity between these educational viewpoints and the hermeneutic theory of Socrates and Plato. Here, the influence of the educator is compared with the skills of a midwife. Knowledge is implicit in the child; the educator merely assists the individual to explicate and become conscious of these ideas. Since the educator will use his skills selectively, however (for instance by choosing certain tasks or toys for a particular child at a particular time), he participates actively in this explication process. After all, the educator, as much as the child, is an active organism. Piaget and, especially, Chomsky have disregarded the educators' participatory role in transforming the historical–cultural conditions for the developmental benefit of the child.

If we were to make our comparisons complete, we would have to search, thirdly, for an interpretation of a passive organism in an active environment. Perhaps Skinner's educational model as represented in *Walden Two* (1948) and in the technology of the teaching machines may serve as cases in point. In comparison to the fourth theory to be mentioned, little emphasis is given here to the structure of the educational input. Since the programs of the more advanced teaching machines are providing some form of organization, however, and since Skinner more than the earlier behaviorists, emphasizes the instrumental acts of organisms, our comparison is all but perfect.

The notion of a passive organism in an active environment is also implied in some sociological theories. Ryder (1965), for example, provided a developmental interpretation in which changes are brought about by generational (cohort) substitutions rather than by psychological growth. Individuals lose successively their places without initial modifications in their own behavior. Also, the early interpretations by Vygotskii can be considered as examples for such a theory emphasizing, in contrast to Skinner, the structure of the environmental conditions. Since in dialectic theories, the penetration proceeds always in both directions, however, i.e., from the environment to the individual and from the individual to the environment, an active role of both is implied. Thus dialectic interpretations lead us to the fourth and most important theory, in which both the organism and the environment are active participants in two-way interaction processes.

It is the merit of S. L. Rubinstein to have proposed a psychological, developmental theory in which both the organism and the environment fulfill an active role and in which, thus, both the conceptual issues and those of social ethics are fully realized. Rubinstein overcomes the Western dualism which, recently, has been delineated so clearly by Reese and Overton (1970). Rubinstein distinguished between external contingencies and what might appropriately be called the organism's internal contingencies. Through two interaction processes, connected with these contingencies, psychic activities emerge into the consciousness and attain their organization. Thus, Rubinstein, on the basis of the dialectic materialism of Marx, Engels, and Lenin, incorporated into a theory of man and his development all three criteria of science and knowledge, namely the enactive–existential, the iconic–phenomenal, and the symbolic–structural. The enactive–existential criterion is realized through the emphasis upon the social relevance of sciences and by viewing consciousness as the result of the organism's activities. The iconic–phenomenal criterion is expressed by viewing sciences and consciousness as reflections of sociocultural contingencies. The symbolic–structural criterion is realized in the organization of changing interactions between the internal and external material conditions on the one hand and the psychic activities of the individual, through which knowledge and sciences originate, on the other. Among the behavioral scientists, only psychological gerontologists, through the explication of developmental research designs (Baltes, 1968; Riegel, 1965; Schaie, 1965; Wohlwill, 1970c), have come to grips with the problem of changing interactions between the individual and society. Most behavioral scientists and educators remain unaware, however, of the far reaching practical and theoretical implications of such interpretations.

ACKNOWLEDGMENTS

This paper is the product of long lasting interactions with teacher-students and student-teachers. The section in "Historical Node Points in the Conception of Man" was written in reaction to our seminar, entitled "Is a Black Psychology of Cognitive Development Possible?" The section on "Open and Closed Developmental Systems in Western Sciences" is a short version of two speeches given in the course of "Cognitive and Language Development" also attended by members of the Black Action Movement during their successful strike for greater social and intellectual participation at the university of Michigan. An extended version of the first part of this section will appear in the *Psychological Bulletin*. The second part has been stimulated through several discussions with William Looft and by his paper on "The Psychology of More" which appeared in the *American Psychologist*. The section on "Dialectic Interactionism in Soviet Psychology" is the result of a long lasting interest in Hegel and of an informal seminar initiated by Robert Wozniak. The section on "Phenomenal, Logical, and Existential Bases of Knowledge and Sciences" summarizes numerous discussions in our seminars on "Models and Research in the History of Behavioral Sciences."

Special thanks belong to Clinton Fink, Joy Hargrove, Lynn Liben, John Meacham, Ruth Riegel, George Rosenwald, Fred Wacker, Peter Weston and to Sue Griffith.

CHAPTER 2

The Early Development of Parent–Young Interaction in Nature[1]

ECKHARD H. HESS

THE UNIVERSITY OF CHICAGO
CHICAGO, ILLINOIS

SLOBODAN B. PETROVICH[2]

THE UNIVERSITY OF CHICAGO
CHICAGO, ILLINOIS

I. Introduction

Gaining a perspective on behavior methodology is difficult. The individual components of behavior are not always readily identifiable, with the result that "controlled" experiments can fall far short of that criterion. In fact, such experimentation often can lack *proper* controls. Variables may be introduced which are overlooked by the experimenter, and the experimenter may also be unable to examine the conditions under which the behavior in question naturally develops and occurs. Not knowing some of the actually relevant factors, the experimenter may easily proceed to blunder into a whole series of artificial constructions, generating data that bear little resemblance to reality.

[1]The research herein reported was supported by Grant 776 of the National Institutes of Mental Health, United States Public Health Service.
[2]Present address: Department of Psychology, University of Maryland, Baltimore, Maryland.

As a result of experimenting exclusively in the laboratory, many of us have fallen into the very same trap against which Watson (1914) warned long ago:

> granting the indispensableness of the laboratory, it is well, after finishing with our animal, to observe him yet again in the field . . . after years of analytical study upon the temperature, visual, olfactory and auditory senses of a given species of bird, one might predict the utter absurdity of that bird's being able to get back to its home when carried out to sea for a distance of one thousand miles. Yet on specific tests we find the bird able to do this. . . . It would seem obvious that there is no conflict between field and laboratory work. The field is both the source of problems and the place where the laboratory solutions of these problems are tested [p. 31].

With Watson's words in mind, this methodological issue in the study of species-specific behavior will be examined in relation to imprinting research.

In the research literature, the term "imprinting" usually refers to the rapid acquisition by young animals of the primary social bond to their parent during early life. Konrad Lorenz's 1935 formulation of the characteristics of this process initiated modern scientific interest in this phenomenon. He postulated that imprinting took place in a highly limited, sensitive period early in the life of the individual, that it had lasting effects, that the imprinting process "selected" species-specific, biologically appropriate cues, that only specific reactions of the young animal, not its entire behavior repertoire, are imprinted to the specific object, and that imprinting could affect behaviors not yet performed by the young animal (such as sexual behavior) when they later appeared.

Imprinting has been subjected to extensive laboratory investigation since the early 1950s. One of the investigators, Hess (1957, 1959a,b, 1964, 1970), has demonstrated several differences between the imprinting process as studied in the laboratory and other types of learning, particularly association learning:

(a) In the imprinting process, there is a distinct critical period, whereas in association learning, the processes are not confined to such life periods.

(b) Certain drugs, particularly muscle relaxants, interfere completely with the ability of ducklings and chicks to acquire an attachment to a surrogate imprinting object.

(c) Massed practice, that is, greater expenditure of effort, rather than spacing of trials, as in association learning, is the factor correlated with greater probability of a young animal's acquiring an attachment to the imprinting object.

(d) That which has been learned first has more influence upon attachment behavior than what has been learned more recently; the reverse is true in association learning processes.

(e) Painful stimulation enhances the acquisition of filial behavior toward the imprinting object, whereas punishment inhibits behavior in association learning.

Reviews of imprinting have been published by Moltz (1960, 1963), Sluckin (1964), Bateson (1966), and Smith (1969).

In recent years, Hess (1964) has proposed that there are other early and extremely rapid learning experiences which result in animals directing specific behaviors in ways that will promote species survival. For example, the process of learning food object characteristics by chicks and snapping turtles (Hess, 1962; Burghardt & Hess, 1966) appears to be much more like the imprinting process than like association learning. Similarly, preference for a particular type of nest site by mallard females appears to be affected by specific experience during the second day of life. Hence, it seems that there may possibly be a maturational sequence of three imprinting phenomena in the life of chicks and ducklings, all occurring within the first days of life: filial imprinting on the first day; environmental imprinting on the second day; and food imprinting on the third day (Hess, 1964).

The effects of *early* experience in influencing environmental preferences is not so well known as social imprinting, although several studies show that there is such a phenomenon in different species. Hess (1959b) exposed day-old chicks to a large cut-out shape and later found that the chicks exhibited a preference for being near this particular shape. Brown (1964) has done work relating early experience and environmental preferences in chicks while Klopfer (1963) did work in this area with chipping sparrows. Bateson (1964a–c) conducted research showing that complex environments during rearing do affect preferences shown in laboratory imprinting experiments involving the same complex patterns used in the rearing environment.

The majority of research on social imprinting has focused upon particular manifestations of the attachment of the young to the parent object: following or staying close to it. Furthermore, most researchers have viewed it as a straightforward learning phenomenon measured in terms of number of feet of following, number of seconds close to the object, distress calls, etc. Mother surrogates usually have been offered to hatchlings at specified ages, in specified places, and for specified lengths of time. Prior experiences from the time of hatching to the imprinting exposure have been limited, often through maintaining hatchlings in visual and social isolation so as to prevent contamination of the young bird's responses to the imprinting object. Hence most imprinting experiments have been conducted as *deprivation experiments*. The hatching, handling, and maintenance of hatchlings in man-made artificial laboratory settings have prevented them from obtaining normal, environmental experiences. Furthermore, the animals usually have been imprinted on *biologically inappropriate* objects, ranging from flashing lights to milk bottles and decoys.

As a result of the deprivation methodology, much information bearing upon the imprinting phenomenon has been missed. Thus, after having run thousands of ducklings and chicks in completely automated apparatus, the research work at the Lake Cove research station, located on a peninsula at the eastern shore of Maryland and near the Black Water National Refuge, has begun in a different direction. This is being done through very careful and detailed observation of female mallards and their offspring in natural settings, beginning with the onset of incubation and continuing through incubation, hatching, exodus from the nest, and the subsequent weeks of life. The current research has as its initial aim the determination of an *ethogram* of imprinting, that is, an inventory of all events, behavioral, physiological, and environmental, occurring during the development of the parent–young relationship. In doing this, the total process must first be studied in its natural setting through methods that do not alter the animals' environment nor interact with their behavior; that is, they must not introduce contaminating variables into the experimental situation.

Other aspects of the research involve manipulation only to the extent that the natural situation is still left as intact as possible with the experimental variation being measured in relation to the natural situation. *Hence the control is always the actual natural parent–offspring relation in a feral setting. It is never a state in which animals are deprived as completely as possible and are permitted to experience only the few variables which are introduced experimentally.*

Figure 1 depicts one of the experimental methods for studying the imprinting process in the natural setting. Sounds that are made within the nest box in which the female is incubating eggs are picked up by means of a concealed microphone. A speaker placed underneath the eggs permits taped sounds to be presented to the female. A thermister probe permits the continuous recording of the nest box temperature at the level of the eggs. Each nest box being monitored is between 300 and 700 feet away from the laboratory building which houses the tape recorders and the telethermometer.

The data reported herein are a part of the ongoing research dealing with the wild and semiwild mallard duck population resident at the Lake Cove research

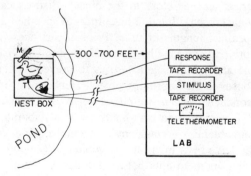

Fig. 1. Schematic representation of one of the experimental methods of studying imprinting in the natural setting. The nest box in which the female mallard is incubating eggs is an elevated structure above the water of a large pond. The different nest boxes in the pond are all located between 300 and 700 feet away from the laboratory building housing the recording equipment. This permits the observation of the natural incubation process without the experimenter disturbing or being seen by the female mallard. T: thermistor; M: microphone; s: speaker.

station. These data, of course, are not fully complete, because knowledge of the genetic and ecological factors that affect early and contemporary experiences and behavior of animals is necessary for understanding the complex interactions in observed events. They do, however, indicate some of the factors which strongly influence natural imprinting events.

II. Incubation and Hatching

A. Duration and Synchronism

It has recently been reported (Hess, 1971a) that there are many differences between natural incubation and hatching of mallard eggs and laboratory incubation and hatching of eggs of the same species. In the laboratory, hatching may occur after 22 to 26 days of incubation, and there is normally a 2–3-day period between the hatching of the first and last eggs. In the wild, hatching may occur after 25–28 days of incubation, and there is normally a 3–8-hour period between the hatching of the first and last eggs. (A possible reason for this difference in hatching times is discussed on page 34.) Records of incubation by wild mallard females, as reported by Hess, indicate that the length of incubation is inversely correlated with mean noontime temperature during the incubation. In addition, experimental data (Hess, 1971a) indicate that daily cooling of the incubating eggs in a $7 \pm 1°C$ room tends to reduce hatching asynchronism in laboratory incubated mallard duck eggs.

Still another possible factor promoting hatching synchronism in naturally incubated mallard eggs is the vocalizations between parent and young that occur before hatching.

B. Female and Duckling Vocalizations during Incubation

It has been observed that a few days before ducklings hatch the female will make certain clucklike sounds. These sounds have been recorded by placing a microphone into the nest as shown in Fig. 1. Sometimes they consist of single clucks, sometimes bursts of three, four, or five clucks. They reach a high output rate when a duckling hatches. This vocalization is initiated before the eggs are pipped and it continues periodically until and during the time of the nest exodus. Since these vocalizations were not observed to be made by females that had been incubating either for a short time or for 2 weeks, this raised the question of whether there were stimuli emitted from the eggs that elicited the vocalizations from the incubating female.

This question was experimentally investigated by installing 3½-in. Quam loudspeakers just underneath the eggs in the nest (Fig. 1). These loudspeakers played sounds from a remotely located Uher 4000 L tape recorder. The tape was a recording obtained from a hatching mallard egg in the laboratory. The sounds of the duckling in the hatching egg consisted of bill clapping and vocalization. A microphone placed very close to the egg transmitted the sounds which were recorded for a period of 1 min on a Nagra IV-D tape recorder at a speed of 3¾ ips. This master tape sound was then used to make the stimulus tape which began with 1 min of silence followed by 1 min of duckling sounds, another minute of silence, and so on, ending with the seventh minute, which was silent.

Each loudspeaker was wrapped in an extremely thin and pliable plastic material to insulate it from water and placed cone upward in the nests at a depth of approximately ½ in. (see Fig. 1). The sound pressures made when a pipped duckling vocalized had previously been determined by a Scott Type 450 sound pressure meter to be approximately 50–60 dB at a distance of about 6–8 in. from the eggs. The Scott meter was used after a loudspeaker had been installed at the nest to ensure that the volume setting on the Uher tape recorder resulted in the same sound pressure as that emitted by an actual hatching egg. By this means, the sounds of the hatching eggs were emitted as the females sat upon their eggs.

Every female except one was tested for only one session during her reproductive cycle. Some were tested during their first week of incubation (Days 1, 2, and 3), some during their second week (Day 10), some during their third week (Days 14–22), and some in their final week, either close to having eggs pipped or actually having pipped eggs. One female was tested twice, on the second and third days of incubation.

Recordings of the females' responses when the 7-min stimulus tape was played at different points during the incubation period revealed that the specific stage of the reproductive cycle of the individual female had a definite influence upon the nature of her responses to the hatching sounds. As shown in Fig. 2, the eleven females in the first few days of incubation gave no vocalization response to the sounds of the hatching duckling. One of these females, tested at the second day of incubation, immediately flew off the nest when the sound was presented. This was the female that was subsequently retested. Two others

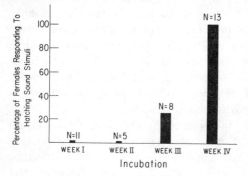

Fig. 2. The responsiveness of incubating female mallards to a tape recording of sound stimuli emitted by a duckling that had pipped but had not yet emerged from its shell, in relation to the incubation stage of the female mallard's own eggs. The bars represent the percentage of females in the particular weeks of incubation that responded by vocalizing when presented with the hatching sound stimuli.

gave a panting sound while fluffing up their feathers, an action regarded by students of mallard behavior as being a threat response.

On the other hand, all 13 females tested during the last days of incubation gave the vocalization response to the hatching duckling sounds. In fact, the degree of vocalization was strongly correlated with when the incubated eggs were going to pip. While it would appear plausible to hypothesize that sounds from the female's own eggs enhance the probability of her making vocalizations to the stimulus tape, two observations demonstrated that this does not need to be the case. In these two observations, the females tested turned out to have been sitting upon infertile eggs and they still made the vocalizations to the sounds of a hatching duckling at the time when the eggs should have been hatching, based on the length of time the female had been on the nest.

None of the five females tested during the second week of incubation responded, and only two of the eight tested in the third week of incubation gave vocalizations. As shown in Fig. 2, this seems to indicate that, in female mallards, there is a rapid development of vocalization behavior toward the end of the normal incubation period. The data, of course, are still preliminary since some of the females were incubating for the first time and thus probably had had no prior experience with hatching eggs. According to the females' identification bands, some of them were in their second incubation season, some in their third, some in their fourth, and two in their seventh. Future research will permit the examination of the effect of previous experience upon the female's vocalization responses to the sounds of hatching ducklings.

In this initial experiment, only one female was tested more than once. Hence, another experiment was conducted involving daily testing of individual females during incubation. Twenty females were studied, five of which had been imprinted to human beings after laboratory incubation. The remaining 15 were females living in the field.[3] Testing with the tape-recorded duckling sounds was carried out *daily* with each female, beginning on the first day of incubation and continuing through the day the eggs were hatched. The data obtained paralleled those obtained in the initial experiment, even though there are differences between the human-imprinted and the field mallards. As shown by Figs. 3 and 4, the differences consisted of the human-imprinted females' responding to the hatching sounds earlier in the reproductive cycle and making more vocalizations in response to these sounds.

Because there were only five females in the human-imprinted group, these differences may well be due solely to sampling error rather than to any early-experience effect. Further research is being conducted to determine whether this is the case.

---

[3]Since there is a possibility that some females that have been released to the field after laboratory experimentation lose their leg bands, it must therefore be kept in mind that one or two human-imprinted females might have been among the field mallards.

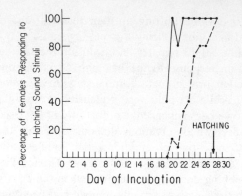

Fig. 3. The responsiveness of incubating female mallards to a tape recording of sound stimuli emitted by a hatching duckling. Five females known to have been imprinted to human beings when they were ducklings during the previous spring (————) and 15 females found incubating in the field and not known to have been laboratory imprinted (·——·) were each tested daily with the recorded hatching sound stimuli. The points represent the percentage of females on that day of incubation that responded by vocalizing when presented with the hatching sound stimuli. Since none of the females responded during the first portion of incubation, none of the zero scores for these days are plotted on this graph.

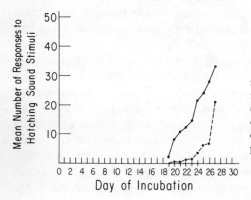

Fig. 4. The mean number of vocalizations made by the five human-imprinted female mallards (————) and by the 15 field mallards (·——·) during the test session on each day of incubation. Again, zero scores obtained during the first portions of incubation are not plotted on this graph.

These two experiments together demonstrate that the female's vocalization response to the sounds of a hatching duckling is not made at every stage of incubation, but is made primarily during the last week of incubation, particularly just before pipping, and during pipping and hatching. The fact that two of the tested females had been sitting for approximately 24 days upon infertile eggs and nevertheless gave very strong vocalizations to these sounds suggests that the females themselves are "primed" to make these responses. Whether this phenomenon is strictly under neuroendocrine control or whether other factors such as experience also play a role and to what extent, will be investigated during the next breeding season. Nevertheless, it does appear presently that there are neuroendocrine factors which "prime" the female's vocalization responses which are then elicited by the sounds made by the young in the eggs.

The question of whether the vocalizations proceeded strictly from young to parent was investigated by playing a recording of a female's vocalization to ducklings which had pipped and were still in the egg. They were scheduled to hatch about 24 hours later. The recording used was a 1-min sample of a female vocalizing to a hatching duckling.

Two groups of three pipped eggs each were used. The test procedure was as follows. The speaker was placed at a distance of about 1 foot away from the eggs and the volume setting on the tape recorder adjusted so that the sound pressure from the recording was at about 55 dB as determined by the Scott sound-pressure meter placed at a point just above the level of the pipped eggs. This level is similar to that which occurs in an actual nest and preliminary experimentation showed that female vocalizations played at the level of 45 dB to pipped eggs resulted in good responses from the hatching ducklings. In this experiment, the eggs were given 10-min trials at six different times: 24 hours before scheduled hatching, 3 hours before scheduled hatching, 2 hours before scheduled hatching, 1 hour before scheduled hatching, during actual hatching, and 1 hour after actual hatching. Each 10-min trial consisted of five repetitions of the 1-min female vocalization each interspersed with 1 min of silence.

The data obtained for the two groups of subjects were highly similar. Try show that the degree to which pipped ducklings initiate vocalization when the female is silent changes as the time of hatching approaches and changes again after actual hatching. This is evident in Table 1 which gives both the number of duckling vocalizations during the silent and female vocalization periods at each test session for both groups and the percentage of all duckling vocalizations that were emitted during the silent periods in each test session. In the first place, there was a progressive decrease in the relative number of duckling calls made during silent periods over a period of hours as the hatching time approached. For example, 24 hours before hatching, 34% of all duckling vocalizations were made during the silent periods, while at 3 hours before hatching 24% were. From that time on, there was a steady, rapid fall in the percentage of calls emitted during silent periods, and during the hour of hatching itself, only 9% of the calls were made during the silent periods of the test session. One hour after hatching, however, the proportion of vocalizations made during silent periods went back up to 37%. There is also a progressive increase in the total number of vocalizations made by the ducklings during the female vocalization periods, starting with 100 emitted at 24 hours before hatching, rising to a level of about 250 from 2 hours before hatching and through the actual hatching hour, and rising still further to a level of 419 1 hour after hatching.

Taken together, these data indicate the possibility that the female's vocalization is initiated by sound stimuli from the young at some point in their development when the female is ready to make such responses to the young. However, once the female's vocalizations have begun, they may possibly serve as a stimulus

TABLE 1

Number of Vocalizations Emitted by Pipped, Hatching, and Hatched
Ducklings during Female Vocalization and Silent Intervals
of 10-Min Test Sessions

Pre- and post-hatch time in hours	Number of duckling vocalizations during five 1-min female vocalization intervals in test session		Number of duckling vocalizations during five 1-min silent intervals in test session		Total vocalizations	Percentage of total vocalizations that were made during silent intervals
	Group 1 (N = 3)	Group 2 (N = 3)	Group 1	Group 2		
Hour − 24	64	36	37	14		
Total		100		51	151	34
Hour − 3	90	77	28	24		
Total		167		52	219	24
Hour − 2	122	127	22	42		
Total		249		64	313	20
Hour − 1	137	132	12	37		
Total		269		49	318	15
Hour 0 (hatching)	116	139	12	12		
Total		255		24	279	9
Hour + 1	209	210	122	124		
Total		419		246	665	37
Total	738	721	233	253	1945	
Total		1459		486	1945	

promoting synchronism of hatching. That is, if ducklings respond to her vocalizations, the activities of all of them become similar and facilitate the occurrence of hatching of all ducklings within 3–8 hours of each other. There may, of course, still be other possible factors promoting the observed hatching synchronism in natural conditions. The young may possibly interact with each other in hearing each other's calls. Vince (1964, 1966a,b, 1968a,b) and Vince and Cheng (1970) have shown conclusively that hatching synchrony in quail is caused by such interaction between the young themselves while in the eggs. Such a phenomenon, of course, has not been demonstrated in the mallard species. Nevertheless, it should not be excluded as a possibility in investigating the

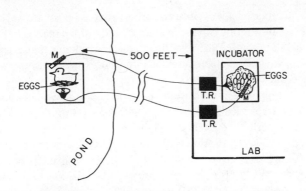

Fig. 5. An experimental method of studying the effects of the parent–young auditory communication upon hatching time and synchrony. In this study, the nests were approximately 500 feet away from the laboratory building housing the incubator with the eggs. M: microphone; T.R.: tape recorder; S: speaker.

fact that incubator-hatched ducklings hatch over a period of days while naturally hatched ones accomplish this in a matter of only hours.

The next step in investigating the parent–young communication in relation to hatching synchronism is to subject eggs in the laboratory incubator to the same sort of auditory stimulation and communication as are given by a real female to her own eggs. This step, which is currently being conducted at Lake Cove, is illustrated by Fig. 5. Microphones and speakers are installed in the laboratory incubator and in an actual nest where a female is incubating her eggs which have begun at the same time as those in the laboratory incubator. This two-way arrangement permits the incubator eggs to have the same auditory feedback as the female's own eggs. That is, whenever the incubator eggs emit sounds, the female can then respond to them. The vocalizations of the female can be received both by her own eggs and by the incubator eggs.

C. Incubation and Developmental Age Data

The question of developmental age must also be considered in relation to hatching behavior. Gottlieb (1961, 1963e) has suggested that the extended hatching period of incubator-hatched ducklings indicates that they are not of the same developmental age at the time of actual hatching: "thus, for example, a bird of post-hatch age 15 hr. can actually be *developmentally* older than another bird of post-hatch age 15 hr. when the former has a more extended incubation period than the latter [Gottlieb, 1961, p. 422]."

Gottlieb's (1961) subjects hatched over a period of 2 days and were imprinted at different posthatch periods. The resulting imprinting data were then plotted in two different ways. One was in terms of days and hours from the onset of incubation until the laboratory imprinting experience and the other was in terms of the number of hours since hatching, that is, posthatch age at the time of the laboratory imprinting experience. As is well known in imprinting literature, Gottlieb (1961) interpreted the resulting data as showing that a critical period could be seen when developmental age measures were used, but not when posthatch age measures were used.

However, the graphic presentations of data for the two measures were not the same. The graph dealing with posthatch age (Gottlieb, 1961, Fig. 1, p. 424) covered a period of 25 hours, with each bar representing data over a 5-hour period. The graph dealing with developmental age (Gottlieb, 1961, Fig. 2, p. 425), however, covered a 48-hour period, with each bar representing 12 hours rather than 5. Because of this, the data in the two histograms are not truly comparable. The developmental-age data cannot be broken down into smaller intervals, but the posthatch age data can be consolidated so that each bar represents a time interval more similar to that in the developmental age graph. Doing this permits some reduction in the discrepancy between developmental and posthatch-age data treatment. In other words, the first bar can be made to represent the age periods of 3 to 12 hours posthatch, an interval of 10 hours, the second bar can be made to represent the age periods of 13 to 22 hours post hatch, an interval of 10 hours, and the third bar to represent the remaining ages, 23 to 27 hours, an interval of 5 hours. When this is done, it becomes apparent that 9 of the 25 ducklings (37%) in the first age group were imprinted according to criteria and that 18 of the 30 ducklings (60%) in the 13–22 hour age group were imprinted. The third age group, as before, would consist of ten animals, six of which were imprinted. Assuming that an equal number of animals tested in the age group 28 to 31 hours would have resulted in none being imprinted, this would reduce the resulting percentage to the order of 30% for a 10-hour age group 23–31 hours. Hence, it becomes apparent that the posthatch data do not constitute evidence against the existence of a critical period on the basis of posthatch age. This is unfortunate in view of the fact that these data have been repeatedly cited as calling into question the notion of the critical period on the basis of posthatch age.

It is certainly possible that developmental age could be involved in the laboratory imprinting situation where animals are used that have hatched over a period of 2–3 days even when incubation is initiated at a precise developmental stage. However, such hatching variability, as has been mentioned earlier, does not occur in the natural setting. Bjarväll (1967) observed that single clutches hatch over a period of 3–8 hours and our own observations of a large number of individual nests for several breeding seasons have shown that hatching is normally complete within 6 hours. In this case, the question of developmental age becomes irrelevant and posthatch age is sufficient to provide an adequate measure. It may be necessary to reevaluate the concept of developmental age in relation to imprinting in view of the fact that in the same ecological setting the normal incubation period can vary from 25 to 28 days. This variation appears to be strongly influenced by environmental temperature changes during the incubation period. Certainly it is not feasible to regard ducklings that hatch in June after 25 days of incubation as developmentally 3 days younger than those hatching in March after 28 days of incubation.

D. Development of the Female Mallard's Vocalization Rate

For a period of 6 years, detailed records have been made of the temporal sequence of pipping, hatching, and nest exodus. Pipping normally occurs sometime between 24 and 27 days after the onset of incubation, with the exact time determined by the total length of incubation, which may be between 25 and 28 days from onset to hatching. Pipping generally occurs during the morning hours, between dawn and noon. The following day, usually during the morning hours, the eggs hatch, with an interval of about 6–8 hours between the first and last ducklings in the clutch. Then during the next day (or very occasionally, 2 days later), the female leaves the nest with the young for the exodus. The exodus generally occurs during the morning, but usually not until the mid or late morning. Therefore, the average age of the ducklings at the time of the nest exodus is normally 24 to 26 hours after hatching, although on occasion they may be as old as 48 hours. Bjarväll (1967) has reported similar observations.

Some 24 hours before actual pipping begins, the ducklings move into the air space within the egg. Observations made prior to this time period have not revealed the occurrence of any spontaneous female vocalization, although this may be due to limited sampling. When ducklings have entered the air space, however, the female vocalizes at the rate of approximately one to four times per minute. The movement into the air space occurs about 72 hours before the nest exodus. Upon pipping, which is approximately 48 hours before the nest exodus, the female vocalizes at the rate of about 10 to 15 times per minute. Sound pressure readings taken of actual females have shown that their vocalization is normally about 50–55 dB at the level of the eggs. The data shown in Table 1 are based upon using this sound pressure. Gottlieb (1965c), however, has played species-specific maternal calls to duckling embryos during the day before they were due to hatch at a sound pressure of 68–74 dB at the level of the eggs. Not only would it appear reasonable to assume that it would be of greater selective value to the species for the female not to vocalize too loudly to her young, since this would attract predators, but the possibility also arises that using overly loud sound stimuli may result in obtaining erroneous data. This would be through forcible elicitation of responses through nonspecific stimulation. After pipping, there is a long time period in which the vocalization rate tends to be quite low, on the order of one to four times per minute. This long period of time is interrupted periodically by 1- or 2-min bursts of vocalization during which the rate rises to a level of 45 to 68 per minute. Where we were

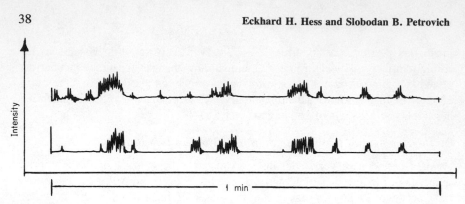

Fig. 6. One-minute recordings of the vocalizations of two different female mallards of the stimulus tape of a hatching duckling. Each upward movement of the recording pen represents a single cluck, with the height of the upward stroke depicting the loudness of the cluck. Comparison of the patterns in the two records reveals some of the kinds of consistent individual differences in vocalization that occur among individual female mallards as well as the agreement between cluck clusters at those times when duckling sounds were emitted by the stimulus tape.

able to check, this was always found to coincide with the hatching of one of the eggs in the clutch. Figure 6 shows the vocalizations made by two female mallards at the hatching of a duckling.

The patterns shown in Fig. 6 were made by transmitting the output of the taped recording of the female's vocalization through a Motorola Model MDA920-7 full wave rectifier and then using the output from the full wave rectifier to activate a chart recorder. Figure 6 thus shows that the female represented by the bottom record made 47 vocalizations, generally in clusters. Each vocalization is represented by one upward stroke of the recorder pen and the amplitude of that stroke indicates the intensity of the vocalization. Numerous analyses, some made at very high chart recording speeds, have shown that when vocalizations occur, that is, during the clusters, they are emitted at an approximate rate of 3 to 3½ per second, with each individual vocalization having a duration of approximately 150 msec and with the silent duration between them being approximately 150–180 msec.

After hatching, the vocalization rate returns to the low level, to be interrupted again by another burst coinciding with another young duckling hatching, and so on. Figure 7 depicts a typical record of a single female's vocalization during hatching, with a single peak indicating the maximum vocalization rate reached upon the hatching of a young duckling.

After all ducklings have hatched, the female is generally relatively quiet for a number of hours. Bjarväll (1968) has reported similar observations. As Bjarväll has pointed out, this is not in accord with Gottlieb's (1965a) statement that female mallards begin vocalizing after hatching and continue to do so until and through the time of the nest exodus, with the call rate increasing during the period. In contrast, the Lake Cove records have shown that the average

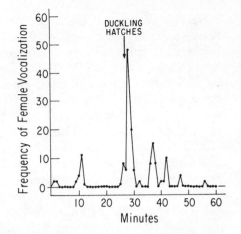

Fig. 7. Vocalization record of a wild ground-nesting female mallard during the hour of hatching. The total numbers of clucks emitted during each minute are depicted by the points.

vocalization rate after hatching until just before nest exodus ranges from 0 to 4 per 1-min intervals. At the beginning of the nest exodus, the female vocalizes at a low rate but, this quickly builds up to a crescendo, not exceeding, at least in our observations, the rate of 40 to 65 per minute. On the basis of these data, it becomes evident that there are two events during which vocalizations are emitted at the maximum rate. The first is whenever a duckling hatches and the second is during the nest exodus when the female takes the hatchlings off the nest. The high vocalization rate during exodus continues for a longer or shorter time period, depending partly on how quickly the young follow the female mallard as she moves away from the nest.

The observations have also revealed that there are clear and consistent individual differences between female mallards in their vocalization patterns. Figure 6, as may be recalled, depicts the vocalization patterns of two different females to the 1-min stimulus tape of a hatching duckling. Each female has its own typical vocalization pattern. Some females make individual clucks spaced out in intervals of 1 sec each; others emit call clusters that consist of cluck triples or cluck quadruples. Still others may regularly vary in the number of clucks they emit within each call cluster with the result that their call clusters are unequal. A few females emit many more clucks in their call clusters than do other females in the same situation. Even so, such females still emit less than 70 clucks per 1-min interval. Despite such individual differences, it can be noted from Fig. 6 that both records are vocalizations in response to hatching-duckling sounds presented by the tape recording.

Investigation is currently being conducted on whether these consistent individual vocalization patterns persist to successive breeding years and whether there are effects of early experience upon characteristic vocalization patterns such as was suggested by the observed differences between human-imprinted and field mallards.

Not only are there individual differences among female mallards, but individual female mallards change their vocalizations during the period prior to and after hatching and during nest exodus. Spectrographic analyses of these changes have been reported (Hess, 1971b). They show that a female mallard's vocalizations not only change in terms of rates, as reported previously by Gottlieb (1965a), but also qualitatively. This is in contrast to Gottlieb's (1965a) report that there are no such qualitative changes. Even with respect to the changes in vocalization rates, however, Gottlieb's (1965a) findings have not been substantiated by observations made at Lake Cove.

In the paper by Gottlieb (1965a, p. 16), there is a graphic presentation of the rate of the female mallard's vocalization during the 22-hour period before the nest exodus. According to this graph, the female mallard's initial vocalization rate is less than two per minute and then rises constantly to reach a level of more than 240 per minute during the nest exodus. High-speed chart recording of 12 female mallards (four ground nesters and eight elevated box nesters) has shown that the normal vocalization rate of the female mallard is between 3 and 3½ per second during the call clusters. This is evident in Fig. 7. This, if prorated to an entire minute, would be equivalent to a maximum of 210 per minute. Hence, it would be difficult for a female mallard to emit more than 240 clucks per minute even if there were no pauses between the call clusters. The records of the 12 females studied showed that they emitted their vocalizations at the rate of 40 to 65 clucks per 1-min interval during the nest exodus. Bjarväll's (1968) report that females vocalize at the rate of 66 to 200 clucks per minute appears to be based upon prorating call rates on the basis of call clusters rather than upon entire 1-min intervals.

III. Conclusion

This research is of methodological significance because it represents a step in the direction away from the deprivation experience methodology which has characterized the laboratory study of imprinting for two decades. Deprivation methodology has been used in other areas of psychological research, and many investigators in the field of early experience effects have adopted it. Deprivation experiments can be very valuable in giving information regarding the nature of the processes involved in a specific phenomenon, but it is well to be aware of the potential pitfalls in relying upon them exclusively.

This research, though a beginning, has demonstrated that an auditory interaction between the female mallard and her young begins even before hatching. As soon as ducklings enter into the air space within the egg, usually 3 days before the actual nest exodus, the female and the ducklings vocally interact with each other. After actual hatching, the ducklings are with the female on the nest for 24 hours before the nest exodus begins. In this way, even though the young do not follow the mother, there is an overabundance of opportunity for a strong affiliation to develop between parent and young, particularly in view of the fact that 10 min with a real female on the nest is sufficient to cause an incubator-hatched duckling to form an irreversible attachment to her to the extent that it refuses to follow other objects (Hess, 1971b).

Furthermore, this vocal interaction may possibly lead to the observed hatching synchronism in nature. Investigations should be conducted on this question. This research, however, has suggested that seasonal temperature can affect both hatching synchronism and the length of incubation. Hence, there may be several factors working simultaneously to effect hatching synchronism.

The study of imprinting in its natural setting has also revealed that the female mallard is in the nest with the offspring past the 13–16-hour critical period for imprinting that has been determined for the laboratory situation, a fact which has already been pointed out by Bjarväll (1967, 1968). This fact has several consequences. First, the attachment between the parent and the young is not based solely upon visual characteristics, but includes the auditory modality as well. Ramsay and Hess (1954) early demonstrated that auditory factors are important in eliciting following and attachment in laboratory imprinting, and Gottlieb (1963a,c,d; 1965a–c, 1966) has also shown that both auditory factors and prenatal experiences are important in the filial parent attachment process. Second, all young, even the late hatchers, appear to be fully imprinted to the female mallard when the nest exodus occurs. The completion of the imprinting process can thus occur when each individual duckling is maturationally ready. Third, such completion before the occurrence of the nest exodus is advantageous to the survival of the young since the nest exodus can thus be delayed due to bad weather conditions without resulting in harmful effects upon the parent–young relationship.

There are certainly many factors in addition to the ones touched upon in this report which require investigation in relation to parent–young interaction in the natural setting. It is very important, for example, to determine the effect of semidomestication upon the observed behavior. Much of the literature has demonstrated that behavior often can reflect particular adaptations to specific ecological situations. Not only is the specific ecological complex of importance, but also the effects of early experience upon later behavior. For this reason it is necessary, to take but one example, to be cautious in making generalizations to wild mallards on the basis of data obtained from semiwild mallards.

While a great deal more work remains to be done in the study of imprinting in the natural situation, it has already become evident that behavior research must not only utilize the best techniques that the laboratory has to offer, but employ them in the actual settings in which the behavior in question naturally occurs. In the case of imprinting, biologically appropriate objects must be used in relation to each other in order for the relevant variables to be adequately investigated. Finally, it has become important to understand that all findings and data generated by the scientific investigation of behavior must be interpreted and explained in terms of actual reality. This means that the "control" in imprinting research is the actual imprinting experience between the female and young in the feral setting. That is, the actual imprinting experience must not only be studied but also must serve as the yardstick for measuring the effects of any experimental manipulation.

These experiments serve to show how actual events in their natural settings not only can be studied in themselves though sophisticated techniques, but also to investigate the questions that have been raised by earlier published results from laboratory experimentation. Such questions as those involving the critical period, the primacy versus recency effects, the effects of certain kinds of drugs, the effects of punishment, the effects of massed versus spaced practice or experience, can all be examined by utilizing the normal, natural imprinting object and the feral setting. Formerly, field work was limited to identification of problems worth investigating and could do little more than suggest solutions, because of the lack of precision in methodology. For this reason, it has not been the normal procedure to do research outdoors. But it now appears that the time has come to realize that in at least some respects, laboratory research, through an overly developed concern for experimental precision at the cost of relevance in the larger biological-environmental context, can lead to a sterile dead end in which the behavior being investigated bears no resemblance at all to what actually occurs in nature.

The work herein reported has implications that go beyond the study of behavior in ducklings and female mallards in relation to imprinting, and even beyond the study of species-specific behavior in general. Any developmental analysis, particularly when the entire life span is involved, is inadequate without the use of field work which demonstrates the applicability or generality of findings generated by the laboratory. This, at the very least, is absolutely essential. Both Baer and Willems (Chapters 9 and 10 of this volume), starting from perspectives different from ours, have also concluded that observations in the field both suggest problems and test solutions to these problems. Certainly, cross-checking between the field and the laboratory can discourage the dogmatism that tends to be engendered by the exclusive use of a particular methodology (see Overton and Reese, Chapter 4 in this volume) and to encourage a potentially fruitful openness to fresh viewpoints and strategies. The use of *synthesis*—that is, the employment of sophisticated laboratory techniques *in the field* so that actual behavior events may be studied with a high degree of precision—may become the way of the future as far as research in ethology, developmental psychology, and the study of behavior in general are concerned. Such synthesis permits actual reality to serve as the *control* for measuring the effects of any experimental manipulation, *not* highly artificial and contrived laboratory situations which are divorced from the real world. Just as we must study man to learn about man, we must study reality to learn about reality. Otherwise, our scientific endeavors lead solely to the construction of a fantasy world which does not exist.

CHAPTER 3

Methodological Issues of Cross-Cultural Research in Developmental Psychology

LUTZ H. ECKENSBERGER

UNIVERSITÄT DES SAARLANDES
GERMANY

I. Introduction

What Wilhelm Wundt said, as early as 1911, with regard to "Voelker-psychologie" still holds true for its follower, cross-cultural psychology:

> The fact that new scientific fields, or, as there are no such phenomena in the narrow sense of the word, new forms of scientific observation [of the same topic!] are obliged to struggle for existence over a certain period of time is not only understandable, but, to a certain extent, may even be useful. In this way, the up and coming new discipline receives its most effective incentive for securing its own position by means of concrete achievements and for defining its most significant tasks through discussion with neighboring disciplines, and thus, it moderates excessive claims and limits those already existing to an increased degree [p.1].[1]

Thus, if methodological issues in the nascent[2] discipline of cross-cultural

[1] Translation by the writer.
[2] It was not until 1966 and 1970, respectively, that the *International Journal of Psychology* and the *Journal of Cross-Cultural Psychology* first appeared, to name but two indicators of the late development.

psychology are to be related to the issues in life-span developmental psychology, this is certainly possible only if its subject matter has been delimited from neighboring disciplines. Therefore, a definition of cross-cultural psychology will be elaborated, first, mainly in order to separate it from cultural anthropology (Section II). Second, the contribution of cross-cultural psychology to life-span developmental psychology will be clarified (Section III). Third, turning to the actual methodological issues, after pointing to the efforts to operationalize the culture concept (Section IV), the central issue—the problem of equivalence of measurements—will be discussed in detail (Section V). Finally, the main implications of a strategy for cross-cultural research in life-span developmental psychology will be summarized and a look to future research will be taken (Section VI).

The questions raised here are intentionally of a fundamental nature. Thus, not all of them deal directly with developmental aspects, but, nevertheless, all of them are relevant for cross-cultural research in developmental psychology. Single problems, e.g., those arising with regard to the application of a special research instrument, are not taken into account. The viewpoint present below regarding the fundamental methodological problems in cross-cultural psychology is variously based on Frijda and Jahoda (1966), Przeworski and Teune (1966) to mention only a few, and previous publications of the author (Boesch & Eckensberger, 1969; Eckensberger, 1970). The approach to life-span developmental psychology is in line with the work of Baltes (1968), Baltes and Goulet (1970), and Schaie (1965, 1970). Nevertheless, some conclusions drawn here will differ from these authors' in various respects.

II. Toward a Definition of Cross-Cultural Psychology and Cross-Cultural Research

Traditionally, cross-cultural research is a strategy used in cultural anthropology (cf. Whiting, 1954, 1968), which is concerned with group performances and group products (material, immaterial, or symbolic) in their dependency on external material or social conditions (climate, geography, history; cf. Tolman, 1952). The culture concept is used as an intervening variable or hypothetical construct (cf. Mandelbaum, 1968). Beginning with Tylor (1889), cultural anthropologists have used cross-cultural research with the aim of (1) validating the culture concept itself, and (2) describing concrete cultural groups.

In contrast, *cross-cultural psychology* (as a specialty branch within the discipline of psychology) is concerned primarily with the individual living organism. Especially, it *attempts to ascertain the different expressions of behavior that occur as a consequence of the interaction of the individual with his specific cultural environment*. Thus, cross-cultural research can be used to uncover that part of systematic variance in behavior due to different cultural environments with which individuals cope. That means, strictly speaking, to uncover "if-then relations" (Barker, 1968), wherein "if-conditions" (independent variables) are different cultural conditions with which behavior (dependent variable) is covarying. Principally, this approach is comparable to that of general or experimental psychology. Nevertheless, in contrast to experimental psychology, the independent variable in cross-cultural psychology is an "assigned" variable (Kerlinger, 1964) that can, only with great difficulty if at all, be manipulated arbitrarily by the experimenter. But in most cases, the uncovering of "if–then relations" is possible only on an *a posteriori* basis, because the interaction between the individual and his specific cultural environment has occurred *before* psychological research is undertaken.

In light of the above restriction, a provisional definition of *cross-cultural research* might then read: *Cross-cultural research* (as a strategy), *is the explicit, systematic comparison of psychological measures obtained under different cultural conditions,* in which cultural conditions—the operationalized culture concept of cultural anthropology—serve as the independent variables. Psychological concepts are used as intervening variables or hypothetical constructs. Since not all variables involved in cross-cultural research are part of psychology as generally understood (the independent variables are adopted from cultural anthropology), cross-cultural psychology may be called an interdisciplinary approach.

When the distribution of cultural conditions in various populations is known, cross-cultural research can be used to compare the describable groups by means of these various cultural conditions. [However, this would be the subject-matter of anthropology, sociology, or as LeVine (1966) called it, "psychology of populations."] Unfortunately, most data from various cultural groups—usually nations—are typically compared without defining the distribution of cultural characteristics in each group and without defining the dimensions on which they differ from each other. The result is that in these cases, no meaningful basis is provided for interpreting differences occurring in the data.

The following discussion refers to problems associated with uncovering the "if–then relation." An *a priori* distinction of special conditions understood as cultural (Frijda & Jahoda, 1966) is demanded, thus pointing to the necessity for making the global culture concept operational. In addition, arguments for a systematic (i.e., hypothetico-deductive) research approach will be presented. The cross-cultural approach is meaningful whenever the hypotheses to be tested (1) demand maximal variation of the independent variable or (2) refer to behavior which does not occur in the investigator's own culture (Sears, 1961).Both of these uses mean a test of an experimental, quantitative hypothesis (i.e., not the null hypothesis). Cross-cultural research is not advocated, however, when a generalization of data to "different cultural groups" is desired, because, in principle, this means a test of the null hypothesis. This viewpoint differs from that of other authors (e.g., Baltes & Goulet, 1970; Campbell, 1961; Cattell, 1960; Gutmann, 1967; Jinks & Fulker, 1970), but it seems defensible since, if results contraindicate generalization (of processes and principles), this would at worst lead to several "culture specific" psychologies (cf. Baltes & Goulet, 1970) which in turn would prevent the development of a general body of knowledge and would also hinder the explication of the principles whereby different cultural conditions are related to different forms of behavior, both quantitatively and qualitatively. The discrimination of "cultural groups" ("cultures") from "cultural conditions" may appear somewhat artificial but, in the interest of clarifying methodological problems, it seems to be productive. Despite this discrimination, the writer shall occasionally use terms like "cultures" or "cultural groups." When he does it, he in fact means groups which are definable and separable by one (or more) "cultural condition(s)" or "cultural dimension(s)." The terms are used only because they are convenient marker terms with which to reference the concepts involved.

In concluding this section, some remarks will be made concerning the underlying theoretical view of the problems stated up to now. The basic model of man, or "world hypothesis," implicit in the definition of cross-cultural psychology obviously is neither purely "mechanistic" nor "organismic" in terms of the dichotomy discussed by Reese and Overton (1970). This is intentional, since each world view alone seems to be insufficient to explain all aspects of psychological phenomena.

For a European psychologist, the recent emphasis on organismic models in American psychology, e.g., as represented by Werner or Piaget, seems to be the countermovement against the extremely one-sided experimental tradition in America. Paradoxically enough, it seems disadvantageous, given the necessity of developing a synthetic model of man which takes into account the spontaneous activity of the organism as well as the modifying influence of environment, that the results of stimulus–response (SR) approaches were so tremendously successful in predicting behavior under stimulus-control (i.e., using a mechanistic model of man). But, unfortunately, it was left to the future for psychologists to make explicit that these results were elaborated (1) under artificial (i.e., systematically manipulated) conditions in the laboratory and (2) working with species lower than *Homo sapiens*—both of which lead to an underestimation of the human "organism as inherently and spontaneously active [Reese & Overton, 1970, p. 133]." Therefore, these results are not unreservedly transferable to natural life situations, because influences of the natural environment are not as systematic as "stimuli" in experiments.

It is the undeniable merit of Reese and Overton (1970) to recall these problems. But the pendulum should not be permitted to fly to the opposite extreme. Rather, a "wedding of insufficiencies" should be consummated, as Osgood (1968) suggested with regard to the rival theories—general behavior SR theory and nativistic linguistic theory—in the area of language learning and behavior. Possibly, cross-cultural research in psychology as defined previously will contribute significantly to the necessary construction of a "brand new" theory in developmental psychology that is more than just a synthesis of terms from purely mechanistic and organismic models (cf. Reese & Overton, 1970, p. 121).

III. The Contingency between Cross-Cultural Psychology and Life-Span Developmental Psychology

According to Baltes and Goulet (1970), "human life-span developmental psychology is concerned with the description and explication of ontogenetic (age-related) behavioral change from birth to death [p. 12] ." The approach to explicating ontogenetic change in terms of antecedent–consequent relationships can be summarized in the paradigm presented by Baltes and Goulet (1971): "Change $A_f \{f(H, E_{pr}, E_{pa})\}$, where A_f indicates an age-performance function, H denotes heredity, and E_{pr} and E_{pa} summarize present and past environmental events [p. 5]." As Baltes and Goulet (1970) pointed out, it is a "crucial problem—that the basic dimensions of heredity and environment are largely unknown" and that " most of the research with humans must invoke indirect methods for assessment of nature–nurture relations, [because] the core variables making up heredity and environment are biotic in nature and not under full control of the experimenter [p. 11]."

Cross-cultural psychology, as understood here, may be helpful in looking for solutions to these problems. In order to explore the processes which lead to different forms of behavior, cross-cultural research can serve as a fruitful complement to heredity-oriented approaches by *maximizing that part of the systematic variance due to E_{pr} and E_{pa}*, i.e., "cultural conditions." This obviously is to be done by introducing the cross-cultural approach into the general designs of developmental psychology as in the case where: (a) nature–nurture ratios are established for different "cultural groups" (c.f., Cattell, 1969, p. 357), and (b) single (or combined) psychological measurements are used. This viewpoint is in line with a conclusion drawn by LeVine (1970) who states: ". . . that, if the etiological model of research is adopted, there are obstacles of measurement to be faced and overcome, that cross-cultural studies cannot fruitfully be separated from other developmental studies, [and] that anthropological data should attend the research process in all its phases [p. 570]."

To include the cross-cultural approach systematically in designs of developmental psychology, seems to be a task for the future. How it can be managed will be discussed later (see Sections V, E).

IV. Operationalization of the Culture Concept

As stated previously, cultural conditions function as the independent variables in cross-cultural research. That means the global culture concept as used in cultural anthropology has to be made operational before it can be explicitly incorporated into psychological designs. Usually, in order to clarify the concept, reference is made to the comprehensive work of Kroeber and Kluckhohn (1963), who collected more than 150 definitions and an equal number of statements on the culture concept, thereby demonstrating how ambiguous this concept is in science. Therefore, Smith (1954) was correct in stating: ". . . it is important to note that culture is a concept, not a theory. The term itself embodies no articulated proposition from which consequences can be drawn and put to test. It asserts nothing about reality [p. 40]."

Instead of referring to verbal definitions, it seems more fruitful to look at what cultural anthropologists do when classifying "concrete cultures." In summarizing their efforts to look for operational indicants of the culture concept, three approaches require mention:

(1) In 1964 Naroll presented his description of a "cultunit" as the entity of investigation in anthropology. His considerations were extended and modified by Whiting (1968), who suggested focusing on characteristics which should maximize the "cultural homogeneity" of a certain group. But these criteria are of no benefit for cross-cultural research in psychology, because they either are purely formal (e.g., the group should have a name) or too unspecific (e.g., the group should have a certain degree of sovereignty).

(2) A more concrete idea of the scope of cultural conditions is gained after analysis of the catalog of characteristics used by anthropologists in classifying cultural units. Several classifications are available which, however, are not independent of each other (Murdock, 1967; Murdock et al., 1950; and particularly Textor, 1967). Textor's (1967) tabulation, probably the most extensive one, uses 43 raw characteristics which are subdivided into 536 raw attributes. He referred to such aspects as settlement pattern, diet, writing system, linguistic affiliation, political organization, societal complexity, work organization, marital residence, family organization, authority within the family, status of women, etc. Not all of the 43 characteristics are of equal relevance for psychological research, but they distinguish quite different aspects of the whole material, social, and symbolic ecology usually subsumed under the concept of "culture."

Of course, there are some objections to this approach. On the one hand, there is the question of whether the statistical independence of the mentioned characteristics is guaranteed ("Galton's problem," cf. Marsh, 1967; Naroll, 1964a,b). On the other hand, it is debatable whether, in principle, it is possible to define "cultural" characteristics "transculturally" ("Malinowskian dilemma," cf. Berry, 1969; Goldsmith, 1966) or whether only "functional equivalent characteristics" can be compared (Duijker, 1955; Nadel, 1951).

(3) Although the criticism of treating "nations" as "cultural groups" (Holtzman et al., 1969, pp. 128–129) is justified, it nevertheless seems useful to employ statistics from educational and economic areas compiled on a national

basis. Reference to such stored data and statistics is made by Berstecher (1970), Hastings (1964), Kapferer (1964), Mitchell (1964, 1968), Rokkan (1964), and Scheuch and Bruening (1964). Such data can be handled and reduced by factor analysis techniques which allow one to define either "cultural" or "national characteristics" (R-analysis), "cultural" or "national groups" (Q-analysis), or even "cultural change" (P-analysis) (Cattell, 1949, 1953a, 1965a; Driver & Schuessler, 1957; Hofstaetter, 1951).

In evaluating the usefulness of these three approaches for making operational the global culture concept, only the last two seem to be available as independent variables in cross-cultural psychology. In some respects, however, they are still insufficient and require further methodological considerations to be discussed later (Section VI).

V. The Problem of Data Comparability

According to Campbell and Stanley (1963), "Securing scientific evidence involves making at least one comparison [p. 176]." What is to be compared in cross-cultural psychology when the emphasis is on developmental aspects? With regard to the definitions of life-span developmental, and cross-cultural psychology stated previously, the comparison not only refers to change in behavior during the life-span, that is, the comparison of behavior at varying age-levels but, in addition, to its expression in varying cultural environments. In the following, the problems involved in making a comparison are emphasized primarily with regard to the cross-cultural strategy. Developmental aspects will be referred to in considering the construct validity of measurements.

Since the central hypothesis of cross-cultural psychology is that facing different cultural realities results in different forms of behavior, in both quality and quantity, the problem is to ascertain whether formally identical behaviors in different cultural environments have the same meaning and whether formally different behaviors have different meanings. This implies the concept of "functional equivalence" (conceptual equivalence of measures, equivalence of meaning) which soon will be considered in detail. Although the problem of comparability and equivalence of data is inherent in numerous areas of psychology (cf. Gulliksen, 1968), nowhere is it as immediately evident as in the case of cross-cultural research. As Gutmann (1967) vividly stated: "[in the same way as] we find out that we are air breathers, and 'air' only becomes an objectified datum, when we first fall into the water . . . cross-cultural experience . . . gets us out of our social skin, out of our accustomed psychosocial ecology [p. 189]." The central problem that emerges is to delineate an underlying rationale by which to equate obviously different forms of behavior and to compare them, as, for example, Heckhausen (1967) does in the following example: "Competition with a standard of excellence can be recognized as easily in an Indian tribe hunting game as in middle-class business activity in our civilization [p. 28]."

What are the basic assumptions involved in the specification of activities as homologous in different cultural environments? It was not until the last few years that these problems were elaborated within a general frame of reference concerning the relation between theory and data (Berrien, 1968; Gordon, 1968; Gordon & Kikuchi, 1966; Przeworski & Teune, 1966). It is now evident that *equivalence can be determined only with reference to the underlying psychological construct* or latent variable; this implies the basic assumption that psychological constructs (processes and structures) exist transculturally.

A. Assumption of Psychological Universals

All material justifications for assuming the transcultural existence of psychological constructs (e.g., Hofstaetter, 1956; Piaget, 1958; Sears, 1961; Werner, 1959) have to do, more or less, with the specific biological endowments of the human species. Reference will first be made to the positions of Hofstaetter (1956) and Sears (1961). Piaget's basic viewpoint will be considered subsequently.

Hofstaetter (1956) has presented eleven "theorems of psychology" with a view to the "essence of man [p. 105]" and has enumerated culturally independent universals of man and his interaction with the material and social environment. Somewhat less systematically, Sears (1961) has argued in the same direction. Both Hofstaetter (1956) and Sears (1961) started from the fact that man is born with universally valid initial conditions, e.g., a specific human morphology, a central nervous system with a certain structure and a relatively slow speed of maturation, etc. Regardless of his different material and social environments, for example, each newborn requires care because of the slow speed of maturation. This leads to institutions of care (e.g., family organization) and, consequently, *homo sapiens* is confronted with a series of unavoidable situations which call forth "secondary universals [Sears, 1961, p. 449]," e.g., learning processes. These, in turn, activate the development of cognitive structures, standards of judgment, and affective mechanisms, so that it can be stated that all human beings show something akin to attitudes toward objects, have or acquire motivation, etc. In this manner, all these psychological constructs can be considered as being "genotypically" transcultural, whereas their "phenotypical" manifestation may be unique, that is, culturally peculiar.

B. Determination of Equivalence of Measurements

Despite the problem of comparability and equivalence of data probably being the most frequently mentioned pitfall in cross-cultural psychology, there seems to be no commonly accepted systematization or solution for it. Formulating the problem of equivalence with regard to psychological constructs requires a logical prerequisite. For the purpose of identifying different forms of behavior as equivalent, there must be available "stable reference points" or "transcultural baselines" (Hudson *et al.*, 1959), which have the logical status of a "tertium comparationis." Although a framework could be presented, using set theory concepts, with which to formally describe the basic logic common to all approaches, the logical prerequisites, and the main criteria for determining the functional equivalence of data, space limitations dictate that the writer turn to an examination of the more concrete solutions for establishing the equivalence of measurements.

Although Anderson (1967) proposed not to distinguish "psychological equivalence" of items and/or tests from "linguistic equivalence," the writer suggests that the distinction be made. A research instrument composed of verbal items may cover, in one community speaking the same language, the range of behavior representing an intended construct. These items can be optimally translated into another language (linguistic equivalence). Doing so, however, does not guarantee that the range of behavior is also representative for the intended construct in this (second) language area (psychological equivalence).

C. Linguistic Equivalence

Since, within one language, there are several possibilities by which to express the same content, there cannot be one and only one translation of a phrase from one language into another one. Given this, all translation procedures can only result in approximate solutions. Fortunately, several excellent discussions of translation problems in cross-cultural research have already appeared (cf. Brislin, 1970; Campbell *et al.*, 1971). Therefore, only a brief mention of the most important methods will be made here.

In order to secure linguistic equivalence of verbal material approximately, the "semantic differential" or "bilinguals" are utilized most frequently. Bilinguals may function as "translators" or as "respondents." But in both cases, their efforts are supported by those of monolinguals. Historically, bilinguals have been used primarily to translate verbal material from one language (original version) into a target language only. This procedure then was completed by obtaining independent back-translations from the target language into the original one. However, the most sophisticated proposal seems to be that of Campbell *et al.* (1971), who propose a "multiphasic–iterative process" consisting of several independent translations and back-translations with the resulting several forms in the original as well as in the target language then being compared by monolinguals. Beyond other advantages, it is to be emphasized that this procedure leads to changes within the original version.

When bilinguals are utilized as "respondents" (cf. Anderson, 1967), they are presented the two versions of the same test or questionnaire in the original *and* (already translated) target language. Then the reliability of the test in a monolingual application is used as a criterion for the quality of the translation. The differences between the versions in different languages should not be greater than the retest reliability. However, in using bilinguals there are some cautions to be considered. For example, only "coordinate" and not "compound" bilinguals seem to be able to produce approximately equivalent versions in different languages (for a more detailed discussion of this problem see Ervin, 1964; Lambert, 1955; Lambert *et al.*, 1958). Furthermore, even though we cannot pause here to discuss either the general problem of using verbal material in developmental studies or the problem of retest reliability, it seems worthwhile to point out the facts that (a) the development of language itself is confounded with other—mainly cognitive—variables, and that (b) the very concept of retest reliability is contraindicated, in principle, in the measurement of change.

A completely different approach to surmounting language barriers is the one of Osgood and his co-workers who seek to establish culture-adapted scales of the well-known "semantic differential." In this case, concepts like house, man, sky, hand, dog, etc., selected by anthropologists as "universals," are the "identities." These concepts comprise the so-called common denominators for the choice of semantically equivalent scales (cf. Jakobovits, 1966; Osgood, 1960, 1964, 1965, 1967; Osgood *et al.*, 1957).

D. Psychological Equivalence

In the following discussion, a distinction is made between two closely related approaches for determining the functional equivalence of data. One is statistical and the other theory-oriented. But, because they are complementary, they only stress different aspects of the same issue. For in determining the functional equivalence of data, a psychological theory as well as a model of measurement is needed.

1. Statistical Approaches to Determine the Equivalence of Measurements

In pure life-span developmental psychology the *same subjects* can be used as "stable reference points" (e.g., in longitudinal designs) in determining the functional equivalence of items. But in investigations of cross-cultural age–performance functions, the subjects, as well as the items, may be different. As a consequence, "stable reference points" have to be created on a statistical basis first. This takes place in two steps: (1) "identities" (Przeworski & Teune, 1966) are sought which are formally and substantively identical across cultures and which therefore indicate the "identical dimension" (Duijker & Frijda, 1961) or "transcultural baseline." (2) "Equivalents" (Przeworski & Teune, 1966) are assigned which are formally different but, by providing their relation to the identities, one ensures that they mean substantively the same.

Establishment of identities and equivalents can be realized by means of various statistical methods, the results of which will be conditioned by the method.

Before turning to some of them, the question as to whether it is sufficient to use identities only should be settled. Neglecting equivalents entirely would miss the real cross-cultural issue of concern, for the different expressions of behavior occurring as a consequence of specific cultural environments would not be taken into account. It should be emphasized in this context that the fundamental concern of cross-cultural psychology is not to compare individuals (*a, b, c*) of different cultures (*X, Y, Z*), but, rather, to determine which form of behavior in different cultural environments is the indicant for the construct in question. Not until then should individuals be compared.

a. Coefficient of Difficulty.   The concept of item difficulty is indirectly contained in the discussion of Berrien (1968). He proposed the use of all items in all investigated cultures. "Such a procedure would probably result in some items being nondiscriminating in culture *X* that would be highly discriminating in *Y*, and *vice versa* [p. 5]." Gordon (1968) also used this concept, to define the "level" of items. According to his viewpoint, "identities" are those items which are formally identical and which have an identical level of difficulty. "Equivalents" are those items which are formally different, but which have an equivalent level of difficulty. Irvine (1968, 1969) applied the concept in order to prove the identical meaning of a whole test by correlating the levels of difficulty of different items of the same (i.e., formally identical) test applied in different cultures.

b. Factor Analysis.   Gordon (1968) recommends the use of factor analysis for the purpose of defining the equivalence of item-meaning, because the level of difficulty alone does not permit one to segregate "content" (internal consistency, homogeneity, unidimensionality) and "level" (difficulty) of items. Items are "identities" according to "content" if they have equal factor loadings, thereby building up the same factors. Items are "equivalents" according to "content" if, despite being formally different, they show equal factor loadings on factors which are marked by a large number of invariant identities. Since the comparison of factor structures and factor scores for different populations is handled in detail elsewhere (cf. Cattell, 1969, 1970a) and in the present volume by Baltes and Nesselroade, Bentler, and Nunnally, here only two problems will be pointed out: (1) As indicated by Gordon (1968) ". . . if a significant amount of content substitution is necessary, one might be led to question, whether comparable constructs are being measured in the two cultures [p. 15]." (2) Normally, factor analysis is used to define dimensionality regardless of whether data are dichotomous (Lienert, 1967, p. 251) or continuous. As Sixtl (1968) has stressed, however, use of factor analysis is mostly contraindicated in the case of dichotomous items (yes–no; right–wrong). A factor analysis based on ϕ-coefficients of items which have different levels of difficulty, even though they are homogeneous in the sense of a Guttman-scale, does not result in one factor, as one would expect. The resulting correlation matrix is a simplex which leads to several characteristic factors. Therefore, factor analysis seems to be applicable only in case of continuous variables, i.e., mainly on "test level." But then, obviously, the unidimensionality of these tests has to be proved beforehand.

c. Coefficient of Homogeneity. The most stringent proposal for defining items as "identities" and "equivalents" within classical test theory seems to be the one of Przeworski and Teune (1966), who used the coefficient of homogeneity (Scott & Wertheimer, 1962). According to their proposition, "identities" are those items which do not lose their 'homogeneity when applied transculturally. "Equivalents" are defined by correlation with these "identities." It would be more powerful, however, to define the "equivalents" also according to the criterion of homogeneity. For this, it would be necessary to prove their specific intracultural invariance of homogeneity (unidimensionality) by splitting each cultural group at random and reexamining the homogeneity of the items. Under this proposal, "equivalents" are items which are homogeneous with regard to one culture only and which lose their homogeneity when applied in another culture. This procedure does not permit one to distinguish between "level" and "content," but it defines whether a given set of items is basically scalable or not.

d. The Probabilistic Model of Rasch. All statistical procedures mentioned so far are afflicted with a fundamental shortcoming of classical test theory: The test parameters (in both unidimensional and multidimensional cases) are dependent on the sample used. Sixtl (1967) called classical test theory "circular" because, e.g., on the one hand, the difficulty of an item is defined by the number of subjects who supplied the correct response, while, on the other hand, the performance of a subject is defined by the difficulty of the items he responds to correctly.

In order to circumvent this dilemma, "it should be possible to determine the degree of difficulty from the item itself [Sixtl, 1967, p. 99]." Test items must therefore form an "objective measuring board" which is independent of all reference groups in its construction (cf. Fischer, 1968). Thus, it seems to be meaningful, particularly in cross-cultural research and also in developmental psychology (cf. Spada, 1970), to revert to probabilistic models in test construction. According to Fischer (1968) the one of Rasch (1960) is most exhaustive.

Rasch's model emphasizes the obtainment of independent formulations of item parameters and subject parameters. Rasch (1966) called this "specific objectivity" and stated:

> The comparison of any two subjects can be carried out in such a way that no other
> parameters are involved than those of the two subjects—neither the parameter of any

other subject nor any of the stimulus parameters [and that] similarly, any two stimuli as well as the parameters of the subjects having been replaced with observable numbers [pp. 104-105].

Although difficulties with the methods used to estimate these parameters remain (Fischer, 1970; Fischer & Scheiblechner, 1970; Rasch, 1960; Scheiblechner, 1970), as soon as they are resolved, this model may well prove to be superior both for checking transculturally invariant tests and for examining invariance in the meaning of tests at various age-levels.

After determining unidimensionality of tests, factor analysis is very useful for determining both the transcultural identical and the cultural equivalent manifestations of the psychological construct in question. Because the "identities" are already proved by testing their specific objectivity, they can be used as "reference tests" in order to mark equivalent factors (analogous to Irvine, 1968, 1969).

A few remarks must be made concerning the utilization of factor analysis in this context. (1) The solutions of factor analyses not only depend on the samples investigated, but also—trivially enough—on the tests used. An *a priori* inclusion of specifically objective tests in the analysis could therefore influence culture-specific solutions. For this reason, an *a posteriori* incorporation of the marker variables (the specifically objective tests) seems to be more meaningful and useful (Dwyer, 1937). (2) Every factor analysis entails the problem of stability (reproducibility) of the factors. Therefore, samples which have been selected according to different cultural conditions and for which factor analyses have been set up, should be split and, through procedures of similarity—or criterion rotation (Sixtl & Fittkau, 1968), the different factor structures compared (e.g., Baltes *et al.*, 1969). This splitting need not be done at random, but can be directed by definite hypotheses. In this case, an attempt should be made to control extraneous variance. (3) Gulliksen (1968) made reference to the issue of test variables with low communalities. Normally, such variables are not taken into consideration with regard to interpretation of factor structures. As it is not possible to decide whether erroneous or specific variance is the major component of a variable's uniqueness, with variables of low communalities it is useful to determine additionally whether they have high or low reliability. In the case of high reliability, there is evidence that the variables are specific. Thus, in cross-cultural research, reliable variables of high specificity can determine "culture specific" characteristics and, consequently, are of particular importance.

2. Theory-Oriented Approaches to Determine the Equivalence of Measurements

In addition to the purely statistical ones, there are, as mentioned above, approaches by which to tackle the comparability of measurements from a theoretical frame of reference. The latter, of course, is connected somewhat more closely to the assumption of psychological universals.

a. Psychophysiological Measures. Mainly, with regard to motivation- and attitude-research the writer suggests, following a proposal of Frijda and Jahoda (1966), to make use of "psychophysiological indicators" as "identities" in cross-cultural research. The underlying principle is that cultural conditions exercise such meager influence on psychophysiological processes that they can pass for culturally invariant variables. "Equivalent" items, however, have to be determined by aforementioned statistical procedures.

b. Piaget's Tasks. According to Piaget's theory, thought processes develop in irreversible order and it can be said that the construct of intelligence at various stages is marked by specific formal logic operations. The "difficulty" of a task is defined with reference to these operations, independently of the sample of persons [therefore Sixtl's (1967) demand concerning one characteristic of a test item is fulfilled]. Only the material and the circumstances necessary to identify the operations are dependent on environment. Transposed into the terminology used here in cross-cultural research, the formal operations can serve as "identities," indicating that the construct of intelligence is being focussed on regardless of the varying cultural conditions.

Indeed, the use of Piaget's tasks in cross-cultural research is very encouraging. Greenfield (1966), Price-Williams (1961, 1962), Sigel, Anderson, and Shapiro (1966), to mention only a few, argued for the invariance of development of logical operations under various cultural conditions. Nevertheless, they showed that the various stages of cognitive development are reached with varying rapidity according to material used, verbal ability of subjects, diversity of training, and schooling (Brunswik, 1956; Hooper, 1969; Klingensmith, 1953). Such a result is also familiar outside cross-cultural research (cf. Aebli, 1965; Braine, 1959; Davis, 1965; Haney & Hooper, 1971; Weinert, 1967). Pertinent to these results, however, methodological objections which question the comparability of tasks and/or samples are made (cf. Jahoda, 1958a,b). However, the reader should realize that the very sources of variance which are one focus of cross-cultural research are (a) differences in the generality of judgment, (b) differences in the need of stimulus support, and (c) differences in the use of action (cf. Goodnow, 1969). It must be remembered, however, that these theory-oriented approaches must be complemented by statistical proof of unidimensionality, which helps assure that no variables are investigated other than those intended (by the theory). When other constructs are measured by identical tasks in different cultural groups, they obviously lose their unidimensionality order due to such influence as e.g., the authority role of the tester. Indeed, that particular influence, which had an unintended effect on the application of Piaget tasks with Wolof children (cf. Greenfield, 1966, p. 250) could have been defined by the proof of unidimensionality of the tasks.

E. Inclusion of Cultural Dimensions in Research Designs of Life-Span Developmental Psychology: Construct-Validation

In view of the contingent relationship between cross-cultural psychology and life-span developmental psychology, all attempts to incorporate cultural conditions systematically into the designs of developmental psychology by specifying simultaneously the underlying theory and the method used can be characterized as construct-validation. Looking at an age–performance function under different cultural conditions means that special predictions of behavioral change (according to quantity or structure) eventually can be made from information about particular cultural conditions. In the following section, no differentiation is made with reference to the quality of the dependent variable, e.g., whether it is a nature –nurture ratio (cf. Cattell, Chapter 6 in this volume), a single variable (cf. Baltes, 1968; Schaie, 1965), or a whole set (or structure) of variables (cf. Baltes & Nesselroade, 1970). The emphasis primarily is placed on the independent variables. From this point of view, the inclusion of cultural dimensions in the developmental design can take place by (1) selecting cultural conditions in reality, (2) actively manipulating cultural conditions by planned social change, and (3) simulating cultural conditions.

1. Selection of Cultural Conditions in Reality

In the designs of developmental psychology (cf. Baltes, 1968; Schaie, 1965, 1970), changes over time in cultural variables are inferred through time-lag effects. But the mere proof of such effects does not make possible a substantive interpretation with reference to certain kinds of cultural change. Baltes, therefore, suggested refraining from interpretations according to content. Obviously, however, it is more consistent to include cultural conditions in the designs systematically. In the following paragraph, a differentiation is made between (1) naturally existing cultural groups and (2) individuals who have been selected to form groups that are homogeneous with regard to only one cultural dimension.

   a. Seeking Out "Naturally Existing Cultural Groups."   A graphic representation of a possible result of this procedure is shown in Fig. 1. The systematization of designs of developmental psychology is shown on the right side (three cohorts examined in a psychological function in 10-year intervals). The left side shows how the measures of this function react in various cultural groups if they have been selected on the degree of intensity of a single cultural condition. For example, a hypothesis could be formulated that angle frequency in the environment (cultural condition)[3] influences the size of the Mueller–Lyer illusion (Segall, Campbell, & Herskovitz, 1963). Three cultural groups having maximal difference

---

[3]The use of angle frequency in environment is chosen for simplicity only, and one could doubt whether this is at all a "cultural condition." Such ecological variables, however, can justifiably be called "cultural" according to the tabulation of "cultures" by Textor (1967).

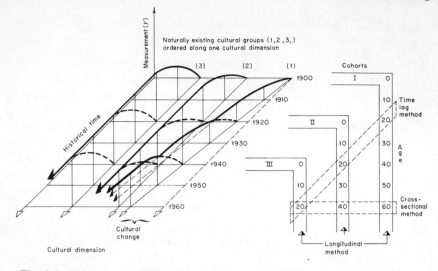

Fig. 1. Inclusion of cultural dimensions in the "general model for the study of developmental problems." Groups (1), (2), and (3) are naturally existing cultural groups. They are sought out to represent the same cultural dimension in varying degrees. In Group (1), cultural change is observable between 1900 and 1960.

with reference to angle frequency ("carpentered world") in the environment might be selected (maximization of experimental or systematic variance). The first group (1) could be selected in a prairie, the second (2) in rural areas, and the third (3) in a large city. In these groups (cf. Fig. 1) the course of development of illusion sizes in various cohorts (I, II, III) can be compared with each other.

In preparing Fig. 1, it was assumed that no changes in angle frequency had taken place between 1900 and 1960 in cultural Groups (2) and (3) (no cultural change occurred), but that there were changes in Group (1). Perhaps, what once was open country was settled and became a village. Therefore, cohort effects would not be observable in Groups (2) and (3), but would be in Group (1).

This approach, however, does not permit generalization of the results on the cultural condition of angle frequency alone. The "naturally existing groups" can also differ. systematically from each other with regard to further conditions which produce extraneous variance $(X_2 \cdot \cdot \cdot X_n)$, e.g., in child-rearing practices which can lead to more or less field-dependent perception (cf. Dawson, 1967a,b). Of course, the usual approaches in controlling extraneous variance could be used (matching, covariance analysis, inclusion of additional conditions in the design). However, they are either very intricate or lead to extensive complications in the design and again presuppose that a theory exists which permits a definition of not only the systematic variance, but also of the conditions producing extraneous variance.

There are also several *statistical* problems involved in using naturally existing cultural groups. Whenever a cultural change occurs in longitudinal studies in cross-cultural research, it leads to unequal frequencies in the cells of analysis of variance designs, i.e., to nonorthogonal designs. Methods for estimating values in empty cells, or for analysis with unequal frequencies, require the inequalities to be unsystematically distributed, i.e., random across cells. In the present example, correlations between factor cohorts and cultural conditions exist. Therefore, the omissions are systematic. The same is true if the extraneous variables which are included in the designs are correlated (Terhune, 1963). The critical question is whether the analysis of variance model is violated. Control of extraneous variance through the use of covariance analysis poses similar problems (cf. Evans & Anastasio, 1968).

Finally, the question should be asked whether trend analyses would be more appropriate in exploiting longitudinal designs. If they were employed, age (or time of testing) would no longer be an independent variable, but would be part of the dependent variable (cf. Wohlwill, 1970a,b). There are not only methods which enable trends to be described through orthogonal polynomials (Edwards, 1960), but which also permit one to compare differences in trends which came about under various conditions (cf. Grant, 1956; Rao, 1958).

b. Selection of "Artificially Created Groups." The problems of the control of extraneous variance in particular lead us to reject the use of "naturally existing cultural groups" and to consider, instead, designs permitting one to select individuals who are homogeneous only with regard to systematic (experimental) variance. On other cultural conditions they may be highly heterogeneous. Such a design is represented in Fig. 2. The measures are independent because cultural change is to be eliminated, and for this reason no cohort effects are expected. For example, it is possible that the individuals of Group (1) (cf. Fig. 2) come from very different "cultural groups" which are homogeneous only with regard to the frequencies of angles in their environments, e.g., from the Sahara, Greenland, and the steppe, and are highly heterogeneous with regard to all other conditions. In Group (1), carpentered-world angle frequency may be very rare; in Group (2), the condition may be medium frequency of angle (individuals could be selected from rural areas of various countries and nations); and in Group (3) the maximum possible occurrence of angles in the environment could prevail (individuals could be selected from various big cities).

A disadvantage of this approach is that the increase in control of extraneous variance goes hand in hand with a large increase in error variance since extraneous variance is added to error variance. Thus, repeated measurement designs are no longer possible (cf. Winer, 1962, p. 298). Interpretations of the results would be conservative in any event. The use of artificially created groups also weakens the objection of LeVine (1970) that

. . . the demonstration of a statistically significant difference in means between groups, necessarily supports the investigator's hypothesis concerning the causes or cosymptoms

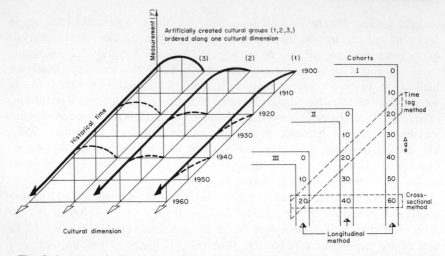

Fig. 2. Inclusion of cultural dimensions in the "general model for the study of developmental problems." Groups (1), (2), and (3) are artificially created to represent the same cultural dimension in varying degrees. With regard to all other possible cultural dimensions, they may be highly heterogeneous.

> of the difference. As Bakan points out, such reasoning confounds the inference from sample difference with the inference from the population difference to the nature of the behavioral phenomenon. . . [p. 571].

This problem does not occur in the case of artificially created groups because the mean differences are interpreted only as indicating differences in behavior.

2. Variation of Cultural Conditions by Manipulation

In cross-cultural research today there is an issue of extreme interest to all social sciences from the viewpoint of scientific theory-development. The issue in question is the possibility of "manipulating" cultural conditions through what is known as "planned social change [Boesch, 1966, p. 335]" or developmental aid. Unfortunately, developmental aid is still viewed within a service context and, so far, research on the topic lacks a theoretically integrative viewpoint. If, however, political institutions could be convinced that it is more productive to seek solutions to practical problems from a superordinate theoretical frame of reference, social change could be brought under control. Then, "social science would have the rare possibility to work at a quasi-experimental level, being able to make *a priori* statements on future processes, wherein conditions would be largely controllable and applicability (or nonapplicability) could be tested [Eckensberger, 1968, p. 124]."[4] [See also Campbell (1969).]

It is obvious that problems of developmental psychology in cross-cultural

[4]Translation by the writer.

research could also benefit from this approach, for, in this case, cultural conditions would no longer be "assigned" or "organismic" variables, and effects on psychological measurements during the developmental process of individuals could be interpreted with greater validity. In the case of planned social change, the assignment of cultural conditions to individuals or groups (experimental variation of cultural conditions) would control extraneous variance, and thereby would greatly improve the internal validity of research plans.

The only shortcoming is that effects of planned social change will appear relatively late after treatment. Thus, though promising, this approach is time-consuming.

3. Manipulation of Cultural Conditions by Simulation

Simulation, in accordance with Abelson (1968), is understood as "the exercise of a flexible imitation of processes and outcomes for the purpose of clarifying or explaining the underlying mechanisms involved [p. 27]." Cross-cultural research is interested in the underlying mechanisms that refer to interactions of individuals and conditions that are more or less present in their cultural environments. It follows that one can try systematically to induce "time compressed" cultural conditions where they are not (or almost not) present and where they are present in a certain amount. Fundamentally, this entails an attempt to grasp "culture by treatment[5] interactions" or, including developmental aspects in the design, to grasp "culture by age by treatment interactions."

This approach has been used with some success in cross-cultural research on intelligence. The intent is to increase, by compensatory test presentations, the testing experience of culturally deprived groups in order to raise these individuals to the level of experience present in groups that are not thus deprived. In this context, it is possible to distinguish "practice," "coaching" (Wiseman & Wrigley, 1953), and "test sophistication" (Vernon, 1954; Wahrstrom & Boersma, 1968), although these methods are slightly overlapping.

In all cases of releasing behavior, these techniques are defensible. If treatment involves restriction or suppression of behavior, however, there are ethical issues to consider.

VI. Requirements for a Cross-Cultural Research Strategy in Developmental Psychology

In the foregoing sections, the most important problems, demands, and assumptions involved in the definition of the independent variables ("cultural condi-

---

[5]The term "treatment" is not used here as it is, for instance, by Cronbach (1957, 1970) in the sense of different "treatments" of individuals in selection or classification procedures but, rather, as an experimentally *induced* process.

tions''), the dependent variables (psychological measures), and their interrelationship (process of construct validation) in cross-cultural research of life span developmental psychology were discussed. Despite the presentation being extremely theory-oriented, there have been several places where strategical aspects have been pointed to (directly or indirectly), but this, necessarily, was unsystematic since the major organization of this chapter is along other lines. Therefore, the main requirements for a cross-cultural research strategy will be summarized more systematically here. The aspects emphasized intentionally represent ''ideal conditions'' which can not yet be realized simultaneously within a single study.

a. Hypothesis-Oriented Approach. The most important prerequisite for a meaningful cross-cultural research strategy is a psychological theory out of which hypotheses can be formulated according to the different expressions of behavior under various cultural conditions. It should be stressed that the dependent, not the independent variable, should be used as a starting point (LeVine, 1970, pp. 565–566). The three basic questions are: (a) Which psychological variable (Y) may be generally influenced by (or covary with) a specific cultural condition (X) in time? (b) Where are these cultural variables present and to what amount? (c) Which cultural conditions $(X_2 \cdot \cdot \cdot X_n)$ are still present which could also influence the psychological variable (y) in time? The strict demand for a hypothetico-deductive approach does not in the least hinder the contemporaneous hypothesis-generating function of cross-cultural research stressed by several authors (Campbell, 1961; Gutmann, 1967; Strodtbeck, 1964).

b. Sampling. According to Subsection *a,* the samples should be selected with regard to specific hypotheses stated about the relationship between cultural conditions and behavior in time. In cross-cultural research of developmental psychology, therefore, the intended generalizations from samples concern (a) cultural *conditions* rather than cultural *groups* (as in cultural anthropology), and (b) age-specific conditions.

Consequently, the subjects under study must not be representative of a cultural population (e.g., in the sense of a nation) and not necessarily of all existing age-groups. But (a) they *should* be representative primarily of the cultural condition *in question*, and (b) in any case, those age-groups should be considered which represent the *''critical period''* with reference to the development of the *dependent variable*. The limitations in interpreting, for instance, the results of studies of perception in cross-cultural research, may be due to failure to include individuals younger than four years of age (cf. LeVine, 1970). Likewise—as discussed in Section V in more detail—instead of seeking out naturally existing groups in cross—cultural research, it seems defensible to create groups artificially by looking for individuals who, regardless of being different in all other aspects, are scalable with regard to the one cultural condition under investigation.

c. Number of Levels of the Cultural Dimension.   Contrary to the usual practice, more than two levels of a cultural condition should be investigated. There are two reasons for this demand: (a) It is well known from experimental psychology that a comparison of two levels on one factor only (independent variable) is not sufficient for stating general laws concerning its relationship to a certain dependent variable. (b) The principle of maximizing the systematic variance, defined as one of the most important advantages of cross-cultural research in developmental psychology (see page 45), should be complemented by trying to ascertain also the *minimal* amount of the systematic variance that still leads to "just measurable" effects on (or covariations in) the dependent variable. In the case of naturally existing cultural groups, this can be realized by complementing "cross-cultural research" by "intra-cultural research" (cf. Campbell, 1961; Frijda & Jahoda, 1966; Holtzman, 1965; Holtzman *et al.*, 1969, LeVine, 1970). In the case of "artificially created cultural groups", no distinction between "cross-cultural" and "intracultural" research can be made.

d. Cross-Validation.   Whether naturally existing groups or artificially created groups are used, the generalizability of the results will be tremendously increased if planned cross-validations are elaborated. Cross-validation should be carried out by splitting the groups which represent the same cultural condition in varying degrees and comparing the results of these groups.

e. Necessity of a Two-Stage Research.   Cultural anthropology is pointed to as an auxiliary science aiding cross-cultural psychology in the determination of where cultural variables are present and to what amount. Unfortunately, however, the data of cultural anthropology can be used only for orientation purposes because "in anthropology customs and jural rules are normative, not normal [Leach, 1968, p. 34]." Thus, empirical investigations often show that anthropological statements concerning a whole group may hold rarely, or not at all, for single individuals (e.g., Powell, 1957). Beyond that, anthropological data are criticized with regard to their methodological level (Driver, 1953; McEwen, 1963; Mitchell, 1967; Stavrianos, 1950). Therefore, as the first step in cross-cultural research, the "collective data" of anthropology have to be tested concerning their applicability and significance for the individual observed. Only afterward, in a second step, should the actual cross-cultural research be carried out.

f. Inclusion of Cultural Conditions in the Designs of Developmental Psychology.   Cross-cultural research by itself indicates that neither the cross-sectional nor the longitudinal design alone is suitable with regard to the concerns of developmental psychology. The "general model for the study of developmental problems" (Baltes, 1968; Schaie, 1965), complemented by the inclusion of cultural conditions, however, becomes highly attractive. Unfortunately, the only cross-cultural research study which used overlapping age-groups (Holtzman *et al.*, 1969), did not choose this design to define generation effects and cultural change, but only to save investigation time.

g. Multivariate Methods. Finally, the great attraction of multivariate methods for cross-cultural research has to be emphasized. Because they simultaneously handle more indicants of a given construct, they may help to answer the question of how constructs are manifested across cultures. It is just this attraction, however, which sometimes leads to an enthusiastic, but unreflective and careless application of these methods.

Most of the requirements mentioned, if incorporated, would lead to an upgrading of the experimental level of traditional cross-cultural research. If utilized in future empirical studies, the level of design would no longer be that of ex-post-facto strategy, but that of quasi-experimental design and, therefore, would lead to more valid interpretations of data. If only measures of two "cultures" are compared, and differences in data are interpreted as "cultural"—a procedure, which most frequently is found in the literature—one has the type of evidence which Scheuch (1967) justifiably referred to as *petitio principii*, because nothing is proved by interpreting "cultural differences" by means of "cultural differences." It is hoped that some of the aspects covered in this chapter may help to avoid such interpretations in future cross-cultural research.

ACKNOWLEDGMENTS

The writer generally wants to express his gratitude to the editors for inviting him to participate in this very stimulating conference. Beyond this, he especially wants to thank Margaret Baltes for her valuable help in translating the initial version of this paper and the editors for their patience in improving the style of the written version. Last, but not least, he wants to thank Uta Eckensberger for her assistance.

CHAPTER 4

Models of Development: Methodological Implications

WILLIS F. OVERTON

STATE UNIVERSITY OF NEW YORK AT BUFFALO
BUFFALO, NEW YORK

HAYNE W. REESE

WEST VIRGINIA UNIVERSITY
MORGANTOWN, WEST VIRGINIA

I. Introduction

In an earlier paper (Reese & Overton, 1970), we presented and explored the thesis that various metaphysical and epistemological models form the determining context within which lower-order, more specific, theoretical models are formulated. Basic metaphysical models are categorically incompatible, and this incompatibility is maintained through the descending *levels of models* to the level of theory construction. Theories formulated within different, basic models are therefore irreconcilable and irreducible to each other. However, theories formulated within one basic model constitute a *family of theories*. The theories in a family may differ in content, e.g., focus on cognitive or social–emotional dimensions, and may differ with respect to specific theoretical issues, but such differences will be compatible or resolvable.

This categorical determinism based on model presupposition, does not terminate at the level of theory construction. Rather, it extends further to influence what are and are not considered to be meaningful problems for investigation, what types of methods are to be employed, and what alternative explanations may be applied in the interpretation of the data generated.

In the present paper, we shall examine some of these research implications of models. Specifically, we shall consider the implications of the two models that have had the greatest impact on developmental psychology—the *mechanistic* (reactive organism) model and the *organismic* (active organism) model. To accomplish this task, we shall first review the general nature, origin, and levels of models as well as the nature of the mechanistic and organismic models. We shall describe the structural corollary issues which derive from these basic models and then turn to the functional or explanatory issues that form the groundwork for the differential research implications of the models.

Portions of the material presented in Sections II, III, and IV, A and B were covered in detail in our previous paper. Hence, this material is presented in these sections as a summary, without detailed development and exemplification. Wherever clarification or supporting argument seems to be needed, the reader is referred to our previous paper (Reese & Overton, 1970).

II. Models

A. Structural–Theoretical Models

The essential characteristic of any model is that it entails an entity which in some manner stands for or represents something other than itself. Beyond this invariant feature, models—as employed in scientific activities—have been classified according to numerous criteria (for a sample of studies that deal with the problem of the classification of models, see Apostel, 1960; Beament, 1960; Black, 1962; Braithwaite, 1962; Gregory, 1953; Hesse, 1966; Hutten, 1954; A. Kaplan, 1964; Lachman, 1960; Rosenbleuth & Wiener, 1954; Turner, 1968). For purposes of the present discussion, the type of models of interest may be referred to as *structural–theoretical models*. These are "theoretical" in the sense that although they are separate and distinct from specific theories, they form the existential meaning context for the construction of theories as well as, at another level, for the interpretation and application of theories.[1] In scientific

---

[1]We remain purposely vague concerning the specific nature of theories because we agree with A. Kaplan that there are several legitimate types of scientific theories. These include *concatenated* or *pattern* theories, in which laws form a network of relations constituting a pattern, and *hierarchical theories*, in which laws are deductions from a small set of basic principles (Kaplan, 1964, p. 298). Within developmental psychology, Werner's and Piaget's theories are representatives of the former type and Hull–Spence theory illustrates the latter. It should also be noted that any attempt to argue in favor of one to the exclusion of the other of these types of theories must derive from the acceptance of a particular model concerning the nature of knowledge. That is, as we shall later discuss, models have a determining influence on epistemology and hence on the particular philosophy of science one adopts.

communities which eschew theory construction except in its inductive mode
—e.g., the experimental, operant, or functional analysis of behavior—these
models serve, generally implicitly, as theory substitutes to guide data collection,
analysis, and interpretation.

The term "structural" is applied to the models we are focusing on in order
to distinguish these from the abstract calculi or formal models of some theories.
Formal models are those which provide no empirical interpretation for their
basic terms. Their validity depends only upon the patterns of relationships existing
among the symbols themselves (A. Kaplan, 1964, p. 261). Structural models,
in contrast, contain terms which "are interpretable in an existential medium
different from that of the thing modeled [Turner, 1968, p. 76]." The actual
medium employed is inconsequential and therefore although structural models
may in some circumstances literally be built or drawn, i.e., may be physical
models, this is not a necessary condition for their acceptance as models. Structural
models may be semantic or conceptual, in the sense of consisting of specific
ways of talking about the domain being modeled (Black, 1962; A. Kaplan,
1964). Mathematical models of learning constitute familiar examples of formal
models; representations of the eye as a camera or a processor, the mind as
a switchboard or a computer, psychoanalytic concepts of instinct as a hydraulic
system, drives as a homeostatic system, and the development of the child as
an equilibration system, are examples of various types of structural models.

B. The Nature, Origin, and Functions of Models

It is generally agreed among philosophers of science and scientists that in
both their nature and origin, structural–theoretical models are metaphorical (e.g.,
Black, 1962; Braithwaite, 1953; Chapanis, 1961; Ferré, 1963; Kuhn, 1962;
Lachman, 1960; Rashevsky, 1955; Schon, 1963; Seeger, 1954; Toulmin, 1962;
Turner, 1968). In an effort to understand and explain an area of inquiry in
which there are some observed facts and regularities, one first selects another
area of knowledge which presents fewer problems or is better organized. This
selected area provides a model or representation of the problem area, but only
after the model-builder has surmounted the further problem of retaining in the
model the properties of the model area which are appropriate to the original
area of inquiry, and rejecting those which are not (see Hesse, 1966).

In our discussion of structural–theoretical models and their nature and origin,
we have already alluded to their functions. Most generally, as representations,
models aid in the understanding and explanation of the subject matter, or as
Black (1962) suggested, a model acts as a lens through which the subject matter
is viewed in a new way. Within this context, models fulfill several other functions.
First, to the extent that theory building is involved, models establish the basic
categories which determine the introduction of certain classes of theoretical
constructs and the exclusion of others. For example, it is no accident, but

rather a reflection of the adherence to a particular model that Erikson (1950), Piaget (1967), and Werner (1948) all introduced constructs which explicitly postulate the direction of developmental change while general behavior theorists do not introduce constructs of this type. Second, models explicate particular features of theories. Examples are the two-stage or mediational model (e.g., Kendler & Kendler, 1970) operating within general behavior theory, and the equilibrium model operating within Piaget's theory (Piaget, 1967). Third, models aid in the deployment or extension of theories (Lachman, 1960; Toulmin, 1962). Finally, regardless of whether explicit theories are employed or not, models function to define meaningful problems for investigation, to suggest types of methods for exploring these problems, and to provide types of explanations for interpreting the data (Fodor, 1968, p. xvi; Kessel, 1969; White, 1970). We shall briefly review the theory-related implications and then focus more directly on issues about methods.

C. Levels of Models

There are levels of models extending from the most circumscribed and concrete to the most general and thus most basic. These levels of models exert a categorical determinism—a restriction on the definition of basic categories—which extends from the most general level "downward" through the construction of scientific theories to the generation, analysis, and interpretation of empirical data. The most general models are metaphysical systems (Peters, 1962, p. 34), variously designated as "paradigms" (Kuhn, 1962), "presuppositions" (Pap, 1949), "cosmologies" and "ontologies" (Bunge, 1963), "world views" (Bunge, 1963; Kuhn, 1962; Seeger, 1954), and "world hypotheses" (Pepper, 1942). Ideally, these have such generality as to be capable of incorporating all phenomena, they are models of the essential nature of reality, including man.

According to Pepper (1942) and Kuhn (1962), differences between world views are irreconcilable and impede communication, because of differences in such basic categories as truth criteria, the nature of substance and change, and the meanings of "explanation" and even "fact." It follows that attempts to synthesize approaches built upon different world views, such as Piaget's on the one hand and American behaviorism on the other, are futile (see Kaplan, 1966). This kind of synthesis or eclecticism must lead to confusion because it involves mixing different world hypotheses, hence mixing truth criteria, conceptions of substance and change, etc.

At a less general level are models that are more explicit, but nevertheless formulated within the context of some metaphysical system. These models have been called "ideals of nature" or "principles" (Toulmin, 1962), "paradigms of science" (Kuhn, 1962), and "suppositions" (Kaplan, 1964). Finally, at the least general level are the relatively specific and precise models which have most commonly been designated by the term "model" (see A. Kaplan, 1964; Turner, 1968).

The levels of models constitute a hierarchy which in any specific case begins with a metaphysical system and in which each more general model determines the nature of the acceptable categories in the models at less general levels (Black, 1962; Kessen, 1966; Pepper, 1942; Toulmin, 1962).

III. Basic Categories in the Mechanistic and Organismic Models

A. The Mechanistic Model

The basic metaphor in the mechanistic model is, of course, the machine. Different models can be constructed, depending on the specific machine considered (e.g., the lever or the computer), but all mechanistic models must entail the same fundamental categories, and hence ultimately result in the same theoretical attitudes (Pepper, 1942). This model has been analyzed in depth elsewhere (Matson, 1964; Pepper, 1942; Reese & Overton, 1970; Schon, 1963), and we need mention here only some of its more salient and pertinent categories. Causes must be external, hence must be forces. There can be chainlike sequences, but involving only efficient, material, or immediate causes; purpose is seen as a mediate or derived cause. Complete prediction is therefore possible, *in principle*, since complete knowledge of the state of the machine at one point in time allows inference of the state at the next, given a knowledge of the forces to be applied.[2]

The mechanistic world view has been employed for further model construction in diverse areas of inquiry (see Cassirer, 1951; Matson, 1964; Mumford, 1970). In psychology, the resulting model is the *reactive organism model of man*. In its ideal form the reactive organism model characterizes the organism, like other parts of the universal machine, as inherently at rest, and active only as a result of external forces. Cognitive activities such as thinking, willing, wishing, and perceiving are viewed as complex phenomena ultimately reducible to simple phenomena governed by efficient causes. Novelty or emergence—the appearance of qualitative change—is considered to be an epiphenomenon or reducible to quantitative change.

B. The Organismic Model

The basic metaphor in the organismic model is the living organism, an organized whole. The whole is organic rather than mechanical, and rather than

[2]Although Heisenberg, Niels Bohr, and others believed that the principle of indeterminacy leads to rejection of the principle of causality in atomic physics, Bunge (1963) noted that it actually only precludes any possible *test* of the causal principle. The principle of indeterminacy refers to epistemological indeterminacy, or uncertainty, and has nothing to do with ontological causality or determinacy.

being the sum of its parts, the whole is presupposed by the parts and gives meaning to the parts (Cassirer, 1951, p. 31).

Through progressive activities of differentiation or individuation, the whole is in continuous transition from one state to another. This progressive change does not involve the chainlike mechanical connection of efficient cause and effect, but rather involves a teleological relationship. For Leibnitz, this relationship was preformistic or vitalistic rather than epigenetic, but regardless of the specific details, teleological causes rather than efficient causes are accepted as basic constituents of the explanatory process. A strictly predictive and quantifiable universe is impossible in such a system.

In psychology, the organismic model is reflected in the *active organism model of man*. In this model, the organism is inherently and spontaneously active; the organism is the source of acts, rather than being activated by external or peripheral forces. Man is represented as an organized entity, whose parts gain their meaning and function from the whole. The category of form (see Merleau-Ponty, 1963) becomes a basic category for the analysis and understanding of behavior, and psychological structure–function or means–ends relations become central rather than derived. Inquiry is directed toward the discovery of principles of organization and the explanation of part–whole and structure–function relations, rather than toward the derivation of these from elementary processes.

In the active organism model, change is given; it is not explainable by efficient or material cause, although efficient causes may inhibit or facilitate change. Rather, the basic causes are teleological.[3] Furthermore, change is qualitative as well as quantitative, because the active organism model represents man as a system in which the parts and the configuration of parts change. New properties emerge, irreducible to lower levels and therefore qualitatively different from them.

The assumption of spontaneous activity entails denial of a complete causal determinism—whether in a substantive or statistical form—and rejection of the ideal of (in principle) complete prediction and control. This point merits special emphasis because there are other meanings of "active organism" which are consistent with the mechanistic position and therefore consistent with a complete causal determinism. For example, the organism may be said to be active in the sense that we do not now know what empirical (efficient or material) causal determinants lead to the emitting of responses. With respect to the active-reactive dichotomy discussed here, this usage is trivial because it refers to factual ignorance rather than to the basic model of the organism.

---

[3]In our earlier paper (Reese & Overton, 1970), we considered only formal cause in relation to the organismic position. In the present paper, we are including teleological causes generally, in order to expand upon the explanatory dimensions of the models.

IV. Corollary Model Issues

A. Introduction

Our general position is that descriptively, psychologists and others do in fact, either explicitly or implicitly, accept some one model and use it as a guide and rationale for both their theoretical and empirical work; furthermore, the acceptance of one model has logical implications which are incompatible with another model. We have called these implications corollary model issues in order to emphasize that the issues that exist at this level are model-like or pretheoretical in character, and hence are not open to empirical test.

In the following section, we shall review some of the corollary model issues described in our earlier paper (Reese & Overton, 1970). These may be best thought of as *structural*-corollary model issues to distinguish them from *functional* or *explanatory* issues to be described in Section V. Structural issues are related to organization of the content of the model; functional issues are related to the organization of the explanatory influences of the model. Actually, the sets of issues represent two sides of the same coin—the determining influences of structural–theoretical models—and are closely interrelated and mutually supportive. For expository purposes, however, they are treated separately.

B. The Structural-Corollary Model Issues

1. Holism versus Elementarism

The assumption of holism derives from the active organism model. The organism is represented as an *organized* totality, a system of parts in interaction with each other, such that each part derives its meaning from the whole. This assumption has the status of a regulative principle for the general analysis of behavior. It proscribes the conclusion that behaviors have identical meanings solely because they are physically identical; it prescribes that behavior be assessed in terms of its function in the whole or context in which it is embedded, i.e., according to the function, ends, or goals of the organism.

The assumption of elementarism is derived from the mechanistic model. The organism is represented as a collection of elements which cannot combine to yield emergent qualities. In principle, the whole is predictable from its parts and physically identical elements have the same "meaning."

2. Structure–Function versus Antecedent–Consequent

From the viewpoint of the active organism model, a major task is to define functions or goals and to investigate the structures or means which serve them. In psychology, the structures are psychological and are not physical or physiological. Psychological structures are the relatively stable, organized patterns or specific behavioral systems of transformations (Piaget, 1970b).

From a reactive organism model, analysis is based on antecedent–consequent relations (e.g., Bijou & Baer, 1963)—not structures, but causes and effects, and not functions, but contingent relations.

The analysis of structure–function clearly implies that such a position is teleological, in that it involves the attribution of purpose, goal, or function to the organism. This is not necessarily a subjective purposivism, nor is any ontological assertion necessarily made (Taylor, 1964). As is the case with holism, the teleological principle involved here is viewed as a regulative principle which directs one to act *as if* there are inherent functions, just as the elementaristic position directs one to act as if there are no inherent functions. It follows that purpose (or more generally, form) is a basic category for a theory constructed on the active organism model, and is a derived category for a theory constructed on the reactive organism model. That is, purpose is explanatory in the one model and is to be explained in the other.

3. Structural versus Behavioral Change

The preceding leads to the primary area of concern for developmental psychology: the nature and direction of developmental change. For the active organism model, structures and functions change during development; for the reactive organism model, it is behavior that changes. In the active organism model, change is determined by the form of the structure or organization. The nature and direction of change are given by the general end state or goal, which acts as a principle for ordering change. Here, as earlier, the teleological aspect is interpreted as regulative rather than constitutive. There is a denial that environmental *determinants* can completely explicate developmental changes, but they may facilitate or inhibit the change as given. This relation between environmental conditions and teleological concepts will be explored further in Section V.

According to the reactive organism model, change is completely determined by efficient or material causes. Changes in behavior, whether over several trials or several years, occur as the result of external events, such as reinforcement history. Direction of change is a derived category, explained, for example, by treating age as an intervening variable that is independent of stimulus conditions and is unidirectional and linear with time (Berlyne, 1966).

4. Discontinuity versus Continuity

The essential model issue here is whether successive behavioral forms are reducible (continuity) or irreducible (discontinuity) to prior forms (Werner, 1957). As a model issue, it is irrelevant whether change is gradual or abrupt and small or large.

In the active organism model and its holistic corollary, changes in the parts or in the organization of the parts result in a whole with new or novel systemic properties. These new properties are *emergent* in the sense that they cannot be predicted from the parts. Thus, there is a basic discontinuity of development.

In the reactive organism model and its elementaristic corollary, all change is continuous in the sense of being predictable from earlier states. Developmental change, then, can involve only *apparently* emergent qualitative differences. What looks like emergence is actually predictable from the history of the organism.

C. *Implications for Research*

In our earlier paper (Reese & Overton, 1970), we presented examples to illustrate the specific influences of the structural corollary issues on theory construction and interpretation. Before turning to functional corollary issues and examining their role, we shall present examples of the effects of the structural issues on the generation, analysis, and interpretation of data.

Fodor (1968) described the general influence of the active and reactive models on the selection of alternative precedures for the study of perceptual development. According to Fodor, the discrimination experiment is eminently suitable from the viewpoint of the reactive organism model, because the discriminable physical inputs are the efficient causes. In contrast, from the viewpoint of the active organism model, in which the organism actively contributes to processes of perceptual organization, the suitable design is not the discrimination experiment, but rather "experimental designs that permit the study of such phenomena as perceptual ambiguity, perceptual illusion, and perceptual bias [p. xvi]," in which the organism's contribution is directly revealed.

In his analysis of the learning theory tradition and child psychology, White (1970) provided a further elaboration of this influence as it operates within the "learning theory point of view" or "S—R tradition." After describing the assumptions which constitute the learning theory viewpoint—assumptions which parallel at a lower level our mechanistic structural corollary issues—White described a "family of procedures" employed within this viewpoint. These constitute a family of procedures, "because they have special characteristics in common, differentiating them from other procedures through which one might conceivably make observations about learning processes [p. 667]." This concept of a *family of procedures* is the direct analogue, at the procedural level, of the concept of a *family of theories* discussed in the introduction to the present paper and in our previous paper (Reese & Overton, 1970). Both families are lineal descendents of models. To pursue this metaphor, the specific family analyzed by White clearly reflects the hereditary features of elementarism, antecedent–consequent analysis, and continuity, which are transmitted by the mechanistic model.

Kessel (1969) carried this kind of analysis a final step by observing that presuppositions (model implications) tend to ensure the generation of empirical evidence which supports the basic theoretical position.[4] As an example, Kessel referred to Spence's (1964) acknowledgment that higher mental processes play a significant role in conditioning and his subsequent treatment of these processes as confounding variables which mask the role of basic theoretical factors such as $_s H_R$ and D. The point is that theory determines what kind of data are relevant and consequently determines what kind of procedure is appropriate, and overriding these determinations is a requirement of consistency with the general model within which the theory is formulated.

In the same vein as Kessel, and especially White, but at a more general level, Kessen (1966) has introduced the concept of "constrained analysis," which refers to "the limits imposed on psychological analysis by premises that are not fully explicit and often not testable [pp. 57–58]."

Other investigators have proposed research strategies which either explicitly (Gollin, 1965) or implicitly (Wohlwill, 1970a) acknowledge an accommodation to organismic implications of structure–function (the role of cognitive and perceptual structures as constituents in developmental change) and discontinuity. We shall discuss specific features of such strategies in Section V.

One last example of the determining influences of structural-corollary issues is Kagan's (1967) plea for relativistic definitions in psychology—i.e., definitions "in which context and the state of the individual are part of the defining statement [p. 131]." Such a plea has echoes of a holistic commitment. Kagan presented several specific examples in the areas of self-concept, learning, and attention, and the examples reflect the differences between a relativistic (holistic) orientation and an absolutistic (elementaristic) orientation.

Further specific examples of model implications can be found in Langer (1969).

V. Functional Corollary Model Issues

The mechanistic and organismic models lead not only to structural implications but also to implications concerning types of explanations which are viewed as acceptable and the relations between various explanations. Our specific concern here centers less on the general structure of different explanatory forms than on the substantive types of determinants that enter into explanations of behavior and development.[5]

---

[4]Feyerabend (1968) viewed this lack of autonomy of facts from theoretical viewpoint as the prime rationale for the necessity to develop mutually inconsistent theories (i.e., between-model theories): Such theories provide alternative viewpoints and thus aid in the process of criticism which prevents any theory from becoming dogma.

[5]A. Kaplan (1964) suggested that there are two general explanatory forms: The *pattern model* explains an event when the event is shown to fit within a known pattern. The *deductive* model explains an event when the event is deduced from other known facts (p. 332). We would note in passing that these forms correspond to the types of theories described in Footnote 1 and that pattern theories and pattern explanations are closely related to the organismic model whereas hierarchical theories and deductive explanations are closely tied to the mechanistic model.

A. Types of Explanatory Determinants

1. Historical Review

A brief review of the types of determinants historically accepted as explanatory will provide an introduction into these functional model implications. Aristotle maintained that the complete explanation of a phenomenon requires a specification of four causal determinants, i.e., material, efficient, formal, and final causes. (Ross, 1959. For some Aristotelian influences on contemporary scientific thought generally and developmental psychology specifically, see also Bunge, 1963; Grinder, 1967; B. Kaplan, 1967; Langer, 1969; Peters, 1962; Rychlak, 1968.)

The *material cause* of an object is the substance which constitutes the object. Granting historical changes in the scientific conception of substance, a present-day example of material causes would consist of the physiological, neurological, or genetic substrate that is a necessary condition for behavior. *Efficient cause* is the external agent, antecedent condition, or independent variable which moves the object. *Formal cause* is the pattern, organization, or form of an object. Thus, the specification of psychological structures, for example, constitutes a formal cause. *Final cause* is the end toward which an object develops. The attribution of an endpoint of development, such as differentiation and hierarchical integration, is an example of final cause. It should be explicitly recognized that formal and final causes are openly teleological.

A modern illustration of the relationships among these determinants is provided by the paradigmatic Piagetian theory (Piaget, 1967; Piaget & Inhelder, 1969) in its presentation of a necessary and sufficient account of development. In this account, genetic and maturational factors (material causes), although left unspecified, are presumed to interact with the physical and social environment (efficient causes) to produce a series of structures (formal causes). These factors, while being *necessary* conditions for development, are not *sufficient* to explain development. The equilibration process (final cause) is introduced to provide a sufficient explanation for the "oriented development" of the successive stages of structures (see also the analysis in Overton, 1972). Note that Aristotle's material and formal causes are causes of *being*, while efficient and final causes are causes of *becoming*.[6]

With the advent of Galileo, Bacon, and more generally the adoption of the Newtonian machine model of the universe, formal and final causes were banished as irrelevant to scientific activity and material and efficient causes were left to carry the full burden of explanation in the mechanistic model. In other scientific views, such as reviewed by Pepper (1942) and discussed by Bunge (1963), the teleological principle was never abandoned, and continued to share the explanatory load.

---

[6]Langer (1969, 1970) stated that material causality is applicable to the developmental task of determining the relationship between stages (forms) of development (1969, p. 8). However, his interpretation seems to ignore the fact that the Aristotelian material cause constitutes a category of being, not of becoming. Actually, final cause (becoming) accounts for the order of stages.

2. Contemporary Usages

In addition to presenting an historical reconstruction, the preceding review fairly reflects—with certain qualifications—the current explanatory contexts generated by the organismic and mechanistic models. That is, on the one hand, the organismic model requires all four types of determinants for the complete explanation of developmental phenomena, while on the other hand, the mechanistic model maintains that material and efficient causes are sufficient for explanation. The task now is to present a finer-grained analysis of the implications arising from each view, but first it is necessary to consider the more important qualifications needed to make this schema reflect contemporary usage within each viewpoint.

The first qualification is in the use of the term "cause" within the reactive organism position in psychology. Stemming from the Humean analysis of cause as the mere constant conjunction of events and Russell's (1953) attack on the concept of cause, many psychologists have asserted that "cause," even the efficient variety, is no longer a viable concept. In place of "cause" these psychologists generally prefer to substitute concepts of statistical determination, conditional relationship, or functional relationship [in the sense that $x_i = f_i(y_i)$, rather than the structure–function meaning of function].

However, even though the reasoning behind this position is clear, we do not believe that it in fact obviates either a causal analysis or the implications thereof. The point here centers around the concept of "production." Insofar as it is maintained that one event is productive of another event, regardless of whether those events are cloaked in the garb of conditional or functional relationships, a causal analysis is in fact being performed. This state of affairs seems to hold for most psychologists who work within the reactive organism framework. This is quite clearly demonstrated in the writings of Baer (1970), for example, who in a discussion of behavioral change stated, "I want to know the process which *produced* the change. . . . Learning procedures . . . are exactly behavior change processes [p. 243; italics added]" and "It seems to me implicit in modern behavioral technology that there must be quite some number of environmental programs, or sequences, which will *bring an organism to any specified developmental outcome* [p. 244; italics added]." More explicitly, "Experiments . . . demonstrate that the experimental procedures were instrumental in producing the change in the measured behavior; i.e., they demonstrate causality [Risley & Baer, in press, p. 3 in preprint]." [See also Bijou & Baer (1963).]

A second qualification emerges within the organismic position generally and consequently in the active-organism position in psychology. Here, the concept of cause has frequently been limited to the efficient and material varieties and causal analysis in those terms has been contrasted with "other determinants." These "other determinants" include the substantive meanings of formal and final cause, but the labels themselves are avoided. Thus, for example, in analyzing developmental laws Sutton-Smith (1970) approached the problem from an organismic viewpoint and distinguished between "causal laws" which include the determinants described by Baer and "noncausal developmental laws" involving considerations such as the direction of change. The latter clearly refer to final cause. The motivation for this type of usage is evidently the avoidance of some of the historical connotations once attributed to formal and final cause. Among these was the idea that formal and final cause imply designs in nature (as in Morris, 1875) rather than the contemporary view of them as regulative principles, and vitalistic rather than contemporary epigenetic interpretations. While it is important, in order to comprehend the model clearly, that such antiquated connotations be rejected and that contemporary meanings be emphasized, to do so by distinguishing between "causal" versus "other" determinants appears to create various confusions. One such confusion is the often held notion that only causal determinants explain, other determinants being "merely descriptive." Another and related misunderstanding is that causal determinants are somehow more basic than other determinants. It is because these views are even more pernicious to an understanding of the organismic framework that we shall continue to discuss the various determinants involved in the explanation of behavior and behavioral change as material, efficient, formal, and final causes. The reader should make allowances for contemporary versus historical usages.

We shall now turn to a closer examination of how the mechanistic and organismic models influence explanation, and the implications of these influences for research strategies. The two most significant influences concern the unidirectionality and linearity of causes generated within the reactive organism framework. For this reason, we shall focus on these mechanistic corollaries and present organismic corollaries as alternatives.

B. The Issues

1. Unidirectional versus Reciprocal Causality

In the mechanistic model, not only are efficient causes external to the system under consideration, but also there is an asymmetric relationship between cause and effect. As the very concept of a reactive organism implies, only the efficient cause is active and productive; the effect is merely the recipient of this activity. Thus, within this view there is a *unidirectionality* of causal application or a one-way causality, in which effect is strictly dependent upon cause (von Bertalanffy, 1968; Bunge, 1963). This unidirectionality permits the isolation of S-R relationships, and the explanation of change in terms of efficient stimulus determinants.

The organismic model leads to a quite different type of representation. The view that the organism is inherently and spontaneously active means that an external condition can never in itself be the sole determinant of an effect. Rather, cause and effect or environmental event and organism stand in a relationship of *reciprocal action* in which each member affects and changes the other. Here, then, we have reciprocal causation, or *interaction*, and this accounts, in part, for the organismic rejection of mechanistic analytic procedures which maintain that a complete efficient causality is possible.

The term "interaction" has several meanings, which are not model-independent. The dictionary meaning of interaction as "reciprocal action" (*American College Dictionary*, 1958) is synonymous with reciprocal causation, and has been retained by the organismic position. In contrast, for those working within the mechanistic frame of reference, the term has been given meanings consonant with the unidirectionality concept of cause.

In the analysis of variance model, "interaction" refers to an interdependency of determinants. The determinants may be causal or noncausal in Bunge's (1963) sense, and therefore may be said to *produce* effects on criterion variables or to be *related to* the criterion variables. In either case, the determinacy is one-way in any given analysis of variance; the interaction is not between cause and effect, but between causes. The interaction between causes amounts to a "conjunctive plurality of causes," which is actually a variety of simple efficient causation (Bunge, 1963). Because the concept of interaction in the analysis of variance model is consistent with the unidirectionality principle, this meaning of interaction is consistent with the mechanistic position and inconsistent with the organismic position. (The analysis of variance model will be further discussed later.)

This same usage is also found in Spiker's (1963) "stimulus interaction hypothesis," which is a mathematical formulation stating that the response to a stimulus depends on the context of the stimulus. It is not the stimulus that changes as a result of the interaction, but the response (the effect). Therefore, in this hypothesis, stimuli function as a conjunctive plurality of causes, acting unidirectionally.

Another example of a mechanistic concept of interaction appears in the work of Bijou and Baer (1961): "An interaction between behavior and environment means simply that a given response may be expected to occur or not, depending on the stimulation the environment provides [p. 1]." Here, one-way causality is clearly maintained despite the dictionary connotation of "interaction." Staats, also working within the context of Skinnerian principles, has taken a similar position in a book subtitled *Principles of a Behavioral Interaction Approach* (1971). Staats described several principles of interaction which employ a one-way causality; for example, "There is an interaction between behaviors the individual has learned and what he will do in future situations, because the former have a cause and effect link with the latter [p. 8]." He then rejected the concept of interaction that asserts reciprocal causality on the grounds that it is primarily philosophical and that it attempts to sweep the nature–nurture controversy under the rug (Staats, 1971, p. 29).

Others, operating with a more general learning-theory orientation, have interpreted interaction to mean that material causes set the limits of development and efficient causes operate from this material base. Thus, Gagné (1968) stated, "everyone will agree, surely, that development is the result of an interaction of growth and learning. . . . Within the limitations imposed by growth, *behavioral development results from the cumulative effects of learning* [p. 178]." In this type of view, there is a recognition that material factors are present, but they are seen as reactively significant and therefore causality remains unidirectional.

In the light of these several mechanistically defined concepts of interaction, it is relevant to restate and slightly expand the organismic position. Interaction refers to the reciprocal action occurring between various elements, specifically between various parts or subsystems of the organism or between the organism, its subsystems, and the environment. This means most generally that from this vantage point an efficient causal explanation is incomplete, for as Bunge (1963) pointed out:

> Efficient causes are effective solely to the extent to which they trigger, enhance, or damp inner processes. . .[p. 195].

> An adequate picture is provided by a synthesis of self-determination [organismic activity] and extrinsic determination [environmental activity]. . . . The two exaggerations of environmentalism and innatism . . . are thereby avoided [p. 197].

With reference to a level involving specific research strategy, interactions in the organismic sense may be considered to be either weak or strong. To the extent that they are weak, as would be the case in most short-term learning studies, it is possible to introduce the convenient fiction (as seen from the organismic view) that the independent variable (efficient cause) is operating upon the dependent variable and thus to introduce the various experimental procedures and modes of statistical analysis traditionally employed in experimental psychology. To the extent, however, that the interactions are considered to be strong, as would be the case, for example, with development over relatively long periods of time, the traditional analytic procedures break down (see von Bertalanffy, 1968) as do explanatory forms based on the same model as these procedures. It is at this point that the mechanistic fiction is abandoned by organicists and *different types of questions* are asked, specifically about (strong) reciprocal causality, and *different types of explanations are given*, i.e., formal and final causal explanations.

The concept of weak and strong interactions introduces one point of possible interrelationship between the mechanistic and organismic views. That is, interaction as organismically defined subsumes efficient causality, and therefore the mechanistic model may be viewed as a limited case of the organismic model (see Bunge, 1963, for a discussion of the divergent views of Russell, Kant, and Hegel on the possible relationship between interaction and efficient causality). We doubt, however, that many committed to the mechanistic model would accept this type of "compromise."

The model issues associated with unidirectionality versus reciprocal causality or interaction influence the research process in many ways. For example, in the sphere of theory, Piaget codifies the notion of reciprocal causation in his concepts of assimilation (the influence of the organism on the environment) and accommodation (the influence of the environment on the organism); in contrast, the learning theory tradition requires the independent identification and definition of stimulus and response (White, 1970). This contrast will mediate a difference in research strategies. Researchers who look for interactions between higher-order mental processes and environment will seldom use the same research approach as those who look for nothing more complex than covert mediators.

A more immediate consequence of these divergent issues (in terms of research strategy) concerns the directions they dictate for the assessment of ontogenetic change. Specifically, this includes the strategies employed to analyze the role of material and efficient factors in development, or to give the problem its traditional title, the nature-nurture controversy. It was only a little more than a decade ago that Anastasi (1958b) was able to write confidently, "Two or three decades ago, the so-called heredity–environment question was the center of lively controversy. Today, on the other hand, many psychologists look upon it as a dead issue [p. 197]." Shortly after this, Hunt (1961) helped to prepare the cadaver for burial via his critique of the use of the analysis of variance model to determine the proportion of a given behavior contributed by hereditary and environmental factors (i.e., material and efficient causes). Hunt's major points attacked (a) the assumption of additivity, which is basic to the analysis of variance model in general (see the following section for a general discussion of additivity), and (b) the assumption—required for this particular use of the model—that there is no interaction (in the statistical sense) between heredity and environment.

Given this background, what accounts for the fact that over the past few years we have seemingly witnessed a second coming, a resurrection of this dead issue? Part of the answer undoubtedly lies in recent methodological advances produced by the behavior geneticists (Hirsch, 1967). This is not sufficient, however, to account for the vitality we are currently witnessing (see, for example, Anandalakshmy & Grinder, 1970; Jensen, 1969). It seems, rather, that the diagnosis was premature. Anastasi's (1958b) analysis implied that psychologists had come to agree that the questions of "Which one?" and "How much?" are meaningless with reference to the individual contributions of nature and nurture to individual development. But this was not true, because as long as a group maintains the mechanistic position and its corollaries of unidirectionality and linearity, at least the more sophisticated of these questions—"How much?"—will continue to constitute a meaningful issue. As long as this model is accepted, its corollaries will continue to dictate research strategies which attempt to partial out hereditary and environmental (Jensen, 1969; Nichols, 1965; Vandenberg, 1962) or endogenous and exogenous (Cattell, 1970b) components.

In marked contrast, for a group that accepts the organismic position and its corollary of reciprocal causation—more particularly, the idea that across development, strong interactions (in the organismic sense) exist between material and efficient causes—the questions of "Which one?" and "How much?" lose all meaning and consequently *for this group* such questions truly die. This is not a case of sweeping an issue under the rug; rather, it is a reflection of the fact that different models yield different questions. From the organismic point of view, questions of "Which one?" and "How much?" are meaningless because the model postulates reciprocal causality or strong interactions. For example, in Piaget's theory, the basic hereditary structures (material causes) are imposed on the environment and provide it with meaning (assimilation) at the same time these structures change (accommodation) in accordance with environmental demands (efficient causes). There is thus a strong interaction between material and efficient causes. As a consequence, research strategies which attempt to partial out components are similarly meaningless.

The viable question from the organismic position is the question "How?" also discussed by Anastasi (1958b). That is, given that it is impossible to generate an adequate explanation for the general course of development based entirely upon either efficient or material causality, or the proportional contribution of each—given, in other words, that some form of a final causal explanation will be required for the course of development *per se*—it is reasonable to ask *how* efficient causal factors and *how* material causal factors relate to the rate and terminal level of development.

On the nurture or efficient causal side of the ledger, Beilin's (1971b) general review of studies focusing on training and acquisition of logical structures provides a number of examples of research strategies produced within the organismic framework (Genevan variety) (see also Inhelder & Sinclair, 1969). Furthermore, in its attempt to explicate the ways in which the developing organism confronts its environment, much of the current ecologically oriented research (e.g., B. L. White, 1971; Willems, Chapter 10 in this volume; Wohlwill, 1966) demonstrates strategies compatible with the organismic model.

On the nature or material causal side, in addition to current ethnological work and neurophysiological studies, proposals by some behavior geneticists (e.g., Rodgers, 1967; Thiessen & Rodgers, 1967) for a *structure-function* or mechanism-specific investigation of genetic determinants are particularly relevant to the organismic framework (see also Lockard, 1971, for the differences between a mechanistically oriented and an organismically oriented approach to comparative work and the relationship of these to developmental psychology).

In concluding this section, we may note again that from the organismic perspective, efficient and material factors are viewed as necessary but not sufficient causes for the explanation of normal developmental change. Sufficient explanation involves the introduction of teleological formal and final causes. This is not, however, to deny that efficient and material factors may be sufficient explanations for the breakdown of normal development or changes in rate of development. Thus, for example, some forms of environmental deprivation or happily appropriate matching of organismic state and environmental events may sufficiently account for changes in rate of development, while brain lesions, genetic defects, or other factors may provide a sufficient explanation for a nontypical terminal level of development (see Hamlyn, 1957; Peters, 1958; Taylor, 1964, for an expansion of this argument).

2. Linear Causality versus Organized Complexity

A second functional corollary of the mechanistic model presupposes the unidirectionality of cause and effect. As already noted, the machine model as a general representation pictures both the universe and its parts, e.g. organisms, as operating through the application of forces, resulting in chainlike sequences of events. In terms of explanation, this means it is assumed that only *linear* relationships exist between efficient causes and effects. Cause and effect are viewed as standing in an invariable or unique one-to-one relationship such that any particular cause will result in a specified effect and this effect will be completely determined by the initial cause. This view has several concomitants including the notions that it is possible to isolate causal chains; that individual causes are additive in their effects; and, of course, that causation is unidirectional. As both von Bertalanffy (1968) and Bunge (1963) pointed out, traditional analytic procedures and the very idea of efficient-causality analysis require the concept of linearity. "Nonlinearity entails a failure of [efficient] causality, since the effects can no longer be decomposed into a sum of partial effects every one of which can be traced to individual events . . . [Bunge, 1963, footnote, p. 168]."

The organismic position, however, does not totally reject the concept of linearity, but rather maintains that this principle becomes extended beyond its useful scope when applied as a *complete* explanation of behavior and development. A major task from the organismic vantage point is to explain the *organized complexity* (von Bertalanffy, 1968) entailed both in the definition of an organism as an organized system, and in the ordered changes that occur in such systems:

In the world view called mechanistic, which was born of classical physics of the nineteenth century, the aimless play of atoms, governed by the inexorable laws of causality, produced all phenomena. . . . No room was left for any directiveness, order, or telos. . . . The only goal of science appeared to be analytical, i.e., the splitting up of reality into even smaller units and the isolation of causal trains [p. 45]. . . . Organization . . . was alien to the mechanistic world. . . . In biology, organisms are, by definition organized things. . . . Characteristic of organization, whether of a living organism or a society, are notions like those of wholeness, growth, differentiation, hierarchical order . . . etc. [von Bertalanffy, 1968, p. 47].

From the organismic perspective, the explanation of this order is not to be found in antecedent, efficient conditions, but rather in the discovery (not as an empirical generalization, but as an invention—Toulmin, 1962) of principles or laws or organization, i.e., in the discovery of teleological formal and final determinants of this order.

The point at issue here is so critical to an understanding of the organismic position and so frequently misunderstood that it bears repeating. First, teleological explanation consists in the postulation of regulative principles and does not necessarily involve individual awareness of needs, motives, or desires (B. Kaplan, 1967).[7] Second, teleological explanations are not *reducible* to or translatable into efficient causal laws. *Teleological laws are viewed as basic and hence they subsume efficient and material causal laws.* In a specific developmental context, this may be expressed by the statement that development subsumes learning and maturation rather than the converse. Or, in terms of specific theories, again, it may be said that Werner's (1948) orthogenetic principle and Piaget's (1967) equilibration process are developmental (final cause) laws which explain the course of development and subsume laws of structure (formal cause) as well as efficient and material causal laws.

The primary significance of accepting teleological laws as basic is that this acceptance asserts an account of explanation that is an epistemological rival to that presented by the mechanistic position and as such leads to different theoretical attitudes and research strategies. Most broadly, it means that at some *specified* point in the research process the search for empirical determinants will be terminated. Hull (1943, p. 26) once termed this stance a "doctrine of despair," but it is only such from a mechanistic view, where it is held that complete empirical determination is possible. From the organismic view, the frequent appeal made by mechanists to wait for empirical solution to complex problems until less complex problems have been "worked out"—i.e., the appeal to simple complexity—might just as readily be seen as a "doctrine of despair."

[7]A distinction between the general organismic position and specific humanistic theories is that the latter entail conscious goals as a necessary feature of the explanatory process (see Rychlak, 1968).

In fact, neither represents desperation; rather, each is an independent but rival account of the problem.

What, then, are some of the consequences of the linearity corollary and the organized complexity corollary for research strategies? The linearity corollary is most obviously reflected in the linear components-of-variance statistical model from which derive the univariate and multivariate analysis-of-variance experimental designs. The basic assumption of this model is that each score is a linear function of independent elements, i.e., the score is the sum of component effects (e.g., Winer, 1962, p. 151). Although interaction effects reflect nonadditivity of the main effects (Winer, 1962, p. 148), the interaction effects combine additively with the main effects to determine the score. Furthermore, the interaction effects are themselves linear, since they are defined as population cell means minus the sum of main effects (plus the population base rate).

It is beyond the scope of this chapter to attempt a demonstration of the extent to which these linear concepts have influenced psychological thinking or to explore alternative nonlinear procedures (for examples of some influences and alternatives, see Beilin, 1971a, p. 188; von Bertalanffy, 1968; Wohlwill, 1970c). However, it should be clear that linear procedures entail the basic categories of the linear corollary issue. We have already considered the mechanistic nature of the analysis-of-variance interaction term in an earlier section. The assumption of summativity or additivity of scores rests on the prior corollary model position that it is feasible to isolate causal chains and reasonable to ignore the possibility of strong interactions, or reciprocal causation. In conjunction with the view that cause and effect stand in the invariable relationship discussed earlier, this means that causes act independently and their joint action merely adds to or subtracts from the effect. The joint action of causes can produce only quantitative change, not novelty. In order to admit novelty into the system, one must move from the linear corollary to the organized complexity corollary which permits causes to act not merely as an aggregate, but as a synthesis or whole having characteristics that are not present in the separate parts (Bunge, 1963, p. 166).

At a more general level of research strategy, but including specific design problems, a recent reconsideration of the age variable in psychological research (Wohlwill, 1970a) further demonstrates the influences of the linear versus organized complexity issues. The essence of Wohlwill's proposal is the suggestion that age be removed from the realm of the independent variable and be considered as a part of the dependent variable. Age would consequently be a dimension along which developmental changes are investigated, analogous to the manner in which time is employed as a dimension for the plotting of behavioral changes in, for example, perceptual adaptation studies. This proposal is a radical departure from traditional positions which have either introduced age as a shorthand for an unspecified, but specifiable set of variables acting over time, or attempted to replace age completely with functional variables that determine behavioral changes (Baer, 1970).

From a model point of view, the significance of Wohlwill's proposal lies in its explanatory implication and its justification. The most critical feature is that to the extent to which the proposal is accepted, age-related change or, more broadly, the general course of development is excluded from the arena of complete efficient or material explanation. That is, developmental change *per se* is accepted as given. In fact, from this approach *developmental variables* are *defined* as those variables "for which the general course of development (considered in terms of direction, form, sequence, etc.) remains invariant over a broad range of particular environmental conditions . . . as well as genetic characteristics [Wohlwill, 1970a, p. 52]." *Nondevelopmental* variables are conversely *defined* as "Variables . . . which show consistent age changes *only* for individuals subjected to specific experiences . . . or other responses acquired through direct teaching, differential reinforcement or exercise. . . [p. 52]."

It is apparent that this proposal is derivable from the organismic position that in the light of reciprocal causality and organized complexity, complete explanation of the course of development is not possible in terms of either efficient or material factors. In a similar vein, Wohlwill's argument that specific environmental conditions may affect rate and terminal level of development is entirely compatible with the organismic position. In contrast, both the general proposal and its specifics are obviously not compatible with the mechanistic position, which maintains that complete empirical determination is in principle possible.

Perhaps the weakest point of Wohlwill's proposal, again as seen from a model perspective, lies in its justification. Wohlwill recognized that not everyone will accept this approach to developmental research, but he implied that the decision to accept or reject is to be made on strictly empirical grounds. Two criteria are established for acceptance:

(a) that substantial, reasonably situationally independent changes occur with respect to the given behavior and (b) that the changes are not readily handled in terms of highly specific experience in the sense of the individual's reinforcement history, of practice or learning experiences with a given task, or of particular events impinging on him [Wohlwill, 1970a, p. 62].

However, the question at issue here is exactly on what basis the decisions will be made that changes are "*reasonably* situationally independent" or that they *cannot be readily handled* in the context of specific experiences. It is, of course, our contention that such decisions will never be made solely on the basis of empirical investigations; rather, they will represent the influence of structural–theoretical models, corollary issues, and perhaps some combination of the hopes and frustrations of empirical studies.

For those who explicitly or implicitly maintain a mechanistic viewpoint and the corollaries of unidirectionality and linearity of causes, these forces will lead to the rejection of any proposal which maintains that some portion of behavioral change is in principle not explainable in efficient causal terms. Parenthetically, they will also reject attempts to *define* development or developmental variables in such a manner. However, those who maintain the organismic position and the corollaries of reciprocal causality and organized complexity will consider Wohlwill's general proposal to be eminently reasonable. This group will maintain that the course of development *per se* is explainable by teleological laws and they will view Wohlwill's further suggestions concerning specific methodological and design problems, which he elaborated in greater detail in another paper (Wohlwill, 1970c), as important additions to their research tools.

VI. Summary and Conclusions

In this chapter, we have tried to demonstrate several ways in which very basic and incompatible structural–theoretical models differentially affect the research process. We have, of course, explored only a small sample of such effects. If space permitted, we might have, for a more extensive analysis, examined the other chapters which composed this volume. For example, both Baer's and Risley and Wolf's chapters evidence a clear commitment to the mechanistic model and its unidirectional and linear corollaries. Willems' focus on interdependencies within behavior–organism–environment systems, in contrast, bears the mark of a concern for the organismic reciprocal causation corollary. Similarly, Riegel's presentation of the dialectic, at least when shorn of its materialistic implications, represents a further specification of reciprocal causation. The interested reader may himself inquire into the extent and ways issues raised by Baltes and Nesselroade, Schaie, Hooper, and others are influenced by these pervasive model determinations. It is our contention that such an inquiry provides a fruitful avenue for evaluating the implications of diverse research strategies and for avoiding theoretical and empirical ambiguity.

CHAPTER 5

Research Strategies and Measurement
Methods for Investigating Human Development

JUM C. NUNNALLY

VANDERBILT UNIVERSITY
NASHVILLE, TENNESSEE

As is typically the case when a scientific discipline begins to mature, people concerned with life-span research are taking stock of their goals, theories, research methods, and findings to date. The purpose of this chapter is to discuss in general terms research strategies and measurement methods for investigating human development. References will be given to detailed matters regarding each topic; critical reactions will be given to previous recommendations; and some new methods and strategies will be outlined.

I. Change Scores

Since life-span research is, in essence, concerned with change over time, it is tempting to assume that the basic psychometric datum with which one works is the change score. Thus, if one is making comparisons of intelligence test scores at two points in time (symbolized by X_1 and X_2), it is assumed that the interest is in $X_2 - X_1$ and that such scores should be computed as one of the first steps in performing analyses. Actually, both the history of the problem and the logic of investigation indicate that the last thing one wants to do is think in terms of or compute such change scores unless the problem makes it absolutely necessary. As is generally known, the major problem in working directly with change scores is that they are ridden with a *regression effect*. The variables X_1 and X_2 can be thought of as the raw scores obtained on the same test at two points in time, or the raw scores obtained on alternative forms of a test administered at two points in time. As necessarily must be the case, there is a regression line; and if the correlation is less than unity, the phenomenon of regression toward the mean is present. If one computes change scores, he finds that the people who scored above the mean on the first occasion tend to have negative change scores, and that the people who scored below the mean on the first occasion tend to have positive change scores—all of this being purely an artifact of the way such scores are computed and the phenomena of regression toward the mean.

The modification of change scores that has been advocated most frequently is that of *residual change scores*. Quite simply, residual change scores consist of deviations of scores on a second occasion from those predicted by regression analysis from a knowledge of scores on a first occasion. Thus, all persons above the regression line would have positive residual change scores, and all below the regression line would have negative residual change scores. The advantage of working with residual change scores is that they circumvent the regression effect that is inherent in absolute change scores $(X_2 - X_1)$. However, this is not the end of a happy story, because a great deal of ink has been spilled over exactly how to compute such residual change scores. (An extensive review of the arguments is given in Cronbach and Furby, 1970.) Such residual change scores encounter both conceptual and psychometric problems.

The major psychometric problem with residual change scores is that they fail to take account of the measurement error inherent in both measurements. Thus, if X_2 were administered on the day following X_1 rather than an appreciable time later, scores would not be exactly the same, the correlation would probably be appreciably less than unity, and residual change scores could be computed and inspected. Of course, such residual change scores would be due almost entirely to measurement error (unless the trait actually changed overnight) rather than to any systematic change in people. To take account of the measurement error inherent in residual change scores, it has been advocated that the correlation between X_1 and X_2 be corrected for attenuation before residual change scores are computed. However, there are questions as to exactly how that should be done.

A direct method for studying change scores is available when a control group is compared with one or more treatment groups. A simple example is a new program of training fifth-grade mathematics. Because an achievement test is routinely given in the school, scores are available at the beginning and end of the year. Students would be randomly sorted into an experimental group and a control group. The control group is developmental in the sense that no new treatment is applied. Similar designs could be used to compare treatments of motor skills and perceptual skills with purely developmental control groups. A correlation coefficient and regression equation can be obtained between pre- and posttest for the *control* group. These statistics are what would be expected if the *treatment* condition had no effect. In contrast, if the condition actually had an effect, this would be shown in differences in regression equations for the two groups. Differences might be in correlations, means, and/or variances. Statistical methods are readily available in most advanced texts for assessing all of these differences. A logical and direct approach to obtaining residual change scores in the treatment group is to compute them with the regression equation constants for the control group. Of course, the problem in most developmental research is that no treatment groups are being investigated, and in essence one is studying the control group only.

As a general rule it is wise to avoid working with change scores if at all possible. Some of their major faults are that (1) they are based on sometimes shaky assumptions about the estimation of measurement error and the characteristics of the bivariate relationship between two variables, (2) they are difficult for some people to understand and are open to misinterpretation, and (3) as can be seen previously, they are computationally somewhat complex. As Cronbach and Furby (1970) showed, most problems in research regarding the measurement of change can be handled without thinking in terms of, or actually working with, residual change scores. This is the case in nearly all analyses of age trends and in investigations of the structure of individual differences at different points in time.

II. Experimental Designs for the Study of Age Functions

Depending on the purposes of the investigation, there are many experimental designs that can be considered for the study of age-related variables. Essentially, all of these should be considered as variants of trend analysis, mainly as encompassed in analysis of variance designs. For these purposes, much statistical hardware is available, and there is no shortage of opinion and controversy regarding what should be applied when. (Two excellent general sources for information on this topic are the volumes edited by Harris, 1963, and by Goulet and Baltes, 1970. References are provided there for discussions of numerous specific issues. Some recent thinking on the topic can be found in other chapters of this volume.) The number of issues involved and the scope of the related literature necessarily limit the discussion in the foregoing section to only some of the major issues. References will be given to in-depth discussions of some of the issues that are mentioned only briefly.

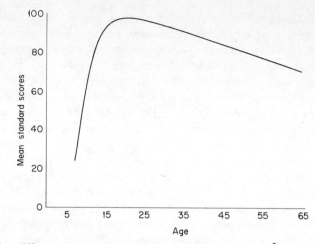

Fig. 1. Age differences on the Wechsler Bellevue Intelligence Scale. [Adapted from Wechsler (1944).]

A. Changes in One Variable over Time

The classic problem in the study of human development is the investigation of age changes in a particular variable. This section will consider some of the major approaches to investigating such changes in one variable over time.

1. Cross-Sectional Designs

One approach to investigating changes in one variable over time is to compare measurements on that variable for different age groups investigated at approximately the same time. A classic example is shown in Fig. 1, which depicts the mean scores at different ages on the Wechsler Bellevue Intelligence Scale from childhood up to age 65. The curve suggests a steep rise in intelligence up through the early teens, a leveling off in the late teens, and a steady decline from that point to old age.

There are two major reasons for performing a cross-sectional investigation of one variable. The first is simply to survey differences in people of different ages at one point in time on some attribute of current intellectual or applied interest. It is important to investigate such matters relating to age in our present population, even if such relationships are not at all indicative of processes relating to maturation and aging. In such cases, longitudinal studies (to be discussed in the next section) actually would be inappropriate.

If one wants to perform cross-sectional investigations purely to understand differences at one point in time, the major problems are (1) obtaining comparable samples at different age levels, and (2) ensuring that measures mean the same thing at different age levels. The former is a straightforward matter, although there may be attendant practical difficulties. That is, one must ensure at least a quasi-random sample at each age level from the same population. The population might be everybody in the country, white males in college, women teachers in elementary schools, or whoever. The usual cautions should be applied in drawing representative samples at each age level.

The second problem, that of ensuring comparable measurement at different age levels, is theoretically more complex and more difficult to handle in practice. The problem will be discussed more extensively in a later section.

The second reason for performing cross-sectional studies is to estimate, or at least provide hints about, developmental sequences that could be obtained only from longitudinal studies. For example, the curve depicted in Fig. 1 has been taken to represent, at least approximately, the growth and decline of intelligence for individuals. Thus, one could interpret the findings there to say that a boy who is now 8 years of age can be expected to rise very sharply in intelligence until he is in the early teens, level off in the late teens, and start a steady decline in the late twenties.

There are a great many other instances in which cross-sectional investigations have been used to estimate longitudinal age changes. Of course, as is now widely recognized, cross-sectional studies completely confound age at time of testing and generation of the subjects. Thus, in looking at Fig. 1, one is looking at the results from people who differ not only in terms of age, but also in terms of the kinds of lives they have led up to the time they were tested. There is no reason to believe, for example, that the people who were 20 years of age at the time of testing would themselves decline in measured intelligence over the ensuing years. Indeed, true longitudinal studies have shown that many functions underlying intelligence do not level off in the late teens and decline, but rather keep growing throughout middle age. (See the discussion of this matter by Baltes, 1968, and the chapters by Schaie, Wohlwill, and others in the volume edited by Goulet & Baltes, 1970. Other papers on this topic appear in the volume edited by Harris, 1963.)

2. Longitudinal Designs

When they are feasible, longitudinal studies have three advantages over cross-sectional studies for investigating age changes. First, they permit a direct analysis of age *changes*, uncontaminated with generational differences. Second, they encounter less severe problems with respect to the sampling of subjects. The major sampling problem in cross-sectional designs is to obtain comparable samples at each age level, which is no easy accomplishment. Of course, in longitudinal investigations there is no major problem in this regard, because the *same* subjects are investigated at each age level. (If, for one reason or another, there is marked attrition from age level to age level in the developmental study, of course what one should do is to investigate the relationship between age and the variable in question for only those subjects who survive throughout all age levels up to the time at which statistical analyses are undertaken. If the attrition is so large that only handfuls of subjects are available at the older age levels, then questions regarding comparability of samples at different age levels are formidable indeed. This matter is discussed in detail by Baltes, Schaie, and Nardi, 1971.)

The third advantage of longitudinal investigations over cross-sectional approximations is that the former allow one to employ more powerful statistical methods. A purely longitudinal study offers a within-subjects design, in which the error term consists of the interaction of subjects and age levels rather than the pooled variance of individual differences. This advantage is particularly large when measures correlate substantially from age to age, as is the case with most measures that are investigated.

Two major criticisms have been leveled against the longitudinal design in age-span research (see discussions by Schaie, 1970, and Baltes, 1968). One is a rather down-to-earth concern about "practice effects" entering as an influence in successive testings. This, however, is a problem that can be handled in most cases. One can test for practice effects over relatively short time periods (e.g., periods of 1 month). If there are no major practice effects at the time of retesting, there are not likely to be any effects in testing once a year or less frequently. If marked practice effects are found for an instrument (e.g., a vocabulary test), there are methods to offset the bias. The principle method is to employ several alternate forms of the measure and counterbalance these over subgroups and testing occasions in such a way as to provide unbiased mean responses at each age level.

The second criticism of longitudinal studies is rather esoteric and concerns theory rather than practical matters of research. The criticism is that such studies confound genetically programmed unraveling of behavioral characteristics with cumulative effects of the interaction of organismic states with the environment (e.g., nutrition, learning). If one views this argument as sensible, and if (by some method or other) one wants to separate the two processes, the longitudinal study completely confounds them. More about this matter will be said in the following section.

If feasibility were not such a major problem, it is undoubtedly true that longitudinal designs would be employed in most life-span research. However, very few investigators are motivated to undertake research that might not be completed even in their own lifetimes. Also, it is very hard to find commitments of grant support and support from universities and other institutions for such very protracted research. The exceptions to these principles are so few they are negligible. (A discussion of these investigations is included in Charles, 1970.)

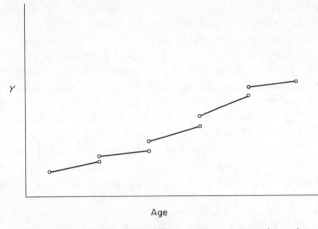

Age

Fig. 2. Hypothetical results of a study in which different age groups are each tested on two occasions.

3. Mixed Designs

Because of the shortcomings of cross-sectional studies for the estimation of longitudinal trends and because of the unfeasibility of performing true longitudinal investigations in many cases, it would be very useful to employ designs that combine some of the economy of the cross-sectional design with the conceptual advantages of the longitudinal design. Also, as will be seen, such mixed designs potentially can supply some useful forms of information that cannot be supplied either by cross-sectional or longitudinal designs separately.

One purpose of such research strategies would be to estimate truly longitudinal curves from partially cross-sectional data. An example is depicted in Fig. 2 which shows the scores of various generations (cohort groups) tested on two occasions rather than on the one occasion that is typical of pure cross-sectional investigations. One notes, for example, that the first cohort group is slightly below the second cohort group at the time of the second testing of the former. The slope of the curve can be determined for the increase in each of the two testings of each cohort group. The fact that successive cohort groups do not have the same score on Y as at the second testing of the previous cohort group suggests generational differences. How can this knowledge of generational differences be used to estimate a purely longitudinal function from mixed information about longitudinal and cross-sectional effects? (For discussions of this matter and attempts to achieve solutions, see Baltes, 1968; Schaie, 1965, 1970.)

Some attempts have been made to specify precise methods of estimating actual developmental trends from designs containing both cross-sectional and longitudinal data (see Baltes, 1968; Schaie, 1965, 1970). Although the available models provide interesting estimates of longitudinal curves, inevitably, the results must be considered highly approximate. To obtain precise estimates requires one to make a series of untenable assumptions. For example, whereas one can see in Fig. 2 that there tends to be a positive generational effect (succeeding generations tend to be higher on Y), it would require too much in the way of assumptions to adjust the cross-sectional data even by only an additive constant. To do so would be to assume that curve shapes for generations are the same at all points, maxima are the same, declines in old age are the same in shape, etc. Obviously, also, the kinds of assumptions that would have to be made would differ in terms of the types of attributes being tested (e.g., a measure of dogmatism or a measure of short-term memory). In order to feel secure in making these very complex and tenuous assumptions, one would need to obtain the longitudinal data. If one actually has the longitudinal data at hand, there surely would be no need to make such dubious, statistical adjustments of largely cross-sectional data to estimate truly longitudinal data.

Unless one has full longitudinal data, any effort to estimate such data is tantamount to predicting the future. This requires numerous assumptions about some variables remaining constant and others changing in a manner that is predictable from what has gone on up to a particular point in time. The number of variables involved is large and quite varied, e.g., many aspects of the gene pool in a particular population, medical practices in the future, states of the physical environment, and numerous others. If, by the year 2000, drugs are developed for preventing the decline in sensory–motor functions for persons above age 60, obviously the actual developmental curve for people who presently are 30 years old will be quite different from anything that conceivably could be estimated from data now available.

Although mixed designs can provide only approximate estimates of longitudinal curves, they have two other useful purposes. A second use is in mathematical models for extrapolating the various components of cross-sectional and longitudinal curves. If one has *both* types of information available, some interesting estimates can be made of the differential contribution of generational and cultural effects on human development (see discussions of these models by Baltes, 1968; Schaie, 1965, 1970).

In addition, a third, very practical, use of such designs is for testing some simple hypotheses about aspects of longitudinal curves from mixed longitudinal and cross-sectional designs. An outstanding example is provided by Schaie and Strother (1968). The hypothesis they investigated concerned the supposed decline in mental abilities that occurs from the middle twenties through old age. A battery of tests was administered to a cross-sectional sample of people, ranging from 20 to 70 years old. All subjects who could be obtained for testing were retested 7 years later. Although, as was said previously, one could not employ such data to obtain precise estimates of future developmental curves, the data were sufficient to provide highly critical information about the hypothesis being investigated. Obviously, if there are declines in mental ability during the thirties, forties, and fifties, then the 7-year segments for each cohort group should show declines. There was strong evidence against the hypothesis in a general form: Some factors of ability kept growing well into middle age, some fell off very little even into the sixties, and those that fell off at earlier ages mainly concerned speeded tasks.

Whether or not mixed designs can provide critical information concerning hypotheses about actual developmental curves depends upon the hypothesis. A more complex hypothesis than the one in the example above might not be as susceptible to such investigation.

4. Repeated Application of Longitudinal Designs

It is this author's judgment that, rather than rely on any one of the types of designs discussed in this section, in the long run, we will see repeated applications of longitudinal designs, either throughout large segments of the life span or in more restricted segments. It is conceivable that in the not-too-distant future, series of longitudinal investigations will be planned to run indefinitely. An example would be to investigate factors of human ability in the range from 10 to 80 years old. A new longitudinal study could begin every 20 years. This would provide a series of longitudinal curves ranging over hundreds of years. The changing character of the curves would tell us much about abilities at different ages and the changing influence of genetic factors and impacts of different environmental facets.

B. Comparisons of Changes in Two or More Variables over Time

Frequently, the concern in life-span research is with differences in growth rates and change of two variables rather than with only one variable. A typical example would be in comparing age functions for two types of memory—recall memory and recognition memory. Many of the considerations in the study of one variable over time are also relevant to the study of more than one variable over time, but the latter involves additional considerations, which unfortunately cannot be detailed here because of space limitations. In brief, the simplest design is the within-subjects design, in which one group receives all measurements at all measurement points. Closely related are designs in which randomly matched groups or *a priori* groups are each given a different measure, but the same one at all measurement points. Finally, mixed designs can be used, for example, with *a priori* groups, each given all measurements at all measurement points. It appears obvious that the first design is most desirable when feasible, and when not, the mixed designs are most desirable.

These designs can also be used for the study of treatments superimposed on age. An extensive discussion of the logic and methodology of such investigations is presented in Baltes and Goulet (1971; see also Campbell & Stanley, 1966).

C. Induction of a Posteriori Groups by Multivariate Analysis

By far the best approach to investigating individual differences in age trends is to hypothesize differences between different types of people and then to investigate these in longitudinal research. For example, there have been many investigations of differences in curves that typify males and females. Such designs concern changes in one variable for two or more *a priori* groups, a matter that was discussed previously.

In many instances, the interest is not in testing hypotheses regarding available *a priori* groups, but in inducing groups or types statistically. The overall results of any longitudinal study can be thought of in terms of N curves, one for each person in the study. The curves will differ in terms of general level, slope at various ages, inflection points, and other characteristics. The question concerns whether or not these N curves evolve into a relatively small number of types, and if so, what these typical curves are. There are some straightforward statistical approaches to these questions, which essentially concern factoring or clustering persons rather than the more usual factoring or clustering of tests. (Tucker, 1966a, discussed this matter in relation to the factor analyzing of learning curves.)

The problem can be conceived in terms of *generalized components analysis*. (The logic and method for performing such analyses are discussed in Nunnally, 1967, pp. 372–388.) The mathematical problem really is no different from that of any type of profile analysis performed to group people in terms of their similarities and differences on a collection of tests or other variables. Each person has as many scores as there are testing times in the longitudinal study. For example, if a particular test of motor coordination were administered each 6 months for 40 occasions, then each individual would have 40 scores. A $40 \times N$(number of people) matrix of scores would then be available for analysis. The method of analysis (Nunnally, 1967) is rather straightforwardly undertaken. One finds sums of cross products of raw scores between individuals, resulting in an $N \times N$ symmetric matrix of sums of raw score cross products. These are then subjected to factor analysis in the usual way. Any available method of factor analysis can be employed, and the resulting factors can be rotated either to theoretical positions or in terms of methods that optimize certain statistical properties of the solution.

A hypothetical set of results is depicted in Fig. 3. In this case, imagine that two strong factors were obtained and subsequent factors had only small loadings and did not appear very interpretable. Each factor is a hypothetical curve underlying the individual differences. The loading of each person on

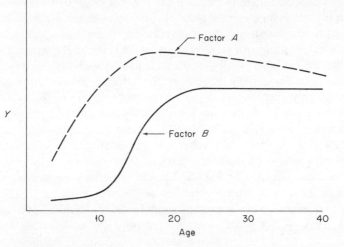

Fig. 3. Hypothetical example of age functions for two types of people derived by factor analysis.

each factor tells to what extent he "belongs to" one or the other types or is a blend of the two. In the analysis of persons, persons have factor loadings, and the variables have factor scores. In this case, the variables are points in time at which the same measure is administered (or alternative forms are administered). Factor scores can be calculated in the usual ways (see Nunnally, 1967, pp. 358–361). Figure 3 shows factor scores for two types of people corresponding to the two factors obtained from the factor analysis. The curve for Factor A underlies individuals who start off at a rather high level on the particular variable (say a particular motor skill), rise rather steadily, level off around 16 years of age, and decline gently thereafter. Factor B is typical of people who start off lower than people typified by Factor A, have a slow growth up to the early teens, spurt up markedly after that, and then level off at a lower level than that in A, but do not decline.

Of course, in an analysis such as that just illustrated, it is recognized that most people are blends of factors rather than representatives of pure types. There probably would be a sizable percentage of the subjects, however, whose age functions rather closely resemble one of the underlying factors. These would be the people who have very high loadings on one of the factors and near zero loadings on the others.

There are numerous procedural details as to exactly how the person-factoring of age functions should be undertaken. Some of the considerations are summarized by Nesselroade (1970), who provided references to more detailed discussions. R. B. Cattell has written extensively on various multivariate designs that can be employed to investigate individual differences in growth curves (see, e.g., Cattell, 1952b, 1963b).

It is more important here to examine the logic of these methods of analysis, their appropriateness for empirical research, and their success to date in investigations of the life span than to go into details regarding fine differences in approaches to the statistical induction of *a posteriori* groups. Despite the elegant mathematical methods that are available and despite the undeniable possibility that developmental types (subgroups) might exist, the evidence for the use of the methods is, I think, not highly encouraging. Some of the problems are as follows:

The methods are predicated upon the assumption that neat types, such as those pictured in Fig. 3, actually underlie masses of individual differences in growth functions. If that is the case, no one has found them to date. I do not know of a single example of clear-cut separation of underlying growth curves like those depicted in Fig. 3. Usually it is the case that most of the individual differences in growth functions can be accounted for by differences in levels, as represented by the average score for each individual over all testing occasions. This average score would be precisely the same as the loading of each individual on the first centroid factor in a raw score components analysis, and it would be very much the same as the loading on a principle axis first factor. If the first factor has very large loadings and a large variance of loadings in comparison to subsequent factors, then it means that nearly all of the individual differences in growth functions result from overall differences in levels. Of course, one can either split up the variance of the first factor in the rotations or, if one is not interested in differences in levels but only differences in curve shapes, one can inspect and/or rotate only factors subsequent to the first one. However, if factors in addition to level are mainly ''noise,'' the aforementioned statistical considerations will be of little help.

There are other problems with employing general components analysis to induced *a priori* groups. One problem is the sheer difficulty in performing the analyses that are required. A typical longitudinal study would employ 200 or more people. If analyses are undertaken on all subjects, then one would be dealing with a 200×200 symmetric matrix of raw score cross-product sums. If five factors were extracted from the matrix, which would strain the best of computers, then one would end up with 1000 factor loadings, which boggles the imagination. Other aspects of the analyses would be equally complex to undertake and comprehend. Combined with this complexity of analysis are many opportunities to take advantage of chance in generating factors that will not stand up under subsequent investigation. In all this complexity and capitalization on chance, there are many opportunities to see faces in the fog and thus come to erroneous conclusions.

Despite the aforementioned difficulties, *a posteriori* methods of inducing groups of people should be given their day in court. Even though there have been many suggestions over the years for employing them, only a few examples are available to date, and they produced nothing that has had a substantial impact on developmental psychology. Hopefully, more thorough tests will be given of the multivariate methodologies for deriving *a posteriori* groups, and hopefully such efforts will lead to important new lines of research.

D. Structure of Individual Differences over Age Spans

In addition to investigating developmental curves for people in general and comparing curves for different groups of people, it also is important to investigate correlations among individual differences over the life span. It is important to investigate such correlations both for the resolution of basic research issues and for applied purposes. Regarding the former, high correlations between measurements taken early in childhood and in adulthood suggest that the traits in question are genetically endowed and intractable to learning experiences. In contrast, low correlations suggest that training programs would be successful in improving people with respect to the particular trait. In terms of applied issues, the stability of individual differences over time has important implications. If, for example, intelligence test scores at age 8 correlate very highly with intelligence test scores at age 20, one can use the results at the earlier testing for long-range prediction and guidance, and to make many decisions about educational activities. Those tests given at an earlier age which have higher correlations with later criteria, such as success in college, can be relied on more heavily than instruments that are less predictive of future success.

1. Comparisons of Factors

In the investigation of the structure of individual differences over time, psychologists usually are more concerned with constructs rather than with separate variables. Thus, psychologists are interested in such broad-gauged constructs as intelligence, anxiety, dogmatism, and extraversiveness. Such constructs usually are supported by factor analytical studies of individual differences on a collection of measures. There are two very important unresolved questions with regard to the investigation of constructs over the life span. First, is the factor structure underlying constructs in a particular domain of variables the same over the life span? Second, if the answer to the first question is yes, how does one measure the constructs in a comparable manner at different age levels? The first question will be discussed in this section; the second question will be discussed in a later section. Unfortunately, no final solution will be offered in this paper, but efforts will be made to clarify the issues and to state some principles regarding final solutions. (See discussions of these issues by Baltes and Nesselroade, 1970, and by Cattell, 1966c.)

Attempts to answer the first question have been posed largely in terms of comparing matrices of factor loadings of tests in a particular domain at different age levels. Thus, one would compare matrices of factor loadings for reasoning abilities in 10-year olds and 18-year olds and attempt to reach conclusions about the similarity of the factor structure (or composition of constructs) in the two groups. As I have pointed out elsewhere (Nunnally, 1967, pp. 367–368), one cannot reach precise conslusions about similarities of factors in different analyses by comparing matrices of *factor loadings*. To attempt to do this violates a logical principle and leads to various paradoxes. The logical principle concerns the fact that factors (either determined directly or only estimated) are mathematical combinations, usually linear, of the variables. Strict comparisons of factors in different analyses, whether in different populations studied at the same time or different populations in a developmental sequence, can be made only by correlational investigations of the factor scores defining the factors. Consequently, it is hopeless to make any strict comparisons of factor analytic studies at different age levels unless one uses the same subjects at different age levels.

In addition to these logical considerations, it is very easy to find cases in which the patterns of factor loadings in two investigations are similar, but the variables concern very different domains of content. This would be the case for any domain of variables that relate to a general factor or any domain of variables that relate to a hierarchical pattern of factor loadings. Indeed, the patterns of factor loadings in the two cases could be exactly the same, and the factors themselves would be entirely unrelated. As was mentioned previously, fallacious conclusions could be reached by investigations of matrices of factor loadings because the loadings are not the factors; rather, the factors are either represented directly or estimated in terms of factor scores. Such comparisons of factor loading matrices at different age levels are interesting, and they offer circumstantial evidence regarding the similarity of factors at different age levels; but they cannot be used to reach any precise conclusions at all.

If longitudinal data are available for a battery of tests, direct statistical tests can be made of the similarities of factor structures obtained at different age levels. The logic and technique of making such statistical comparisons are clear. A real question arises, however, as to whether the same tests (or comparable tests) measure the same things at different age levels regardless of the "true" underlying factor structures. As will be discussed more fully in a later section, it is frequently the case that different factors are involved in easy as opposed to difficult items on the *same* test. Thus, whereas it might be possible (at least theoretically) to measure the same factors at different age levels, the sheer practicalities of composing items might lead to apparently dissimilar factor structures. As with so many other issues that have been discussed in this paper, the problems are severe only if one investigates a large segment of the life span (e.g., over 10 years) rather than more restricted segments. In particular, the problems are severe if one makes comparisons of children below the age of, say, 12 with older groups rather than working with the age segment above about 13 years of age.

Rather than becoming involved in the aforementioned logical and empirical morasses attendant upon testing for the similarity of factor structures at different age levels, it is better to pursue a different approach. The approach starts by defining the factor structure for any domain of variables as that found at maturity, i.e., between ages 18 and 25 years. There is nothing necessary about selecting this particular age group for defining the factor structure, but one could think of this as an interesting bench mark for examining traits in younger and older people. After this factor structure is found for a domain of variables, then one can examine the standings of people at different age levels with respect to the indicants of each factor. In this way, one could measure the maturing of individuals with respect to indicants of the factor and also examine the changes, if any, in correlations among the indicants of a factor from age to age. The examination of the life span in reference to bench-mark factors of this kind seems much more sensible and much more fruitful than searching for illusive methods of determining the similarity of factor structures at different age levels. Even if the latter were more feasible, the inevitable result would be that factor structures at different age levels are somewhat the same and somewhat different. Then what would one do with that finding?

2. Statistical Methods

Regarding the investigation of individual differences over the life span, two considerations regarding statistical methodologies are worth noting. First, there are numerous mathematical models regarding the structure of individual differences over time. A mathematical model that has received considerable promise in that regard is the *simplex*. However, there are various other mathematical models that should be investigated. If a model fits the data well, it lends credence to the supposed underlying processes as explanatory devices for age changes.

The second consideration is that a very general method of analysis is available for investigating correlations among sources of individual differences at various times. The method—*progressive partialing analysis*—is explained in detail in Nunnally (1967, pp. 151–171). This might concern, for example, a group of predictor variables and scores on one variable which is being investigated over a large segment of the life span. Progressive partialing analysis would allow one to pick apart the influence of the various predictor variables on performance in the developmental study and to determine the predictiveness of measurements taken early in the developmental sequence with respect to those taken later.

Table 1 provides an example of how progressive partialing throws light on developmental sequences. The first variable is an intelligence test administered in the second grade. The remaining four variables are tests of reading achievement administered at the ends of the third, sixth, ninth, and twelfth grades, respectively. Progressive partialing consists essentially of performing a square-root factor analysis (see discussion in Nunnally, 1967, pp. 318–321) of a matrix of correlations. The first column of the factor matrix shows the correlations of the predictor

TABLE 1

An Example of the Use of
Progressive Partialing Analysis as an
Aid in Understanding Correlations among
Variables at Different Points in
the Life Span

Tests	Square-root factors			
	I	II	III	IV
Predictor test				
Reading 1	.70			
Reading 2	.60	.50		
Reading 3	.50	.45	.30	
Reading 4	.40	.35	.25	.20

test with each of the four measurements of reading achievement. As would be expected, the predictor test correlates more with the results from earlier testing than those from later testings. The subsequent columns of the factor matrix show the correlations of each earlier testing with later testings when the influence of the predictor tests and earlier testings are removed. Thus, when the influence of the predictor test is removed, one sees a residual correlation of the first testing with the second testing of .50. Similarly, in the third column, one sees the correlation of the second testing with the third and fourth testings when the influence of both the predictor test and the first testing are removed. Progressive partialing analysis offers a flexible tool for taking apart matrices of correlations concerning developmental trends.

III. Some Major Problems in Psychometric Theory for Life-Span Research

In discussing research strategies and methods of analysis for life-span research in previous sections, some important issues regarding psychometric theory were purposely not mentioned. Some major issues in that regard will be discussed in this section.

A. Reliability

Measurement error serves to complicate life-span research. One frequently finds that distributions of test scores differ from age to age not only in terms of means, variances, and factorial composition, but also in terms of reliability. Here reliability is being discussed in the usual sense of the extent to which measurements are repeatable and thus are free from measurement error. (The estimation of reliability coefficients and the use of formulas for dealing with measurement error are discussed, for example, in Nunnally, 1967, Chaps. 6 and 7.) In life-span research, the first problem regarding measurement error is to obtain good estimates of reliability for the instruments administered at different points in time. An important caution in this regard is that the reliability coefficeint should be obtained from populations that are reasonably similar to those with which the life-span research will be undertaken, and the number of subjects should be 300 or more. If these conditions are not met, the estimated reliability may be quite inaccurate. It is not uncommon to find extensive statistical manipulations (such as corrections for attenuation) made with respect to reliability coefficients obtained from small, unrepresentative samples, by poor methods of estimating reliability.

Reliability coefficients have different uses in studies of group trends and in studies of the correlational structure of individual differences over time. Regarding the former, measurement error becomes part of the error term in examining any type of group trend. On numerous occasions, it has been suggested that a knowledge of the measurement error should be used to make corrections in analysis of variance with respect to the significance of different facets of the experimental design; but that remains an unsettled issue, and consequently analysis of variance is undertaken without considering unreliability as a special source of error. A knowledge of measurement error is useful, however, in interpreting the results of trend analyses. If, for example, reliabilities tend to be rather low, then one would not expect to find clear trends over time.

Information about reliability coefficients not only provides cautionary notes in studies of the structure of individual differences over time, but also leads to some concrete "corrections." The term corrections was put in quotes because really what one does is to estimate what certain statistical relationships would be if measurement error had not been present. The primary type of correction in that regard for life-span research is the correction of correlation coefficients for attenuation. For example, before undertaking a progressive partialing analysis, it usually is wise to correct every correlation in the overall matrix for attenuation. Of course, one has to have excellent reliability estimates for each variable (as discussed previously) before this can be done. Such coefficients should be corrected for attenuation in life-span research, because the need is to estimate "real" correlations rather than those that are artifactually reduced (and reduced to different degrees by measurement error.

B. *Factorial Composition of Measurements*

Whereas there are some straightforward methods for investigating measurement error and making appropriate corrections, the wider problem of "validity" is a much more illusive and intractable matter in life-span research. The severity of the problem is proportional to the number of years being investigated. Thus, if one is comparing 7-year olds with 8-year olds, the problem is negligible;

but if one is comparing 4-year olds with people in their sixties, the problem is extremely severe.

Regardless of whether or not one employs statistical methods of factor analysis, it is almost inescapable to think of psychological measures of individual differences as being underlain by some parsimonious, conceptually meaningful set of dimensions or factors. One can argue about the most appropriate methods for deriving such sets of factors, and about which sets of factors are best in a particular domain of variables. However, it is rather difficult to argue against the proposition that studies of the structure of individual differences need such parsimonious bases as those illustrated by simple factorial equations. If this logic is accepted, then one must face a number of problems in *long-range* life-span research. The problem encountered with respect to the investigation of developmental trends is that the exact shape of most curves depends to some extent on the factorial weights from age to age. Let us consider the situation in which an age curve is being investigated (either cross-sectionally or longitudinally) with respect to development of quantitative skills. Let us further suppose that a very long test, covering a very wide range of difficulty, is administered to students in grades 2 through 12. (Of course, one usually would not administer exactly the same test to all students since the majority of the items would be totally out of the range of some of the younger subjects, and older subjects would breeze through many items of trivial difficulty for them.) Even if one did administer exactly the same test to all students, would one be measuring the same thing at various age levels? The most probable answer is "not exactly." It quite usually is found that, on any test, the easy items tend to measure something partially different, factorially speaking, from the harder items. A test of quantitative skills was chosen as an example, specifically because one typically finds somewhat different factorial composition for the easier items than for the more difficult items. The easier items tend to measure raw numerical facility, as involved in addition, subtraction, estimating square roots, etc. The more difficult items tend to tap factual information, specific training in school, and various reasoning factors, in addition to raw numerical facility. Consequently, to some extent, examining age curves with respect to such a measure of numerical facility, can be likened to comparing three apples at one point in time with four bananas at another. The problem here is not so severe as to make all such comparisons useless, but it requires one to water down any strict interpretations of the exact curves as depicted on graphs.

In addition to changing importance of factors at different age levels, the exact shapes of developmental trends also are influenced by the particular ways in which items are selected for measuring instruments. In order to rule out any major problems with respect to changes in factorial composition over time, let us choose a very simple attribute—spelling ability. One could administer a very long spelling test to students in grades 1 through 12. Each item would consist of two versions of the spelling of a word and the task of the subject

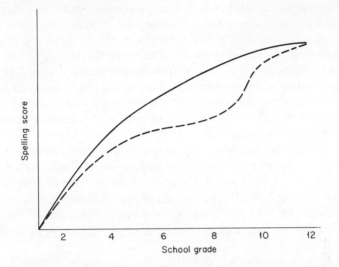

Fig. 4. Comparison of age curves for spelling ability on the original test (——) and a modified test (– – –).

would be to circle the correct spelling. Analysis of the results produces the solid curve in Fig. 4. One notes a rather rapid growth during the primary grades, a less rapid growth in grades 5 through 7, and a further deceleration of the growth function in high school. The exact shape of that curve, however, could be changed markedly by the way items were selected for the test. This can be dramatically illustrated in the situation in which one selected spelling items for the test that were either very easy or very difficult. Then the curve would tend to resemble the dashed line in Fig. 4. Because the easy words are still present, the growth curve is not affected very much for students in the primary grades. Since the average high school student performs well with respect to the relatively difficult words, the section of the curve from the mid-teens upward is largely the same. But the section of the curve in between would look entirely different from that produced by a test that had the full range of difficulty represented.

Of course, no one would construct such an oddball test as that in which the items are composed half of very difficult items and half of very easy items. But what should the distribution of difficulty levels for items be? (See a discussion of this matter in Nunnally, 1967, Chap. 8.) The customary approach to developing tests from item statistics is to develop a homogeneous scale relating to a particular factor of ability or personality. In developing measurement methods by this approach, one is concerned almost exclusively with the nature of individual differences produced by the test and not by mean differences of age groups or of other groups. So far as I know, no tests have been developed specifically for examining age trends. If they have been, I seriously doubt that they faced up to the crucial problem regarding distributions of item difficulties. If one did face up straightforwardly to that problem, what would be his standards regarding selection of items in terms of difficulties? Obviously, I do not have the answers to these questions, but two principles can be asserted: (1) highly precise interpretations of the exact characteristics of age functions are not justified with present measuring instruments, and (2) more attention should be given to relationships between the psychometric properties of measuring instruments and the results of life-span research.

Regarding the former consideration, there are some hopeful signs. First, to the extent to which rather similar age functions are obtained with different measuring instruments, one can begin to place some faith in interpretations of those age functions. Second, not all psychological measures that are of interest for life-span research are put together statistically in terms of test items. For example, there is no problem with investigating the pursuit rotor or tachistoscopic recognition at various age levels.

Regarding future psychometric investigations of measures employed in life-span research, there are some theoretical models that would be useful. For example, measurement models can be developed in which one deals with the percentage of change in responses from age to age, e.g., working with the finding that the percentages of persons who answer an item correctly are 50 at age 9, 62 at age 10, 68 at age 11, etc. By dealing with items on which no age group is close to 0% or 100%, one could develop scales based on such percentages of overlap. However, the details of how to do this have not yet been fully worked out. There are other possible approaches to obtaining "age equivalent" tests. This is an important area for psychometric research.

IV. Summarizing Comments and Guesses about Future Developments

Looking back on this survey of research strategies and measurement methods in life-span research, a number of points become clear. To set the stage for summarizing those points, let it be reiterated that life-span research requires at least the following major steps: (1) developing measurement methods for important human attributes, (2) selecting and implementing research designs with those measurement methods, and (3) employing powerful and appropriate methods of analyzing the results. At this vantage point, it can be seen that, at least conceptually, points (2) and (3) are rather simple, yet sometimes difficult in terms of time, effort, and money.

Working backward in terms of the above-mentioned order, there really are no major problems with respect to most methods of analysis that are required. (The real problem is obtaining meaningful data.) The two classes of analysis that are employed are trend analyses for age functions and correlational analysis for investigating the structure of individual differences over time. Psychology is richly endowed with appropriate, powerful methods of analysis for all these purposes. (If anything, the problem is that so many Rube Goldberg statistical monstrosities are available that they distract us from more germane and perplexing problems.)

Regarding research designs, if there were no practical problems involved, it would be very easy to specify the more appropriate approaches, e.g., large N, longitudinal studies should be undertaken over the entire life-span. However, experimenters do not live forever; granting agencies are not unlimited in their benevolence; and the "reprint race" makes it difficult for competent researchers to survive in a working environment where publications will not be forthcoming for many years. Consequently, in many cases, some compromises will have to be reached with the ideal research strategies. Cross-sectional studies will have to be employed in many instances, because nothing else is feasible and/or because there is no reason to believe that generational effects are large.

As has been the case in the past, heavy reliance probably will continue to be placed on longitudinal studies during crucial periods in the life span rather than across very large segments of the life span, such as investigations of Piaget's principles during childhood, changes in social behavior during the years surrounding puberty, and changes that occur in people after 70 years of age. Such investigations not only are more practicable than longer-range longitudinal investigations, but also largely avoid many of the severe problems that occur in the latter, e.g., comparability of measures employed at different age levels.

As is widely recognized, cross-sectional studies confound generational effects with effects of aging, and longitudinal studies confound effects of aging with effects due to cultural changes. It has been suggested that unconfounded effects of generations and of culture could be obtained by various designs that combine longitudinal and cross-sectional data. These designs have been used for three purposes: (1) to provide estimates of longitudinal data, (2) to provide information concerning simple hypotheses regarding limited aspects of developmental data, and (3) to test the explanatory power of mathematical models concerning various components of human development. With respect to these three purposes, it was concluded that (1) whereas interesting suggestions might be obtained about true developmental trends, these are based on untestable assumptions about what people and the world will be like in the future, (2) the designs do provide strong critical information about some hypotheses, e.g., supposed declines in ability starting in the early thirties, and (3) the mathematical models are interesting, quite abstract, and more useful for stimulating research than for analyzing actual data or for forecasting future trends.

As an ultimate design for investigating most of the life span, it was suggested that the future would find series of longitudinal investigations, one starting, say, every 20 years. Each curve would tell us about current generations, and comparisons among curves would allow us to ferret out effects of different causal factors.

Even if one employs ideal research strategies and methods of analysis, life-span research is beset by some perlexing problems in terms of psychological measurement. First, there are problems concerning differential reliability at different age levels. Fortunately, these problems are not very severe, and some hardware is available for handling them. Far more severe are problems concerning the factorial composition of measures at different age levels. By argument and by example, it can be shown that the exact shapes of developmental curves are to some extent artifactually related to the way measuring instruments are composed. Consideration in research should be given to developing mathematical models concerning age-equivalent tests. This is an important and entirely new arena for psychometric research.

The factorial composition of measures at different age levels also plagues studies of the correlation structure of individual differences over time. Unfortunately, much of the theorizing regarding comparisons of factor structures at different age levels has been based fallaciously on statistical comparisons of matrices of factor loadings at different age levels. It was argued that strict comparisons of factor structures can be made only in terms of factor scores rather than matrices of factor loadings. Such comparisons require longitudinal investigations. Even with such data available, however, I am rather pessimistic about the possibility of making any highly precise statements regarding similarities and differences in factorial structure at different age levels. Mainly, this is because either different instruments are given to people at different age levels or different factors are involved at different levels of difficulty in the instruments. Thus, the question of whether or not a particular factor of spatial visualization exists from childhood through adulthood is rather hopelessly confounded with questions regarding comparability of measuring instruments. Other difficulties were mentioned in performing research on this matter. It was suggested that, in general, a more fruitful approach is to fix the factor structure at a particular age level (e.g., young adulthood) and examine age trends up to and beyond that point.

In general, it can be concluded that problems of ensuring comparability of psychological measurement are very severe only when (1) large segments of the life span are investigated, e.g., from 15 to 70 years of age, and/or (2) included in the investigations are children (e.g., below 10) or old people (e.g., above 70). Regarding the former, one must be concerned about such matters as practice effects, dated test materials, large changes in the social and physical environment, and other problems. Regarding the latter consideration, the marked differences in abilities and personality characteristics of children and adults make comparable measurement difficult (e.g., because of artifacts in ways that tests are constructed, as illustrated in this paper in relation to selection of test items in terms of difficulty). Some of the same problems may be encountered in comparing persons in the final declining years with less aged adults.

The status of life-span research is not much different from that in psychology as a whole nor much different from that in any emerging science: Interesting ideas outstrip the available methodology for their investigation; measurement techniques are crucially important, but difficult to develop in many cases; research strategies either are doomed to produce equivocal results or are unfeasible in the light of available resources and technical developments; but despite all the difficulties, the questions are intriguing, and the search for answers is fun.

CHAPTER 6

Unraveling Maturational and Learning Developments by the Comparative MAVA and Structured Learning Approaches

RAYMOND B. CATTELL

UNIVERSITY OF ILLINOIS
URBANA-CHAMPAIGN, ILLINOIS

I. Two Proposed Technical Innovations and Their Associated Models

When psychologists are able to predict, with moderate accuracy, an individual's score on a trait some years ahead of time, knowing only his present score and the intervening environment, psychology will have some claim to have "arrived" as a science. At present, the only trait on which most psychologists would agree that we can approach such prediction is intelligence; and here we succeed because it is largely a simple outcome of genetic maturation and the volution law[1] is essentially understood. We flounder in any instance less simple than this primarily because we have only crude models for recognizing the distinct actions of maturation and learning, and for putting their effects together. Moreover, our predictions remain weak also on the pure learning

---

[1] Our vocabulary for concise, intelligent discussion of hereditary and environmental interactions is at present quite inadequate. Elsewhere, I have suggested the term "volution" for what we do not yet have, a concept to cover both maturation and involution, i.e., the internally unfolding components of personality change. It derives from the Latin *volvere*, to roll. It could happen that maturational and involutional curves are part of a single process, incorporating the same parameters, in which case it would be particularly apt to refer to volutional curves and volutional laws.

theory side. Though the reflexological generalizations which preempt much of what should be a broader approach to learning do well enough with the speed of rats in a maze, or the human eyelid reflex, they are quite inadequate to give equations for the learning of the complex patterns which the personality theorist now measures as traits or processes. Some advance in the latter is promised by the new branch of learning theory we have called structured learning theory, which we shall bring to bear here on the general nature-nurture problem.

Because of its bristling technical difficulties, a majority of developmental psychologists in this generation have fought shy of handling the problems in separating maturational and learning curve components in their obtained developmental curves. Yet the "developmentalist's" basic understanding of the fabric of personality will get nowhere unless he faces the conceptual problems of separating the warp of the genetic threads from the woof of experience. As the ancient Greeks believed, it is the Fates who throw the shuttle of events to and fro across our lives, weaving the unique patterns of our personalities. Yet the patterns which Destiny weaves speak not only of the play of the shuttle, but also of the quality of the supporting warp of our genetic fibers.

Because of the timeliness of such a turning of the spotlight on to the analysis of genetic, volutional components in distinction from threptic,[2] experiential components during the present surge of interest in developmental analysis, the present chapter will concentrate on new concepts in the "nature–nurture" of development. Precision in use of terms being important, Table 1 is presented as the quickest way of indicating how such terms as learning, means–end learning, classical conditioning, maturation, induction, modulation, endogenous, etc. will be used here. It corresponds to the use in Structured Learning Theory (Cattell, 1970b).

One might suppose that the analysis of developmental change curves into threptic (or exogenous) and genetic (or endogenous) components would have to depend on obtained nature–nurture or kindred breakdowns (see next section) for a given trait at each of a number of points in time. As we shall see, the cross-sectional nature–nurture method is an important avenue, but not the only one by which we can approach these issues. In fact, we propose here to cover the following conceptual and methodological innovations:

(1) The use of the *comparative* method with the Multiple Abstract Variance Analysis (MAVA) and twin method tools, across ages and cultures;

---

[2]At present, behavior geneticists and psychologists have no term for "environmentally, experientially determined" and I have proposed elsewhere (Cattell & Nesselroade, in press) and here Aristotle's (De Anima) apt term "θρεπτικη." Thus *threptic* contributions are those from the whole environment (both learned and induced) and the term is truly complementary to *genetic*, from the same Greek cultural period. The word *threption*, in Table 1 is the natural brief English derivative for "the acquisition of behavioral modifications by all kinds of environmental, experiential action."

	Stable trend change	Modulation[c] or Reversible change
Behavior change (personality is modified)		
1. Threption[d] (Personality is Modified by Experience)	**(a) Learning[a] (and forgetting)**	*Reversible change*
	(i) CE. Coexcitation learning (classical conditioning, CRI) (principle: coexistent excitation)	*(i)* Exogenous situation-determined temporary states.
	(ii) ME. Means–end learning (operant or instrumental conditioning, CRII) (principle: connected reward)	Diurnal and other imposed rhythms.
	(iii) IE. Integrative learning (integration among immediate ends) (principle: goal-hierarchy formation)	
	(iv) GM. Ergic goal modification (sublimation, some imprinting) (principle: second-best, modified goal acceptance)	
	(b) Induction[b] (Induced change from direct physiological modification by environment)	
	Examples	
	Central nervous system and brain injury; hormonal over development and exhaustion; vitamin deficiency, altitude, oxygen shortage, etc.; drug exposure, poisoning; energy-economic changes;	
2. Volution (Personality is modified by endogenous genetic, time controlled constitutional life processes)	(a) Maturation or evolution (genetic capacities)	
	(b) Aging or involution (genetic capacities)	*(ii)* Endogenous time-determined cyclical changes and appetitive effects

[a] *Learning* defined as change in the response usually given to a particular stimulus and which can be shown to be *adjustively* related to events specifically connected with the response.

[b] *Induction* defined as nonadjustive change from direct modification of the organism by the environment.

[c] *Modulation* defined as reversible, temporary change in reactive capacity of the organism due to either exogenous, situational effects or endogenous physiological-appetitive effects.

[d] *Threption.* A new term needed to cover inclusively *learning* and *induction.* It is derived from *threptic* (see page 112) as opposed to *genetic* or *volutional*, and means any kind of change due to experience of the environment.

(2) Attempting to trace the components not merely as "heritability" or "nature–nurture" ratios, but as specific scores assignable to individuals and correlatable with external observations;

(3) Attempting to use factor analysis directly to abstract genetic and threptic patterns and score contributions and,

(4) Attempting direct analysis of personality life curve plots into threptic and genetic components.

In discussing these possible methodological advances, we shall also need to discuss variations in basic models for heredity–environment interaction including (a) the alternatives of composite, *uniform* mixed genetic and threptic, and purely genetic and threptic *dissective* factorial source traits, and (b) the successive investment model for the acquisition of discovered source trait patterns.

II. The Convarkin and MAVA Methods of Genothreptic Analysis

From here on it will be accepted as a truism that the developmental level which a person reaches on any trait is a joint outcome of genetic and threptic influences and that the true problems concern (a) what model of interaction is most promising? and (b) how do we collect and analyze data to yield information on the parameters of the accepted model? Developmental curves, the primary stock-in-trade of developmental psychology, rest on *points*. Our choice is between taking two sets of the points initially, plotting separate volutional and threptic curves, or plotting the points of our actual measures and finding ways of splitting the curve—as a set of parameters—into two curves.

Now as to locating the genetic component in any measured behavior, the clinical–genealogical method will sometimes tell us the gene action of a trait like Huntington's chorea, or taste blindness, and correlation of the behavior with physical signs of known heredity will tell us about phenylketonuric amentia. But these comparatively simple approaches fail when, as in traits like stature or intelligence, the hereditary part is polygenic. Distributions on such traits are likely to be continuous, even before the further smoothing action of environment occurs. Then we must turn for a solution to methods which divide up the measured total variance on a continuous trait into the fractions contributed respectively by heredity and environmental learning. These experimental methods we have called (Cattell & Nesselroade, in press) the *convarkin* methods because they handle *con*tinuous traits, by *var*iance analysis methods applied to *kin*ship groups. The two main convarkin methods in present use are single pair methods, (as in parent-child regressions and, especially, the twin method) on the one hand, and the complex MAVA method on the other.

Multiple Abstract Variance Analysis (MAVA), means that the design takes several *concrete*, observable variances (on any trait) and breaks them down into *abstract* components, such as *within family environmental variance, within family hereditary variance, between family environmental variance,* and *between family genetic variance,* as well as the effects of *correlations of hereditary and environmental variances.* The MAVA method has many advantages over the older twin method, such as being able to yield *inter*familial (*not* just *intra*-familial) environmental variance sources, as well as the *correlations* between the two influences. The typical breakdown of two examples of concrete, experimentally measurable variances into the abstract variances is shown in Eqs. (1) and (2), while the calculation of an abstract variance is given in (3). Note that what are sometimes symbolized by subscripts "h" and "e" for hereditary and environmental, we have here and later symbolized by "g" and "t" for *genetic* and *threptic.*

$$\sigma^2_{UA} = \sigma^2_{wg} + \sigma^2_{wt} + \sigma^2_{bg} + \sigma^2_{bt} + 2r_{wgwt}\,\sigma_{wg}\,\sigma_{wt} + 2r_{bgbt}\,\sigma_{bg}\,\sigma_{bt} \qquad (1)$$

$$\sigma^2_{ITA} = \sigma^2_{wt} + \sigma^2_{bt} \qquad (2)$$

σ^2_{UA} = variance between unrelated persons, i.e., the general population variance

σ^2_{ITA} = variance between identical twins raised apart (sometimes written MZA for "monozygotic twins raised apart")

σ^2_{wt} = variance within family environmental ("t" for threptic) variance component

σ^2_{wg} = variance within family hereditary ("g" for genetic) variance component

σ^2_{bt} = between family environmental (threptic) variance component

σ^2_{bg} = between family hereditary (genetic) variance component

The terms on the left, with subscripts UA and ITA, are taken as instances of concrete, experimentally measured variances. That in the general population called "between *u*nrelated persons reared *a*part" is written UA and the familiar *i*dentical *t*wins reared *a*part is written ITA.

By juggling such simultaneous equations, we can obtain solutions for the abstract unknown variances, such as σ^2_{wt}, σ^2_{bh}, etc., in terms of the measured concrete variances. For example, using just ten equations, for ten concrete variances, we can solve for between family environmental variance by (3) as follows:

$$\sigma^2_{bt} = \sigma^2_{SA} - 2\sigma^2_{UA} + \sigma^2_{BNF} \qquad (3)$$

BFSF is sometimes used for "between full sib families" instead of BNF "between natural families." Here, besides σ^2_{UA}, the variance in the general population, one needs the concrete variance for sibs reared apart, σ^2_{SA}, and "between natural families," σ^2_{BNF}, i.e., the variance among the means of ordinary families (calculated as that between the means of sibs, a pair from each family.) For the reasoning on the composition of these equations, in their development and solution, the reader must be referred elsewhere (Cattell, 1953a, 1960, 1963a, 1965b; Cattell & Nesselroade, in press).

To proceed to the newer methodological approaches to be studied here, it will be necessary to assume that basic ideas of the convarkin methods, i.e., the twin and MAVA designs, are understood. What they yield is, (a) a statement of the magnitude of the genetic variance on a continuously distributed variable, and (b) a statement of the magnitude of the part that is environmentally determined.

Three objections are sometimes raised by newcomers to the results delivered by this whole convarkin approach. It is felt to have the shortcomings that: (1) as far as genetics is concerned, the analysis tells us only what *proportion* of the variance is due to gene action, but does not tell us what the hereditary mechanisms or gene structures are for the given trait. For example, it does not tell us whether there are few or many genes, or that they have dominant or recessive action. (2) These variance ratios or heritabilities are admitted to be specific to the cultural ranges and racial mixtures studied. Thus they might be expected to alter to some extent if derived from experiments with different racio-cultural groups. (3) The statement about relative variance applies to the population in general and does not tell us the proportions in any given individual. These comments are true, but they turn out not to be criticisms. The sufficient answers to them are as follows: (1) There simply does not exist, where continuous combined genetic and environmental variables are concerned, any way of calculating from variances *directly* to gene mechanisms, i.e. to single gene actions. (However, in some instances, e.g., open field mobility in mice, a single gene seems to account for most of the variance.) As far as we yet know, the convarkin methods remain the indispensable, basic step for proceeding eventually to gene mechanisms. From them, we can hope later to employ new *population-genetic analyses* to isolate gene action. (2) The fact that the abstract variance components may vary from one population to another is not a defect but a valuable new piece of information, being the means by which we proceed to analysis of specific environmental and genetic associations, by following methods proposed below. Actually, as Whitney, McClearn, and De Fries (1970) have suggested, the variation in this ratio may not be large. (3) The amounts in a given *individual* can ultimately be estimated, by methods introduced in what follows.

As to utilizing comparisons among cultural, racial and age groups, if we were to find the threptic variance contribution ($\sigma^2_{bt} + \sigma^2_{wt}$) to intelligence greater in a group of 30-year olds than in a corresponding MAVA analysis of 20-year olds, we should conclude that it is after the adolescent period that environment has its chief dispersing action. Or, if, in MAVA analyses of groups chosen at the same age level, we found the variance in superego strength to be greater in a culture with many religions than one given to a single, uniform religion, we might tentatively conclude that the form of religious education is important in determining a level of superego formation. Incidentally, in this first illustration, we have not introduced the complication of separating the *ecogenic* from the *epogenic* effect (in this case in environment). That is to say, the environmental variance in 30-year olds might differ from that in 20-year olds not merely on account of age, but because the *epogenic* (epoch-tied trend) effects (Cattell, 1970b) were greater in one historical epoch than in another. The separation of these has been systematically set out by Baltes *et al.* (1970) and Cattell (1969).

Thus, what we may call the *comparative MAVA method*—involving comparisons of variances and correlations from different populations strategically chosen—is actually a powerful new tool. It is capable of telling us, on the environmental side, at what age and largely from what sources the environmental component arises, or, on the genetic side, the differing genetic variances associated with various gene pools. But it has been my experience that those who (like Yeatman & Hirsch, 1971, for example) come to human genetics from studying plants or fruit flies, where they can directly "see" what a gene does to the physical phenotype, are under some kind of illusion that they can likewise directly see the behavioral phenotype for a genotype. In other words, they assume some royal road to knowing what the genetic component has contributed in a given organism. Consequently, their initial reaction is that variance analysis is a lot of complex work which yields only a relatively abstract outcome. This emotional reaction is understandable, but the abstractness is a reality of research, and the physical geneticists, untrained in the novel problems of behavioral genetics in humans, have absolutely no alternative to offer when it comes to unraveling the complicated components in continuously variable human behavior. It would be easy, of course, if we could, as with some insects and plants, obtain clones—sets of people all guaranteed born with identical heredity—and divide them into groups, subjecting each to a different, graded environment. Or, alternatively, if we could obtain known variations of genetic makeup and expose them all to an identical environment. But, in the first place, neither the physically possible controls, nor the ethics of exercising such controls permit experimenters to subject other human beings to the prolonged and powerful manipulated environments necessary to produce measurable changes of personality. And, second, we cannot obtain clones, or indeed, manipulate human genetics at all.

Accordingly, the realistic path in human behavior genetics research is to let life do the experimenting and to tease out by superior statistics what cannot be isolated by manipulation. This is what the comparative MAVA method seeks to do, using existing racial and cultural groups and utilizing the differences in gene distributions and cultural–environmental influences that naturally exist.

The first outcome of the comparative MAVA method, as pointed out on page 115, will then be statements of *the genetic variance itself* for different racial groups, groups with different degrees of inbreeding, etc., forming a basis for inferences about gene action. In that same first harvest will be information about the different threptic variance magnitudes themselves, for different cultures and subcultures. It will also supply evidence on the magnitudes of the correlations of genetic and threptic effects in the various cultures. A novel possibility we should discuss is that an extension of the usual application of the MAVA design might be effective in breaking down not only the *effects* of genetic and environmental influences on the individual, but also the causes. This has no meaning or use for the genetic component which is entirely of genetic origin, but it has meaning for the physicosocial environmental features of the individual. For such external environmental features, as, say, income or years of education have a fraction of their variance associated with genetic features of the individual and a fraction associated with the threptic part of an individual's trait. For example, some variation in length of education is associated with the genetic part of an individual's intelligence and some part with environmentally acquired (threptic) parts of his intelligence. At this point, we do not need to ask which is cause and which is effect; it suffices if one part of the external environmental feature, e.g., years of education, can be associated with the genetic variance in intelligence in individuals and another part with the threptic variance.

Now, if we consider this purely environmental measurement—say, years of education—to be scored for siblings, twins, children raised apart, etc., the usual application of the MAVA method should yield genetic and environmental variance parts to *it* just as for a personal trait. In the next section, we shall discuss how pursuing this into *comparative MAVA* may lead to estimates of an *individual's* endowment in genetic and threptic components.

Meanwhile, let us round off the view of the MAVA method itself by pointing out that prior to its *comparative* design here discussed, the behavioral geneticist has considered it a sufficient goal to obtain actual *absolute* variances in a given trait due to within and between family threptic variance, and to within and between family genetic variance as well as the two or more genetic–threptic correlations. And this incidentally, is no mean advance on the more restricted convarkin methods (or on no method at all), for, as Burt has pointed out (1971), obtaining reliable values for these variance fractions is of great help in guiding the practice of the teacher and the clinician.[3] These variances can either be

---

[3] For example, if a trait such as intelligence is largely inherited, the teacher does not infuriate the child by drill and exhortation intended to change it, and if superego strength is largely environmentally determined (threptic) the clinician can hopefully bring to bear influences to modify it. A poorly defined concept "teachability," which has recently come into use, better defined by a "modifiability index," requires precision treatment here. It is asserted that σ_e^2 gives no index of how much environment *could* modify the trait, but only how much it *does*. However, the

left as they stand or used to derive a *nature–nurture* ratio, N as in (4), or a heritability ratio H as in (5). (Incidentally, the latter is generally written h^2, which confuses it with communality in factor analysis. It seems best to keep the variance ratios as N and H, and hence the sigma ratios, rarely used, as $\sqrt{N}$ and $\sqrt{H}$.)

$$N = \frac{\sigma_{wg}^2 + \sigma_{bg}^2}{\sigma_{wt}^2 + \sigma_{bt}^2} \tag{4}$$

(or partial N's, such as $\sigma_{wg}^2/\sigma_{wt}^2$ and $\sigma_{bg}^2/\sigma_{bt}^2$). The heritability *ratio* as in in Eq. (5), proceeds, as in (4), as if the actual magnitudes of the variances might be irrelevant.

$$H = \frac{\sigma_{wg}^2 + \sigma_{bg}^2}{\sigma_{wt}^2 + \sigma_{bt}^2 + \sigma_{wg}^2 + \sigma_{bg}^2} \tag{5}$$

III. Estimating Genetic and Threptic Parts of an Individual's Score through Regression on Real World Influences: Comparative MAVA

As pointed out previously, the notion that we can get to measures of the genetic and threptic components in a single individual's trait score has been a myth. The ordinary use even of comparative MAVA will not directly yield this, and we have to turn to a novel approach here proposed as Environmental Feature Nature–Nurture Analysis or EFNA as a possible approach. One must stress that it is previously undiscussed and untried, and therefore to be critically evaluated.

The variances we obtain from MAVA and comparative MAVA deal, of course, with what in this frame of reference are *dependent variables*. The threptic and genetic components *in the individual's trait* itself are the effects of influences

---

further assumption is then made in "teachability" that with sufficient attention, any trait could be modified indefinitely. The only way to put this type of discussion on a firm footing is to establish a relationship between some environmental variance, e.g., in hours of teaching, or rewards per increment in performance, and the resulting threptic variance. We could thus calculate a *modifiability index* for the trait *with respect to some definite environmental influence*.

Meanwhile, extreme environmentalists have been having phantasies that the teachability could be quite unrelated to the present environmental variances. Since there are only 24 hours in a day, and only so much available economic resources for education, so that heavy concentration on modifying one trait means less on another, it is highly probable that with an agreed set of priorities, the "teachability" of any trait would not be very different from that indicated by the ratio of threptic to genetic variance which our cultures now produce. "Teachability" or "modifiability" has no meaning except as a ratio to some measured environmental variance. An advance to such a concept is made possible by the second methodological innovation proposed above.

(independent variables) in the actual physicosocial environment, and in the chromosomes, respectively.[4]

Now it turns out that the problem of tracing the causal action, and that of estimating a component in an individual are related, and that the former must be tackled first. But if we are to proceed in the direction now proposed, it is necessary that the psychometric, scaling foundation should first be firm. Over this, we shall pass quickly because it deals with comparatively familiar needs. What follows, indeed, requires but two conditions: (1) that the original measurements be made in terms of psychologically meaningful, factorially unitary source traits (as proposed and practiced, for example, in Cattell, Stice & Kristy, 1957; Cattell, Blewett & Beloff, 1955); (2) that they should be in scale units— *ideally universe-standardized scores based on pan-normalization procedures* (Cattell, 1971). This permits factor scores in different racio-cultural groups to have significant differences of means and variances (rather than a standard score variance of unity in each group) which is necessary to the operation of the comparative MAVA method.

The outcome of comparative MAVA is a set of genetic and threptic variances and correlations for racio-cultural groups for which environmental and chromosomal features are to some degree known. What use one makes of this depends upon further developments of method. The main use which comparative MAVA contemplates is the relating of these variances on the one hand, to the genetic, chromosomal features and on the other, to the measurable features of the external climatic, social, etc., environment. Since most readers in the present context are interested in relating development to environment, we shall pass over the former briefly. However, it will involve some questions as "With what polymorphisms in the genetic structure (established on some physical basis) can the genetic–behavior variance be associated?" "When such and such a change in absolute population genetic–behavior variance occurs with such and such a change in assortive mating or inbreeding, what must the genetic structure be?" The various backcross experiments possible with animals cannot be performed (or, indeed, even found) with humans, so this branch of investigation is likely to face a slow and complex development awaiting insights in population genetics of the kind pioneered by Fisher, Haldane, Wright, and Malecot.

It is in the understanding of the environmental causations that the methods here discussed offer the more immediate advances. It is also one of those ironies

---

[4]We cannot call all significant associations between an environmentally determined trait in the individual and some measure of his environment proof that the *latter* is the *cause*. A corresponding correlation between a genetic feature and a gene structure *is* evidence of cause, because the gene had to come first. A comprehensive analysis of the directions of causality in the case of threptic features has been made elsewhere (Cattell, 1963a). However, it can readily be seen that, say, a good acquired skill in the Spanish language could be either a cause or consequence of a greater amount of travel in South America.

not infrequent in pure science that a method originally developed to help solve genetic problems—MAVA—should turn out to be the means of unraveling an otherwise insoluble environmental effect problem. The problem is that there is no direct way to correlate scores on that *part* of some environmental feature, e.g., years of schooling, which is associated with threptic effects in the individual, with scores on the threptic effect. For example, how much is the variable "years of schooling provided for the individual regardless of his genetic makeup" associated with improvement in that part of intelligence which is environmentally produced?

It must be understood that at this point, of the two theories of trait structure discussed in the next section—the homogeneous and the divisible—we are holding cautiously to the former, which is best supported. This supposes that by the observable nature of our measurement, *there is nothing in it which will tell us which part of the trait score is an hereditary and which part an environmental component.* Just as in putting a ruler into a can of water collected from two rain showers there is no way of saying, from any intrinsic characteristic of the inches, how much came from one shower and how much from the other. Thus we assume, if the generality of our approach is to be maintained, that there is no way of telling *from the character of the measures themselves,* how much of Tom Jones's 132 points of IQ came from genetic and threptic components, respectively.

What we actually have from MAVA is variance components, and if we find that σ_g^2 has a value of 9 and σ_t^2 a value of 4 for the given group, then the regression of the observed score would lead to an estimate that a person who measures 5 points above the mean on the observed score is 3 points above on the genetic component and 2 points on the environmentally caused part (using what we call the two way regression or collation method; Cattell, 1971[5];

---

[5]The regression coefficient r_{ab} of A on B, which gives A_1 as the equivalent of B_1, will, in reverse as the regression of B on A, give a new value B_2 as the equivalent of A_1. This is, in each direction, the best estimate. The reason that these two equivalences are different is that some two *specific* sources of variance reside in A and B besides that which is *common* to them, and produces the correlation. However, suppose we have reason to believe that the specific source is nothing but random error, or, alternatively, that it is irrelevant to the conclusions we wish to make, e.g., that it does not affect other uses we make of the A and B measures. In that case, we can logically argue that we do not want the ordinary two-way, different regression equivalents, but what we may call the *codistribution* or *collation equivalent.* This derives, by a formulation which DeYoung has set out in detail, from making a least-squares-fit line to the scatter plot of A on B. An approximation to the same is to set the same percentile scores in the distributions of A and of B as equivalent. (We can, of course, convert this conversion table to standard scores when the distribution happens to be normal in both.) This might be called "two-way regression" because it insists that the conversion must have the same result either way. However, I have suggested it be called *codistribution conversion*, or more briefly, a *collation* equivalent of A and B. Thus *collation* and *regression* are the two possible alternatives to be considered in any mutual conversion of scores, with the differences of outcome here described.

Lewis & DeYoung, in press). But that 3 : 2 ratio would divide up *every* person's observed deviation from the mean in just the same way. We know also that that is most unlikely to be true. It is only a crude approximation, since different people get the same observed total deviation more for one reason than another.

However, now let us consider the possibilities if we knew the regression of the threptic component upon a variety of measured environmental features, and could measure those features for any given individual. We could then make a more personally adapted estimate of his threptic component and therefore of his genetic component (which would be the remainder). But the calculation of that regression is denied us because we do not have on the one hand, the individual threptic scores, nor do we have on the other, the scores on that part of the environmental feature which is associated purely with any individual's threptic component. For, as we have seen previously, some part of any environmental feature is correlated with the individual's heredity. Thus we are caught in a vicious circle—the absence of the true individual environmental part (threptic) scores denying us the correlation and the missing correlation denying us a good estimate of the threptic score for a new individual from his known total score. Nor will such devices as the part-correlation (Dubois, 1957), save us, for they will in this case, leave the individuals' rank orders the same in the threptic as in the total measure.

Two steps are necessary for a breakthrough here. The first we have called Environmental Feature Nature–Nurture Analysis, EFNA, which aims to find that fraction of the feature variance which is (in any way) associated with the threptic variance in individuals. The second is called the Comparative MAVA Variance Correlation method—the CMVC method, for short. As to the first, it may suffice, as stated before (page 118) to point out that any feature of the environment upon which a person can be assigned a score as "his own," e.g., his years of schooling, his parents' income, the mean temperature of the town he lives in, the number of hours he has played baseball, can, in principle, be analyzed into variance portions associated with hereditary and with threptic aspects of his makeup, just like any other "trait" he possesses. This still leaves causal directions unspecified: it merely says how much is "associated."

Incidentally, the reader who ponders this issue further will run into the question "What is the meaning of *within family* and *between family* threptic components when we come to features such as 'hours spent reading.' " This could be determined both by the fact that as, say, a later child, the individual encounters more books on the family bookshelf than did his brother and by the fact that his family is, in any case, more given to reading than other families. This problem is not new to the EFNA approach: it has existed all the time in the ordinary convarkin methods, where the sophisticated investigator recognizes that what statistically we call the within-family threptic variance σ_{wt}^2 has substantial parts of itself associated with environmental differences between sibs, e.g., number of friends that have nothing to do with differences in their treatment arising within the family, but lie in "accidental" influences to one sib or another from remote encounters outside the family.[6] This constitutes, therefore, no new problem in EFNA, and can, if necessary, be avoided by our dealing subsequently only with the population environmental variance, σ_{pt}^2 which for simplicity of exposition we will now do, where:

$$\sigma_{pt}^2 = \sigma_{wt}^2 + \sigma_{bt}^2 \tag{6}$$

In any case, granted that we have used EFNA on top of comparative MAVA to obtain for each of several racio-cultural groups the following values:

σ_{gx}^2 the total genetic variance for a trait x;

σ_{tx}^2 the total threptic variance for a trait x;

σ_{tf}^2 the threptically associated variance in an environmental feature f;

σ_{gf}^2 the genetically associated variance in the environmental feature f,

we are in a position to calculate the regression coefficient, $r_{tx \cdot tf}$, granted certain assumptions, by the CMVC method.

[6]It is customary to think of the within family threptic variance σ_{wt}^2 as that fraction of the variance of the sibling difference which is due to differences of position, parental treatment, etc., within the family, while the σ_{bt}^2 component is thought of as what the sociologist is concerned with in differences of economic and cultural status among families. However, this is an oversimplification. If two sibs go to different schools, choose different peer companions, marry different wives, and so forth, it is evident that there threptic differences, which constitute the σ_{wt}^2 value, will arise not only from differential treatment *within* the family from the birth order, parental age, the behavior of other sibs, etc., but also from events far *outside* the family, such as having different teachers in school, though we label it "within family environmental variance." Reciprocally, the *between family* threptic component does not arise only from what the sociologist conceives as family differences of earnings, social status, religious affiliations, cultural descent of the parents, and other outer forces. The between family threptic variance includes the effect also from psychological atmospheres for the whole family that are generated in the family itself by the interactions of the given parents and children themselves. In short, the abstracted within and between parts are *effects* kept within these categories by the mode of analysis (between brothers and between the family means of brothers); but the *influences* which produce these effects (or, as we shall prefer to say later, *associated* with them) are not to be divided into environmental features that operate within the family, on the one hand, and in the world generally, e.g., in the social status of families, on the other. This complicates our attempts to trace and apportion the origins of the total observed environmental variance, but it might reasonably lead to the argument that regression of a trait on one of the influences that causes it should be the same in the "within family" as the "between family" variance (with due allowance for the latter being the *mean* of two or more individuals), and this could be a check on the regression value. There are, of course, some features not susceptible to being divided into a within and a between influence, e.g., family income, except where different at the rearing period of one child from that at the period for another.

TABLE 2

*Possible Analyses of Associations between Threptic and Genetic Variances
and Outside (Feature and Chromosomal) Variances by the CMVC Method*

Parameters yielded for groups by the comparative MAVA method

1. Abstract variances and correlations concerning traits in people

   a. σ_g^2 = trait variance of genetic origin (= $\sigma_{wg}^2 + \sigma_{bg}^2$)

   b. σ_t^2 = trait variance of threptic origin (= $\sigma_{wt}^2 + \sigma_{bt}^2$)

   c. r_{tg} = general population correlation of genetic and threptic components in persons (derivable from $r_{wt.wg}$ and $r_{bt.bg}$)

2. "Outside" variances (causes or associates) in environmental features and chromosomal, genome observations

   a. σ_f^2 = total observable variance on some environmental feature f (theoretically analyzable into σ_{wt}^2 and σ_{bt}^2, the components acting within and between families)

   b. σ_c^2 = total observable variance in chromosomal features (or indirect evidence of such features)

   c. r_{cf} = general population correlation of environmental and chromosomal (genic) features

   It will be noted that the variance in the phenotypic trait itself, resolved into its two components, is represented by g and t subscripts, in 1a–c whereas the "physical" environment and the chromosomal facts are represented by "f" and "c" subscripts in 2a–c.

3. Expected magnitudes of possible correlations of variances (or sigmas) employable in the CMVC method, across groups. These are the six mathematically possible correlations among four score series: those for f, the environmental feature score; c, the chromosomal value; t_x, the threptic component on trait x, and g_x, the genetic component in trait x.

   a. $r_{\sigma_{t_x}\sigma_f}$ = degree of association of actual environmental features f's with threptic trait x endowments. (= $r_{t_x \cdot f}$)

   b. $r_{\sigma_{t_x}\sigma_c}$ = this association of environmentally produced variance with chromosomal features should be zero unless there is some tendency (Cattell, 1963) in society to produce causal relation of genetic endowment to cultural position.

   c. $r_{\sigma_{g_x}\sigma_f}$ = this also should tend to be zero unless associations of the same general nature as in (b) arise.

   d. $r_{\sigma_{g_x}\sigma_c}$ = this is the genetic "corresponding" correlation to (a), and should have high values when the investigator hits on the chromosomal, genic feature correctly representing the genetic personality expression measured in "g."

   e. $r_{\sigma_{t_x}\sigma_{g_x}}$ = this should be a zero correlation except through such connections of community genetic and threptic variances as are brought about through the media of some actual t and c connection in the environment.

   f. $r_{\sigma_c\sigma_f}$ = this is the correlation of purely observed sigmas. It could have some low but significant value and should, if assumptions hold, be the same as the mean value of 1c across all communities.

For the CMVC (comparative MAVA variance correlation) method, we need for a correlatable series of, say, 60 communities, the σ_{tx}^2 and the σ_{tf}^2 values for each. We would also have the raw, observed score means of these communities, but we are not proposing any immediate use for these.[7] In passing to our analysis of the environmental correlations, we may also note on the side, as indicated in Table 2, that there are other correlations that can be explored.

As has been said previously, we are unable to calculate the $r_{tx \cdot tf}$ correlation because we do not have the scores of individuals on tx, the threptic part of their observed scores on trait x, or on fx, the score on that part of an environmental feature f that is associated with purely environment-originated variance. The talisman by which the CMVC method attempts to break through this barrier of ignorance consists of the assumption that *the correlation of the two variances, σ_{tx}^2 and σ_{fx}^2, across groups will be the same as the correlation of the two scores, tx and tf within the population represented by those groups.* To make this assumption, it is necessary that the 60 or more racio-cultural groups here supposed to enter the correlation be random samples from a conceived world population. The normal distribution obtained by Cattell, Breul, and Hartman (1952) for cultural measures on 80 countries justifies to some degree the hope that this assumption can be made. If it is made, then it can be shown by comparatively simple statistics (McNemar, 1962, p. 399) that the average within group $r_{tx \cdot tf}$ is estimated from the obtainable variances as follows:

$$r_{tx \cdot tf} = r_{\sigma_{tx} \cdot \sigma_{tf}} = \frac{\sum^N \sigma_{tx} \sigma_{tf}}{N \sigma^2_{\sigma_{tx}} \sigma^2_{\sigma_{tf}}} \tag{7}$$

where N is the number of groups involved.

With this instrument, we may hope to track down what a social and developmental psychologist most wants to know, namely, the extent to which particular environmental features account for the threptic part of an observed trait measurement. Since we know that the threptic score must be wholly accountable for by various environmental features, $f_1, f_2, f_3, \ldots, f_n$ (each as a tf part only), as follows:

$$t_{xi} = b_1 tf_{1i} + b_2 tf_{2i} + \cdots + b_n tf_{ni} \tag{8}$$

it is up to the psychologist, by hunch, theory, or trial and error to find the features of the environment that *will* entirely account for t_{xi}. The b's in (8) are, of course, beta weights in a multiple R, to be derived by finding correlations of the tf's with the tx in question, and transforming them according to the correlations among the tf's.

---

[7]One possible way of involving this extra information as a check is to make the assumption (as in modulation theory, Cattell, 1963c, 1971) and in real-base true zero factor-analysis (Cattell, 1971) that in true scores, the mean and sigma of a group will hold the same ratio for the same trait across groups. The total observed mean M_{t+g} would then be divided into means M_t and M_g in the proportion of the sigmas.

Parenthetically, a time saving strategy here must be to factor the features of the culture itself, either, as already done by Cattell (1952), Gibb (1956), Rummel (1970), and others across cultures, or in terms of the scores of individuals on features of environment. (For example, how are the number of books a person possesses correlated with the number of his siblings, or the hours his mother spends at home?) Instead of trying an almost endless set of f variables in $r_{tx \cdot fx}$ correlations, e.g., years of marriage, age of parents, use of corporal punishment, etc., one might then correlate only the *factors* among the f's (and thus also permit canonical solutions). Regardless of which is done, one will hope to finish with a multiple R of the form (treating the tf's for simplicity as outright f's).

$$R^2_{tx(f1, f2, \ldots, fn)} = b_1 r_{tx \cdot f1} + b_2 r_{tx \cdot f2} + \ldots + b_n r_{tx \cdot fn} \qquad (9)$$

that offers a substantial prediction of the threptic part of an individual's score. As a check, it should turn out that the limit one is approaching as additional significant dimensions are added to (9) is a variance σ_{tr}^2 equal to that reached by the MAVA method for the threptic component.

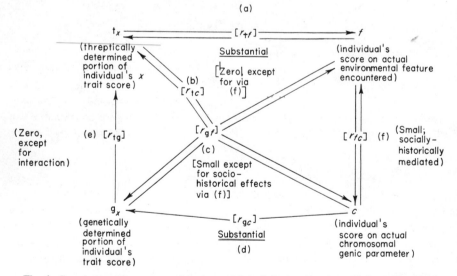

Fig. 1. Causal connections assumed in the model, and the associated correlations. The (a)–(f) beside the correlations refer to their designation in Table 2. This figure aims to set out (in the individual not the group comparison form) correlations in Table 2, Section 3 together with the causal connections which theoretically they are assumed to be expressing. Some of these causal connections are immediately in the individual's own life, some in historical effects in his society (Cattell, 1963). A correlation represents however, more than the causal connection over which it is directly written; it is the outcome of the full chain of causal connections around the diagram.

A corresponding course through the separate chromosomal parameters should ultimately, theoretically produce an $R_{g(\bar{c}_1 + \bar{c}_2 + \ldots + \bar{c}_p)}{}^2$ in which the genetic variance is fully accounted for by everything one knows about the gene structure of the population. How far either the environmental features or the chromosomal indices we hit upon for measurement will succeed in accounting for a substantial fraction of the threptic and genetic variance, respectively, remains to be seen. However, in the CMVC (the comparative MAVA variance correlation) method, we have a means—the only one yet available—for relating each of the two separate contributions as such to the extra-behavioral conditions with which they are associated.

As far as the estimation of individual part-scores which we promised, it will be through the weights of Eq. (8) if they are substantial enough, that we can obtain tolerable estimates, from scores on the individual's actual environmental features and gene endowment, of his personal endowment respectively in the threptic and genetic contributions in his individual trait score.

To state *associations*, as we have so far done, is not necessarily to state causal connections. Indeed, the derivation of causal connections is commonly a further and more difficult task. However, it behooves us here to state what causal connections are assumed in the model used above in connection with associations. The more outstanding have been stated, e.g., that the environmental features, f's, will affect traits, and the genetic part will in turn affect the individual's environment. In Fig. 1, a more comprehensive summary of the causal connections one must assume is set out diagrammatically.

IV. Amalgamated and Divisive Source Trait Models: The Divisive Possibility of Directly Factoring Out Nature and Nurture Components

So far, we have assumed that a source trait is what may be called "amalgamated." That is, there is supposed to be no change in the pattern of various measures which go to estimating the factor that would permit one to realize when one is measuring the threptic part or the genetic component, which are inseparably amalgamated in a single pattern of influence. This assumption of ignorance—this inability to fission the trait measure directly by subsets in the factor battery—has been the reason for the development of the convarkin methods, the MAVA method within them, and the further approaches in the last section previously.

However, an alternative model has long been considered (Cattell, 1946; Fuller & Thompson, 1960) in which, factor analysis is conceded to be capable of *directly* pulling apart the threptic and genetic subpatterns in any source trait. This presupposes that what would normally be a single, indivisible factor pattern for a particular source trait, over all its range, is capable of being factored by more sensitive methods into two distinct images or *eidolons* (as we may call them, to avoid confusion with the use of trait *image* term in instrument factors, Cattell, 1965a), one corresponding to the threptically established part and one to the genetic. (In more general terms not restricted to a genetic and threptic component, the possibility of getting two kinds of factor for one trait has been stated in the idea of *wholistic* and *conditional* factors; Cattell, 1946.) A now well-investigated instance is the splitting of Spearman's general factor, *g*, into *fluid, g_f*, and *crystallized, g_c*, intelligence factors. They are sufficiently different in content, and, what is more important, in their hyperplanes, i.e., in what they leave *un*affected, to separate quite readily on rotation (Cattell, 1971) despite a correlation between them of .4 to .6. In this case, g_f is the genetically given factor. And through its investment in learning a second factor g_c is created. In this case, g_c does not turn out according to nature–nurture evidence, to be a purely threptic factor. But this we would not expect it to do, because, according to the investment action (Cattell, 1971, p. 255), it is partly environmental, partly genetic in its literal nature and score (unless we partial g_f out of it).

The two models—the amalgamated and the divisive source trait theories—can be stated and contrasted in Eqs. (10)–(12) as follows. First, in Eq. (10), which represents the amalgamated model, the trait may be considered to have two parts, e.g., T_{1g} and T_{1t} for trait T_1, which represent the genetic and threptic parts. These have the same factor pattern and behave in the same way, however, as shown by having the same behavioral indices and acting as a uniform whole.

$$a_{ij} = b_{j1} (T_{1gi} + T_{1ti}) + \cdots + b_{jk} (T_{kgi} + T_{kti}) \tag{10}$$

From this model, in which each of the k source traits has two part scores, T_g and T_t, it follows that the heritability of any specific kind of behavior, such as a_j above, is expressed by:

$$H_j = \frac{\sum^{x=k} b_{jx}{}^2 \sigma_{xg}{}^2}{\sum b_{jx}{}^2 \sigma_{xg}{}^2 + \sum b_{jx}{}^2 \sigma_{xt}{}^2} \tag{11}$$

Knowing the $\sigma_g{}^2$ and $\sigma_t{}^2$ values for each factor (here expressed as fraction of a unit total variance), and the specification equation for the behavior in question the heritability of any specific behavior can then be estimated.

In the case of the divisible model, however, we suppose there is some difference of pattern, slight or substantial, between the paired "eidolons," such that T_{1g} and T_{1t} are no longer parts of the same, but two distinct source traits, each requiring its distinctive b, as follows:

$$a_{ij} = b_{j1g} T_{1gi} + b_{j1t} T_{1ti} + \cdots + b_{jkg} T_{kgi} + b_{jkt} T_{ku} \tag{12}$$

Here, each source trait is wholly genetic or wholly threptic, and it is not implied that the two kinds of traits are necessarily of equal number. In the image or eidolon case, they *would* be in pairs, and the first and last appear in this equation as pairs. However, the divisible model which follows could develop clear of this eidolon restriction. In any case, the behavior in a_j is still genothreptically heterogeneous though the factors are homogeneous, and the heritability of a_j is still fractional, as we ordinarily know that it is, as follows:

$$H_j = \frac{\sum^{xg=d} b_{jxg}^2}{\sum^{xg=d} b_{jxg}^2 + \sum^{xt=f} b_{jxt}^2} \tag{13}$$

where there are d genetic and f threptic uniform source traits, and unit variance is supposed as usual for all factors.

From the standpoint of current genetic theory there are, however, difficulties in accounting for a continuous single genetic factorial source trait. If such a trait has p different manifestations, and if the genetic increment on any one of them is due to, say, the dominant allele of some additional gene coming into action, how do we account for the same kind of increment in general, i.e., with some exceptions, occurring simultaneously on all the p manifestations, loaded by the genetic factor T_{xg}? There are two possible conditions that would produce this: (1) a series of genes all with roughly the same pleiotropic pattern, or (2) a linkage effect among a set of genes each responsible for only one of the p manifestations, but producing a tendency for one-step increment in one, to be associated with a one-step increment in any other. The third possibility that will occur to the reader, that a *single* large gene pleiotropically accounts for all manifestations, is not being entertained because this would produce a dichotomous rather than continuous score. Instances are very rare and confined to specialized behavior rather than broad traits.

Since neither conditions (1) nor (2) are *very* probable, the possibility has to be considered that the eidolon model is of limited applicability and that where the divisible model obtains, with a distinct genetic pattern of trait contribution, the latter will appear more frequently as some broad second order factor, representing the effect of some set of genes unrelated in their inherent behavior genetic effect, but for some reason, e.g., racial isolation, tending to segregate and move about as a single body. The possibility that quite *small* (not massive factor) patterns could, in this model, ultimately be traced to single genes, is at present technically unencouraging. For, to trace and isolate these, we should have to factor more variables than genes, and since the latter might be 10,000, we are stopped.

Some small support for the eidolon model appears in the phenomenon of "cooperative factors" having forced itself upon us (Cattell, 1952a, 1966b). Moreover, the recent investigation of the fluid and crystallized intelligence cooperativeness of pattern suggests that we already have a case which is indeed an eidolon in the genetic–threptic sense. Further support for this interpretation comes from the novel factoring of identical and fraternal twin differences, by

Vandenberg (1965) and Loehlin and Vandenberg (1968). Consistent with the fluid and crystallized intelligence theory, they obtained one general ability factor of a genetic kind peculiar to the fraternals, but in both a general ability factor seemingly of environmental origin.

Another suggestive finding in this area is that of Hegmann and DeFries (1970) with mice. It is true that this does not reach the degree of structuring involved in demonstration of a unitary factor, but it does show that in one investigated instance where the genetic components in two pieces of behavior are positively correlated, the threptic components are also significantly positively correlated, as would be expected from the eidolon model.

Let us scrutinize more closely how a genetic pattern which so arises (by whichever of the preceding processes manages to produce it) could generate its threptic eidolon. A simple theory is that a genetic predisposition multiplies rather than merely adds to the effect of environment in any area. Another is that an animal or man tends to seek out more experience in areas where he is more gifted. Another is that natural selection favors both particular combinations of genes and similar particular combinations of learning, in a given area. The problem is really that of accounting for the genetic pattern itself, as we have tried to do up to now, rather than that of accounting for its threptic eidolon once it is formed.

Thus let us suppose, from both the Horn (1966) and Cattell (1971) and the Loehlin and Vandenberg (1968) work that a fluid, general intelligence factor, g_f, exists and is paralleled by a largely threptic crystallized intelligence eidolon factor, g_c, as stated. In this case, it can be argued that we get a well defined genetic general factor mainly because the variables examined are all in the cognitive area, likely to be uniformly enhanced by any gene which contributes to the total associative brain mass which is the origin of proficiency on those variables. However, by genetic expectations, each of these genes which does something to the brain mass would, pleiotropically, have effects in quite other parts of the organism, and without the special pleading for parallel pleiotropies above, these would not act cumulatively in these other areas. Consequently, we can argue that if Cattell in ability factoring, or Vandenberg and Loehlin in their twin studies had taken a wider range of variables, including length of toe, alkalinity of urine, etc., it is logically to be expected (a) that their g_f factor would lose its typical *ability* flavor and extend to many other things, and (b) that it would lose its character as a substantial variance general factor as it straggled across these new domains. This can be illustrated if we look at the matter in a small number of variables, in equations:

$$a_j = \left[b_{j1}G_1 + b_{j2}G_2 + b_{j3}G_3 \right] + b_{jc}g_c \qquad (14)$$

$$a_k = \left[b_{k1}G_1 + b_{k2}G_2 + b_{k3}G_3 \right] + b_{kc}g_c \qquad (15)$$

$$a_l = b_{l1}G_1 + b_{kh}H + b_{km}M \qquad (16)$$

$$a_m = b_{mp}P + b_{mx}X + b_{m3}G_3 \qquad (17)$$

Here (14) and (15), i.e., a_j and a_k, represent cognitive variables and a_l and a_m variables outside the cognitive field. (The i, for individual i, subscript is dropped for simplicity.) The genes G_1, G_2 and G_3 are all genes that affect associative brain mass. So long as we keep within cognitive variables, they will "maneuver" as a single general factor, each individual having more or less of G_1, G_2 and G_3 (square brackets). However, when variables like a_l and a_m are included, this behavior as a block ceases.

The unity joining a_j and a_k is the unity of a few genetic contributions—almost an accident in genetic terms. However, this causal "substation" is itself then the origin of a wide array of cognitive consequences in a clear general factor. The summary of what is being implied here is not easy to make for readers unfamiliar with the design of factor analytic experiment. Nevertheless, we are saying essentially that certain organs, e.g., the brain, the thyroid gland, are affected by genes which probably also affect several other aspects of the organism. However, in a set of purely behavioral measurements, a wide pattern of cognitive variables may be affected by the brain and a wide pattern of temperament variables by the thyroid. These will appear as typical first or lower order factors. If it should happen that the gene group which affects the brain also affects the thyroid, and we include both intelligence and temperament variables, the illusion of a single "genetic intelligence factor" would vanish, and we should have to recognize that the genetic factor is quite different in pattern from any threptic pattern and indeed, operates (and is to be discovered) only at a higher-order level. In that case, factor analytic investigation in this area becomes, in practice, quite difficult. One must start with enough variables to get enough factors at the *second-order level* that are of the same order of frequency as single powerful genes.

Thus, when genetic probabilities are pursued far enough, the whole idea of a source trait simply splitting into two eidolons—two "cooperative" factors of distinctly similar image, one genetic, one threptic—becomes less convincing. If we get to this position, there is no longer any particular expected "paired" relation between the forms of genetic and threptic factors. However, if we *do* suppose that effects as in fluid and crystallized intelligence are likely to be found elsewhere (and the geneticists' notion of phenocopies, in which an environmental pattern mimics a genetic one encourages this view) then we have still to account for the image-like quality, and clearly this must arise in one of two ways: (a) a genetic unity creates a corresponding threptic pattern, or (b) a cultural pattern produces by natural selection over many generations a collection of linked genes favorable in combination to the required cultural pattern. Thus families like the Bach's, long concerned with music, might

TABLE 3

Possible Models for Relation of Genetic to Threptic Trait Patterns
(Illustrated by Numerical Loading Values)

A. The divisive model

	(a) Cooperative, eidolon					(b) Independent			
	F^1_t	F^1_g	F^2_t	F^2_g		F^1_t	F^2_g	F^3_t	F^4_g
1	.7	.6			1	.4			
2	.4	.2			2	$-.7$		.4	
3	$-.3$	$-.8$			3	.5			
4	.4	.5			4	.3	$-.4$		
5			.3		5		$-.3$		.4
6			.6	.4	6		.6		
7	.2				7		.7		$-.3$
8			.7	.7	8			$-.5$	
9			$-.4$	$-.6$	9			$-.4$	
10			$-.5$	$-.4$	10			.6	
11		$-.2$			11				$-.8$
12			.5	.6	12				.4

B. The amalgamated model

(c) As a higher-order factor

Primaries of amalgamated type	F_{II_g}	F_{II_t}	F^1_t	F^2_t	F^3_t	F^4_t
F^1	.6		.6			
F^2	.4			.7		
F^3	.5	.6			.6	
F^4	.8	.4				.4

accumulate a favorable genome for this educational experience. However, culture is so recent for *Homo sapiens* that one would surely refuse to credit many truly genetic aggregates to this source.

In summary of the possible models here, Table 3 shows the loading patterns that are supposed by the divisive eidolon model (in which one factor somehow generates another resembling it) the divisive independent model, and the amalgamated model with the genetic factor (as well as a threptic factor) at the second order. As a technical issue worthy of note, Fig. 2 shows the special rotation problems that are likely to confuse resolution in the cooperative, eidolon case.

Parallel pleiotropy, linkage, and racial gene pools are not very strong *a priori* arguments for purely genetic (divisive) trait patterns emerging in factor analysis.

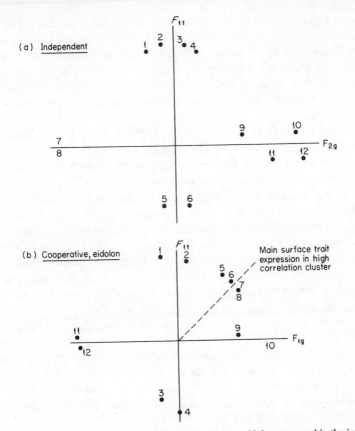

Fig. 2. The problem of resolution in the cooperative pattern, eidolon case, and in the independent case.

Despite this, there does seem to be suggestive evidence even apart from what is possibly a pseudoinstance in Loehlin and Vandenberg (1968) previously noted, for factor analysis pulling out wholly genetic and wholly threptic source traits.[8]

[8]Incidentally, the MAVA approach and the pair-difference factoring of Vandenberg and Loehlin, introduced with the idea of separating genetic and threptic source traits admit of being usefully combined. There is no need to confine the latter method to twin differences for it could be usefully extended to difference scores of pairs in all the constellations—sibs raised together, sibs apart, unrelated children together, etc.—of the MAVA method. Only in the comparison of identical and fraternal twins would factors in one disappear *entirely* in the other, but systematic quantitative relations of factor variance would be expected to be consistent with the MAVA equations, as in (1) and (2) here. So far, this would be only an alternative approach to the same results as by the ordinary MAVA. However, a real addition to knowledge might ensue from comparing the pattern of factors when resting largely on *within-family* compared with *between-family* variance, since the influences in trait formation might be interestingly different in the two situations.

It is to be found, first, in the distribution of nature–nurture ratios for objective test personality factors, as found in 1955 by Cattell, Stice, and Kristy (1957). The distribution of these N values (admittedly not over more than a score of factors) shows a distinct tendency (at least when Loehlin's (1965b) implied correction for error reducing the genetic component is applied) to pile up at the extremes. In short, there is a suggestion of relatively pure genetic and threptic patterns.

Second, the factoring of dynamic traits (Cattell, 1957, 1965a; Horn, 1966; Cattell and Kawash, in press; Krug, 1971; Sweney & Cattell, 1961) has repeatedly shown two distinct kinds of patterns corresponding to what have been called ergs and sentiments. Although no convarkin research has yet explored nature and nurture variances on them, the first kind of factor pattern clearly "checks" in possessing every association usually assigned to drives on the one hand, as the second does in fitting the meaning of a purely acquired, cultural–institutional, learning pattern on the other. The divisive model is certainly supported by factor analysis in the dynamic modality of behavioral measurement.

As the divisive model equation (12) brings out, if all trait structure were of this kind, it would be appropriate to talk of an N ratio, or an H heritability percentage for specific pieces of behavior, but not of such values for unitary source traits, since they would be wholly one or the other. However, investigation of N and H for source traits is not wasted, for we have as yet no proof as to which model holds in various domains. What probably *is* wasted, relatively, is effort to determine N's and H's for all sorts of specific behaviors, for they are infinite in number and whether the amalgamated or the divisive model holds the values for any of these can be simply estimated once the values for the source traits are known, as Eqs. (11) and (13) show.

V. Assistance from Structured Learning Theory and the Successive Investment Theory

Three possible models for the way in which genetic and threptic influences may combine to produce structure—the amalgamated, the divisive eidolon, and the divisive higher-order-source trait models—have already been discussed, and the limitations of our present methods for elucidating the structures have been examined.[9] Assuming that one may be true—or indeed, that each may operate

---

[9]A definite choice in any given domain between the uniform factor and the dissectable factors model is generally impossible chiefly because of the following reasons: (a) the samples have hitherto been too small in convarkin studies; (b) source traits have been insufficiently defined, factorially; (c) estimates of factor scores have been of insufficient validity; (d) fraternal and identical twins have been insufficiently separated, etc. All these would tend to push findings that are really consistent with Model 2 [Eq. (13)] toward those of Model 1 [Eq. (11)].

in certain areas—we shall leave the matter for further development and proceed to explore an entirely new approach. This constitutes a third general approach, beyond the convarkin–MAVA variance analysis methods, and the refined factor analytic approaches previously discussed in succession.

A passing dream which must have occurred to many psychologists in the developmental field is that by examining the character of *the mathematical parameters of a developmental curve* one might hope directly to recognize which components are genetic and which threptic. That is, one would analyze by properties of the curve, without any prior cross-sectional separations by convarkin experiments. For example, where subjects are uniformly given a very great amount of practice, might not the final plateau reached by each represent his *innate* limit? Perhaps, but if so, it seems the better strategy not to spend time attacking the problem in this crude bivariate form of a single performance curve since more promising elaborations of the learning curve approach lie in (a) a *multivariate* longitudinal approach and (b) in manipulative experiment that may be called a maturation-learning contrast design.

Before explaining these, it is necessary to state some fundamentals of structured learning theory (Cattell, 1970b). The aim of structured learning theory is to operate on a model that will account for the personality (including dynamic and ability) trait changes that we actually find in personality research. It does so by using the factor specification equation for any performance under change and expressing a learning change as (a) the difference of two such equations—a difference affecting T (trait), b (behavioral index), and s (modulator) terms, and therefore a *trivector* change, and (b) seeking to explain these T, b, and s changes in an equation which is essentially the initial specification equation to which a term for reward and experience (reinforcement) has been added. The trivector description of learning change has been fully set out elsewhere (Cattell, 1970c), and here we shall concentrate on the second. It differs from the prevalent reflexological learning formulation in two important ways: (1) the reinforcement is expressed as ergic tension gratification in terms from the dynamic calculus (Cattell, 1958), and (2) the existing traits and states of the individual, e.g., abilities, anxiety, etc., are brought in as important predictors.

For the sake of being open to either assumption about genetic action (the amalgamated or the divisive model), we set the structured learning theory formula down with three types of traits (genetic, threptic, *and* mixed) as follows:

$$(a_{ij_2} - a_{ij_1}) = \sum^{g=m} b_{jg} T_{gi} + \sum^{(g+t)=n} b_{j(g+t)} T_{(g+t)i} + \sum^{t=o} b_{jt} T_{ti}$$
$$+ \sum^{e=p} b_{je} (E_{it_1} - E_{it_2}) [c + (t_2 - t_1)^{-d}] \qquad (18)$$

Here there are m divisive, pure genetic traits, n amalgamate genetic and threptic traits, and o divisive threptic traits. Instead of using T, b, or s as the dependent

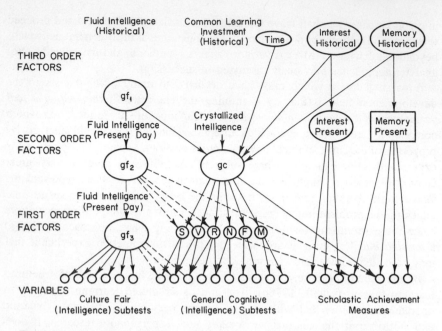

Fig. 3. Example of the successive investment theory of trait pattern generation. This illustrates the whole structure in the ability field from test variables, through primary abilities, to fluid and crystallized intelligence. The part which graphically represents Eq. (19) is the genesis of g_c, crystallized intelligence, from g_f, the original genetic fluid intelligence and the coordinated curriculum learning experiences (memory, time, interest).

variable we have taken specific behavior a_j as an intermediate, for reasons to be seen. The term requiring special explanation is the last, covering the learning experience. Though complex in appearance, it states only that the learning gain is a function of the magnitude of the individual's reward ($E_{it1} - E_{it2}$), expressed as the drop in ergic tension between the beginning time (t_1) and the response correctly ending the task (t_2). The last expression in brackets simply states that learning varies inversely as the time lapse (d is some exponential) between correct action and reward of that response. (c is a suitable constant and the b's are, as usual, loadings or weights.) Of course, the whole equation would be multiplied by some function of N, the number of repetitions (or integrated over N occasions) if the learning experience is one that is repeated. Parenthetically, the psychometrist need not worry about the fact that the ordinary factor analytic equation would ignore the mean gain of the whole group, since it is supposed that the above is written in terms of *real-base factor analysis* (Cattell, 1972), in which both an individual's score and the mean score change.

The central question in structured learning theory with which we are here concerned is "How does learning account for the emergence of unitary, structured trait patterns?" The answer is that a factoring of learning gains, as on the left of Eq. (18) should, by the nature of the variables producing the gain, yield the same personality factors, T_g, $T_{(g+t)}$, and T_t as existed before the learning, plus a new factor corresponding to the learning term at the end. *This will be a common broad factor, i.e., not a specific, only if several learned variables, a_j, a_k, a_l, etc., have for some reason shared the same magnitude of learning reward and frequency of repetition.* A social arrangement that would produce such a learning schedule would be the impress of a common sociological institution, for which action we have found evidence so far in the formation of sentiments.

Let us next recognize that in infancy—say the first year of life—when differential learning experience will have operated little, there will be virtually no terms in (18) of the type T_t or $T_{(g+t)}$. Such terms must therefore gradually appear by what we shall call the *successive investment model* from the T_g's and the common learning experience—$(E_1 - E_2)\left[c + (t_2 - t_1)^d\right]$—for certain groups of variables. If we consider the first equations as having only T_g terms and later T_t terms, a mystery arises as to why an equation for some postlearning prediction—as of a_{j2} taken from Eq. (18)—can come to have a $T_{(g + t)}$ term. For although the b's in (18) are likely to be different from those for the same factors in the specification for a_1, the summed effect of the latter and (18) would still $\left[\text{if (18) is now considered to begin with no } T_{(g + t)}\right]$ contain only factors T_g, T_t, and the new learning factor.

The problem is quite real, since it represents precisely what we believe to be happening in the instance of fluid and crystallized intelligence. Why, when we factor cognitive performances, do we not simply get a g_f and a factor corresponding to length and intensity of schooling, orthogonal to the first, instead of a new factor g_c, much positively correlated with g_f? In this case, a psychological explanation has been offered (Cattell, 1971) to the effect that the new "variable cluster," created by the investment of g_f in schooling, takes on "a life of its own" and itself becomes a new, active, psychological influence, giving it the status of a new factor. This is illustrated for fluid and crystallized intelligence factors in Fig. 3 which shows g_c as a new product and also depicts the continuation of one factor g_f at different order levels, as discussed in the following. However, an alternative to be considered in all such cases is that the noninteractive, simply additive factor model does not hold, and that the interaction of g_f and schooling produces new variance not present in addition of the two parent influences.

The rather unusual factor structure then required can be shown by considering the equation for a_{j2} would contain the old factors T_g and T_t, plus the newly generated factor $T_{(g + t)}$ through learning. Let us write this expanding the last into its generators, as in (18) (but, of course, starting from only T_g's and T_t's and assuming no $T_{(g + t)}$), though including now an interaction term, thus:

$$a_{ij2} = \sum^{g=m} b_{jg} T_{gi} + \sum^{t=o} b_{jt} T_{ti} + b_{jn} \left\{ \sum^{g=m} b_{jg} T_{gi} + \sum^{t=o} b_{jt} T_{ti} \right.$$
$$+ \sum^{e=p} b_{je} (E_{it1} - E_{its}) [c + (t_2 - t_1)^{-d}]$$
$$\left. + \text{ interaction of } T_g, T_t \text{ and the learning term} \right\} \tag{19}$$

(The form of the factor specification equation is preserved here, though the presence of an interaction term would require special handling.)

The whole learning effect is here placed in long brackets because it *could* emerge from factoring as a single primary. Then, however, if it were factored with other primaries that also shared T_g, T_t, etc., it would yield T_g, T_t and the learning term as second orders. Thus we would have a new primary at the first order, $T_{(g + t)}$, which would reveal substantial variance from second orders already present directly as first orders elsewhere (see Cattell, 1964, for analyses of this type), but which would indubitably have specific primary variance. Incidentally, another instance beyond that of g_f and g_c that one would theoretically expect to have this form would be in second-order factoring of ergs and sentiments in the dynamic realm. Here, since the genetic ergs have been instrumental with learning experience in generating the sentiments, they should appear not only with the sentiments at the first order, but again at the second order. This remains to be investigated.

The general strategy suggested by the preceding for understanding the genetic and threptic components in development is (a) a coordination of cross-sectional factoring at a_{j1} and a_{j2} (with a_{k1}, a_{k2}, etc., of course) and of dR-technique factoring over the growth interval, and (b) an attempt to arrange experimentally such factorings over two kinds of periods, one with more maturation and less learning and another with more learning and less maturation. Since, by definition, we are dealing with human beings, for whom important and massive learning influences cannot be manipulated, as in a laboratory, the learning influences have to be naturally occurring and a matter of more or less, e.g., children in a school period compared with a vacation period, a group of married young people compared to unmarried, and so on. This approach in (b) must be given more extended examination in the next section, but so far as (a) is concerned, the argument is that if the loading pattern for the learning term at the end of equation (18) resembles that for a trait term in Eq. (12) predicting some absolute level, the latter may be assumed to be a threptic pattern. (This assumes that in general, incremental and absolute scores have a similar loading pattern.)

The *successive investment model* inherent in structured learning theory tells us that a genetic trait pattern will "invest" itself, in some pattern of rewarded and repeated learning offered by the environment, to produce a new trait pattern, which typically is not merely a cluster fully resolvable into the parent influences. Instead, by interaction effects and a psychological autonomy—in fact by taking the role of an influence—it tends to appear as a new factor, with specific primary variance. The successive investment continues, when this in turn helps generate new patterns. Light on these relations is gained from comparison of the successive factorings.

Few domains are accurately enough worked out in research to permit full checks on this theory, but I have already instanced the ability field and I would add that in the personality field as researched by Q data, it is true that (a) more factors are found at later ages, though only by the order of 10% to 20%, as shown by contrasting the factors found in the ESPQ (aged 6–8) and the CPQ (aged 8–12), with the additional factors present in the HSPQ (aged 12–18) and 16 PF (adult), and that (b) the higher order structure definitely enriches in going from the HSPQ to the 16 PF (CPQ data are not yet available).

VI. The Maturation–Learning (or Volution–Threption) Contrast Method of Isolating Genetic and Environmental Influence Effects

The second possible attack on developmental analysis now to be proposed from the basis of structured learning theory in the preceding section, is the maturation–learning contrast method. Obviously, it would be possible to contrast maturation and learning gains on some single arbitrary variable, without the benefit of structured learning concepts; but, as the following should show, the definition will not then be as clear. Only in a designed or natural learning situation where one set of several variables is simultaneously subject to the same learning schedule, and perhaps another set to a different schedule, would this be possible. For with structured learning, using many variables, we can add up the effects on the separate variables to contribute to what the model suggests are the truly wholly genetic or threptic components, and this we can do either from successive R-technique analyses or in the case of a single subject, a P-technique analysis.

Since maturation can be assumed to proceed at a rate beyond our control as a simple function of time, whereas learning rates can either be *controlled* (in the case of trivial personality and ability learning) or *selected* by taking groups in different situations in the culture (in the case of typical major trait development), the possibility exists of experimental designs in which the T_g and T_t traits would change their relative rates of growth (or in factor analysis, their relative variances) when one time span is compared to another. (It is perhaps unnecessary to point out here that just because a T_g trait is genetic, we cannot expect it to stand still, i.e., not to grow. It will mature or involute according to its inner physiological basis.)

The essence of the design is therefore such that one group be found in which learning goes on at a much faster rate than in some otherwise comparable group, *through more frequent repetitions of the learning situation, or magnified rewards*. In such a design, we would want to arrange that the groups are biologically similar, so that the maturation rates will be much the same. Theoretically, the converse arrangement would do just as well, if we have reason to believe that maturation is naturally faster in one group while learning influences are similar. (Though with differences of the age, etc., of the groups to produce maturation differences, some factor analytic complications might arise.)

Let us assume that two (or more) groups of subjects are chosen such that the ages and the time period are the same, but where one is getting intensive education or life experience over the period and the other is getting only moderate education. For example, one might be in school 6 hours a day, the other only 4; or one might be attending church regularly and the other sporadically or not at all; or one might be a university student group in the dormitories, and another a group living at home. Some interesting examples of uneven alternation of learning and maturation in the seasonal school system are discussed in the paper by Baltes, Baltes, and Reinert (1970), and would be excellent for an experiment as here proposed.

The developmental curve on any *one* of the variables measured could of course, be broken down in theory by MAVA into components from genetic and threptic factors. However, if only one variable were used, there would be no way of knowing what the factors are that account, respectively, for the genetic and threptic variance. The experimenter in the maturation–learning analysis experiment described here would probably be interested in such univariate analysis only as a special and later study, and his main concern would be to obtain and plot the scores over the given period for the distinct meaningful factors, some of which should be following a purely maturational course, while others would be taking shape as T_t's, i.e., factors newly generated by the learning experience. In the R-technique study, these could be obtained by an overall multiple subject entry analysis (Tucker, 1966a), or by successive analyses at several points in the learning process using the isopodic principle (Cattell, 1971). The multiple subject entry method is illustrated in Table 4a by a case of just three entries.

The outcome, as seen in Table 4c, is a series of factor scores, suitable for plotting to show either individual or group mean trends on the T_g and T_t factors over the period concerned. According to our theory, if the subjects in the moderate and intensive learning situations are of the same age, the trends for those factors which are wholly genetic should be the same in the two experiments, whereas those which respond to learning should show a statistically significant difference.

Such an experiment must not be expected to yield a decision as to the genetic or mixed genetic–threptic nature of *all* factors taken out from such a set of variables. The factors constituting the second term in Eq. (18) and now recognized to be factors already in existence before the beginning of the learning, yet which are not genetic, but of mixed nature, might change their level in the given experiment no differently from a factor affected by nothing but maturation. The limitation of this *maturation–learning recombination design* is, therefore, that it will separate the newly learned pattern from the others, but not the genetic from the older patterns.

TABLE 4

Multiple-Subject Entry Design on a Maturation–Learning Analysis Experiment[a]

(a) Score matrix			(b) Factor matrix			
Variable: a_1 ... a_j ... a_n			T_g^1 T_{gk} T_n^1 T_{np}			
Allen 1			a^1			
Allen 2			$\vdots$			
Allen 3						
Brown 1			a_j			
Brown 2						
Brown 3			$\vdots$			
Clarke 1						
Clarke 2			a_n			
Clarke 3						

(c) Factor score matrix

	T_g^1	T_{gk}	T_n^1	T_{np}
Allen 1				
Allen 2				
Allen 3				
Brown 1				
Brown 2				
Brown 3				
Clarke 1				
Clarke 2				
Clarke 3				

[a] These matrices (there is no need to enter "scores") are meant to show how the treble entry (from three occasions, pre-, during, and postlearning) of each individual in the score matrix at (a) will yield a set of factors common to all three occasions, as at (b). These will be partly genetic factors—g's—the scores of which should not change, and partly "investment factors"—n's—which would be expected to reveal their nature by a change of score. This change of score (or absence of change) will be shown in matrix (c) where the V [factor estimation matrix, from (b)] yields scores for each individual in his "before," "during," and "after" condition.

VII. Summary

(1) Although there is, of course, a general descriptive usefulness in gross developmental curves, until methods are applied to separate maturational from learning experience effects, the real possibilities of psychology as *an explanatory science* cannot begin to be employed. For example, an understanding of something as simple as the age curve in auditory acuity needs resolution into an endogenous (genetic, volutional) curve on the one hand, and an exogenous (threptic) curve on the other, and the latter particularly needs breaking down again into ecogenic (average environment) and an epogenic (special epoch) component, especially in the present noise-polluted epoch.

(2) Methods are becoming available for these analyses. For example, the epogenic can be separated from the ecogenic curve by comparisons of cursive, longitudinal, and simple cross sectional data as set out by Baltes (Baltes *et al.*, 1970), Cattell (1969) and Schaie (1965). The separation of the exogenous from the endogenous requires the determination of nature–nurture variance ratios at each of several age levels. At present, the only known effective methods for doing this are what have been called the convarkin (continuous variable variance analyses in kinship groups) and the MAVA (multiple abstract variance analysis) methods, where graded, continuous variables are concerned.

(3) The first of these, convarkin, has a more limited yield, and has, in fact, been content to stop at heritability H and nature–nurture N ratios. MAVA, on the other hand, yields four (not three) absolute variances (σ_{wt}^2, σ_{wg}^2, σ_{bt}^2, σ_{bg}^2) as well as two or more intercorrelations of hereditary and environmental effects not given by convarkin, twin methods. Nevertheless, from data by MAVA on *one* society, there is no known means of (a) relating pure genetic and threptic contributions to their chromosomal and environmental feature sources, or (b) assigning scores on these components to an individual. The step from MAVA to *comparative* MAVA now permits a new array of possible inferences. For example, by comparing results for different age groups, one can locate the periods where maturation and experience reach different relative action, or by comparing cultures, find the particular cultures which produce most effect on a given trait, or the gene pools which produce certain genetic variances (leading by population genetics to analysis of gene action).

(4) A necessary preliminary to further comparative MAVA is environmental feature nature–nurture analysis (EFNA) which aims to discover how much of the variance of some environmental feature, e.g., years of schooling, is associated purely with environmental variance in the individual and how much is to be associated with (and potentially accountable for by) genetic variance. This can be achieved by applying MAVA to environmental feature measures. A general model is proposed for causal connections among genetic and environmental features and genetic and threptic components in the individuals, which involves circular and feedback effects.

(5) The regressions of environmental and chromosomal features upon components from genetic and threptic sources can be discovered by a new method designated comparative MAVA variance correction (CMVC), if the assumption can be made that the various racio-cultural groups in the comparison are random samples from a "world" population. This involves determining the correlation between (a) the magnitudes of threptic variances and of environmental condition (feature) variances, across racio-cultural groups, (b) similarly, the correlation of genetic variance components with any information on chromosomal, gene variances. When combined with the EFNA approach, this leads to a regression being calculable between an environmental feature score separated from any genetic association in that feature and the purely threptic component score in the individual. If this approach can be realized in practice, it will mean progress from making statements only about general variances to making estimates of separate threptic and genetic component levels in a given individual. This assumes that enough potent environmental feature can be found to give a multiple R approaching unity between the genetics-free environmental feature scores and the threptic score.

(6) It is uncertain at this stage of the research knowledge whether we need a source trait model of what is here called (a) an *amalgamated trait* kind, in which every trait measurement battery gives an inseparable composite of genetic and threptic contributions, or (b) a *divisive trait* kind in which quite distinct factor trait patterns are discernible and measurable with respect to the distinct genetic and threptic effects, or (c) a mixed model involving both. In (b) again it is possible to entertain an hypothesis (*i*) that the genetic and threptic patterns will correspond, in pairs of "eidolons" imaging each other, or (*ii*) that there will be no resemblances, and that the genetic factors will tend to be broader, second order influences behind mixed, amalgamated primaries.

(7) If the divisive model holds, then a sophisticated factor analytic methodology should alone suffice to pull out the separate genetic and threptic source trait patterns. From estimates of scores on these, the volutional and learning curves and influences could readily be separately studied. In this case, any *variable* can have a nature–nurture ratio, but any *source trait* is wholly of one kind or the other.

(8) A third main independent approach to separating exogenous and endogenous developmental curves is through *structured learning theory,* using the *successive investment model,* by which existing traits in combination with a learning experience develop new traits. Some threads of evidence already support the concepts here involved, notably, (*i*) that the number of primary factors, e.g., in the questionaire area, increases as we factor at later ages, (*ii*) some indications that factors appearing at higher orders, e.g., exvia (Cattell, 1957; Eysenck, 1967) are more likely to be genetic, as the model would require, (*iii*) that in both the 16 PF and in the investigation of fluid and crystallized intelligence, certain primaries (notably G, superego and g_f, fluid intelligence) tend to reappear

at the higher order, as Eq. (19) would require. This approach, like Method 2 $[$Eq. (7)$]$ may solve the nature–nurture problem by leading to direct estimates of the separate divisive factors. Even if amalgamated primaries of certain of the higher-order factors turn out to be exclusively genetic, a separation of genetic and threptic components would be directly obtainable by factor analysis.

(9) A fourth and last methodological avenue is possible through studying curves of change (or difference measures) by the maturation–learning contrast experiment. Here, naturally occurring situations are found in which learning influences are at work (a) intensively, and (b) less intensively over the same time interval for two genetically similar groups (or the same group on two occasions). Since maturation is time bound only, a separation of threptic effects is possible, though its full meaning cannot be brought out with single variables. The approach requires preferably simultaneous study of several variables leading to a comparison of factor variances for matchable factors under the two conditions.

This method is applicable even to a single individual (with several variables) using P technique across successive learning and nonlearning periods and recognizing preexisting threptic source traits by their resemblance to newly acquired patterns.

It is recognized that many technical proposals in the preceding need to be set out in more detail, e.g., the use of real-base factor analysis, the choice of variables to give the best factor separations, but the aim in this space has been to sketch the basic MAVA method with its many applications, and to add four new methods in outline, whereby developmental analysis can be made.

Acknowledgments

I wish to express a debt of gratitude to Drs. John Loehlin, Tom Klein, and John Nesselroade for valuable, insightful criticisms of the original text. I am also much indebted to Dr. Gerrit De Young for overhauling the 19 equations set out in this chapter.

CHAPTER 7

Assessment of Developmental Factor Change at the Individual and Group Level[1]

P. M. BENTLER

UNIVERSITY OF CALIFORNIA
LOS ANGELES, CALIFORNIA

I. Introduction

There are two main goals to be met by this chapter. First, a nontechnical survey of methodology in assessing multivariate change is provided for the developmental psychologist who is interested in finding an overview of techniques of analysis available to him in certain types of data situations. Second, a number of recently developed, novel methodological procedures are discussed in detail. The latter section is quite technical in nature, and will require the understanding of matrix algebra. However, an introduction to the techniques is provided in the first portion of the paper so that the developmentalist can consult a measurement specialist to implement the more complex techniques if he judges that these are likely to be of benefit for him.

Before proceeding to the heart of the chapter, it may be helpful to orient the reader by contrasting the goals of this chapter with those of other writers in this book. Some of the general issues involved in the selection of methods of analysis in the developmental framework are described in the chapter by Nunnally (Chapter 5). Nunnally's scope is far broader than that to be presented here, where we focus primarily upon factor analytic methodology. Measurement

[1]This work was supported in part by USPHS grants MH17072 and MH16992.

problems faced in a cross-cultural setting are discussed further by Eckensberger (Chapter 3). Eckensberger's topic is not oriented in a multivariate fashion as ours, though the problem of matching measured qualities across cultures, discussed by Eckensberger in detail, is similar to the problem of establishing cross-age equivalence of measures to be discussed. Finally, some of the problems alluded to in this chapter, involving the use in a developmental context of loadings and factor scores, are also touched upon by Baltes and Nesselroade (Chapter 11), though these writers do not provide the general survey of methods that is described herein. This chapter differs from the writings of others at this conference primarily in the following ways: It analyzes the advantages and disadvantages involved in choosing a multivariate model for the analysis of developmental data; it surveys the extensive variety of factor analytic tools that are available; and finally, it describes a set of new techniques that have not been published elsewhere in the psychometric literature.

A. The Data of Interest

The developmental psychologist will quite frequently be faced with data of the following sort. A large number (N) of subjects has been administered n measures on a given occasion. For example, all the subjects have been tested with a set of personality measures such as the Minnesota Multiphasic Personality Inventory, or a set of ability measures such as the Primary Mental Abilities. The investigator has on hand a multivariate set of data for that occasion, data that can be placed into a matrix X_1. We let the $N \times n$ matrix represent the responses of all individuals to all variables. We would like to consider a situation in which the investigator has on hand a second set of data for N individuals on n variables, data that can be arranged into another data matrix X_2. The developmental psychologist may have two data matrices of this sort from a cross-sectional study, in which data X_1 represent the responses of 5-year-old children, say, and data X_2 those of 10-year-old children. The two data matrices come from different sets of subjects. Alternatively, the developmental psychologist may gather data that are longitudinal in nature, where the responses X_1 are obtained on a given occasion and the responses X_2 are generated by the same subjects somewhat later in time, perhaps 5 years apart, as in the previous example. We are interested first in deciding whether or not the typical developmental psychologist will want a multivariate analysis of these two sets of data, such as is provided by factor analysis; and second, how he might choose an appropriate type of analysis for the problem in which he is interested. Since factor analysis has become an extremely popular tool, it behooves us to look in some depth at the first major point to be made by this paper: Traditional types of factor analysis should be avoided in many instances.

B. When Not to Factor Analyze

It is important to remember that any factor analysis attempts to break up a set of observed scores into various parts—common parts and unique parts. Any given variable will, of course, contain a certain amount of error variance; and the portion of any individual score that represents random error certainly is not of interest to an investigator. Consequently, he may well wish to subtract out the error scores from the observed scores, if he had some estimate of these error scores. Factor analysis does this. It allows an investigator to subtract out the error scores from the observed data. In addition, factor analysis suggests that each variable possesses a specific score that is not shared with any of the other variables. This specific score, like the error score, is uncorrelated with similar specific or error scores on other variables. The argument is generally made that since this score is specific to a given variable and does not overlap with others, it may as well also be subtracted out from the original scores. The specific and error scores, together called unique scores, are generally considered to be irrelevant in a factor analysis and an attempt is made to eliminate them from the observed variables. What remains are common scores. Factor analysis is a technique for analyzing the common scores into further uncorrelated portions, called factors.

To those persons already well acquainted with factor analysis, it should be noted that factor analysis itself usually is not performed on the raw scores in the data matrices X_1 and X_2, but upon derived correlation matrices. Here, we have emphasized the conceptual nature of what a factor analysis attempts to accomplish.

Thus, a factor typically focuses upon that aspect of the data which various variables have in common. Here we would like to suggest that in many instances the investigator is *not the least bit interested in knowing what the variables have in common.* He is rather more interested in the reliable part of the unique score—the specific portion of the variable that does *not* overlap with other variables. For instance, if the variables in the data matrix represent traits of personality such as achievement, aggression, impulsivity, and thriftiness, the investigator may well be interested in the aspect of variables that serves to differentiate them from one another; in other words, the specificity. That which the variables share in common, such as mental health versus lack of health or social desirability would be of little interest. Similarly, relatively independent traits of intelligence such as verbal meaning, spatial ability, reasoning, numerical ability, and word fluency no doubt share a certain amount of overlap—general intelligence or G. Yet while the investigator may be interested in G at certain times when he gathers multivariate data, he is probably more interested in keeping his traits distinct and measuring this distinctness rather than combining all the variables. So it is probably fair to make the generalization that when the variables used by an investigator already represent measures of various *factors*, such as personality factors or intellectual factors, the investigator will rarely if ever be interested in what the variables share in common. We shall later describe one method, multiset factor analysis, that is able to identify common, specific, and error variance components of each variable's total variance.

It should also be noted that the factor-analytic definition of the common portion of a variable can often be quite arbitrary, changing from study to study depending upon the particular set of variables included in the analysis. In the case of the primary mental abilities, just described, if the set of variables included several measures of vocabulary, the verbal meaning variable would no doubt be highly correlated with them and a common factor would be created. If the investigator did not add such variables, the verbal meaning variable would be relatively unrelated to the other variables in the analysis and a common factor would not appear.

In addition to focusing upon aspects of the observed data that may not be of interest to the investigator, the typical factor-analytic approach to cross-sectional or longitudinal data also assumes that the investigator is rather naive about what is being measured by the variables that he has chosen. If he has chosen the variables carefully, he will be interested in precisely the variables for which he obtained data. He will have no interest in any transformation of these variables, such as would be provided by a principal component analysis or a factor analysis. Factor analysis could provide a new set of derived variables that may be quite meaningful. Yet if these derived variables are obtained by the experimenter for the first time in his investigation, it should be clear that psychometric criteria of adequacy of the derived variables are not met, such as acceptable data on cross-validation, internal consistency, or reliability. Ideally, if the investigator had an interest in a factor, he would have identified it prior to the start of the cross-sectional or longitudinal study and would have been able to provide ways of measuring the factor with adequate statistical precision.

Finally, if the investigator's data matrices consist not of variables but of items, and these items are scored in a binary 0-1 fashion, factor analysis is not appropriate. The interrelations among binary items or variables are generally not linear, and some other technique such as monotonicity analysis will have to be used. This problem is described in greater detail later.

Granting then, that the investigator has made an appropriate decision, and that the multivariate methods of factor analysis may be relevant to his aims, how then should he proceed? Our plan will be the following. Initially, we shall describe principles to which an investigator might want to adhere in the selection of a methodology relevant to his aims. Thereafter we survey the various methods that the investigator might choose to meet his goals.

C. Principles for Choosing Analytic Methods

Most psychometric writers who have discussed the issue of factor analyzing data matrices such as our X_1 and X_2 have recommended that the subjects in such analyses be highly homogeneous, for example with respect to sex, education, or social class (e.g., see Nunnally, 1967). This recommendation is one with which we do not agree. For example, if one believes the following principle, the recommendation must be ignored.

1. Derived or latent variables should be defined with respect to a particular population of individuals;
   a. the population should include all subpopulations to which the derived or latent variables are intended to apply, and
   b. the derived or latent variable is inapplicable to other populations unless it is *proven* to be applicable.

The factors of factor analysis are usually called latent variables, but we describe them here as derived or latent variables to emphasize that ultimately any latent, unmeasured variable must become an overtly measured, derived variable—usually depending upon a number of indices combined in some fashion to provide an estimate of the factor. Thus, ultimately any latent variable must be measured by some operational technique.

If a factor analysis is performed using a population of girls only, the above principle suggests that there is no reason to expect the results to have any relevance whatever for boys. Similarly, we propose that one can assume that factors derived at a given age have no relevance or applicability at other ages unless there is positive evidence that the factors are so applicable. A factor derived from a homogeneous population may well describe that homogeneous population. However, if one intends to generalize to other more heterogeneous populations, factors derived only from homogeneous groups may be irrelevant in the larger case. For example, it appears that the domain of intelligence becomes multidimensional as soon as the groups being tested are highly homogeneous with respect to age, sex, education, social class, and the like. A factor derived in such a homogeneous population can be orthogonal or uncorrelated with these variables. But what kind of intellectual factor has no correlation with age? Certainly none in which one usually has interest. One can expand the first principle to the following.

2. Rules defining derived or latent variables should be based upon the entire population of individuals.
   a. The defining rules should be derived using one or several adequate samples from the population.

This subprinciple is not startling, but it suggests that any factors derived upon small samples, or unrepresentative samples, can have no relevance to questions of interest to most investigators.

b. The minimal criterion for the psychometric acceptability of a derived or latent variable is the internal consistency of the components that determine that variable.

We are suggesting that a factor becomes acceptable for empirical investigation when it meets the standards that are described in most elementary discussions of test theory—namely that the items that compose the factor, or the variables that are combined to yield a composite variable, are in fact internally consistent in the sense of coefficient alpha or the Kuder–Richardson Formula 20. Thus it is suggested here that different manifestations of the same trait should be positively interrelated. This subprinciple is spelled out separately because most discussions about the acceptability of factors, such as that by Baltes and Nesselroade (1970 & Chapter 11 in this volume), suggest that an entire factor pattern remain equivalent in various samples from the population. Such a requirement is far more stringent than the one suggested here, because it suggests not only that components should remain internally consistent but also that irrelevant variables having no particular bearing upon a given construct must maintain their same relationship to the construct. For example, we suggest that a variable irrelevant to mental age, such as height, might be correlated one way with mental age at one point in the life span, but may have a rather different correlation at another point in life. In such a case, the different manifestations of mental age should still be highly interrelated, but the irrelevant variable may correlate quite differently with it. A coefficient theta for determining internal consistency, which has been proven to provide a better lower-bound estimate than coefficients alpha and $K\text{-}R$ 20, is presented by Bentler (1972).

c. Psychometric criteria such as reliability, validity, and internal consistency should be established for these variables in confirmatory or cross-validational samples.

With this subprinciple, we are again emphasizing a quite traditional aspect of scientific investigation, yet one that tends regularly to be ignored in factor analytic investigation. A single factor analysis of a given set of data usually does not meet this criterion since the cross-validated psychometric adequacy of the derived measure is not at all established in this case.

d. If psychometric criteria are inadequate in any well defined subpopulation, the derived or latent variable is inapplicable in that subpopulation.

All too often it is simply assumed that a factor derived in one situation will be directly applicable to other situations. The above subprinciple again places the burden of proof on the investigator to demonstrate psychometric adequacy for a factor if he plans to utilize a particular latent variable in some subpopulation.

3. Derived or latent variables should be sensitive to changes in distribution of the scores on the variables, such as shifts in mean or variance.

The reader may well wonder why this obvious principle needs to be spelled out. After all, virtually any observed variable measured by some standard operational procedure, such as a test being defined by a certain set of items, provides data which are sensitive to shifts in the distribution of the variable. Yet it cannot be emphasized too strongly that virtually all factor analytic models assume that factors have equal, standardized variances, and that their means are zero. Thus a factor analysis of vocabulary scores at age 5 yielding a vocabulary factor, taken alongside another analysis yielding a vocabulary factor at age 10, would require the mean performance of the individuals at ages 5 and 10 to be exactly the same. Quite obviously this is patent nonsense if one thinks of vocabulary skill as growing from age 5 to 10. The average knowledge of words has surely increased radically from age 5 to 10, yet most if not all traditional factor analytic methods cannot discover such a difference at all. Similarly, most methods of factor analysis standardize the variance of the factors, so that it becomes impossible to determine whether or not the variability in a given sample varies, as with age for example. This is a serious shortcoming of factor analysis in most instances. Later in the paper we shall describe techniques that aim to overcome these gross limitations.

4. Rules defining derived or latent cross-sectional variables relevant to a longitudinal study should be based upon a population composed of subpopulations that are structurally equivalent to the longitudinal population at various points in time.

As we shall describe in greater detail, there are a number of analyses that can be performed with longitudinal data that are impossible with cross-sectional data. Obviously, with cross-sectional data there is no possibility for assessing, for example, the stability of a factor. Yet there are some models that allow one to obtain certain equivalent information if the structural attributes of two cross-sectional samples are similar to those of a longitudinal sample at two points in time. If the interrelations of the variables, their means and standard deviations, their reliabilities, and the like, are highly similar in the two situations, the resulting factor analytic results can be equivalent. It should be pointed out that some investigators, such as Schaie (Chapter 12 of this volume) doubt whether such equivalence is ever possible, since time of measurement and cohort differences make it quite unlikely to find the degree of equivalence we are discussing here. Yet if such structural equivalence cannot be demonstrated, the results obtained with a cross-sectional analysis cannot be assumed to hold for the longitudinal data.

5. Rules for defining latent variables should be obtained from a well-defined universe of variables.

It was mentioned before that the results of any factor analysis depend upon the particular selection of variables that enter into it. This well-known truism becomes highly relevant, however, since if the investigator does not realize when performing his factor analysis that his results may be limited to the particular set of data in hand, he may be severely criticized by colleagues who consider the variables a poor selection as compared to those that might have been used. Thus this final principle serves to reiterate the ideal procedure of defining variables for study independently of the cross-sectional or longitudinal investigation, and of making sure that this definition provides a sampling of the relevant universe of interest.

II. Methods of Analysis

It will be helpful to review how factor analysis works. The factor-analytic model specifies that an observed data matrix X can be decomposed into the sum of two other matrices $C + U$. The matrix X can be any matrix, such as the matrices X_1 or X_2 that we have described previously. It can be a matrix of raw scores or, alternatively, a matrix of scores that have been standardized for the variables. Standardization can include giving all variables a mean of 0, or a standard deviation of 1, or both. In factor-analytic theory, the data matrix X is itself not of interest because, as already mentioned, it contains error and specific scores that should be eliminated from the observed scores; these scores are presented in the matrix U, mnemonically to represent uniquenesses. Interest in factor analysis centers on the matrix C, the matrix of common scores. This matrix itself is divided up into two other matrices, a matrix S of scores representing the scores of individuals on factors and a matrix L of loadings representing the loadings of variables on factors. Consequently, the factor-analytic model specifies that $X = SL' + U$. The matrices are illustrated visually in Fig. 1. Hopefully, there are many fewer columns in the score matrix S than in the data matrix X, since the number of columns of S equals the number of factors. An ideal factor analysis requires only a few factors, relative to the number of variables n, to account for all common variance among the variables.

In the usual case, the data matrix X that is being analyzed is actually a matrix of deviation scores, which we may represent by the X matrix minus the matrix of means $\bar{X}$ for the variables so that $X = \bar{X} + SL' + U$. In the case of standardized scores, the formula looks the same, but is "postmultiplied"

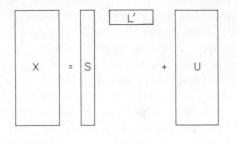

Fig. 1

by a diagonal matrix. The nonmathematical reader should not be frightened by this equation. He should look at it to notice the very important characteristic that the observed data matrix X is *not*, in fact, decomposed into a sum of the factor-analytic matrices SL' and U alone, but also involves a separate matrix $\bar{X}$ of means; these means are not included in the usual factor analysis. This very important observation indicates that in virtually all factor-analytic situations the factor scores S for individuals must have a mean of 0, and the means of the observed variables simply do not enter into the determination of the common factor space. While in any given single analysis (for example, of the scores X_1 only) it may not matter that the factor scores S have a mean of 0, the imposition of that same requirement on several sets of data matrices X_1 and X_2 can cause havoc. In this case, as mentioned previously, one must assume that factor scores do not change on the average or that their means are equal, an assumption that might be highly inappropriate in many applications.

We have also emphasized the score matrices X and S because they call attention to the data matrices involved in performing a factor analysis. The scores S, just like the scores X, actually represent scores for individuals. At this point, we prefer not to place much emphasis upon matrices derived from these score matrices, such as the correlation matrix derived from the observed scores X. If one is interested in making inferences about the mean factor scores for individuals, it is necessary to know the factor score matrix S, or at least an estimate of it. Just as if one is interested in knowing the performance of a particular individual on a factor, it is also necessary to have available the score matrix S. Factor-loading matrices are irrelevant to this problem. As will be shown, many techniques of analysis fail to provide the appropriate data when attempting to assess developmental factor change either at the individual level or at the group level. In a later section, we shall develop in detail some methods that do allow one to look at individual scores in a useful fashion.

At this point, we provide a general overview of factor-analytic methods that an investigator may use to analyze his data matrices X_1 and X_2. It will not be possible to describe each of the models in great detail, since each of the methods could require its own chapter for an adequate discussion. Wherever possible we shall present a reference that an investigator can utilize to obtain more information. We shall provide a name for each method, although it should be clear that this is done primarily to simplify communication rather than to imply that there are consensually agreed upon names for all of the methods.

While certain techniques accept identical input matrices, but provide for different computations in the analysis process, in most cases the problem of analysis revolves around how the data matrices should be altered, if at all, prior to any analysis (e.g., should the variables be standardized or not), and around how the data are to be arranged prior to the computation of indices of association (e.g., should matrices X_1 and X_2 be analyzed separately or simultaneously). As has been mentioned previously, there are obviously more options open to the investigator who has longitudinal data rather than cross-sectional data. However, we shall devote somewhat more space to cross-sectional methods since such data are more frequent, and because many problems encountered with these methods also occur in longitudinal methods. We shall deal first with the case in which the two data matrices X_1 and X_2 are obtained from different subjects, or the investigator wishes to analyze his data as if that were the case. In this case, the investigator is, in essence, not interested in the cross-correlation between variables of X_1 and X_2 (if he has longitudinal data which might make such computations feasible), or he cannot compute the correlations (because different subjects have generated X_1 and X_2).

A. Separate Standard Score Method

The data matrices of raw scores, X_1 and X_2, can be modified prior to analysis into standard score form Z_1 and Z_2—each variable is transformed so that all variables have a common mean of 0 and a common standard deviation (or possibly sum of squares) of unity. Each of the Z matrices in turn generates a separate score matrix and loading matrix, S_1L_1' from matrix Z_1 and S_2L_2' from matrix Z_2. This is simply the traditional method of factor analysis applied separately to the two standard score matrices, as described in any standard text on factor analysis (e.g., see Harman, 1960). As the sophisticated reader will recognize, the analysis is usually not carried out upon the Z score matrix directly, but rather upon the correlation matrix derived from it. Thus this method generates two correlation matrices R_1 and R_2, representing the correlations among all n variables for each of the two sets of data. Each correlation matrix is analyzed to generate the respective loading matrix L_1 and L_2. Without spelling out the many problems involved in generating any loading matrix, it should be noted that there are always issues involved concerning the number of factors, the method of factor analysis to be utilized, and the rotation of an initial solution. There are also important issues involved in choosing a methodology to estimate the factor scores S (e.g., see Harris, 1967). We will assume throughout this paper that these issues have been dealt with appropriately. We shall assume that we are dealing with a finally selected loading matrix L and the corresponding factor scores S.

Since the factors for each of the matrices are derived independently of each other, in this method the problem remains of whether the factors in one solution are similar to those in the other solution. Ideally, of course, they would be identical—exactly the same thing being measured in the two data matrices. (See Nesselroade & Bartsch, in press, and Baltes & Nesselroade, Chapter 11 in this volume, for some important issues regarding factor matching.) There exist two ways of handling the problem: rotating the solutions to make them maximally similar (e.g., see Kristof, 1964), or rotating each of them separately to an identical hypothesis (e.g., see Bentler, 1971a; Gruvaeus, 1970). On the one hand, congruence rotations may generate maximal similarity, but may not be particularly meaningful; on the other hand, hypothesis rotation procedures will generally lead to more meaningful results, but will not generate maximum similarity for the two separate analyses. In either case, the degree of similarity of the two solutions can be evaluated by some index of factor similarity.

The separate standard score method is frequently utilized, but it has some very important limitations. Factors will seldom, if ever, match perfectly. Consequently, one is uncertain whether or not the "same" factors are being measured in the two sets of matrices. Principle 2, already described, has not been utilized, since the defining rule for factors in X_1 will differ from that for X_2 unless the two loading matrices L_1 and L_2 are identical. In the case where all data Z_1 and Z_2 are based on the same subjects, it remains uncertain to what extent the individuals obtain the same factor scores in the matrices S_1 and S_2, even when congruence is very high. Just because the loading matrices L_1 and L_2 match, one cannot conclude that the score matrices match. Ideally one would like to have a method that allows one to conclude how similar the factor scores are as well. The longitudinal method, described later, does this.

Perhaps the most serious problem from the point of view of the developmental psychologist is that standard scores are used—requiring the mean factor-scores in S_1 and S_2 to be equal. This method ignores Principle 3, since the solution cannot verify any real shifts in distribution of latent factor scores. As was mentioned previously, if the two sets of data are mental age data obtained at ages 5 and 10, for example, this method will give ridiculous results since it assumes that the mean factor scores for the two occasions are identical. There are ways of dealing with this problem (e.g., Cattell, 1970a). For example, one can estimate the factor scores using the combined distribution of subjects' raw scores. The matrix is illustrated in Fig. 2. Thus a matrix X_3 is obtained that has $2N$ subjects and n variables. This matrix is standardized and factor scores are estimated using it. It will be noted that X_3 maintains information

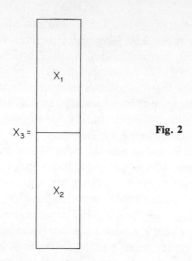

Fig. 2

regarding the two sets of means. However, this technique is technically inappropriate, since it does not follow from the factor model utilized, in which the scores S_1 and S_2 have equal means.

A practical solution to the difficulties inherent in the use of this method is to rely on the loading matrices to group the variables into clusters. All variables that load highly are added together to yield a single cluster score. How the cluster scores interrelate and how they are distributed in each of the two measuring situations can be determined. It is also possible to find differences in means of cluster scores for X_1 and X_2. However, in this case the factor analyses are used solely to provide an indication of internal consistency of components entering the cluster, and the factor model is in essence abandoned in favor of Principle 2b, specifying the acceptability of any derived variable in terms of the internal consistency of the components.

B. Separate Raw Score Method

Rather than transform the raw score matrices into standard scores, it is possible to factor analyze the raw scores themselves. The focus can be directly upon the raw score matrices X_1 and X_2 and the matrices of cross-products of X_1 with itself and of X_2 with itself; the analysis is performed on the cross-products matrix rather than the correlation matrix. Aside from this, the methodology relevant earlier is applicable to this situation.

All of the problems of factor matching described above will also remain with this method. But since the means are retained in the analysis, the factors themselves will reflect the means. This is one important advantage, as Principle 3 is met. Changes in means from X_1 and X_2 can be attributed to the latent factors. Some discussion of this technique can be found in Tucker (1966a), for example, although he described the related-component analysis model rather than the factor-analysis model (see also Horn, 1969).

Since information about the means as well as the scatter or standard deviation of the scores is maintained in the factor-analytic solution, it may be difficult to match factors across X_1 and X_2 when one attends to the loadings, since these are usually affected strongly by the means themselves. However, it is possible to avoid this problem by specifying that the loadings be normalized for each factor, thus absorbing the differences in scale and mean in the factor scores S rather than the loading matrix L. This suggestion has not been tried in practice.

From time to time it is asserted that the factor model cannot be applied to raw scores, because communality and uniqueness become confounded (e.g., Cattell, 1970a; Nesselroade, 1967a). This is not necessarily true, as we shall show in a later technical section (see also Nesselroade, 1973), who comes to a similar conclusion).

Rather than work directly with the raw scores, or alternatively with standard scores having a common mean and standard deviation, as suggested by the two methods previously described, one can eliminate information about only the means so that the solution reflects differences in variance from X_1 and X_2. In other words, it is possible to work directly with the scores $Y_1 = (X_1 - \bar{X}_1)$ and the scores $Y_2 = (X_2 - \bar{X}_2)$. Then the previous discussion is also relevant. It will be noted explicitly, however, that this method again throws away information regarding average performance.

C. Within-Group Covariance Method

It has been suggested by Tucker in unpublished work (Cattell, 1970a) and by Bentler (1966) that a compromise solution is possible, by finding a single factor-loading matrix for X_1 and X_2 while allowing the scores for individuals to vary. This result is obtained by placing the deviation-score matrices into one large matrix (as shown in Fig. 3), which is again $2N \times n$ and analyzed by usual methods. The correlations are computed across all $2N$ subjects in the matrix Y_3, but the data have the means separately removed from X_1 and X_2 prior to pooling. This procedure has the distinct advantage of not being confounded by factor matching problems, since only one factor-loading matrix is used to describe the data. In addition, individuals may have different factor scores for the two occasions if the two sets of data are longitudinal in nature. A person's score in S_1 need not be identical to his score in S_2; the extent to which the factor scores remain stable longitudinally is an empirical question. This is to be contrasted with some approaches, described later, in which individuals' factor scores must remain identical across time—perhaps an unrealistic

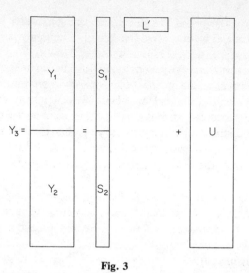

Fig. 3

situation in developmental psychology. Again it is a severe drawback of the method that the average performance of individuals in X_1 must be identical in X_2 (Principle 3 is not met). However, it is possible to abandon the model and to estimate the factor scores by using the combined distribution of scores, as described previously.

It will also be obvious that instead of using the deviation scores Y as already described, one could use standard scores Z in a similar fashion. This method would give different results unless the variances in X_1 and X_2 happen to be identical.

D. Simultaneous Analysis Method

The technique that most persons who are naive about factor analysis would utilize is also the one that we recommend above all of the other methods described previously. Indeed we recommend it more highly than virtually all the specifically longitudinal methods. The raw-score data matrices X_1 and X_2 are placed end to end in the way described for the within-group covariance method (but it is the raw score matrices X and not the deviation matrices Y that are analyzed). This results in the $2N \times n$ matrix X_3, described previously. The analysis is thus simultaneous for both groups; a single loading matrix describes all the data, but factor scores S_1 for X_1 need not be identical to the factor scores S_2 for X_2. If the data were longitudinal, individuals could grow from occasion to occasion.

In practice the $2N \times n$ data matrix that is obtained by placing X_1 and X_2

end to end need not be analyzed directly, since one obtains the correlation matrix that is generated from X_3 and works with it.

This is the only method that meets the various principles for selecting among techniques that were described earlier in this chapter. All subjects to which generalization is intended have their data analyzed simultaneously, and any derived score holds for all subgroups that enter the analysis; distributions can shift. Horst (1965) and Bentler (1966) have described this method previously. However, there remain various technical issues that have not been analyzed; these are described later in the quantitative portion of this chapter.

It has been asserted that the simultaneous-analysis method is not appropriate because when combining two sets of data X_1 and X_2 into a single data matrix X_3, the differences in means between the two data sets can completely distort the resulting analysis. For example, various variables in each of the data sets might represent height and mental age. At measurement X_1 height and age would most likely be uncorrelated; as they might be at measurement X_2; and they should remain separately measured, since they are independent constructs. If the X_1 data are obtained at age 5, and the X_2 data are obtained at age 10, it is quite likely that the mean height would be radically different at the two ages, as would be the mean mental age. This large difference in mean height could lead to a very large correlation between height and mental age scores computed for X_3, since the taller children would no doubt have a much higher mental age than the shorter children. Thus the huge mean differences could generate high correlations, perhaps in the .90's, which would make it appear as if height and mental age are identical constructs. To avoid this problem, the previously described techniques have been recommended.

However, we have pointed out that the preceding methods do tend to throw out precisely the variables of interest. What kind of a developmental factor is it that shows no mean change with age? Obviously one must find a method of maintaining information about means while not making dissimilar variables look alike. The technique of partial correlation is often recommended in this context. For example, in this instance, one could partial the effects of age out of both height and mental age as well as the other variables and use the remaining correlation to generate factors. The obtained factors would show no correlation with age. This procedure, while appearing to meet the problem head-on, unfortunately faces an important philosophical problem: What type of developmental factor would be completely uncorrelated with age? In the case of mental age, we would be defining a mental-age factor unrelated to chronological age! Or we would be describing a height factor which shows no increment with age! Clearly this partial correlation technique is inappropriate to most situations of interest. (See Wohlwill, 1970a,c, 1971, for a further discussion of this issue, as well as Nunnally, Chapter 5 in this volume.)

There are two solutions that can be recommended. In the first place, if various factors are intended to be correlated with age, it will be possible to identify age as a variable in the analysis. A rotated-factor solution can then be obtained, using a hypothesis-transformation method, which shows a high positive loading of age on each of the factors that are developmental in nature. Thus the factors will be separable, though each of them will correlate with age. Second, Principles 1 and 2 suggest another way out of this dilemma. Surely most factors are intended not only for the two specific ages investigated, but for an entire age span—perhaps a life span. The analysis should include subjects from the entire age span and not only for two ages if generalization is intended to other ages. For example, height and mental age as variables are most likely meant to be basic variables at all points of the age spectrum. And it will be obvious, though it has not been pointed out by other writers, that although height and mental age may be correlated in a narrow, restricted portion of the age span (such as ages 5–10), they will be quite lowly correlated across the *entire* age span. To be very specific, then, we are suggesting that the only appropriate methodology relevant to such variables as intelligence is based upon a simultaneous analysis of the entire age range. A similar recommendation is made by Eckensberger (Chapter 3) for the case in which the two data sets X_1 and X_2 are obtained from two different cultures.

E. Monotonicity Analysis Method

In case one does not wish large differences in scores to reflect the results of any analysis unduly, one can use any method of analysis that maintains the rank order of the data points, but ignores the distances. Score difference between children of differing ages will be maintained as differences in the analysis, but the distortion that can be caused by a large gap in scores will be avoided. All gaps are essentially considered equally large, and any score that is larger than another score maintains its ranking.

One technique that works well is monotonicity analysis. It is a type of nonmetric factor analysis that has been described by Bentler (1970a, 1971b). A loading matrix L summarizes the projection of variables on dimensions. Variables that have high monotonic intercorrelations have similar projections on dimensions in the loading matrix; i.e., they are at the same place in multidimensional space. These variables can be combined to generate a derived variable whose components are internally consistent, in accordance with Principle 2b. There is no linear matrix of factor scores S available from a monotonicity analysis, however, since variables can be combined in many linear ways while maintaining their monotonic internal consistency. The scoring method that proves easiest to use in most cases is a simple equally weighted sum of raw scores.

Thus, monotonicity analysis operates on the raw-score matrices X_1 and X_2.

However, these matrices can be analyzed separately or simultaneously end to end, as previously described. The advantages and drawbacks of the two options have already been summarized. As stated earlier, we generally recommend a simultaneous analysis.

Monotonicity analysis is the only technique that deals adequately with binary variables, such as dichotomous test items, since such items are only rarely linearly related. Being a multivariate technique, it is able to place items in multidimensional space according to their monotonic interrelations. Two sets of items at orthogonal positions in the space have their observed scores unrelated in a linear or monotonic sense. Thus monotonicity analysis can identify multiple Guttman (1944) scales, absolute or relative simplexes (Bentler, 1971c), as well as multiple homogeneous tests (Loevinger, 1947), since all of these are composed of items that are monotonically interrelated. It can deal equally well with items that interrelate according to classical test theory (e.g., Lord & Novick, 1968), since linear relations are special cases of monotonic relations.

We turn now to longitudinal data—data in which the score matrices X_1 and X_2 are obtained from the same set of subjects. In this case, it is possible not only to intercorrelate variables within each set of scores, but also to correlate across the two sets of data. Rather than placing the scores end to end, with longitudinal data it is in general also possible to place them side by side, obtaining an $N \times 2n$ data matrix X_4, which can be intercorrelated to generate a $2n \times 2n$ correlation matrix, as shown in Fig. 4. The symbols R_1 and R_2 represent the within-set correlations that we had previously described for cross-sectional data; R_{12} represents the correlation across the two sets of data, the correlation between first occasion and second occasion scores. Several of the longitudinal methods described in what follows work directly on the above-mentioned matrices. However, the first method places the matrices back to back—one behind the other—and analyzes the data cube that is formed in this fashion.

Fig. 4

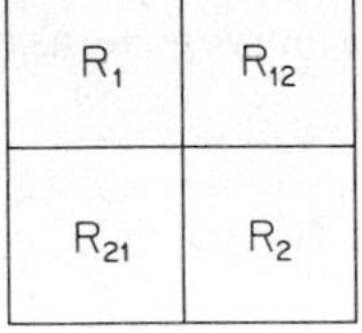

R_1	R_{12}
R_{21}	R_2

F. Multimode Analysis Method

While the usual factor-analytic method analyzes two-dimensional matrices, Tucker's (1966b) method is able to find not only trait dimensions, but also dimensions that describe idealized individuals and occasions. Relevant loading matrices can be obtained for the various dimensions. In addition, the interrelationships of these dimensions are described in a core "box," since the three sets of dimensions cannot generally all be orthogonal to each other. This technique is the most general one devised for dealing with developmental data, since it can handle the time dimension in a rather straightforward manner. One can utilize any number of sets of data matrices, generating a data cube of any size. It is also possible to generate more complex analyses for data that can be classified in more than three ways, such as persons, variables, occasions, and groups.

The method is quite complex and cannot be described adequately without matrix algebra. Levin (1965) provides an introductory account. This method has not been applied to developmental data as yet, and it is likely that it will not be so applied until more psychometricians become acquainted with the technique and teach it to their students.

G. *Identical Factor Score Method*

The $N \times 2n$ data matrix X_4 can be submitted to a single factor analysis, usually performed on the correlation matrix that includes the cross-correlations R_{12}. This produces a single factor-score matrix S, so that each individual has only one factor score per factor, which is taken to be the same for the two occasions. The loading matrix L, however, contains loadings from each of two separate occasions, so that one obtains an L_1 and an L_2 that need not be identical. This model is presented visually in Fig. 5. Individuals are assumed to remain identical from occasion to occasion—only the tests change. This model thus assumes no growth for individuals from occasion to occasion—either on the average or in terms of individual differences. Consequently, the model would have limited relevance to developmental study.

This model has been utilized by several investigators, including Harris (1963). Evans (1967) has provided a more general model, one that allows factor scores

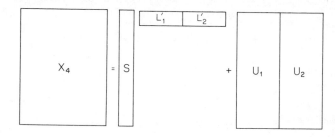

Fig. 5

to change from occasion to occasion, on the average. However, since all individuals are nonetheless assumed to retain their exact ranking, this model also has its limitations.

An important additional problem with this method is often unrecognized. It deals with a different factor space than that of the cross-sectional models. It will be noted that the correlation between the same variables across occasions is incorporated into the common factor space. But this correlation may simply represent reliable variance that is specific to the variable, not correlating with other variables in the analysis. Thus the specific variance is artificially included in the analysis, when it should be eliminated. Equivalently, one can say that the unique scores U_1 for variables on Occasion 1 are uncorrelated with unique scores U_2 on Occasion 2. Although U_1 and U_2 are shown side by side in Fig. 5, it will be clear that this method assumes that any pair of columns picked from either U_1 or U_2 will be uncorrelated. Yet if one is interested in allowing the column in U_1 corresponding to a given variable to correlate with the corresponding column in U_2, representing that which a variable measures specific to itself on both occasions, one must allow the uniquenesses to be related. This would produce a "communality" problem in the *diagonal* of R_{12} —the correlation between height on the two occasions being too high, for example, compared to the variance shared by height and other variables. The identical factor-score method does not take this problem into account. The multiset and longitudinal methods, described later, can do so.

H. Interbattery Method

One solution to the difficulty caused by the identical factor-score method is to perform an interbattery analysis (e.g., Kristof, 1967). One accepts the factor solution for the method of Section G, but attempts to rotate the factor scores and loadings so as to obtain a new set of scores and loadings. The factor loadings can be divided into three sets of loadings L_1, L_2, and L_{12}. The loadings L_1 and L_2 describe factors that exist only on Occasions 1 and 2, respectively—factors that are not measured on both occasions. The loadings L_{12} describe factors that are identical on both occasions. The factor scores are broken down similarly, so that one set of factor scores is identical on both occasions.

The problem remains, of course, that individuals must necessarily retain their exact standing on both occasions for the interbattery factors. This is an undesirable feature of the method, since no growth can occur in the individuals. In addition, as mentioned previously, the specificity can be inappropriately drawn into the common factor space. Tucker (1958) and McDonald (1970) have attempted to deal with this problem in this context, but the methods do not provide measurement of the specificity.

I. Difference-Score Factoring Method

One way around the problems caused by the preceding methods is simply to calculate for every variable the difference, for every individual, between the score he received on Occasions 1 and 2. Each person has n difference scores, so there results an $N \times n$ matrix of difference scores X_5. This matrix can be analyzed by the many ways described previously for cross-sectional data.

This approach has been advocated by Cattell (1966b) and others, and the advantages and disadvantages of the method have been spelled out in detail by Nesselroade and Bartsch (1973). It is particularly applicable when states or other fluctuating variables are being measured, since stable traits may not be discovered with the method. In some situations the loadings that are obtained are also loadings of differences between loadings on the two occasions—loadings that may be difficult, if not impossible, to interpret.

J. Longitudinal Factor Analysis Method

If factors are ultimately to be measurable, it should be possible for individuals' scores to vary from occasion to occasion, as indicated by Principle 3. The model described by Corballis and Traub (1970) does this, while ensuring that specificity is not brought into the common factor space. The data matrix X_4 is broken up into two sets of scores and loadings, $S_1 L_1'$ and $S_2 L_2'$. But the scores are interrelated so that the scores on the second occasion are a linear combination of scores on the first occasion plus an increment that is independent of the initial score. Thus $S_2 = S_1 D + W$, where D changes the variance of factor scores S_1, and W is the increment that is uncorrelated with S_1. The model is ideal because it guarantees that the same factors are measured on the two occasions, while still allowing individuals' scores to vary from occasion to occasion.

Unfortunately the mean factor scores on both occasions are taken to be 0—again violating Principle 3. One requires that there is no mean growth from occasion to occasion, surely an unacceptable requirement in developmental contexts. To obviate this difficulty, we have devised a generalized longitudinal factor analysis method, to be described later in the technical section of this paper, that does allow mean change to occur across occasions. The means can be estimated from the model. The Corballis–Traub model is a special case of this generalized model.

While most of the methods previously described have allowed rotation of factors, allowing one to choose a loading matrix that is relatively interpretable, the longitudinal solution has the characteristic that there is no rotation possible for the factors. On the one hand, this attribute is desirable, because it avoids the problem of picking a "meaningful" rotation from among the infinite number possible; on the other hand, the given set of loading matrices derived with this method, though uniquely defined, may be uninterpretable. As has been pointed out by Nesselroade (1972), the factors that are obtained are those for which the factor scores are most stable. While this may be an acceptable set of factors for the study of stable traits, when one studies fluctuating moods the solution could be quite undesirable.

In principle, the longitudinal model is the most important one to be developed in the last few years, because it at least allows factor scores to change across occasions. It turns out, however, that one special case of the longitudinal model is that in which the factor scores remain perfectly stable—that is, identical on both occasions. In that case the increment scores W equal 0, and $S_2 = S_1$. Such a model may fit a given set of data more accurately than a model that allows the scores to fluctuate. Indeed this turns out to be the case for the illustration provided by Corballis–Traub of their method. We shall present a solution that fits their data better than that originally provided, with the end result that the factor scores are identical. Unless it can be demonstrated in the future that it is possible to obtain a more accurate description of the raw data when the factor scores vary than when they are considered identical, the Corballis–Traub model will have limited applicability despite its more interesting theoretical properties.

K. Multiset Factor Analysis Method

Taking a hint from the special case of the longitudinal model, we have developed a method that allows factor scores to remain identical from occasion to occasion but also eliminates the specificity from the variables. Factors common to all variables are obtained, as are cross-set specific factors defined only by matched pairs of variables, and error factors defined only by single variables. Thus common, specific, and error variance components are estimated.

The technique has the same difficulties as that of Corballis and Traub regarding Principle 3, since no shifts in factor scores are allowed. However, it does allow the common factors to be rotated, so that they can be placed into a meaningful, interpretable position. Even more importantly, perhaps, it has the still greater advantage of being able to deal with more than two sets of data; a three-set example is presented later. Measures taken on any of a number of occasions can be analyzed by this model, so that the two set restriction of the longitudinal model is avoided. Logically and computationally, the method represents a special case of the regression model for factor analysis (Bentler, 1970c). A related model has been described by Jöreskog (personal communication, 1970).

L. Common-Score Growth Method

The longitudinal factor method requires factor scores S on the second occasion to be a linear combination of scores on the first, plus an independent increment. It is this feature of the model that insists that only a particular set of factors can be obtained, with no rotation to a meaningful position being possible. In the later part of this chapter, we describe a model that suggests that the *common* scores C on the two occasions be related in the fashion described above, $C_2 = C_1 D + W$. With this change in the model, rotation to a meaningful position becomes possible. However, it should be pointed out that this method has not been tried in practice.

M. Summary

We have now concluded our general survey of methodology. It will be obvious that the discussion has been limited in many places, and that comparison among methods has perhaps been underemphasized. However, we hope that the reader has been informed about the relative advantages of the various methods so as to be able to make an intelligent choice among them when facing data of the X_1 and X_2 type. Primarily because of the allowed changes in factor scores that are possible with the simultaneous analysis method, we recommend it. Where the data are only monotonically related, we recommend monotonicity analysis.

Other models have also been developed recently that we have not discussed. They are, however, not publicly available, and so we do not emphasize them. We turn rather to a technical section in which we expand mathematically upon the points that have been made in previous sections.

III. Technical Considerations

A. Effects of Means in Factor Analysis

We wish to demonstrate that if a factor model applies to the raw scores, such a model also fits standard scores, given a suitable assumption. We define the common factor model by $X = C + U$, with $C'U = 0$. Then $X'X = C'C + U'U$. Standard scores Z can be obtained using a scaling diagonal D and the matrix of means $\bar{X}$ with $Z = (X - \bar{X})D$. Consequently $Z = (C + U - \bar{X})D$. Let $\bar{C} = \bar{X}$, so that the means $\bar{U} = 0$. Then $Z = (C - \bar{C})D + UD$. If we let $C_1 = (C - \bar{C})D$ and $U_1 = UD$, it can be readily verified that $C_1'U_1 = 0$ so that the cross product of Z scores is decomposed as $Z'Z = C_1'C_1 + U_1'U_1$, which is equivalent to the decomposition of $X'X$. If $U'U$ is diagonal, so is $U_1'U_1$. Similar results obtain if $\bar{U} = \bar{X}$, so that the means can be absorbed into the unique space or the common space. However, the assertion that common and unique spaces become confounded in raw-score analysis can be seen to be false.

B. Simultaneous Factor Analysis

Since the algebra of the simultaneous model has not been described previously, we shall do so here. Let $X' = \begin{bmatrix} X_1'X_2' \end{bmatrix}$ be the $n \times 2N$ matrix X_3' (transposed) described earlier. Then we assume the factor model $X = C + U$, which is equivalent to $X_1 = C_1 + U_1$ and $X_2 = C_2 + U_2$. Even if one makes the traditional factor-analytic assumptions that $C'U = 0$ and $U'U = $ diagonal, it need not be true that $C_1'U_1 = 0$ or that $C_2'U_2 = 0$, although this is possible. Similarly although $U'U$ may be diagonal, the equivalent single set statement $U_1'U_1 = $ diagonal may not be accurate.

The common scores C can be decomposed into factor scores P and loadings QD, with P and Q orthonormal and D diagonal, as in Horst's (1965) basic structure. Thus $C = PDQ'$. Let $P' = [P_1'P_2']$, with P_1 and P_2 representing nonorthonormal factor scores. These scores can differ in mean and variance, a desirable feature.

Although the entire matrix P is orthonormal, the matrices P_1 and P_2 will not be so. The factor scores may indeed not even be orthogonal within each set. It is also true that $C_1 = P_1DQ'$ and $C_2 = P_2DQ'$, so that there results a solution that maintains identical factor loadings for the two sets. This is an important feature of the solution; these results hold for any rotation of the loadings as well. Finally, the score matrix P must be estimated by the usual methods of factor-score estimation. The estimated matrix will contain the relevant information on individual and group performance, and it is possible to estimate factor reliability by correlating estimated factor scores.

One can conceive of a separate basic structure for C_1 and C_2. However, the loading matrices would not be identical, the factors would not automatically be aligned correctly, and the factor score variances would be artificially equated. Indeed, the rank of the two matrices may be different, indicating an unequal number of factors for X_1 and X_2. With the analysis performed simultaneously, however, no factor-matching problem is created. Consequently, there is little reason for obtaining separate structures for C_1 and C_2.

However, it is possible to generate a more stringent version of both the within-group covariance and simultaneous analysis methods by requiring C and U to be orthogonal within each set. This can be done by estimating the common-score cross-products within each set and summing these matrices prior to analysis for factor-loading matrices. Factor scores can be estimated by estimating the common scores within each set, and analyzing all estimated common scores simultaneously by a single basic structure across sets, as described by Bentler (1966).

C. Generalized Longitudinal Factor Analysis

Given raw-score data matrices X_1 and X_2, scale these for simplicity so that the means of X_1 are 0 and the means of X_2 are deviations from the original means for X_1. This preserves the mean differences between data sets, but makes later computations easier. Assume the factor-analytic model of common scores C and unique scores U:

$$X_1 = C_1 + U_1, \qquad C_1'U_1 = 0 \tag{1}$$

$$X_2 = C_2 + U_2, \qquad C_2'U_2 = 0 \tag{2}$$

We generate the cross products $X_1'X_1 = C_1'C_1 + U_1'U_1$ and $X_2'X_2 = C_2'C_2 + U_2'U_2$, using Eqs. (1) and (2). In agreement with traditional assumptions, we can assume $U_1'U_1$ and $U_2'U_2$ to be diagonal. We further define $U_1'C_2 = U_2'C_1 = 0$. Thus $X_1'X_2 = C_1'C_2 + U_1'U_2$. There now exists the option of assuming $U_1'U_2 = 0$, in which case, there is no "communality" problem in $X_1'X_2$, since all its cross products enter the common factor space. This generates a legitimate model that can be utilized under some circumstances. However, in the remaining section, we assume, along with Corballis and Traub (1970), that $U_1'U_2$ is diagonal. Then there is a communality problem in the diagonal of $X_1'X_2$. It follows that

$$\begin{bmatrix} X_1'X_1 & X_1'X_2 \\ X_2'X_1 & X_2'X_2 \end{bmatrix} = \begin{bmatrix} C_1'C_1 & C_1'C_2 \\ C_2'C_1 & C_2'C_2 \end{bmatrix} + \begin{bmatrix} U_1^2 & U_{12}^2 \\ U_{12}^2 & U_2^2 \end{bmatrix} \tag{3}$$

using a shorthand notation $U'U = U^2$ with the diagonality assumption.

Let S represent factor scores, L loadings, and $\bar{S}$ the matrix of mean factor scores with

$$C_1 = S_1L_1', \qquad S_1'S_1 = I \quad \text{and} \quad \bar{S}_1 = 0 \tag{4}$$

$$C_2 = S_2L_2', \qquad S_2'S_2 \neq I \tag{5}$$

Also, we generate

$$S_2 = \bar{S}_2 + \underline{S}_2, \qquad \text{where} \quad \underline{S}_2'\underline{S}_2 = D_2^2 \tag{6}$$

and the mean of $\underline{S}_2$ is 0; any matrix can be broken down into a rescaled standard score matrix plus a matrix of means. The factor scores are assumed to be related in the following way

$$\underline{S}_2 = S_1D + W, \qquad W'S_1 = 0 \tag{7}$$

where W is a matrix of orthogonal increments. Thus

$$W'W = D_2^2 - D^2 \tag{8}$$

which is diagonal. It will be obvious that S_1 and $\underline{S}_2$ relate in the manner described by Corballis–Traub. However our factor scores have been scaled so as to absorb

N, the number of subjects (alternatively, all raw scores could be divided by the square root of N, so that corresponding Z scores yield $Z'Z = R$, a correlation matrix).

It now follows from (4) that $C_1'C_1 = L_1L_1'$; from (4) to (7) that $C_1'C_2 = L_1DL_2'$; and from (5) to (7) that $C_2'C_2 = L_2(\bar{S}_2'\bar{S}_2 + D_2^2)L_2'$. The structure of (3) can be further specified as

$$\begin{bmatrix} C_1'C_1 & C_1'C_2 \\ C_2'C_1 & C_2'C_2 \end{bmatrix} = \begin{bmatrix} L_1L_1' & L_1DL_2' \\ L_2DL_1' & L_2(\bar{S}_2'\bar{S}_2 + D_2^2)L_2' \end{bmatrix}. \tag{9}$$

It will be seen from (9) that when the mean factor scores $\bar{S}_2$ are 0, $C_2'C_2 = L_2D_2^2L_2'$, and if the factor scores S_2 then are taken to have equal unit variance $D_2^2 = I$, $C_2'C_2 = L_2L_2'$, which is the Corballis–Traub model. Thus it is a special case of the present model.

The cross-product form of the model, as given in (3), can be estimated by multiset factor analysis, described below. Using the Corballis–Traub case of (3) and (9), an analysis of a set of longitudinal Primary Mental Abilities data (Meyer & Bendig, 1961) was performed. The data consisted of five mental measurements taken at two points in time, at Grades 8 and 11. There existed a 10×10 correlation matrix which was analyzed by Corballis and Traub (1970) using their methodology. The results are presented in the left-hand portion of Table 1. Decimals are omitted. It will be seen that two common factors were

TABLE 1

Comparison of Two Longitudinal Solutions

	Corballis–Traub				Bentler			
	L_1		L_2		L_1		L_2	
	I	II	I	II	I	II	I	II
V	78	27	76	15	76	−18	82	−07
S	61	−45	51	−38	42	−37	33	−52
R	57	06	57	32	58	−07	64	06
N	54	39	59	63	71	43	69	38
W	35	22	31	−01	37	−04	29	−11

		D					D	
		I	II				I	II
	I	94	0			I	100	0
	II	0	68			II	0	100

extracted, and the loading matrices for the two occasions L_1 and L_2 are quite similar. The correlation between the factor scores on the two occasions, given in this case by $S_1'S_2$, are presented in the diagonal matrix D. The factors for the two occasions correlate quite highly.

The multiset method for estimating the Corballis–Traub version of (3) generated the loading matrices L_1 and L_2 for the two occasions as presented in the right-hand part of Table 1. The loadings are again highly similar, but the D matrix turns out to be the identity matrix. Factor scores in our solution were perfectly stable.

Since the two methods of estimating the model generated different results, the sum of squared residuals was computed for each method to provide an index of accuracy of fit for the two solutions presented in Table 1. The sum-of-squares discrepancy between off-diagonal input-correlation values and those values estimated from the model was .284 for the Corballis–Traub solution and .113 for the multiset solution. Thus the multiset method estimated the longitudinal model more accurately than the method used by Corballis and Traub. This result would seem to imply that lack of perfect stability in factor scores, as generated by Corballis–Traub, occurred primarily because of a poor estimation method rather than because of some intrinsic feature of the method.

Perfectly stable factor scores, with $D = I$, are, in fact, a special case of the longitudinal model. Consequently the multiset solution represents an appropriate fit for the model. For example, the model is still applicable in the special case in which the off-diagonals of $X_1'X_1 = X_1'X_2 = X_2'X_2$. It is obvious that the solution should then generate identical factor scores for the two occasions. It would seem that the only time to accept a longitudinal solution for which $D \neq I$ would be a case when, for a given number of factors, such a solution fits the observed data with a lesser sum of squared residuals. Although there is some question whether a longitudinal solution with $D \neq I$ will prove to be useful, we shall finish this discussion of the longitudinal model by focusing on estimates of the mean factor scores $\bar{S}_2$ in the general case. We shall assume we have obtained the matrices U^2 of (3) using some procedure, such as the multiset method.

We shall assume a basic structure for $L_1 = PaQ'$ and $L_2 = EbF'$. Then $L_1DL_2' = PaQ'DFbE'$. Let $T = (\bar{S}_2'\bar{S}_2 + D_2^2)$. It follows that $L_2TL_2' = EbF'TFbE'$. Having solved for $C_1'C_1 = L_1L_1'$, we can obtain Pa. Next $a^{-1}P'(L_1DL_2') = a^{-1}P'(PaQ'DFbE') = Q'DFbE'$. Let $B' = Q'DFbE'$. We obtain a general inverse of B, B^i, that we shall represent by $B^i = Q'D^{-1}Fb^{-1}E'$. The product $B^i(L_2TL_2')B^{i'}$ can then be represented by $Q'D^{-1}Fb^{-1}E'(EbF'TFbE')Eb^{-1}F'D^{-1}Q$, which simplifies to $Q'D^{-1}FF'TFF'D^{-1}Q$. If $FF' = I$, as it will when the rank r of L_2 and L_1 is less than n,

$$B^i(L_2TL_2')B^{i'} = Q'D^{-1}TD^{-1}Q. \tag{10}$$

But $T = \bar{S}_2'\bar{S}_2 + D_2^2$ so that

$$B^i(L_2TL_2{}')B^{i\prime} = Q'D^{-1}\bar{S}_2{}'\bar{S}_2D^{-1}Q + Q'D_2{}^2D^{-2}Q. \tag{11}$$

Now the first right-hand part of (11) is a rank 1 matrix, but the second matrix is full rank. This suggests using a rank 1 factor analytic model that fits $B^i(L_2TL_2{}')B^{i\prime}$ with minimum residual in the off diagonal, while leaving a Gramian nondiagonal residual matrix. The regression model (Bentler, 1970c) does this. The resulting residual matrix can then be taken to have the basic structure $Q'D_2{}^2D^{-2}Q$. The matrix of eigenvectors Q can be obtained from an eigenvector routine. Given Q, L_1 can be obtained. Apparently we have no choice but to fix either $D_2{}^2$ or D^2. If we set the factor variances $D_2{}^2 = I$, then the roots of the residual matrix determine D^{-2}. Consequently, we obtain D, and can transform the estimated rank 1 matrix $Q'D^{-1}\bar{S}_2{}'\bar{S}_2D^{-1}Q$ (obtained from the factor analysis) using Q and D to obtain a matrix whose diagonal elements represent the sum of squares of factor means. Thus the factor means can be determined. Alternatively, we could set the factor means equal. For example, we can use Q to transform the estimated rank 1 matrix to $D^{-1}\bar{S}_2{}'\bar{S}_2D^{-1}$, set $\bar{S}_2{}'\bar{S}_2 = I$, and the diagonal of the resulting matrix yields D^{-2}. The variances $D_2{}^2$ can then be obtained from the roots of the residual matrix.

This model needs further exploration, because it appears that once the factor means have been solved for and the factor stability coefficients D are available, it is possible to test the statistical significance of mean factor score differences under the assumption of normality of the factor scores S. Such a possibility is intriguing, because it makes unnecessary the estimation of the factor scores themselves.

D. Multiset Factor Analysis

A model of the type described in Eq. (3) is applicable in many situations, not only those involving changing factor scores. The name multiset will describe any matrices having the assumed structure of (1), (2), and (3). The factor scores across occasions can be assumed identical. Making appropriate assumptions about common scores and unique scores for any pair of data sets analogous to those described above, the model is directly applicable to any number of sets. Data that are found in a multitrait multimethod matrix, as well as retest data, would be of such a nature that it would be useful to identify (a) common factors, existing across data sets, (b) specific factors, existing across data sets but being specific to a given variable, and (c) error factors, existing in a given variable only in one data set. If desired, the common factors can be rotated into interbattery position, separating within-set from between-set common factors.

An example of multiset factor analysis applied to three sets of data is presented in Table 2. The nine variable data were taken by Horst (1965) from Thurstone and Thurstone (1941). They represent three cognitive factors, each measured by three tests. Tests $[1, 4, 7]$, $[2, 5, 8]$, and $[3, 6, 9]$ presumably measure

TABLE 2

*Multiset Factor Analysis: Input (Upper Right) and Residual (Lower Left) Matrices,
Common and Specific Factors, and Variance Components*

				Input and residual matrices				
	1	2	3	4	5	6	7	8	9
1	*76*	25	27	64	18	18	63	37	28
2	01	*61*	40	14	65	26	19	53	36
3	00	02	*61*	18	41	61	22	47	61
4	46	−01	00	*87*	09	15	71	25	19
5	00	*19*	−01	00	*34*	30	10	54	39
6	−04	−03	*30*	−01	00	*75*	18	44	50
7	*41*	01	00	*54*	00	−01	*80*	29	24
8	01	*08*	−01	00	*10*	06	−02	*41*	43
9	01	00	*24*	01	02	*20*	02	−03	*64*

Common factors		Specific factors		
I	II	I	II	III
44	22	*59*	00	00
61	−13	00	*39*	00
63	00	00	00	*60*
29	22	*78*	00	00
66	−47	00	*48*	00
49	05	00	00	*51*
36	27	*70*	00	00
76	13	00	*20*	00
60	03	00	00	*40*

	Variance components		
	Common	Specific	Error
1	24	35	41
2	39	16	45
3	39	36	25
4	13	61	26
5	66	23	11
6	24	26	49
7	20	49	31
8	60	04	37
9	36	16	48
Total	36	29	35

identical functions to a large extent. The correlation matrix among all tests is presented in the upper right-hand portion of Table 2, excluding the diagonal elements. The regression model was applied, with a patterned, nondiagonal matrix of uniqueness being estimated at each iteration; the pattern is illustrated by the italicized values in the lower left part of the first matrix in Table 2. Two common factors were assumed. The final solution for the two common factors is presented in the "common factors" columns. These common factors account for virtually all intercorrelations among variables except the diagonal U^2, and the off-diagonal uniquenesses $U_{12}{}^2$, $U_{13}{}^2$, and $U_{23}{}^2$, where the subscripts represent the across-set submatrices. The residual sum of squares, excluding the uniquenesses, is .017—a very acceptable fit. The communalities for the variables from the common-factor solution are presented in the first column of the lowest part of Table 2, under "variance components."

The patterned, nondiagonal matrix of uniquenesses shown in Table 2 was placed in the minimum trace factor method (Bentler, 1971c). This method finds the minimum trace "communalities" for the specifics that make the uniqueness covariance matrix the correct rank (three in this case). The solution for these factors is presented in the right-most columns in the middle of Table 2. It will be noted that only triplets of variables, across sets, load each of the factors, so that these factors are specific to the variable, but measured in each of the three sets. Exactly zero loadings by irrelevant variables are found for the specific factors.

The sums of squares of the specific factors are presented for each variable in the middle section of the bottom part of Table 2. The final column represents the variance of each variable that is not common nor specific variance. It is displayed in the diagonal of the Gramian matrix of residuals, obtained after the specific factors had been extracted. It should be observed that the sum of specific and error variance for each variable equals the uniqueness as presented in the diagonal of the residual matrix of Table 2. The analysis has thus estimated components of variance for each variable. The proportion of the total variance of all nine variables that each component accounts for is presented in the bottom row of Table 2. In an ideal case where a given test measured the same attribute in each set, and the variables were independent and reliable, the specific variance would be very large in comparison to the other variance components.

E. A Common-Score Change Model

The basic assumptions about common and unique scores made in arriving at Eq. (3) are relevant to the longitudinal model as well as to the multiset model. We now apply these assumptions to a final model for the analysis of longitudinal data. Specifically, we relate C_2 and C_1 as follows

$$C_2 = C_1D + W \tag{12}$$

where $C_1'W = D$. $W'W$ is not diagonal. It follows readily that the structure of the common scores becomes

$$
\begin{bmatrix} C_1'C_1 & C_1'C_2 \\ C_2'C_1 & C_2'C_2 \end{bmatrix} = \begin{bmatrix} C_1'C_1 & C_1'C_1D \\ DC_1'C_1 & DC_1'C_1D + W'W \end{bmatrix} \tag{13}
$$

Factor loading solutions for (13) then remain readily rotatable without destroying the structure of (13). This model allows the common scores to change without making any restrictions on factor dimensions, thus allowing for a meaningful choice of axes. Given various estimates of uniquenesses, $C_1'C_1$ can be factored to yield its eigenvalues Q. Premultiplying $C_1'C_1D$ by the general inverse of $C_1'C_1$ yields $QQ'D$, so that the diagonal D can be obtained by dividing the diagonal of $QQ'D$ by the diagonal of QQ'. In turn $DC_1'C_1D$ can be obtained, so that $W'W$ can be calculated.

CHAPTER 8

Strategies for Analyzing Behavioral Change Over Time

TODD R. RISLEY

UNIVERSITY OF KANSAS
LAWRENCE, KANSAS

MONTROSE M. WOLF

UNIVERSITY OF KANSAS
LAWRENCE, KANSAS

The observation, description, and measurement of changes in behavior over time characterize, if not define, developmental psychology. Tremendous files of longitudinal data now exist and continue to grow. Thus far, developmental psychology has largely used its longitudinal data in passive normative and correlative research. However, *experimental* research in developmental psychology can also employ the procedures of longitudinal observation, description, and measurement.

Experiments are distinguished from other forms of research in that they demonstrate that the experimental procedures were instrumental in producing the change in the measured behavior, i.e., they demonstrate causality. The demonstration of causality involves a comparison between the measured level of the behavior during the experimental procedures and an estimate of the level of that behavior had the experimental procedures not been introduced. This experimental comparison has usually involved comparing, at a single point in time, an average obtained from a group of individuals to whom the experimental procedures have been applied with an average obtained from a control group who have not experienced those procedures. To the extent that the two groups can be said to be identical in all respects excepting the presence or absence of the experimental procedures, the cause of the difference between them can be attributed to those procedures.

Alternatives to such static group designs are now available to developmental research. Designs can be used which demonstrate causal relationships between experimental procedures and changes in behavior over time. These time-series experimental designs usually provide for an experimental comparison between the levels of behavior in the presence and the absence of the experimental variables. Furthermore, the *implications* of a demonstration of causality—that the experimenter has specified and has control over the causal variables—are themselves usually explicitly demonstrated by the experimenter repeatedly exercising that control by replicating the effect with the same individual or group.

Initial repeated measures of the behavior and repeated measures during the application of the experimental procedures, as shown in Fig. 1, are common to all time-series designs. First, the behavior of interest is repeatedly measured over time to establish a *baseline*. This provides a basis for forecasting what level the behavior would be in the future, were the experimental procedures not introduced (see Box & Jenkins, 1970, for a thorough discussion of time-series forecasting). The new behavior level, determined by repeated measures of the behavior during the experimental procedures, is compared with the level forecast from the baseline measures.

It should be emphasized that a simple comparison of the mean and variance of the data points during baseline with those during the experimental procedures, as in Fig. 2, is meaningless. The *trend* of the data over time is the most important consideration for analyzing such data. For example, the data in Fig. 3 would provide the same means and variances as the data in Fig. 1, but the conclusion about the likelihood that the experimental variable caused the change in behavior would be quite different in the two cases. In Fig. 3, the behavior under the experimental condition is little different from that predicted from the rising baseline; in contrast, in Fig. 1 the behavior under the experimental condition is quite different from the level predicted from the baseline.

This A–B design (A, baseline measures; B, measures during experimental procedures) is sufficient to establish whether a *change* in the level of behavior has occurred, and the approximate magnitude of that change. The more extensive and stable the measures under each condition, the more precisely the magnitude of the change in behavior correlated with the experimental procedures can be specified. This design, however, does not strongly establish that the change was due to the experimental procedures. Campbell and Stanley (1966), in their book *Experimental and Quasi-Experimental Designs for Research,* call this simple time-series A–B design a "quasi"-experimental design. There are statistical tests that can be legitimately applied to such simple time-series data (cf. Box

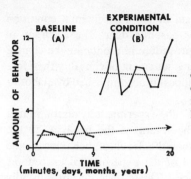

Fig. 1. In the baseline condition, the behavior of interest is first measured repeatedly over time. Then under the experimental condition, the new level of behavior is measured repeatedly and compared with the level that would have been forecast from the baseline measures.

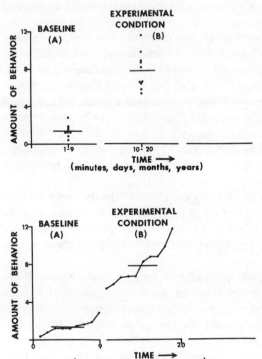

Fig. 2. Comparison of the mean and variance of data points during the baseline condition and within the experimental condition where no information about trends within each of the conditions is provided.

Fig. 3. The same data presented in Fig. 2, now plotted in a manner that reveals the trends in the behavior under each condition.

& Tiao, 1965; Hannan, 1960). By such tests, only large, immediate changes will be found significant, as the range of the forecast from the baseline expands exponentially with each succeeding point in time from the last baseline measure. Thus, the simple time-series *A–B* design is very weak, senstive only to abrupt changes in behavior.

The weakness in this design is that the data in the experimental condition are compared with a forecast from the prior baseline data. The accuracy of an assessment of the role of the experimental procedure in producing the change rests upon the accuracy of that forecast. A strong statement of causality therefore requires that that forecast be supported. This support is accomplished by elaborating the A–B design.

The most common elaboration is to "reverse" the experiment by discontinuing the experimental procedure as in Fig. 4. The return of the behavior to the baseline level supports the initial forecast that the level of behavior would have continued unchanged through the period of the experimental procedures had those procedures not, in fact, been introduced. This A–B–A design is usually further extended by reinstating the experimental procedures—producing an A–B–A–B design—which further demonstrates that the experimenter has specified and does control the causal variables.

It should be pointed out here that there are two levels of experimental comparisons available in an extended A–B–A–B–A–B . . . etc. design—where the same subject (or group of subjects) is repeatedly exposed to the experimental variable. At one level, Campbell and Stanley (1966) call this form of time-series design the "equivalent time-samples design" and suggest that a t test, with degrees of freedom equal to the number of A and B conditions less 2, can be appropriately applied. The resulting experimental comparison is between the distribution of the means of the A conditions and the distribution of the means of the B conditions. The trend of the data points *within* any A or B condition is not considered in this level of comparison.

However, at another level, by considering the trends of the data points within each A or B condition, each A–B–A or B–A–B sequence can constitute a separate experimental comparison. This level of comparison—utilizing time-series forecasting—allows us to make legitimate statements about the cause of any individual A–B or B–A change.

In most cases, we are interested primarily in the *first* A–B change. If we use the information contained in the trend of the A condition baseline, and support the forecast from that trend, we can make legitimate probability statements that our experimental procedures caused the change in behavior in the first B condition.

However, developmental research often produces changes in behavior which are durable, i.e., which persist when the experimental procedures are withdrawn (for example, a change, if significant, may be maintained by the variables which maintain that behavior in older children) so that removal of the experimental procedures may produce no, or only partial, reversal of the change. In such cases, another type of elaboration of the A–B design, called a "multiple baseline" design, can be employed to establish the causality of the experimental procedures with behaviors of a single individual or group over time.

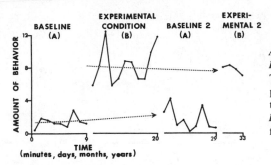

Fig. 4. A *reversal* design where the A represents the baseline condition and B represents the experimental condition. The data in the second A condition support the forecast from the first A condition, and, similarly, the data in the second B condition support the forecast from the first B condition.

With a multiple baseline design, two or more behaviors of a subject or group are measured simultaneously. After baselines are obtained, experimental procedures are applied, first to only one of the behaviors. Any change in the level of this behavior is compared with the level forecast for that behavior from its baseline. The accuracy of this forecast is assessed by comparing this forecast with the continuing measures of the other behavior(s). If the level of the other behaviors remains relatively similar to the level forecast from their baselines (and to the extent that it can be assumed that uncontrolled variables, if such occurred, would have similarly affected all of the behaviors measured) the baseline forecast of the first behavior is supported. Campbell and Stanley (1966) call a similar "multiple time-series design" a "quasi-"experimental design.

This is a somewhat weaker design than the A–B–A design, since it involves an additional assumption: All the measured behaviors are susceptible to the same variables. This assumption can, however, be supported by demonstrating that the other behaviors are also susceptible to the same experimental procedures as the first behavior. This is accomplished by applying those procedures to the second behavior, and so on. Demonstrations that the experimenter has specified and does control the causal variables are made as the experimental procedures are successively applied to each baseline, while the remaining baselines support the accuracy of the forecast of the preceding baseline. It should be emphasized that the strongest experimental comparison is not *between* the sets of data, but between the B condition behavior and the forecast of the A-condition baseline *within* each set of data. The remaining sets of data serve to support the baseline forecast of the first set. In the data in Fig. 5, we can make much stronger statements about the role of the experimental procedure in producing the change in the upper baseline than in the lower, as the forecast from the lower baseline is not supported (with, for example, a third baseline of yet another behavior).

Multiple baseline designs can be employed using not only different behaviors of the same individual or group in a given situation, but also the same behavior

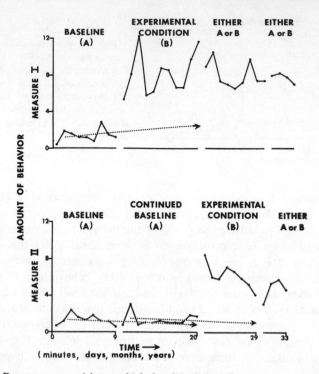

Fig. 5. Data are presented in a *multiple baseline* design. Two or more behavioral baselines are recorded simultaneously. Treatments are then introduced sequentially, first for one behavior and then for the second. The continuation of measure II from one A condition baseline to the next—as forecast—supports the forecast made from the baseline of Measure I.

of a given individual or group concurrently measured in different stimulus situations. In fact, even the same behavior of different individuals or groups concurrently measured in the same situation may constitute the baselines. It may be noted that this last type of multiple baseline design approximates some group-statistical experimental designs.

The "ideal" experimental design would allow simultaneous measurement and comparison of the behavior of a single individual or group in both the presence and absence of the experimental procedures. The usual approximation to this ideal is to compare the averages obtained from two groups of persons—one with and one without the experimental procedures. The "reversal" (*A–B–A–B*) and "multiple baseline" designs—which are common to behavior modification research—are alternative, and in some ways closer, approximations to this "ideal" experimental design. Either of these designs can be further extended to analyze (1) the function of each of the components of the original experimental

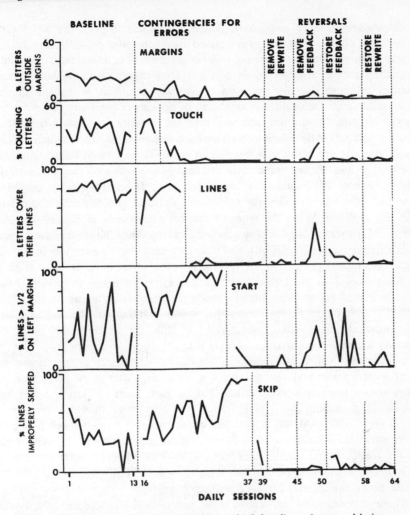

Fig. 6. An example of a study which used both a *multiple baseline* and a *reversal* design.

procedure, (2) the function of various levels of the experimental variables, or (3) the effects of other alterations of the experimental procedures.

Let us illustrate the use of both the multiple baseline and the reversal time-series designs to demonstrate the causal variables in developing the writing skills of a young retarded girl named Marie (see Fig. 6). Tom Sajwaj conducted this study with us several years ago.

Although Marie could form individual letters legibly, her words and sentences flowed freely around the page, unaffected by margins, lines, or the presence or absence of previously written words or letters.

During the *baseline conditions,* Marie was asked to print the alphabet (A . . . Z) in block letters and was praised for each letter regardless of how or where it was written. There were no other consequences or instructions. Beginning with the *margins condition,* Marie was instructed to write the alphabet a specific number of times (usually two to six) and was told that, when she finished that assignment, she could play one song of her choice from any of her favorite record albums. In addition, she was told not to write any letters beyond the four red margins. After Marie completed each alphabet, the experimenter checked each letter. If any letter was beyond or touched the margins no matter how slightly, it was marked through in red and Marie was told that this alphabet did not count. She would have to write it over. If no errors occurred, Marie was told that this was the *n*th completed alphabet and that she could write the next alphabet. When the required number of errorless alphabets was completed, Marie was allowed to play a record. An error, then, had two consequences: It was marked in red (feedback), and it necessitated rewriting the whole alphabet (rewrite), thereby postponing the record. No other attention or praise was given.

After five sessions of this procedure, *touching errors* were added. Marie was instructed not to write letters outside the margins or letters touching each other. If either type of error occurred, it was marked and she had to rewrite the entire alphabet. After five sessions of this, the contingencies were also applied to *out-of-lines errors* (crossing into the line above or below). She then was instructed not to make margin, touch, or out-of-lines errors. If she did, they were marked and she rewrote the alphabet. After eight more sessions, *start errors* (starting a line further than ½ inch from the left margin) were added. Five sessions later, *skip errors* (skipping more than one line on the page) were added. At this point, any occurrences of any of these five errors were marked in red and necessitated rewriting the entire alphabet. This application of the feedback and rewrite procedure to each of these five errors comprises a multiple baseline experimental design, which demonstrates the function of the procedure in reducing each writing error.

Three sessions after skip errors were added to the procedures, the *rewrite requirement* was dropped. Errors were still marked in red, but all alphabets counted toward the number necessary to play a record. Six sessions later, the *feedback for errors* was also removed: Errors were no longer marked in red. Thus, errors had no programmed consequences, but *instructions* were still given at the start of each session not to make any of the errors. *Feedback* was reinstated six sessions later, and the *rewrite requirement* was restored after another eight sessions, thus completing the steps of the reversal experimental design which analyzed the function of several of the components of the original procedure.

The procedures of this program were fairly complex, consisting of instructions, feedback, and a rewrite requirement. In addition, the rewrite component not only involved rewriting the alphabet, but also involved a postponement of the opportunity to play a record. Instructions contributed little to the effectiveness of the program. All error rates increased when feedback and rewrite components were removed during the reversal conditions leaving only instructions. It was originally assumed by the experimenters that the rewrite was the most effective component of the procedure. However, the reversal conditions demonstrated it to be relatively ineffective, while showing the feedback component to be considerably more critical.

In addition to the two time-series designs employed in this study to accomplish two different types of analysis, this subject could have been one child in an experimental classroom where the feedback and rewrite conditions were being used on all children, whose handwriting in turn was being compared to that of children in a control classroom who were receiving another type of instruction.

In conclusion, we wish to emphasize what should already be obvious: These time-series experimental designs simply add to present technology for investigating developmental phenomena. But the reversal and multiple baseline designs are uniquely suited to the procedures of longitudinal observation, description, and measurement which have characterized developmental psychology.

CHAPTER 9

The Control of Developmental Process:
Why Wait?

DONALD M. BAER

UNIVERSITY OF KANSAS
LAWRENCE, KANSAS

I. Introduction

The definition of developmental psychology is not a simple matter. The division of the American Psychological Association which is called Developmental periodically debates who its members should be; and I have occasionally received unofficial invitations to discontinue my membership in that division—not because of the dues which I sometimes do not produce, but because of the research which I sometimes do produce. Worse than that, it is true that during a 1966 symposium on the topic of development, held under the auspices of that division, a discussant concluded that I was not a developmental psychologist at all, but merely a child psychologist (cf. Baer, 1970). I have aged since then—which I thought was the relevant process—and now am rarely referred to as even a child psychologist. Surely, this establishes my credentials for declining to define the concept of development.

Then how am I to discuss "strategies" under a heading of *design of developmental research*? It may be that I can point to certain very common characteristics of research called developmental, even if I am not well qualified to explain why those characteristics are so common in that research. It may be that those characteristics intersect in part with a field which I can define, namely behavior modification. If developmental research shares certain goals with behavior modification research, then possibly the strategies of behavior modification can be recommended as strategies for developmental research as well. Mere recommendation may prove to be no more than a weak example of the courtship which Edwin Willems (Chapter 10 in this volume) tells us in his title is not enough. However, I will argue here that marriage of the two approaches is still premature; if courtship is really not enough, that seems to leave only the possibility of a brief affair. Or perhaps, they can be good friends.

II. Developmental Research and Behavior Modification

Developmental research typically presents two kinds of data. First, it displays behavior change as an orderly function of age. Undeniably, a tremendous amount of very diverse behavior is indeed ordered quite thoroughly by the age of the organism. Thus, while we argue about the environmental conditions that control, say, the emergence of language behavior in the normal child, and occasionally validate the importance of one environmental contingency or another, the most thorough analysis of receptive language is still offered by the simple statement, "Be 1 year old," and of productive language by the statement, "Be 2 years old." This is not to deny that the experimental application of operant-conditioning techniques has often produced selected examples of receptive and productive language in deficient children (e.g., Lovaas, 1967). Nevertheless, most children will come to very broad repertoires of those behaviors simply by living out a sufficient amount of time in the usual environment. Behavior modification places a strong value on breadth of repertoire modified and range of subjects in which the modification was successful, and therefore will nod respectfully to the processes of being 1 year old or 2 years old in the usual environment.

Second, developmental research displays behavior change as an orderly function of sequence. Again, it is undeniable that a great deal of behavior regularly occurs in its turn, which often means simply that it will occur after some other behavior occurs first. And again, while we continue to argue about the emergence of language in the normal child, and sometimes show that we can make it occur according to our own programming, a very thorough analysis of productive language is still offered by the simple statement, "Wait for receptive language to emerge." Again, it is understood that this waiting is to occur in the usual environment.

I suggest that developmental research thus has three hallmarks of considerable relevance to behavior modification. It emphasizes behavior change, which is exactly the subject matter of behavior modification; it emphasizes the time course of behavior, which is again precisely the analytic dimension which behavior modification most often employs; and it emphasizes waiting along that time course, which is surely the antithesis of behavior modification. The philosophy of behavior modification is, in effect, "Why wait?" This philosophy has probably been adopted because behavior modification most often has been used with children for whom waiting, even in the usual environment, has in fact *not* produced some of the usual desirable developmental changes. Those changes either have not emerged, or else very undesirable distortions of them have occurred instead. In either case, the child's behavior is considered a clinical problem, and in recent years, behavior modifiers have translated the clinical problem simply into two sets of behaviors which need changing: one set of undesirable behaviors, too high in strength, which require reduction; and another set of desirable behaviors, too low in strength, which need to be increased.

The strategies which have replaced waiting arose from several sources. First, there was the strong suspicion that further waiting would not repair the behavioral problems already obvious, and indeed, would probably worsen them. Second there was the suspicion that behaviors labeled *clinical*, as well as behaviors labeled *developmental*, might not be different in essence from some extremely significant behaviors labeled *bar-pressing* and *key-pecking* (which, in moments of theoretical grandeur, were often relabeled *operant*). Third, there was the clear evidence, far beyond mere suspicion, that bar-pressing and key-pecking were thoroughly modifiable behaviors, that the tactics for their modification were well known and codified into sets of general principles (called operant conditioning), and that they definitely did not include the technique of waiting in any significant role.[1] Instead, they included techniques of immediate environmental reaction to the behavior undergoing modification, generally summarized as contingencies of reinforcement, punishment, or extinction, typically discriminated to certain cue stimuli, and usually programmed according to a schedule chosen for its own characteristic ability to determine the rate or durability of the behavior which would interact with it (Baer & Sherman, 1970).

In the past decade, behavior modification has demonstrated its ability to analyze and change significantly a wide range of behaviors. It can be instructive for what is about to be argued to consider a sample of those behaviors. They include the rudiments of language (receptive and productive), beginning with simple labels, expanding to requests, going on to short declarative sentences and conversational gambits (e.g., Risley & Wolf, 1967), then encompassing the use of relational terms such as prepositions across a wide range of instances of these relationships (e.g., Lovaas, 1967), and recently emphasizing the use of grammatical cases such as plurals, verb tenses, comparative and superlative

[1]Operant conditioners will recognize that short-term waiting does in fact figure in several important techniques such as time-out, DRO, and aversive and interval scheduling. However, these applications, while valuable, are hardly characteristic of operant conditioning as an analytical or intervention technique.

adjectives, active and passive verb voices, and the basic noun–verb–object sentence format, all in a thoroughly generalized way showing a correct handling of new instances appropriate to each grammatical rule as well as those instances used for the initial training (cf. Guess *et al.* 1968; Schumaker & Sherman, 1970; Wheeler & Sulzer, 1970). This has been done primarily with institutionalized retardates initially deficient in those language skills. In that population and similar ones, thorough control of self-destructive and self-mutilating behavior has been gained, as well as the ability to eliminate or greatly reduce milder forms of disruptive response, such as tantrums, whining, screaming, aggression, and destruction of property (e.g., Lovaas & Simmons, 1969; Risley, 1968; Wolf, Risley, & Mees, 1964). Coupled with that has been the ability to produce toilet-training, proper eating techniques, and the complete range of self-care skills frequently absent in institutionalized children and critical to their continued institutionalization (Lent, 1968; Lent & Childress, 1970; Lent, LeBlanc, & Spradlin, 1970). Some of this capability for modification followed from an earlier development of simple techniques for producing a widely generalized imitative skill in such children, such that any new motor or vocal performance was easily installed in them simply through a few demonstrations of it (e.g., Baer, Peterson, & Sherman, 1967; Lovaas, 1967). Among otherwise normal preschool children, the behaviors successfully subjected to experimental behavior modification have generally been those motor, social, and cognitive skills thought specially appropriate to the preschool environment yet not appearing in the normal course of events in that setting, or quirks of development thought to be prejudicial to the child's future performance in grade school, with his family, or with his peers. Thus, preschool children have been taught to walk, when necessary, and have had their climbing, running, and cycling skills adjusted upward; social isolates have been given social skills; silent children have been given a readiness to speak when useful; aggressive children have lost the violent fraction of that repertoire, while long-standing victims have learned to defend themselves effectively; hyperactive children have been taught the possibility of unbroken attention to a task; and undemonstrative children have been taught how and when to smile (e.g., Baer & Wolf, 1968). School children of the ghetto have been reintroduced successfully to public schooling by teaching them that at least one agency of the Establishment—their experimenter—would reinforce them handsomely for academic achievement, and by allowing them to resume that curriculum where they had last learned any of it, usually at the second-grade level (Baer & Wolf, 1968; Wolf, Giles, & Hall, 1968). Their teachers have been taught not to allow their attention to students to be commanded by disruptive behavior, but instead by orderly, learning-oriented responses, and accordingly, the students of those teachers have learned to display just those orderly, learning-oriented behaviors rather than the disruptive ones (e.g., Hall, Lund, & Jackson, 1968). Predelinquents have been taught school achievement, self-care of their living quarters, friendly speech, cooperative interaction with their families, and an absence of stealing and aggression (Bailey, Wolf, & Phillips, 1970; Phillips, 1969). Jailed delinquents have been taught the academic components of a high school diploma and some salable vocational skills, for their after-jail future (Cohen, Fillipczak, & Bis, 1970). Stutterers have been given fluent speech throughout their range of everyday environments (Goldiamond, personal communication, 1970). And overweight adults have had that development reversed, apparently learning the skills of eating and exercise necessary to ongoing weight reduction and a return to their healthier, albeit less-developed status of earlier life, through the exigencies of a contingency contract with a behavior modifier who, without it, would have no control over those so resistant behaviors (Mann, 1971).

This list is far from complete. It is representative of much, but not all that behavior modification can reliably do (cf. Bandura, 1969). I chose it to suggest two characteristics: (1) that behavior modification is an impressively effective discipline and technology, and thus cannot readily be set aside as a mere intellectual toy of the academic world of psychology; and (2) that some of the behaviors with which behavior modification techniques have shown their competence have considerable relevance to the behaviors that developmental research investigates. Both points are important to the argument that will follow, but the second is primary. It can be restated as a question: How many of the behavior changes considered the special interest of developmental research are, in fact, as thoroughly modifiable by the techniques of behavior modification as the behaviors listed previously? Some of them are, at least; possibly, many of them; conceivably, all of them. No one could assert prudently that all the behaviors studied as "developmental" will experimentally develop under the contingencies of behavior modification technology, because not all the necessary demonstrations have been made. My point is that enough demonstrations have been made, for enough behaviors sufficiently similar to those called developmental, to raise the question, and to suggest that while a prudent scientist would not make the assertion, neither would he bet heavily against it.

In a word, I have suggested an *overlap* between the subject matter of behavior modification and the subject matter of developmental psychology. The question is whether that overlap exists on a large enough scale to have relevance for either discipline, but especially for developmental research. The possible relevance is twofold:

(1) If the overlap is large and important, there arises the possibility that the mechanisms of behavior modification are largely identical to the mechanisms of development. In that case, the reason that age orders developmental change in the usual environment is that behavior modification contingencies usually occur at those ages; and the reason that sequence orders development is either

that some behaviors are easier to shape than others and therefore are done sooner, or that some behaviors are easier to shape after others have been established than before, or that the people doing the teaching have some fixed ideas about when to teach what.

(2) If the mechanisms of development are largely identical to the mechanisms of behavior modification, there arises the possibility that the usual environment represents rather inefficient programming of those mechanisms. In general, the behavior changes affected by behavior modification are prompt, considered one class at a time; they require time, certainly, but rarely in amounts measured in terms of years. For example, the development of a thoroughly generalized, tightly accurate imitative skill in a profound retardate usually requires between 50 and 200 experimental hours. Those hours typically are spread over the same number of days, but that represents only the experimenter's convenience, not the necessities of behavior change—so far as we know. Thus, there may be a great deal of developmental acceleration available, if we should ever value it.

It needs to be emphasized that these two possibilities are exactly that—possibilities. They are possible mainly because of the prior possibility: that there is a considerable overlap in the behaviors subjected to behavior modification and those studied in developmental research. The latter possibilities may be attractive, however: They suggest an integration of two conceptual fields, to the possible profit of both. Development has often been a mechanism-free concept; behavior modification, which is mechanism-rich, has often been pointedly non-developmental in its choice and sequencing of behavioral targets. The fact that both have often gotten away with those practices does not mean that there is nothing to be gained by their reciprocal instruction in the logic and capabilities of one another.

If the potential attractiveness of this integration is to be achieved, there are two very large requirements to be achieved first. One of these is to examine the actual extent of overlap between those behaviors considered developmental and those amenable to behavior modification. This is not a particularly likely outcome, considering current practices. Behavior modifiers, almost of necessity, have dealt with those behaviors having clinical relevance or social importance, especially in those children or adults identified as "problems." Developmental researchers, by contrast, have dealt primarily with the normal case, and for some reason they have particularly valued the ability of a child to know whether he has more water, less water, or the same, after it has been poured into a different container, or more, less, or the same number of marbles after they have been rearranged from a short line to a long one. Those are certainly fascinating behaviors—but they are neither sick nor of obvious social importance, and consequently have not attracted much intensive behavior modification. If overlap is to be evaluated, either the behavior modifiers will be required to turn their efforts toward such conservation behaviors, or the conservation researchers will be required to learn the complete technology of behavior modification and apply it to those behaviors, to see if their timings and sequences are not, after all, susceptible to some degree of arbitrary rescheduling. Thus, evaluation of the relevance of behavior modification research to developmental research will require quite a lot of behavior modification within the researchers themselves. If those of us who are in a position to do so will try it, and if others of us will reinforce them for it, at least a little will get done, and the example may evoke extensive imitation, which is not at all a bad mechanism for the problem. Meanwhile, we might convince behavior modifiers that there are sick theories as well as sick people, and that theories do sometimes control a fair amount of behavior, some of it relevant to the social control of research, as by funding agencies. At the same time, perhaps we can persuade developmental researchers that claims about the immutability of certain developmental patterns are more convincing when they come from connoisseurs of mutation techniques.

The second requirement to be achieved before we can evaluate the possible integration of behavior modification and developmental research derives from a simple logical point: Even if extensive empirical research were to show that the behaviors considered developmental are indeed highly susceptible to behavior modification techniques, that alone would not establish that they result *only* from those mechanisms. Any effect may have several causes; and we are accustomed to considering behavioral change as particularly sensitive to multiple causation. Thus, some future demonstration that conservation skills are readily shaped, in arbitrary orders and at arbitrary ages, by standard behavior modification contingencies, will not establish that it is those contingencies which produce these conservation skills in the usual case. It will establish only that those contingencies *could* produce the skills in the usual case—and it may suggest that any proponent of an alternative causal mechanism should produce an equally clear demonstration of *its* feasibility. However, while any proponents of an alternative mechanism are busy at that assignment, there is yet another program of research necessary for the behavior modification enthusiast: He must examine the environment of the usual case of development to see if the relevant behavior modification mechanisms appear to be operating there. Thus, he would eventually be able to show not only that behavior modification techniques, deliberately applied, result in the specified conservation skills in whatever sequence desired; he would also be able to show that just such techniques do get applied, nondeliberately and nonexperimentally, but recognizably as the same techniques, in the usual case (which is, we presume, an experimenter-free case). Unfortunately, that discovery, while reinforcing to the behavior modifier's argument, still would not establish it beyond doubt. The observation of what appears to be a reinforcement contingency does not establish that the contingency being observed is a *functional* one. It merely establishes that reinforcement could be going on.

It is always possible to describe contingencies which, in all probability, are not functional for the behavior in question. Suppose, for example, that we develop an intense interest in sneezing as a case in point. Laboratory investigation might show that with potent reinforcement, an operant sneezing response could be established, at least in some subjects. If so, we would have established the feasibility of sneezing as one more example of behavior modification, perhaps devoid of all hint of either Piagetian or Freudian significance. An examination of the usual environment of the sneezer probably would show that whenever he sneezes, someone is likely to say "God bless you!" or words to that effect. The contingency is clear: Sneezes typically produce a prompt social consequence of a topographically positive sort. However, it would be imprudent indeed to conclude that since sneezing can be reinforced, and since sneezing in the usual environment is socially answered in a positive manner, it therefore has been developmentally analyzed. Most students of behavior would suggest that the usual organization of sneezing is according to the respondent paradigm, not the operant one: Sneezing is elicited by its antecedents (such as pollen, dust, or pepper) rather than reinforced by its social consequences. Unfortunately, on an issue this grave, we can hardly accept even the informed opinion of the student of behavior. Proof will be required. It will necessitate an entry into the usual environment of the sneezer, and a conversion of some of those nonexperimenters into at least temporary experimenters. They must stop saying "God bless you!" as a consequence of our subject's sneezing; they must greet his future sneezes with silence and impassivity, and if they are to continue saying "God bless you!" it must be at other times than when the subject has sneezed. In other words, we shall attempt the extinction of this hypothetically socially reinforced sneezing. If it does indeed extinguish, then we shall of course reinstate the practice of saying "God bless you!" to see if we can recondition the response, at which point we will triumphantly proclaim a truly developmental analysis of another behavior into nothing more than just plain behavior modification. More likely, though, we will discover that sneezing continues at its old rate despite the absence of a contingent "God bless you!" and we shall thus have one of those numerous examples of usual-environment contingencies that are not functional contingencies. Only this kind of experimental intervention into the usual environment will settle the matter clearly; and if research shows a considerable overlap between the behaviors considered developmental and those changable by behavior modification, then this type of experimental intervention into the usual environment will become mandatory, if the significance of that overlap is to be assessed.

III. Summary

In summary, I have argued for three extensive programs of research:

(1)   an ongoing, diversified attempt to subject all behaviors considered developmentally significant to change through behavior modification techniques;

(2)   if many of those behaviors are found susceptible to behavior modification, then an inspection of the usual environment in which those behaviors develop, to see if apparent behavior modification contingencies operate there on those behaviors at the appropriate times;

(3)   if such contingencies are seen in relevant forms, then an experimental intervention into those contingencies, to see if they are functional contingencies which indeed are responsible for the acquisition and/or maintenance of the developing behaviors interacting with them.

To whatever extent these programs of research produce positive answers, showing that developmental behaviors are shapable, that apparent shaping contingencies do operate on them as they emerge in the usual environment of development, and that those contingencies are demonstrably functional for those behaviors, then *to that extent* the mechanisms of behavior modification and the mechanisms of development may be considered the same; and the fact that I am not sure how to define development will be less important than it is today.

CHAPTER 10

Behavioral Ecology and Experimental Analysis: Courtship Is Not Enough[1]

EDWIN P. WILLEMS

UNIVERSITY OF HOUSTON
HOUSTON, TEXAS

I. Introduction

Taken in one way, the purpose of this chapter is to represent and advocate pluralism at two levels. First, by means of a rather extended set of examples, analogies, and arguments, I shall advocate the adoption of an ecological perspective on behavior, a perspective that demands attention to complexity of an order which has not been represented in the literature on the development of behavior. Second, with that perspective in mind, I shall try to show that the stage is set for a kind of methodological and procedural pluralism which, rather than accepting diversity in a benign fashion, involves methodologies of diverse origins and styles actively in the interdependent pursuit of important problems of behavior and development.

As a discipline, psychology is passing through a phase of renewed polemics regarding the scientific merits of various procedures and some serious attempts at courtship between strategies. I have participated in some of those polemics myself, especially the ones clustering around the naturalistic–experimental or

[1] Work on this paper was supported in part by Research and Training Center No. 4, Baylor College of Medicine, funded by Social and Rehabilitation Services, United States Department of Health, Education, and Welfare, and in part by the Institute of Urban Studies, University of Houston.

lab–field polarity (Willems, 1965, 1967c, 1969). Against that background, I shall argue presently for a position that will sound, on the surface, like heresy to the devotees of extreme positions on that issue. Stated simply, the position is that, when formulated properly, behavioral ecology depends upon experimental analysis as an integral part of its armamentarium of research strategies. In order to clarify why such a simple statement should need any elaboration at all, we will have to move some disruptive furniture out of the way and begin with a brief discussion of ecological–experimental polemics in psychology. Following that discussion, the rest of the paper will treat: (a) a characterization of the ecological perspective, and (b) a brief characterization of the experimental method, and (c) some arguments that demonstrate why I believe that the relationship can move rapidly out of mere courtship and be consummated in effective style.

II. Ecological–Experimental Polemics

Recently, while describing her dissertation proposal to me, a student mentioned that she planned to gather "ecological data," by which she meant that she intended to engage in a program of direct observation of children. Less than an hour later, a colleague offered the proposition that psychologists need to devote more attention to "ecological methods," by which he meant nonexperimental techniques for gathering data. Both of these incidents came shortly after I was invited to prepare this chapter on the general problem of "integrating ecological methods with experimental developmental psychology." In each of these cases, there was reference to a domain called "ecological methods," a phrase which has come into common coinage in psychology. Despite the risk of semantic nit-picking and gamesmanship, I submit that the adoption of the phrase, "ecological methods," is responsible for much of the controversy that has swirled around the evaluation of behavioral ecology. How behavioral ecology has become equated with a particular set of methods is a problem for the history of science. More important for present purposes is my conviction that this has been an unfortunate error that has led to unnecessary and scientifically fruitless debates.

As I shall argue later, behavioral ecology is a perspective, an orientation, or a set of theoretical principles in terms of which the investigator formulates questions about behavior and its habitat and context in particular ways. Perhaps because it is easier and more efficient to demarcate a new and complicated position in terms of research techniques than by its substantive, theoretical thrust, the major authors and devotees of ecological psychology have fallen into the trap of defining and justifying it primarily in terms of naturalistic, nonexperimental strategies for gathering data (Barker, 1964, 1965, 1968; Willems, 1965; Wright,

1967). It is probably true that those psychologists who most eagerly describe their work as "ecological" have preferred naturalistic, nonexperimental methods in their work and it is true that a great many ecological questions lend themselves best to field research. However, the tendency to identify behavioral ecology with naturalistic methods has led to the unfortunate error of implicating behavioral ecology in the arguments, claims, and counterclaims about the relative merits and tenabilities of experimental and naturalistic methods, so that, depending on how those arguments are proceeding at any particular time, the behavioral-ecology baby is thrown out or reinstated with the methodological bath water. Before turning to the ecology-of-behavior viewpoint, a word is in order regarding some of the methodological controversy.

Disagreements about tactics of research are older than psychology, but they took on added heat with the advent of ecological psychology. The phrase, "ecological psychology," or "psychological ecology," has been circulating around American psychology for about 20 years, with a positively accelerating curve of visibility and acclaim. During the first 15 of those years, the major authors and agents of ecological psychology were Roger Barker and Herbert Wright, who, in turn, were co-workers and intellectual descendents of Kurt Lewin. Suddenly, after their lonely pioneering, ecology is now *in*. A few years ago, those of us who stated interests in ecological psychology received quizzical and patronizing looks, but we now receive knowing and appreciative nods and the number of requests for reprints, comments, and consultation has gone up at a remarkable rate. It is my hypothesis that, within the professional atmosphere of the 1950s and early 1960s, what struck the prime movers of ecological psychology was a twofold phenomenon: (1) their work was evaluated (usually criticized) on methodological grounds, and (2) they found little justification and rationale for their naturalistic procedures in the existing literature. The prevailing values within scientific psychology during those years favored the experiment and the literature describing the rationale, merits, and advantages of the experiment was extensive and detailed. So it was that the authors of ecological psychology devoted many of their arguments and examples to buttressing the case for naturalistic research and nonexperimental methods.

Bypassed, perhaps, in this development was the fact that, just as the logic, structure, and merits of the experimental method can be formulated at a general and abstract level, apart from what particular persons are studying, so can nonexperimental, naturalistic methods be formulated at a similar level. Recognition of that fact has led to two developments: (a) generation of a body of literature that presents the rationale, logic, and range of application of naturalistic methods, somewhat independent of the ecological orientation (Brandt, in press; Campbell, 1969; Webb *et al.*, 1966; Willems & Raush, 1969), and (b) recognition that experimental and nonexperimental methods can and should be treated within unified frameworks of methodological argument (Bijou, Peterson, & Ault, 1968;

Brandt, in press; Campbell & Stanley, 1966; McGuire, 1969; Menzel, 1969; Scott & Wertheimer, 1962; Willems, 1969).

This literature, serving to formalize naturalistic research and bringing it into the completely respectable armamentarium of research tools, is still polemical and polarizing in places, but the polemics and special pleading have served the important function of sharpening definitions, issues, applicability, and the problems of inference. That is an accomplishment of some note, both to the sciences of behavior in general and to the behavioral ecologist in particular. However, firming up the separation between the ecology-of-behavior viewpoint and naturalistic methodological developments still leaves the substance and flavor of the ecological point of view relatively unattended. What we need is a new starting point, a formulation that sets the stage for more than superficial desegregation of behavioral ecology and experimental developmental psychology.

III. Behavior in Ecological Perspective

The ecological perspective on behavior places a great deal of emphasis upon interrelationships and interdependencies within behavior–organism–environment systems. This focus gives me pause, because perhaps more than any other issues to which behavioral scientists have addressed themselves, understanding the links among organisms, their molar behavior, and their habitats requires attention to a kind of complexity for which psychology is scarcely prepared. In order to back up this opinion and to provide some of the flavor and substance of an ecological perspective on behavior, I shall discuss a set of examples, ideas, and arguments, some of which can be applied to developmental psychology only by analogy.[2] This is so because some of the clearest illustrations of the principles and problems of the ecological perspective fall outside of the behavioral sciences. However, their clarity outweighs the disadvantages of cross-disciplinary translation and they have much to teach us. I shall proceed by citing several large-scale examples from other areas and then converging on more direct examples and implications for the study of behavior.

A. Large-Scale Interdependencies

We know now that large-scale attempts to rid whole areas of insect-borne diseases and to release crops from the ravages of insects have created very unpleasant but unanticipated results, also on a large scale. Some 20 years ago, with the noblest and most humane intentions, the ''great insecticide experiment''

[2]Recognizing that a great deal of methodological argument permeates the literature of ecology, it would be worthwhile to review that literature (especially the writings of Barker and Wright) in order to glean the substantive hypotheses, findings, and generalizations about person and environment. Space will not permit doing that here. The purpose of this section is to indicate some of the larger, higher-order issues and principles involved in an ecological approach to behavior.

began. Many results of this worldwide experiment are now in, and we have observed (a) new, larger outbreaks of insect pests due to the killing, by the insecticides, of their natural predators; (b) explosive emergence of insect strains that are resistant to even the most advanced insecticides; and (c) the accumulation of high concentrations of insecticides sufficient to do great harm to and threaten the survival of many top carnivores, such as birds of prey and, perhaps, even man. Two things stand out in retrospect. One is that this technological intrusion was mobilized, at least in part, to help someone and to enhance habitability. We cannot question the intentions of the agents of the intrusion. However, the second aspect is that large-scale, *unanticipated* results cropped up everywhere, results that are in some ways worse than the original conditions. There is something pervasively wrong with our understanding of environment-inhabitant systems and the impact of singular intrusions into those systems.

The second example is the building of the Aswan Dam on the Nile River:

> . . . Its purposes were laudable—to provide a regular supply of water for irrigation, to prevent disastrous floods, and to provide electrical power for a primitive society. Other effects, however, were simply not taken into account. The annual flood of the Nile had brought a supply of rich nutrients to the eastern Mediterranean Sea, renewing its fertility; fishermen had long depended upon this annual cycle. Since the Aswan Dam put an end to the annual flood with its load of nutrients, the annual bloom of phytoplankton in the eastern Mediterranean no longer occurs. Thus the food chain from phytoplankton to zooplankton to fish has been broken; and the sardine fishery, once producing eighteen thousand tons per year . . . has dropped to about five hundred tons per year.
>
> Another ecological effect of the dam has been the replacement of an intermittent flowing stream with a permanent stable lake. This has allowed aquatic snails to maintain large populations, whereas before the dam was built they had been reduced each year during the dry season. Because irrigation supports larger human populations, there are now many more people living close to these stable bodies of water. The problem here is that the snails serve as intermediate hosts of the larvae of a blood fluke. The larvae leave the snail and bore into humans, infecting the liver and other organs. This causes the disease called schistosomiasis. The species of snail which lives in stable water harbors a more virulent species of fluke than that found in another species of snail in running water. Thus, the lake behind the Aswan Dam has increased both the incidence and virulence of schistosomiasis among the people of the upper Nile. [Murdoch & Connell, 1970, p. 57. Quoted by permission.]

Taken together, these examples of unpleasant and unanticipated results on a large scale point to several important issues. One is that our humane efforts humane efforts to enhance living conditions, whether by ridding areas of insects or by building up the industrial base, agricultural base, land use, and standard of living of an area, often go awry in the most vexing ways. Second, and more important, we simply do not have enough basic understanding of environmental systems. In the insecticide and Aswan Dam cases, we are now quite sure that they are ecological phenomena whose complexity was not anticipated because we know now what happened—we know the principles that govern such events. Immensely complicated, extended, and expensive studies may well be required, especially when long-term ecological phenomena need elucidation. Many eye-catching examples could be mentioned about which we now know a great deal. I cannot point to any examples in human social behavior that have that degree of clarity, but I am betting that there are such phenomena. The mere *possibility* of their existence is enough to give me pause.

B. Subtle Interdependencies

Consider the following story, for which I am indebted to Robert B. Lockard.[3] An ornithologist with a European zoo wished to add a small, rare bird, called the bearded tit, to the zoo's collection. Noting that other attempts to maintain the bird in captivity had been unsuccessful, he invested a great deal of time and painstaking effort to summarizing what was known about the tit's habitat and life style. Armed with all this information, including many photographs, the ornithologist built an extensive setting for the tits in his zoo, being careful to include exactly the right proportion and distribution of shrubs, trees, grasses, rocks, and lighting. After the designed environment satisfied him, he introduced a male and female to it. He noted that, by all reasonable indicators, the birds loved it. They sang, ate, drank, flitted about, groomed, mated, built an appropriate nest, laid eggs, hatched babies, and fed them. If birds can be said to enjoy their environments, then, by all these behavioral criteria, the ornithologist had created an environment whose habitability the bearded tits enjoyed thoroughly.

Within a day or two, however, the zookeeper came to check the tits, only to find the babies dead on the ground. Since the parents were still so clearly enjoying themselves, he assumed that some accident or illness had befallen the infants, and he waited for the reproductive cycle to recur. When a new brood was hatched, the ornithologist observed carefully and found, to his dismay, that after a day or two the parents pushed the babies out of the nest, onto the ground, where they died. This cycle, beginning with mating and ending with the babies dead on the ground, repeated itself over and over again, and the ornithologist realized that he had somehow created an environment so *un*habitable that he would not be able to keep tits in captivity unless he brought in successive wild-born babies or changed the captive environment in some fundamental way.

He tried modifications, but none forestalled the infanticide. Finally, in desperation, he went back out to observe tits in the wild. After many hours of observation, he noted three clear patterns of behavior. One was that throughout most of

---

[3]If the story has lost or gained anything in the present use, the fault is mine. Lockard's recent paper (1971) on the "fall of comparative psychology" also offers strong corroboration of many of the present arguments.

the daylight hours the parent tits were almost frantically active at finding and bringing food for the infants. Second, the infants, with whose food demands the parents could hardly keep pace, spent the same hours with their mouths open, apparently crying for food. The third pattern was that any inanimate object, whether eggshell, leaf, or beetle shell, was quickly shoved out of the nest by the parents.

With these observations in mind, the ornithologist went back to observe his captive tits and what he found astounded him because of its subtlety, and yet its clarity. During the short time a new brood of infants lived, the parents spent only brief periods feeding them by racing between the nest and the food supply, which the ornithologist had supplied in abundance. After a few moments of such feeding, the infants, apparently satiated, fell asleep. The first time the infants slept for any length of time during the daylight hours, the parents shoved them—two inanimate objects, after all—out of the nest. When, by making the food supply *less* abundant and *less* accessible, the ornithologist made the parents work much longer and harder to find food, he found that the infants spent more daylight time awake, demanding food, and that the tits then produced many families and cared for them to maturity.

There are several important implications of this story. The first implication is the subtlety and elusiveness of the interdependencies among (a) some aspects of a total environment, (b) the ongoing, short-range social behavior of the birds, and (c) some long-range outcome. The second is that all the good will in the world and even the designer's deep love for the inhabitants did not ensure his creating the right environment. We need to remind ourselves continually that good intentions by environmental agents and social engineers do *not* necessarily ensure habitability. The third implication is more complex and has to do with the criteria we use in making inferences about environments. All the indicators in the behavior of the parent tits suggested that their captive environment was congenial and hospitable and that it fulfilled their needs. Yet, the long-range criterion of survival of the captive representatives of the species pointed to a very different conclusion about the environment. The implication is that day-to-day and moment-by-moment behavioral criteria, as well as indicators or expressions of enjoyment, comfort, and satisfaction, can be very misleading indicators of how functional an environment is. Indeed, if we can think anthropomorphically a bit longer, or if we think of human counterparts of the environmental conditions that ensured survival here, the parent birds probably enjoyed the ease and comfort of the first captive environment much more than the effort and strain required by the second environment. The parents had to work and strain much harder in the second environment than in the first, but their babies *survived* in the second and *not* in the first. We must pick and choose our criteria with the greatest care, perhaps flying in the face of what common sense and accepted social wisdom tell us is humane, important, and worthwhile. Many practitioners of behavior modification recognize this principle, but I am chagrined to note how often we depend upon short-term attitudinal measures and verbal expressions for making our judgments. For many purposes, such expressions may be the least important behavioral indicators.

The last implication points to methodology. I take it, since it involves behavior and behavior–environment relations, that the case of the bearded tit and its human analogs would be of direct interest to the psychologist. And yet, our traditional methods of research on humans hardly put us in a position to elucidate the real-life interdependencies of behaviors and environments. Psychologists have been talking about the environment for at least 100 years, but we cannot talk to designers because we do not really know much about environments (Willems, 1967a; Winkel, 1970). We say that systems concepts, complex dependencies, reciprocity, and time-related cycles must be entertained as descriptive and explanatory terms, but they almost never show up in the actual reports of our research. By and large, we continue to study the phenomena of behavioral development as if they were simple, single-file, and relatively static.

C. More Direct Examples

The behavior of the predators of lemmings in Alaska is also instructive (Sears, 1969). Lemmings, living and breeding under the snow, have a kind of pulsating population record, in which high and low density alternate in fairly regular fashion. When the snow melts, they are preyed upon by a variety of animals, such as the Arctic fox, the snowy owl, and the jaeger, a kind of sea hawk resembling a gull. When the lemming population is low or average, the jaegers space their nests and consume their prey in orderly fashion. But when the lemming population is at its peak, so that food is no problem, there is a great deal of fighting over nesting space and food among the jaegers. Few of them raise normal broods and their numbers decline, but not from lack of food. Plenty is not the road to biological success among the jaegers and their behavioral development is somehow involved in this paradox. Again, the governing principles, the interdependencies, are little understood.

Several years ago, Proshansky, Ittelson, and Rivlin, in an architecturally oriented study, attempted to increase the therapeutic effectiveness of psychiatric facilities through appropriate design (Proshansky, Ittelson, & Rivlin, 1970, Chaps. 3, 43). They focused their efforts on one ward of a state mental hospital—a ward with severely disturbed adult women. The ward was laid out on one long corridor, with a nurses' station at one end, near the entrance, and a solarium at the other end, with bedrooms, a bathroom, and a day-room in between. When the psychologists came, the solarium, which was meant to be a place of relaxation and recreation, was overheated, poorly furnished, and generally unappealing, with intense sunlight pouring in through a bank of uncovered windows. It was used very little, even though there was a TV set there. Just about the only thing patients did consistently in the solarium was to stand alone for long periods of time in a state of preoccupation, detachment, and with-drawal—that singular behavior pattern in which severely disturbed persons engage so much. This isolated standing was precisely one of the behavior patterns that the hospital staff wished to change.

The psychologists changed the solarium markedly by adding furniture, drapes, and many other small accessories. Immediately, larger numbers of patients began spending longer periods of time there and the solarium took on the air of a pleasant recreational and social area. More importantly, the rate of isolated standing behavior went down so that very little of it was now occurring in the solarium. The psychologists had achieved their purpose—for the solarium. However, all they had succeeded in doing was to change the *location* of the isolated standing behavior—a great deal of it now took place at the other end of the corridor, by the nurses' station. Luckily, these environmental agents did not restrict their focus to the solarium, but studied a whole environ-ment–behavior *system*, of which the solarium was only one component. Creating the environment conditions for damping down the level of troubling behavior in one part of the system had only shifted the troubling behavior to another part.

Shalom Vineberg, William LeCompte, and I are involved in an extensive program of research at the Texas Institute for Rehabilitation and Research, a comprehensive rehabilitation facility in Houston, Texas. Adults with lesions of the spinal cord, resulting in severe functional impairments, are our target population. We are searching (a) for quantitative behavioral indicators of progress in rehabilitation, (b) for the ways in which the hospital's system of health care links with the patients, and (c) for the ways in which these relationships change over time. In this exercise in the microecology of social behavior, we have confronted some very complicated and elusive problems. For example, we are just now trying to understand why our measures of patients' behavioral independence, initiative, and zest, retrieved from direct observations, wax and wane so dramatically when the patients change from one hospital setting to another, from one type of social encounter to another, and from one type of activity to another (LeCompte, 1970; LeCompte & Willems, 1970; Vineberg & Willems, 1971; Willems, 1970). It appears that differences between hospital settings account for far more variance in patient independence and zest than differences between patients. Clarifying this multifaceted issue is important, not only because it will elucidate the processes by which the hospital does its work, but also because we want to know what will be affected when the hospital carries out some of its planned changes in facilities and programs. We have come to questions and findings such as these because we are working within an ecological perspective and because we decided not to use the most widely used techniques for studying the disabled adult, but rather to observe him as if for the first time, as if he were a strange organism.

Some years ago, New York City police, in work with gangs, engaged in a program of intervention whose purpose was to break up the gangs and their fighting behavior. Several troublesome and unanticipated phenomena accompanied their systematic intervention: outbreaks of vandalism, isolated drug-taking, feelings of alienation, and serious crimes of assault (Philip G. Zimbardo, personal communication, 1971).[4] These phenomena beg for further research, but if the accompanying phenomena can be attributed to the intervention, then they point again to the system-like complexity of behavioral phenomena.

At City College of New York in 1965, a student snack bar was closed for several months in midyear to permit remodeling. On the basis of first-hand observation and tallies of seating patterns and occupancy before and after the closing, it was possible to ascertain that the proportions of occupancy by blacks and whites and the cross-racial seating patterns that had reached a very high level of stability before the closing never reinstated themselves afterward (Zimbardo, 1966).

On a smaller, more molecular scale, we have known for years that whole structures of cognitions, impressions, judgments, and interpersonal behaviors can be changed by substituting one word in the introduction of a person (Asch, 1946; Kelley, 1965). A similar alteration in one word in the brief biography introducing an experimenter can produce strong differences in the verbal conditioning performance of a subject (Sapolsky, 1960). Furthermore, we suspect now that we can produce or eliminate the group-induced shift toward risk on demand by adding and deleting one word in the instructions given to subjects (Clark & Willems, 1969).

D. Some General Implications

If we think of the implications of such phenomena and what they suggest—and I emphasize, *suggest*—about human behavior in general, and if we think, especially, about the new and recent emphasis upon applied psychology and functioning as change agents in the world of everyday affairs, the following striking observation emerges: Though we are, by now, very conservative and sophisticated about introducing new biotic elements and new chemicals into our ecological systems, we display almost childish irresponsibility in our attitudes toward behavioral and behavioral–environmental systems (or should I say "adolescent" irresponsibility—perhaps we have grown up a *little* bit). I am thinking here about many of our favorite sacred cows: (a) intensive psychotherapy upon single,

---

[4] I am grateful to Philip G. Zimbardo for his patient reading and evaluation of an earlier version of the present arguments, for his enthusiasm and encouragement, and for citing this example for inclusion.

perhaps arbitrarily selected members of social and behavioral networks; (b) poverty programs; (c) social change programs, in which simplistic measures of attitudes or values provide the criteria of change; (d) managerial and industrial consultations, in which we intrude arbitrarily into organizational–behavioral systems about which we know little; and (e) yes, even that most solidly empirical of sacred cows—the operant approach to the modification of behavior. Applied behavior modification is a strikingly simple and successful technology of behavior change. Along with a few physiological and pharmacological techniques, it is probably the most precisely successful technology available today. However, its precision and specifiability depend largely upon its application to single dimensions of behavior, one at a time, and the questions of larger and unintended effects within the interpersonal and environmental contexts and over long periods of time beg for evaluation and research. Lessons learned in other areas suggest that we should always be sensitive to "other" effects of single-dimensional intrusions. This is one reason why, in answer to Donald Baer's question, "Why wait to control the developmental sequence" (Chapter 9 in this volume), I would say, "Because we know so little about the phenomena from which you are selecting a few things to control."

There is a rather folksy principle making the rounds of ecological circles that says: *We can never do merely one thing* (Hardin, 1969). Wishing to kill insects, we may put an end to the singing of birds. Wishing to "get there" faster, we insult our lungs with smog. Wishing to know what is happening everywhere in the world at once, we may create an information overload against which the mind rebels. Wishing to increase administrative and educational efficiency and institutional viability by making public schools large, we diminish the rate of participation, the sense of social obligation, and the responsibility that students develop (Baird, 1969; Barker & Gump, 1964; Wicker, 1968, 1969; Willems, 1967b). Wishing to increase the rate of emission of sociable play and decrease the rate of petulant crying in children, we may create altogether new behavior problems. Who knows?

The counterargument often is, "Don't try to immobilize us with all that alarmist talk. We'll deal with side-effects when they come up. After all, we're not stupid!" However, when we think in terms of environment–behavior *systems*, we can see that there is a fundamental misconception embedded in that popular term, "side-effects" (Hardin, 1969). This phrase means, roughly, "effects which I hadn't foreseen, or don't want to think about." What we so glibly call "side-effects" no more deserve the adjective, "side," than does the "principal" effect—they are all aspects of the interdependencies which we need so badly to understand. However, it is hard to think in terms of systems and we eagerly warp our language to protect ourselves and our favorite approaches from the necessity of thinking in terms of interdependent systems. It is quite foreign to us to think of the physical and behavioral environment as inextricable parts of the life processes of organisms and as relating to them in ways that are complex beyond our wildest dreams. Perhaps, though, we will have to.

By now, we should sense the emerging meaninglessness of one of our favorite concepts—the concept of *independence*. Independence forms the very bedrock of most of our models for statistical inference, sampling, and experimental analysis. I am arguing that just the opposite characterizes many of the phenomena we should be studying and that we should study them in ways that assume the opposite.

For the student of behavior, there is much to be learned from this emerging ecological orientation, but if the lessons are learned, then there is an immediate and pervasive need for an expansion of perspective. It seems to me that before we can really play the game of designing and arranging human living conditions, we must know much more about the principles that characterize and govern the environmental systems into which such arrangements must, of necessity, intrude. Seeking that knowledge raises a host of theoretical, metatheoretical, and methodological problems. Many problems of the environment and human behavior need immediate attention, but I think that we should not confuse human ecology and the search into understanding behavioral ecology with social service. The search for understanding is not a missionary endeavor (Darling, 1969); it is a quest for information and insight. We also need a great deal more insight into environments than we now have, before we do the environmental missionary work.

One implication of this line of argument may well be a conservatism with regard to intervention in behavior–environment systems and the clear hint that the most adaptive form of action may sometimes be *in*action. However, if we give these examples and their lessons a slight interpretive twist, we arrive at a second implication that is, perhaps, even more important. This is the clear suggestion that we need a great deal more basic research and theoretical understanding that takes account of the ecological, system-like principles that permeate the phenomena of behavior and environment. Commenting on what he calls the "fall of comparative psychology," Lockard says (1971):

> The whole enterprise of comparative psychology worked itself into an extremely narrow position, scientifically speaking, by ignoring all but a tiny fraction of the behavior of animals and incorporating an elaborate set of premises about animal behavior into a dogmatic tradition [p. 169].

It is entirely possible that an ecological perspective and research guided by it will provide the means to avoid a similar misfortune for other areas of psychology.

E. Key Aspects of the Ecological Perspective

I have not offered a precise definition of the ecological perspective on behavior. I shall resist that temptation to the bitter end, partly because that perspective is elusive and difficult to define, but more importantly, because it is not *a* theory or *a* method. It is just what I have suggested—a general orientation or viewpoint which leads one to view behavior and development and research upon them in certain ways. However, it is only fair that I highlight what I view as some of the earmarks or characteristics of the ecological perspective for psychology. Here they are, in the form of a list, with little amplification and with no regard to order of importance.

First, the ecological perspective on behavior places a great deal of emphasis upon the *mutual* and interdependent relations among the organism, its behavior, and its environment. Craik (1970), Barker (1965, 1969), and Gump (1968, 1969) have discussed what this means and most of the examples I have cited address this issue. The arguments regarding *strong interactions* by Riegel and by Overton and Reese (Chapters 1 and 4, respectively, in this volume) are closely related.

Second, this perspective is largely naturalistic in its methodological orientation. I say "largely" because it is not defined by any particular technique and because I am pointing to an emphasis rather than a necessary condition. The ecologist's methodological statement of faith has two parts. With the Brelands (1966), the ecologist says, ". . . you cannot understand the behavior of the animal in the laboratory unless you understand his behavior in the wild [p. 20]." And, contrary to widely held canons, the ecologist believes that the investigator should manipulate and control only as much as is absolutely necessary to answer his questions clearly, an argument which Menzel (1969) and Lockard (1971) have made so well. The ecologist works with the continual reminder that holding constant experimental conditions while varying a limited phenomenon is a figment of the experimental laboratory which may result in the untimely attenuation of both findings and theories.

Third, the ecological psychologist assumes and *acts* on the assumption that the phenomena of psychology participate in a much larger network of phenomena, descriptions, and disciplines. Thus, ecology tends to be highly eclectic and the ecologist tends to borrow and lend concepts, methods, and hypotheses freely, with little sense of preciousness about boundaries between disciplines.

Fourth, the ecological perspective tends, generally, to place more emphasis upon *molar* phenomena than upon *molecular* ones. Closely related is a relative emphasis upon environmental, behavioral, and organismic holism and simultaneous, complex relationships. This is so in part because, all the way from survival of a species, through adaptive functioning, down to day-to-day and moment-by-moment adaptive processes, the emphasis is upon the organism's and the population's behavioral commerce with the environmental packages they inhabit.

Fifth, this perspective concerns itself with the distribution of phenomena in nature; upon the range, intensity, and frequency of behavior in the everyday, investigator-free environment. Space does not permit the elaboration of this misleadingly simple, but controversial issue (see Barker, 1965, 1968, 1969;

McGuire, 1969; Willems, 1969; Wright, 1969–1970), but King (1970) has documented its importance for behavioral ecology. One vivid and current example on which such descriptive research would shed a great deal of light is the study of bystander behavior, social responsibility, and helping. As is so common in social psychology, following the pioneering work of Latane and Darley (1970), investigators have rushed to the experimental analysis of variables that influence the likelihood of bystander intervention in crises, but the field is muddled greatly because we know so little about *where* intervention and helping occur. The result is that, instead of a concerted attack upon an important social phenomenon, ·ve have another spooky phenomenon—now we have it; now we don't.

Sixth, the ecological perspective concerns itself with one of the great voids in modern American psychology—the problem of taxonomy. What are the units of environment and behavior? Into what types of classification do situations, behaviors, and environments fall? As Sells (e.g., 1969) and Barker (1969) have pointed out, basic taxonomic research is especially critical when we become involved in applied problems and mission-oriented research.

Seventh, the ecological perspective devotes a great deal of effort to the question of *habitability*; that is, to the issue of what kinds of environments are fit for human beings to inhabit. The ecologist does this not only because it sets the stage for applied environmental design and social engineering, but also because he believes that when he leaves his preoccupation with measures of time, latency, errors, number of trials, thresholds, and molecular physiology and concerns himself with such messy problems as safety, convenience, comfort, satisfaction, long-term functional achievement, adaptation, and cost, he may well be on the most direct path to basic theoretical understanding (see Chapanis, 1967).

Eighth, and closely related to what I have already suggested, the ecologist is much more willing than many of his peers to favor working from the complex to the simple as his strategy of choice and to accept complicated, intact phenomena as his arena.

Ninth, as Craik has pointed out (1970), the ecological perspective has a varying, but unmistakable undercurrent of direct moral concern and involvement in prescriptive and proscriptive guidelines for human action. The ecologist reasons that such issues cannot be avoided anyway, so he welcomes them and makes them part of his work.

Tenth, in keeping with the characteristics of behavior–environment systems and the kinds of behavioral dimensions with which he often works (e.g., adaptations, accommodation, functional achievement, long-range behavior, and sometimes even survival), the ecologist not only allows, but sometimes demands, unusually long time periods and time dependencies in his research. Over and above the more traditional search for early antecedents, such long-range research might take the form of monitoring interdependencies continuously, or nearly continuously, for extended periods of time.

Eleventh and last, the ecological psychologist is more willing than psychology as a whole to depend upon rate measures across whole populations in drawing conclusions. I suspect that Americans and American psychologists are used to getting excited only about *whopper* effects; we tend to respond most readily to large increases and decreases in things. We are used to viewing things as effective or ineffective, important or unimportant, good or bad only if they lead to big changes in rate. Another way of saying this is that we do not view things from an ecological perspective. The ecologist lets himself view certain matters in terms of whole populations and in terms of small changes in *rates* in those populations. Small changes in percentages or even fractions of percentages in such phenomena as tuberculosis, metallic poisoning, bubonic plague, cholera, or schistosomiasis can bear unambiguous information that something is afoot in the environment and in the relationships among persons and · the environment. If this is so, then why should it be different with social and behavioral phenomena? Does nearly everyone in a population have to be involved in rape, murder, suicide, drug addiction, alcoholism, assault, irritability, depression, malaise, uncooperativeness, or lack of social amenity before we conclude that there is something fundamentally wrong with the environment or with the interaction of that population with it? I dare say not. However, we are not prepared to take rate measures seriously enough; we know so little about the general adaptive and maladaptive value of behavioral phenomena; and we do not yet have the models and theories that lead us to depend upon such rate measures. These are ecological problems, and I would assert that they are ecological problems for psychology.

IV. Experimental Analysis

Even with a few obvious aspects of oversimplification, a brief characterization of experimental analysis is in order.[5]

To many students of behavior, experimental analysis is the highest and most fruitful form of activity to which the psychologist can aspire. Most professionals qualify their enthusiasm for the experimental method with recognition of the complexity of behavior. However, even though a great deal of human activity does not lend itself at present to experimental analysis, many psychologists believe that the most important issues in complex behavior will one day be solved through experimental procedures. Despite the qualifiers and doubts that have been raised about this set of beliefs (Brandt, in press; Chapanis, 1967;

[5]Two things should be kept in mind here: (a) I am describing a procedural orientation, rather than a substantive one, on the assumption that experimental psychology is not a content area or even a set of content areas. This makes it quite different from the ecological perspective and this difference is precisely one which I hope the present paper will sharpen. (b) Since the experimental mode is so widely known and accepted, it is unnecessary to make an extended presentation.

Willems & Raush, 1969), experimental analysis still resides at the top of our procedural pecking order.

"In psychology, as in any science, the heart of the experimental method is the direct control of the thing studied. When we say, 'let us do an experiment' we mean, 'Let us do something and see what happens.' The order is important: we do something first and then see what happens [Skinner, 1947, p. 20]." What the investigator *makes* happen and what he allows or does not allow to happen are the major stylistic earmarks of the experiment. In other words, an experiment is a *deliberately* contrived, simplified, and artificial situation in which the investigator varies some factors and minimizes the functioning of other factors in which he is not interested in order to measure changes in behavior that result from what he manipulates. The experiment is generally characterized by purposeful limitation of complexity and the optimal setting for the experiment is a special location chosen and arranged by the investigator. All of these procedural strengths, sometimes executed partially and sometimes totally, lead investigators to the experiment as the strategy of choice, sometimes in principle and sometimes because their phenomena cannot be studied by any other means. Control is the guiding principle, and precision of inference and test are the accompaniments. Each of the major dimensions of the experiment—degree of manipulation of independent variables, degree of control over other variables, and degree of restriction and demarcation of the dependent variables—can vary from study to study, but the underlying logic remains the same: control as much as possible. Depending upon the investigator's purpose, these very strengths of the experiment can become its greatest liabilities (Breland & Breland, 1966; Campbell & Stanley, 1966; Willems & Raush, 1969), but cataloging those problems is not part of the present purpose. The major purpose is to explore the integration of experimental analysis with the ecological perspective.

V. More Than Courtship

Metaphors have a way of losing usefulness and applicability rather quickly in science. However, the courtship metaphor might serve a bit longer here because it indicates the kind of relationship between ecology and experimentation beyond which we can grow and, I believe, *must* grow.

I have argued that the ecological perspective on behavior places much emphasis upon complex and system-like regularities and interdependencies (often of a surprising and unanticipated nature and often on a large scale and on a long temporal sequence) among organism, behavior, and environment, and that it has a great deal that is profound and important to offer the behavioral sciences. Second, I have argued that this orientation is not primarily a procedural or methodological one, even though it might have many implications **for** methodology. Finally, I have argued that its domain is not defined by any one model or theory.

In a very real sense, characterizing the ecological perspective in this fashion erases the problem of integration with experimental analysis. The ecological perspective is a multifaceted and demanding, but, most crucially, a highly pluralistic one. Elucidation of ecological issues not only begs for, but, perhaps, *requires* methodological and procedural pluralism, a highly cooperative and interdependent procedural attack on its problems, a maturing beyond the ingratiation and billing and cooing that characterize courtship.

Such assertions and statements of faith are still too abstract. In order to make the argument more concrete, one working assumption must be made explicit. I assume that psychological research is a quest and that investigations of behavior are after something. I assume that the faith of those persons whose interests and activities constitute that diverse aggregate, "psychological research," is that they are contributing to the understanding of behavior in everyday affairs—in nature, so to speak—and that it is this faith that keeps the work going, no matter how esoteric and rarified it may appear at any particular time. Given that, there are three general forms of acceptance of pluralism and integration that I wish to mention.

A. Procedural Cross-Seeding

The first general form is quite familiar and is illustrated by many examples in the literature. This is the case in which one investigator or several independent investigators converge upon their phenomenon of interest or test its generality under the simple strategy: "I wonder what would happen if I changed the conditions" in terms of measures, manipulations, subjects, background variables, or locations. One of the common modes is to compare the results of shifts from lab to natural setting, or vice versa. The conceptual and paradigmatic grounds for cross-situational inferences are often very loose and sketchy, but I mention this form of interplay because it reflects the celebration of pluralism and the hope of substantive progress through an interplay of procedures.

One example of this strategy is Hall and Williams' (1966) investigation of decision-making in groups. Following the long tradition of laboratory analysis of groups, Hall and Williams staged a decision problem for 20 ad hoc groups, groups whose members were randomly assigned from a subject pool. However, they extended the research to include 20 established, intact groups of management trainees on the same decision problems. The ad hoc groups differed markedly from the intact groups in the process of making decisions, the way they dealt with conflict, and in the final products of their deliberations.

Against the background of extensive laboratory research on the perception of size and distance, Brunswik (Postman & Tolman, 1959) found a nearly perfect correlation between physical size of objects and judgments of their linear dimensions in the everywhere environment.

At a more formal level, Bijou, Peterson, and Ault (1968) have outlined a strategy for the interdependent use of naturalistic observation and experimentation. Even though their proposal has severe limitations, it represents a clear emphasis upon procedural cross-seeding.

B. Ecologically Oriented Experimentation

The second form of integration is more unidirectional and more stringent, but also more critical from an ecological viewpoint. In this mode, as Lockard (1971) points out, a new role is emerging for the experiment. This strategy assumes that the many ". . . behavioral adaptations of animals and how these fit particulars of the habitat in which they evolved have a much higher probability of detection in the field [p. 175]." Many of the hunches thus derived can be explored in the natural setting of the field, but, at times, the experimental laboratory is the only feasible location for testing other problems.

The sticky issue here is that, ". . . since animals match their environments, but mismatch the laboratory, severe distortions of behavior are common [p. 175]." In order to eliminate these artifacts, the circumstances of the laboratory must be made to duplicate the natural conditions as closely as possible and must be checked and rechecked for correspondence. This strategy

> . . . allows problems to originate in the real world, avoiding the expenditure of effort on laboratory-born problems which may be irrelevant . . . allows a happy marriage of field and laboratory procedures, exploiting the best of each . . . and it allows the investigator to see how his animal functions in its world, not his [Lockard, 1971, p. 175].

Remembering the assumption that our long-range goal is to understand how the organism normally functions and not only in what he can be made to do takes some of the sting of ecological imperialism and unidirectionality out of this strategy. A great deal of empirical and procedural substance is given to this position by Breland and Breland (1966). The exciting work of Kavanau (1964, 1969) on rodents in ecologically oriented laboratory settings and Hess and Petrovich's ecological–contextual experimentation with ducks (Chapter 2 in this volume) show how it can be done. The case of the bearded tit cited earlier also exemplifies the underlying issues.

C. Pursuit of an Ecological Hypothesis

Perhaps the highest form of integration is found in the pluralistic, but converging attack on an ecological hypothesis. Here, the many-sided activities and findings of an investigator, a team of investigators, or even independent investigators, converge to elucidate a model, hypothesis, or problem that is ecological in flavor. This convergence can come about intentionally or unintentionally. Rather than extend the abstract characterization of this strategy, I shall illustrate it with three examples.

1. Edging

Menzel (1969) reports a program of research on responsiveness to objects and structures in free-ranging primates, a program that can be described as microecological in flavor. Menzel's account is full of discoveries and hypotheses about contextual and environmental aspects of behavior that should give the animal researcher pause, including some fundamental questions about the concepts of *stimulus* and *response*. Through an extended series of remote and first-hand observations, as well as semiexperimental tests, Menzel formulated the hypothesis of *edge effects*: That the edges and ends of structures and patterned concatenations of discrete objects provide the orientation and locations for overwhelming amounts of the individual and communal behavior of primates in the natural habitat. To test this hypothesis and converge on its tenability, Menzel engaged in a pluralistic, but interdependent set of activities.

Naturalistic observation on Cayo Santiago supported the hypothesis. On manmade structures, on rocks, along trails, and at tree lines, the percentages of instances in which sitting, lying, standing, or walking took place at the edges were very high. Furthermore, monkeys tended to locate and cluster at the edges of clearings. Menzel then explored the hypothesis experimentally by taking eight randomly-spaced cinder blocks and placing them in two closely spaced rows of four in a clearing. Out of the first 100 monkeys who approached, 78 sat on or touching an edge of this new structure and the other 22 sat near them. Thus, these primates use only a very small fraction of available space, and the way in which objects are *patterned* seems to be the element of the habitat that governs much of this use.

Space does not permit the delights of reviewing more of Menzel's program, including his generalizations back to the laboratory. The important point for present purposes is that the pursuit of an ecological hypothesis involved the convergent use of various procedures, including experimental analysis, even if in crude form.

2. Location and Role Judgment

In the program of research on persons hospitalized with spinal cord injuries mentioned earlier, we have come upon another curious phenomenon. Despite the best efforts by occupational therapists at professionalism, orientation toward treatment, and communication of their purposes and rationales to patients, patients invariably see occupational therapy as fun and games, time-filling, and entertaining arts and crafts (Vineberg, 1970; Vineberg & Levine, 1969), a tendency that we have measured through interviews regarding hospital roles. Contrary to the most popular hypothesis around the hospital, which is that this happens because the occupational therapists are very unsure and ambiguous in the execution of their roles and communicate badly, we are now quite sure that the manner in which the patients perceive occupational therapy is linked to the *location* in which the occupational therapists work and interact with the patients. Occupational therapy occupies one part of an L-shaped room. The other part is the recreational area, which houses a great deal of recreational equipment and in which patients and staff members (including occupational therapists) spend a good deal of time playing games. Not only do patients have visual access to the recreational area while in occupational therapy, but our systematic observations of patients show that, before and after occupational therapy hours, patients are often left to wait in the area between occupational therapy and recreation, and that they often spend one hour in one place and the very next hour in the other. Our hypothesis is that this juxtaposition of location, the blurring of setting boundaries, and the frequent merging of behavioral sequences combine to determine the patients' judgments and perceptions of the occupational therapist's role. If we are right, then even a massive effort devoted to shoring up the occupational therapists' communicative skills and modifying patients' cognitions directly would not alleviate the problem. We hope to test our hypothesis experimentally through a sequence of interventions involving a portable room divider, a different waiting area, and a rearrangement of patient schedules for occupational therapy and recreation. This is a small-scale ecological-contextual issue, to be sure, but it illustrates the convergent analysis of an ecological issue through the integration of interviews, naturalistic observation of behavior, and experimentation.

3. Attenuation of Social Involvement

Perhaps more interesting from the systematic, ecological standpoint is the converging set of findings, from a wide array of studies, that demonstrate the relationship between size and density of groups and populations on the one hand and the rate of participation in social-behavioral tasks and opportunities on the other. The pattern of findings can only be highlighted here.

In the short-term microcosm of the experiment, increases in group size or available participants produce attenuation of social involvement. Latane and Darley (1970) found that as the number of witnesses available to intervene in a crisis increases, the likelihood of intervention decreases and the latency of intervention increases. When Moede (1927) increased the number of persons per side in a tug-of-war, he found that total amount of pull *per side* increased, but that the average pull *per person* decreased dramatically. Calhoun (1967) found that increasing population size and crowding among rats led to dramatic decreases in indices of social interplay.

In real-life classrooms, Dawe (1934) found that increases in class size led to (a) decreases in total amount of discussion, (b) decreases in percentage of children who participated, and (c) decreases in average amount of participation per child.

Naturalistic studies of public schools show that as school size increases, (a) the number of students available per school activity increases and (b) the average rate of actual participation in activities decreases, especially participation in leadership functions (see Barker & Gump, 1964; Wicker, 1968). Baird (1969) has replicated these findings for a nationwide sample and Wicker (1969), Wicker and Mehler (1971), Indik (1963, 1965) and Ingham (1970) have extended them to churches and business organizations and across a wide range of behavioral indicators.

A similar finding emerges even when the comparisons are made between large and small towns. Wright (1969–1970), in observations and quasi-experimental studies, has found that rates of participation and social interaction are higher for small-town children than for large-town children. Milgram (1970), in a series of studies involving staged encounters and requests for aid, has found small-town dwellers to be much more likely to offer aid than city dwellers.

Beyond the short-term and immediate behavioral effects of variations in number of people, there are also short-range aftereffects. Reported satisfactions vary as a function of participation in small and large groups (Willems, 1964). Students in small schools report more action-oriented satisfaction than students in large schools (Gump & Friesen, 1964; Wicker, 1968). Members of sparsely populated environments retain richer, more detailed recollections and cognitive representations of the environments (Wicker, 1969; Wright, 1969–1970). Students in small schools develop a stronger sense of behavioral obligation than do students in large schools (Willems, 1967b).

However, the picture becomes even more intriguing when we consider the possibility of long-range correlates. Robert A. Aldrich (personal communication, 1971) reported that persons who grew up in small towns and attended small schools tend to be over-represented among business executives and organizational leaders. Davis (1966) reported that students in small schools tend to select careers that are more ambitious and demanding than students in large schools. In the sample of subjects who participated in one of their studies of bystander behavior and intervention, Latane and Darley (1970) found a strong negative correlation between subject intervention within the experimental study and the size of the community of the subject's origin.

I have only scratched the surface of this issue, but several points stand out:

(1) The distribution of persons in relation to attenuation of social involvement is an issue for which an ecological framework can be constructed and it is an issue of some note, both on basic theoretical grounds and in terms of current and projected trends in the distribution of population and the size of population aggregates.

(2)   The phenomenon appears to have both immediate, situational compo-
       nents and cumulative, residual components and, certainly, governing
       principles at many levels that await discovery.

(3)   As Staub (1970) has indicated, involvement in relation to the presence
       of others may have some age-related developmental ingredients.

(4)   As a behavioral tendency that emerges across a wide range of situa-
       tions, across species, and within many procedural paradigms, it is
       even possible that, from an evolutionary standpoint, the attenuation
       of social involvement that accompanies group and population size
       has strong adaptive value in ways that we do not understand.

(5)   Finally, it is important to keep in mind that only a rich methodological
       pluralism has made possible the progress we see in this area. True
       experimental analysis, loosely controlled experiments, field experi-
       ments, naturalistic observation, in-depth interviews, retrospective
       interviews, staged encounters, and questionnaire studies have all con-
       tributed much. However, it is only when the whole set is taken
       together that the single contributions become clear. Considered in
       isolation, each particular study can be criticized and analyzed to
       death. Within the larger ecological perspective, we do not say that
       Study A was a bad experiment, but that it was a good naturalistic
       study; we do not say that Study B was such a tightly controlled
       experiment that its findings do not generalize, but we say that it
       offered a precise test of an explicit hypothesis. A mature ecological
       orientation does not pin its identification and hopes to any particular
       style and it does not eschew either manipulation or naturalism. It
       is neither purely descriptive, naturalistic nor purely manipulational;
       it is capable of being either or all, depending on the problem at
       hand, and it welcomes both into its set of tools.

VI. Concluding Comments

With a set of examples and analogies, I have argued that the theoretical,
investigative, and social-engineering task before us is surprisingly complicated
and demanding if we take seriously an ecological side to our science. In the
process, I have emphasized ideas and possibilities that are quite foreign to
many psychologists, perhaps even to those psychologists whose writings include
ecological arguments and terminologies. If this is so, then my response is that
we must, as a discipline, at least consider these issues with care, even if only
to *deny* that they shall be part of our discipline and its subject matter.

Next, I have argued that, when the ecological perspective is formulated properly, integration with experimental analysis presents no real problem. The argu-

ment is that progress in behavioral ecology depends upon procedural pluralism. Several examples illustrate how such progress comes about.

Kenneth Boulding (1970) has noted:

> Recently I came upon the reassuring news that the year 1910 was a crucial one in human history because this was the year when the medical profession began to do more good than harm. I wonder whether the teaching profession has reached this watershed yet [p. 38].

Whether we accept Boulding's date for the medical profession is really beside the point, because our concern should be with psychology and the processes of development. I know that the essence of science is to reduce uncertainty by discovering unifying and simplifying principles. However, it just *may* be that in the long run, the most direct and efficient path toward scientific understanding in developmental psychology will involve the timely recognition and acceptance of complexity. Perhaps more than helping us reach the point of doing more good than harm, such awareness will place us in a better position to *judge* between good and harm. Working with that awareness, achieving ecological wisdom about good and harm, will require all the methodological ingenuity and commitment we can muster.

CHAPTER 11

The Developmental Analysis of Individual Differences on Multiple Measures[1]

PAUL B. BALTES[2] AND JOHN R. NESSELROADE[2]

WEST VIRGINIA UNIVERSITY
MORGANTOWN, WEST VIRGINIA

I. Introduction

Research approaches to the study of change phenomena differ in the level of conceptual analysis used in organizing developmental products, processes, and antecedents. In principle, the distinction among various levels of analysis when studying a particular object or event is based on the propositions that: (a) there is no absolute set of criteria that specifies the level of complexity on which the analysis should be conducted, and (b) since the variables and attributes examined are construed (invented) rather than detected, differential levels of analysis are warranted and may be useful in explicating a given subject matter. Thus, a variety of scientific attacks, at different levels of complexity or molarity, should be encouraged, and no scientific model seems to warrant, exclusively, the enthusiastic support of any single level of analysis. In short, the level of conceptual analysis is not completely dictated by the precision

[1]Preparation of this paper was facilitated by a grant from the U.S. Office of Education OEG-0-9-580289-4415 (010). The authors acknowledge the valuable assistance of Gisela V. Labouvie with the bibliographic research on which this paper is based.

[2]Present address: College of Human Development, The Pennsylvania State University, University Park, Pennsylvania.

of a theory or model alone but, in addition, by the complexity of the subject matter and the intentions of the researcher.

It seems fair to conclude that the majority of prominent developmental researchers have relied on univariate, experimental approaches oriented toward the explanation or control of developmental differences in relatively specific response units. Such research, however, runs the risk of neglecting complex interactions and interrelationships among behavior systems and of presenting a fragmented picture of the developing organism. Particularly in learning approaches to the study of ontogenetic change, the emphasis is often on a selected set of age-invariant processes and mechanisms (e.g., mediation, attention) rather than on the entire behaving organism exhibiting changes in a multitude of response systems. As Coan (1966), in discussing some of the objectives of developmental research, concluded:

> . . . we must be able to discern both the interrelationships that provide an organic unity to the behavioral system at any point and those that underlie its longitudinal integrity over periods of many years. If we then seek to discover the sources of behavioral changes we are faced with the prospect of relating these changes, both to an immensely complicated system of biological processes and to an entire world of social and physical influences that impinge on an individual over time [p. 372].

Multivariate research, as a model for scientific attack, relies on three assumptions that, at least on the surface, run counter to univariate practices:

(a) Any dependent variable (or consequent) is potentially a function of multiple determinants.

(b) Any determinant or antecedent has potentially multiple consequents.

(c) The study of multiple antecedent-consequent relationships provides a useful model for the organization of complex systems.

Note that in what follows, multivariate research is not seen as being necessarily tied to a particular research strategy such as correlation. To the contrary, similar to Cronbach's (1957), Cattell's (1966a), and Coffield's (1970) positions, it is argued that the prevalent use of multivariate models as descriptive and correlational research tools is an historical accident which needs rectification. Whether multivariate research is experimental or correlational is primarily a function of the subject matter and the experimenter involved (see also Fruchter, 1966). In fact, it is one of the major intentions of this chapter to provide a set of rationales that will exert a unifying effect on the disparate sectors of research approaches inherent in correlational versus experimental and univariate versus multivariate distinctions.

II. Basic Concepts and Methods

More and more frequently one encounters assertions in the developmental literature concerning the potential usefulness of multivariate research strategies (e.g.,

Baltes & Nesselroade, 1970; Cattell, 1969; Coan, 1966; Emmerich, 1968, 1969; McCall, 1970; Nesselroade, 1970; Wohlwill, 1970b, 1971). In the present discussion we wish to circumscribe a rather limited set of multivariate approaches in order to provide ample space in which to focus on a number of intriguing substantive issues related to developmental patterns. To provide some orientation for the sequel, however, we shall digress briefly to remind the reader of a few elementary points.

A. Nature of Data Matrices

With a few notable exceptions such as P-technique factor analysis, integrating multivariate analysis procedures with most developmental-related issues can be seen to involve at least two data matrices (see Bentler, Chapter 7 in this volume). The elements in these matrices may represent scores on repeated multiple measures at two different occasions of measurement (such as age levels or pre- and posttreatment) or they may represent scores for two independent samples of subjects who differ in age or some age-correlated set of treatments. A third example occurs when one data matrix consists of scores for a set of subjects on a variety of measures and the other data matrix contains scores on the same or different measures for another group of subjects, different from the first, but who can be isomorphically identified with them, e.g., children's scores in one matrix, their parents' scores in the other. These are only a few of many possible examples, but they serve to illustrate data which are amenable to a variety of multivariate analysis procedures such as comparative factor analysis. Such paired data matrices may be examined separately, sequentially, or conjointly, depending upon the investigator's purpose.

B. Interrelationship of Multiple Measures

A second point deserving mention is that when one employs multiple measures in a research design, say n of them, there are not only n means and n variances which may be of interest. There are also $n(n - 1)/2$ covariances to be considered. Cooley and Lohnes (1971) remind us that the multivariate researcher is at least as interested in the latter as he is in the former. The use of multiple measures in research is necessary, at this point, if we are to respect the multiple determinants—multiple consequents position stated in the introduction.

It is acknowledged that change in single measures may be profitably studied. However, if one wishes to deal with more abstract concepts, such as patterned change—change in the interrelationships among a variety of measures—then a multivariate approach is necessary. It is from the interrelationships among measures (e.g., covariances), so often ignored in developmental research, that we may eventually extract the raw material that can be efficiently molded into general, but powerful constructs to aid the scientific study of development. A related point is that when research interest centers on change in more molar behavior patterns such as anxiety and aggression, no single variable can serve as a perfect indicator of the target construct. The use of multiple indicators (measures) enables us to form some combination of measures which "locates" the construct more precisely (see Cattell, 1966a, for further discussion of the merits of a multivariate approach).

C. Intraindividual and Interindividual Variation

Numerous writers have offered general definitions of, subclassifications, and a variety of techniques for separating intra- and interindividual change as distinct sources of variability. Still, there remains a number of thorny issues to be solved before both can be integrated into a consistent developmental framework. One significant trend, however, is that more and more people (e.g., Wohlwill, 1970c) are reaching the conclusion that it is the study of intraindividual change and interindividual differences in intraindividual change that constitutes the core of developmental methodology.

At the simplest level, both inter- and intraindividual variation represent variance in the ordinary sense; interindividual variation refers to differences among persons, intraindividual variation to differences within persons. Additional clarification is obtained by heeding the time dimension and construing interindividual variation as among-persons differences extant at a given point in time and intraindividual variation as differences manifest in a given person across a number of points in time. Consideration of time, however, exposes the "Achilles heel," from the developmentalist's viewpoint, of cross-sectional interindividual variation interpretations. Cross-sectionally established interindividual differences may or may not represent relatively stable attributes—no information bearing on this issue is provided in a strictly cross-sectional design. What seems certain is that measured interindividual differences over and above some amount of arbitrarily defined *initial* interindividual ones can only reflect prior intraindividual variation.

One might ask whether the demand for intraindividual change data, since their accumulation requires longitudinal analysis, lays life-span research to rest. In a way it does, since only a few researchers may become sufficiently excited to be willing to risk theirs and their successors' life satisfaction in following up a selected group of subjects (hopefully divided into various experimental and control groups) from birth to death. Here, it is argued that the generation of such long-term change data should either consist of combining several short-term longitudinal studies (see, e.g., Schaie, Chapter 12 in this volume) or be left to a few entrepreneurs who are able to secure and manage the resources for long-term research. Interpreted otherwise, this disconcerting situation decrees that acceptable alternative strategies are needed, and that more attention need be paid to such options as the analysis of simulated intraindividual change patterns (see, e.g., Baer, Chapter 9 in this volume; Baltes & Goulet, 1971), which are assumed to parallel the type of long-term change trends obtained by a few "marker" longitudinal studies.

III. Comparative Factor Analytic Models and Developmental Change

The emphasis in this chapter will be on factor-analytic models, although the writers are aware of a variety of issues (e.g., linearity and additivity assumptions, problems of factor identification and rotation, methodological artifacts, etc.) which have prevented many researchers from enthusiastically embracing factor analytic work. In fact, we share some of these concerns, but since space does not permit otherwise, we must restrict ourselves to mentioning a few of the papers that address themselves, in a critical manner, to some of the limitations inherent in factor-analytic research (e.g., Cronbach, 1967; Digman, 1966; Kallina, 1967; Nesselroade & Baltes, 1970; Nesselroade, Baltes, & Labouvie, 1971; Overall, 1964).

The use of comparative factor analysis as an analytical strategy in developmental psychology has been discussed recently by the writers and others (e.g., Baltes & Nesselroade, 1970; Cattell, 1969; Nesselroade, 1970). The major proposition is that specific factor-analytic techniques offer a powerful methodology for distinguishing between structural and quantitative changes in developmental data. The salient features of the arguments center upon the interpretation, and the unique implications of *factor loading patterns, factor scores,* and *factor intercorrelations* for studying ontogeny. The full spectrum of possibilities and their significance for developmental research is vast indeed; as yet, many remain unexplored. Some implications of such factor-analytic models for the examination of multivariate ontogenetic change will be highlighted in the next sections.

A. Factor Change Concepts

A variety of conceptual models such as stages, sequences, milestones, and differentiation have been proposed to aid us in integrating the complex features of developmental change data. Coan (1966) was one of the first to attempt a conceptual integration of factor change with ontogenetic considerations. He argued that, since the universe of behaviors that we can measure varies from one age level to another, we must accept that the behavioral expression (e.g., loading pattern) of a factor will necessarily differ across age levels even though its "basic nature" remains the same (see also Nunnally, Chapter 5 in this volume). Coan, unfortunately, did not make clear what he meant by the term *basic nature* nor how one can establish that it does, indeed, remain constant over time. He provided, however, some appealing descriptions of factor change types one might observe in idealized developmental studies.

Among the changes over time which may occur in factors, Coan (1966) defined *factor metamorphosis* as a process by which a factor would gradually change to the point that it would appear to be qualitatively different over disparate age levels, even though it is a single, historical continuity. Another factor change process proposed by Coan is called *factor emergence*—appearance of a factor at a given age level from measures that were uncorrelated at previous age levels. *Factor convergence* is defined by Coan as the process of change in which factors remain intact, but become so highly intercorrelated with increasing age that they define a single second-order factor which, at still older age levels, eventually shows up as a first-order factor. An opposite process, characterized by decreases in the degree of interrelationship among measures to the point that a factor at an earlier age breaks up into a number of uncorrelated components at a later age level, is labeled *factor disintegration*. Still other possible manifestations of factor change are presented by Coan, but the ones mentioned suffice to show the variety of possibilities to be considered in trying to account systematically for developmental change by factor analytic methods (see also Chapter 6 by Cattell).

B. Stability and Change in Factor Patterns and Factor Scores

What is currently desirable, then, are models and techniques that allow for the investigation of such change concepts. In discussing some of the models available for distinguishing between stable interindividual differences and intraindividual change, over short time periods, Nesselroade (1967b) proposed a fourfold classification of factors as follows (see also Fig. 2, p. 227):

(a) invariant loading patterns—stable factor scores
(b) invariant loading patterns—fluctuant factor scores
(c) noninvariant loading patterns—stable factor scores
(d) noninvariant loading patterns—fluctuant factor scores

As presented originally, these are descriptive statements about the conceptual nature of factors at a given point in time. One has the alternative of placing his bets, as it were, on invariance of loading patterns or on stability of factor scores, and there are a variety of models available (see Bentler's chapter) which require making an *a priori* decision as to which is of prime concern. What, in the end, is the "best" solution, depends upon the criteria (which the investigator must also select) by which the outcomes are evaluated. Of course, one does not have data to permit accurate classification of a factor in this scheme when only one occasion of measurement is involved.

Type-a factors (invariant patterns—stable scores) have the characteristics of ideal traits, in the conventional sense. The invariant patterns denote a high degree of repeatability, at least over relatively short time spans, of the interrelationships of responses. The stable factor scores indicate that subjects are maintaining their relative positions on the dimensions inferred from these highly repeatable response patterns.

Type-b factors (invariant patterns—fluctuant scores) also evince repeatable response patterns, but the fluctuant rather than stable factor scores indicate that persons do not maintain their relative positions, over time, on the factor-score continua. Factors of this type best fit the traditional notion of state dimensions. To illustrate this more clearly, we might be able to identify, with appropriate measures, a highly consistent and well-known behavior pattern for which a college student scoring high on the dimension on Saturday night would place lower on the scale on Sunday morning than his less enterprising peers. Similarly, in a life-span framework, we might assume that the variable-cluster marking the trait "dependency" exhibits age-invariance, whereas age-specific situational variations (see, e.g., Kagan & Moss, 1962) result in a fair amount of intraindividual variation, that is, low long-term stability.

Type-c factors (noninvariant patterns—stable scores) appear to have a substantive parallel in, for example, behavior patterns displayed during transition, critical, or crisis periods, etc. Suppose subjects in a sample are distributed such that on a set of conservation tasks, some consistently manage to conserve on only three, some on five or six, and some on nine or ten tasks. Regardless of the number of tasks on which they conserve, however, they succeed on different task patterns at different times. Data such as these could show Type-c factors if the loading patterns differed from one testing period to the next while the ordering of subjects along a continuum representing conservation behavior remained stable. Harris (1963), for example, employed this precise notion of perfectly stable factor scores in devising a factor-analytic procedure for investigating change in response patterns over time.

Type-d factors might be summarily dismissed, in a short-term context, as either error factors, situation-specific factors, or some other type of nonrepeatable "transients." In a life-span perspective, however, Type-d factors may be useful. One might assume, for example, that in early phases of ontogeny, responses are somewhat unstable *and* independent of each other, similar to a situation of relative chaos. Subsequent ontogeny would then consist of an imposition of order on the initial state of specificity.

Figure 1, portraying the relationships between observable variables, factor loading patterns, and factor scores, summarizes this bimodel classification scheme and emphasizes some aspects of relevance to developmental research. Each quadrant in the figure represents one of the four cases described earlier in a two-age level, longitudinal research context. Quadrants a and b, corresponding to the labels used on page 224, represent factors whose loading patterns are invariant from one age level to the next. The difference between these two quadrants is noted in the factor score distributions. Persons maintain their relative positions over time in the factor score distributions in the one case (quadrant

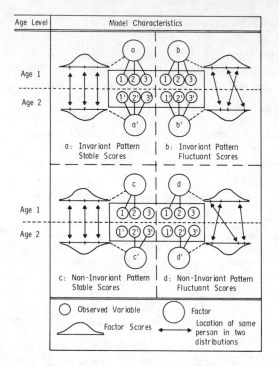

Fig. 1. Hypothetical comparisons of two age levels involving combinations of invariant versus noninvariant factor patterns and stable versus fluctuant factor scores.

a), but not in the other (quadrant b). Although the corresponding distributions shown appear to have the same mean, this need not be the case. Mean change on factor scores from one age level to the next may be the phenomenon for which the investigator is looking. Quadrants c and d show, in similar fashion, the remaining two cases, both reflecting noninvariance of loading pattern from Age Level 1 to Age Level 2. Again, we note that the two kinds of factors represented here differ in the nature of stability of the associated factor scores.

C. Ontogeny of Factor Patterns and Factor Scores

Incorporating the factor-change models described in the previous section more explicitly into a longitudinal research framework raises a number of salient substantive issues. We shall now attend to some of them, especially those relevant to the simulation data to be presented subsequently. To aid us in focusing on these points, one possible example of factor change is symbolized in Fig. 2.

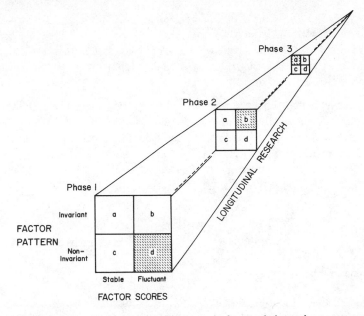

Fig. 2. Hypothetical age-related change sequences in factor solutions: chaos→state→trait (note that different types of factors may prevail at different stages of development for various response systems).

Each of the three rectangles in Fig. 2 depicts the types of factors discussed earlier, any or all of which may characterize the factors derived from a set of multiple measures on a group of subjects at a given time. Although it is only one of a variety of examples and, at that, a somewhat restricted one, the type of change shown here illustrates the following developmental sequence:

Phase 1:   The kind of factor indicated by the shading shows no orderly behavior in the sense of loading pattern being invariant and factor scores being stable. In other words, observed behavior is highly labile in terms of both covariation patterns and individual differences in level of response.

Phase 2:   From the "chaos" of the preceding phase, a degree of order has emerged in that a factor (indicated by shading) derived from the observed measures, exhibits an invariant loading pattern, even though the factor scores are not stable. This is what was previously identified as a state dimension, that is, a stable pattern on which subjects vary differentially in level from one occasion or situation to the next. A more concrete example of this might be situational anxiety, which shows a common behavior pattern across persons, but intraindividual differences in level depending upon changes in situation.

Phase 3:   The factor now falls in the quadrant of invariant pattern—stable scores (shaded portion), which we interpreted earlier as indicating the conventional notion of trait. For instance, what emerged as a state dimension of anxiety at Phase 2 has stabilized through the course of development into an interindividual differences dimension of anxiety at Phase 3.

The developmental sequence represented here emphasizes the molding, over time, of intraindividual change into an eventual pattern of stable interindividual differences. In subsequent sections we shall discuss potential mechanisms by which these patterns of behavior emerge, change with time, stabilize, and are maintained. Moreover, we will present evidence, using intelligence as a sample case, that bears on the explication of such change sequences.

IV. Sample Case: Ontogeny of Intelligence

A. General Overview

Concern with multiple measures of ontogenetic (intraindividual, age-correlated) change always has been an intrinsc part of developmental research as evidenced, for example, in the widespread early use of complex questionnaires or batteries of intelligence tests (see, e.g., Charles, 1970). A number of inter-related factors contributed to this early concern with multiple measures.

First, there was the extensive propagation of a comparative model of development (see Baltes & Goulet, 1970; Langer, 1970; Reese & Overton, 1970; Werner, 1948) whose holistic features imply a convergence on molar behavior systems in their full-blown complexity, both on the level of ontogenetic and phylogenetic change phenomena. Second, psychometrists involved in developmental research, being concerned with measurement, were quite eager to consider chronological age as an important parameter in organizing individual differences. Third, quite a number of prototheories of development (see Emmerich, 1968, for review) such as Werner's, Freud's, or Piaget's were, in principle, multivariate prototheories emphasizing such concepts as stages, structures, integration, differentiation, traits, or types. Finally, there was the impotant influence of longitudinal research. The extraordinary investment necessary for long-term longitudinal research (see Schaie, Chapter 12 in this volume) made it a prime candidate for the incorporation of multiple antecedent conditions and multiple consequent measures.

In the following, one of the major historical contributions will be highlighted to illustrate the potential usefulness of a multivariate model in the analysis of developmental change patterns. The example involves notions about ontogenetic changes in the organizational pattern of intelligence as expressed in Burt's and Garrett's age-differentiation hypothesis of intelligence. An attempt is made to show how multivariate research in this area proceeded from a descriptive to an explanatory attack.

B. Ontogenetic Changes in Patterns of Intelligence

Intelligence, when conceived of as a label for a class of cognitive performances, is typically considered to be the classical example of a complex, multidimensional construct. Various recent reviews (Anastasi, 1970; Baltes & Labouvie, 1972; Horn, 1968, 1970; Reinert, 1970; Riegel & Riegel, 1971; Schaie, 1970) have traced the history of research dealing with the ontogeny of intellectual patterns.

1. Descriptive Evidence

Historically, it was the lack of precision obtained when charting a single ontogenetic function of intelligence (using a global IQ measure as dependent variable) that was the major reason for considering multiple measures. In fact, recent analyses and reviews (e.g., Baltes & Labouvie, 1972; Bayley, 1970; Riegel & Riegel, 1971; Schaie & Strother, 1968b) have shown that developmental functions based on a variety of measures of intelligence not only exhibit deviations in peak and slope characteristics, but also in the overall direction of ontogenetic changes. Horn (1970), for example, presented data which indicate that the developmental functions for fluid and crystallized intelligence dimensions are markedly different, with fluid intelligence showing a steady decline from the twenties onward and crystallized intelligence exhibiting an increase up to late adulthood. Similarly, using sequential strategies involving a series of seven-year longitudinal studies, Nesselroade, Schaie, and Baltes (1972) have shown that, if the adult ontogeny of four major dimensions of cognitive behavior is considered, two of them (cognitive flexibility and visualization) do not exhibit significant longitudinal, age-related changes, whereas the developmental functions for crystallized intelligence and visuo-motor flexibility show discrepant, but age-related trends. All these data represent convincing evidence for the necessity of a multiple-measure approach, at least for the area of intelligence.

There is a second line of research which is more directly indicative of a concern with developmental aspects of a multivariate conception of intelligence. Stimulated by Burt's (1954) and Garrett's (1946) propositions, quite a few researchers (for reviews, see Anastasi, 1970; Horn, 1968; Reinert, 1970) examined whether it is feasible to assume an age-invariant model of intelligence or whether factor-analytic models of intelligence should explicitly incorporate notions about ontogenetic changes in the interrelationships of multiple measures. On the level of observables, such changes refer to the emergence of novel response systems and to changes in the correlational relationships among the response variables. On the level of inferred multivariate constructs, such changes refer to differences in the number and nature of underlying dimensions (factors) and their interrelationships (factor intercorrelations).

Thus far, evidence for the usefulness of the age-differentiation hypothesis is quite equivocal. However, both Anastasi (1970) and Reinert (1970) convincingly argued for the conclusion that the lack of compelling data seems primarily a reflection of inadequate methodologies (nature of factor-analytic techniques, failure to apply factor-matching techniques, use of inappropriate test batteries, predominant use of cross-sectional rather than longitudinal research, etc.). Anastasi (1970) argued, moreover, that another limitation of many of the studies on the differentiation hypothesis stems from their failure to consider the nature of the preexperimental experience (learning) patterns which would allow for the separation of maturational and experiential antecedents.

Nevertheless, it seems fair to conclude that the majority of interpretable studies support the notion that the structural model of intelligence is not age-invariant, but undergoes systematic ontogenetic transformations, although the nature of these transformations is not sufficiently clear. Such age changes in the factor pattern of intelligence are particularly conspicuous if a life-span perspective is considered. In line with Reinert's (1970, p. 472) and Horn's (1970) integrative presentations, the overall trend appears best capsulized by an *integration-differentiation-reintegration* sequence (see also Balinsky, 1941; Lienert & Crott, 1964; Steinhagen, 1970). In early childhood, the major direction seems to be toward the emergence or "building-up" of structure in terms of initially specific (relatively independent) response systems becoming more and more intercorrelated and yielding a strong "general" ability dimension. Subsequently, during childhood and adolescence, the direction of change seems to be toward increasing differentiation or reintegration. The latter segment of ontogeny is the one least investigated.

What are the major methodological and theoretical implications of such research on the ontogeny of intelligence regarding both differential age functions and age-correlated changes in ability organization? The implications are twofold:

(a) It is useful to conceive of intelligence not only as *multidimensional construct*, but also as a construct whose ontogeny, on a descriptive level, involves structural changes in the number of dimensions (e.g., factors) and their relationships (e.g., factor intercorrelations).

(b) It is useful to distinguish between two types of developmental change—*quantitative* and *structural*—where quantitative change refers to age-correlated, intraindividual differences in the magnitude (e.g., on factor scores), and structural change to age-correlated changes in the pattern (e.g., correlational pattern of variables, number of factors, factor intercorrelations) of intellectual measures.

Recognition of the ontogeny of intelligence as a multidimensional construct also has various implications for the evaluation of existing theories or models of intelligence. First, and most important, it is realized that the majority of intelligence modelers (such as Spearman, Thurstone, Guilford) were nondevelopmentalists and made little provision for such ontogenetic changes. Second, the potential existence of structural change implies that none of the various "classical" models of intelligence (e.g., Burt, Guilford, Spearman, Thurstone, Cattell, etc.) possesses universal validity. On the contrary, in line with Reinert's (1970) reasoning, one is tempted to allocate different models to different segments of the life span, for example, the Spearman model to early childhood and the Thurstone model to early adulthood.

2. Explanatory Evidence

As is true for most multivariate models, the amount of effort invested in the explanatory analysis of the differentiation hypothesis is at best minikin, although there are isolated, early studies and papers (e.g., Anastasi, 1936; Tryon, 1935) which draw attention to the need for "inquiries into the conditions that bring about or modify trait organization" (Anastasi, 1958a, p. 371).

a. Genetics.   The ontogeny of trait patterns, of course, potentially is a reflection of both hereditary and environmental sources and their interaction in terms of maturational and learning processes. The emphasis in this chapter is on environmental conditions, since Cattell's chapter (Chapter 6 in this volume) is devoted to a discussion of the developmental implications of heredity–environment research. Suffice it here to sketch briefly how part of the existence and ontogeny of structure can indeed be due to genotypic patterns.

Tryon (1935), for example, pointed out the possibility that correlations between independent gene blocks (due to assortative mating) represent one mechanism to account for the origin of trait patterns. In a similar vein, Vandenberg (1969) has discussed various aspects of hereditary transmission of specific abilities and personality patterns, and has presented specific data on the heritability of various complex ability and personality dimensions. For example, he has published data which suggest significant hereditary components for word fluency, verbal comprehension, and space, whereas the evidence indicates that heredity contributes minimally to individual differences in reasoning and memory.

It should be recognized, however, that from a developmental perspective, the bulk of heredity–environment research is not very convincing. First, concerning the ontogeny of patterns of abilities, the use of twin control designs or multiple abstract variance analysis (MAVA) procedures is not very helpful, since such research varies heredity with respect to overall similarity only, rather than more specific aspects of gene pattern composition. Second, nature–nurture research for the most part has not incorporated chronological age or age-correlated treatments as explicit design parameters (but see Chapter 6 by Cattell). Finally, and perhaps most importantly, the resulting nature–nurture ratios are sample statistics (see, e.g., Jensen, 1969), which reflect the operation of a selected (fixed-level type) set of hereditary and environmental conditions. On the one hand, it is to be noted that developmental processes are under continuous genetic control with different genes being effective at different times during ontogeny. But, on the other hand, neither does the environment consist of an age-invariant set of dimensions. It, too, exhibits continuous variations. Correspondingly, a learning approach to ontogeny (i.e., ontogenetic change patterns represent largely cumulative effects of learning experiences) would necessarily assume that nature–nurture ratios are not fixed, but undergo systematic age-related changes. Furthermore, one may reasonably assume that such learning effects do not necessarily follow a linear growth model. Kessen (1968), McClearn (1970), and Thompson and Grusec (1970), for example, in reviewing comparative research on early experience effects and critical periods, have convincingly argued the need for developmental models that consider Gene × Age × Environment interactions, although the available evidence is clearly univariate in nature and thus far restricted to work with infrahuman species. Finally, the awareness of cultural and/or generational change components (e.g., Baltes, 1968; Cattell, 1970b; Riegel & Riegel, 1971; Ryder, 1965; Schaie, 1965, 1970) further suggests that nature–nurture ratios should change not only with increasing age, but also in conjunction with secular trends in environmental and hereditary characteristics.

In short, while it is quite certain that genetic mechanisms play a prominent role in the formation of intellectual organization, the available body of specific information about hereditary sources and the resulting developmental product is meager. Genetic inquiries into multivariate change phenomena, indeed, presuppose a rather advanced understanding of heredity on a continuum of similarity (identical twins, fraternal twins, siblings, unrelated children, etc.), but also the recognition of gene location, gene-coupling, and gene-repulsion states (e.g., Vandenberg, 1969) as well.

   b. Molar Environmental Conditions.   Evidence for the effect of environmentally based conditions on the life-span ontogeny of intellectual changes is somewhat richer, particularly as it pertains to the study of quantitative ontogenetic changes. It is not the purpose of this section to dwell on research dealing with the global effects of environmental variation (enrichment and massive stimulation versus deprivation and restriction) on univariate intellectual ontogeny. Such research, by and large producing impressive results, has been well summarized, for example, by Bayley (1970), Longstreth (1968), and Thompson and Grusec (1970). In this section, only those salient lines of empirical and theoretical work will be highlighted which contribute directly to the understanding of the ontogeny of structural aspects of intelligence.

A first line of reasoning and research involving the effects of environmental differentials on the ontogeny of intelligence patterns concerns the comparative analysis of correlational and factor patterns derived from criterion groups which supposedly differ in their preexperimental, experiential history or in the nature of their environmental fields. There is a multitude of studies (although rarely using appropriate methodology) aimed at within- and cross-cultural comparisons (see also Eckensberger, Chapter 3 in this volume) which substantiates the effects of cultural, social, educational, occupational, and familial differentials on the development of the pattern of abilities. Both Anastasi (1970) and Horn (1970, pp. 438, 440) have reviewed research focusing on the "shaping of particular abilities" and "the emergence of structure" in conjunction with the process of acculturation. In a related vein, Child (1968) summarized research which illustrates "differing relations among personality variables in different cultures [p. 126]." Similarly, LeVine (1969) in discussing ontogeny within a given societal framework, utilized a Darwinian "variation-selection" model coupled with four environmentally based adaptation processes to account for the developmental transformation of genotypic into more differentiated phenotypic behavior patterns.

Furthermore, models of life-span socialization (e.g., Brim, 1966; Neugarten, 1968; Riley, Foner, Hess, & Toby, 1969), delineating continuous ontogenetic changes in socialization agents, goals, products, and mechanisms, lend indirect support to the proposition that the emergence of structure does not stop somewhere in early adulthood but extends, in correspondence with age-graded value and role systems, into late maturity and old age. Finally, it seems reasonable to assume that the selective disintegration of environmental and biological systems in old age (see, e.g., selective survival effects and the terminal drop hypothesis as discussed by Riegel & Riegel, 1971) should further accentuate systematic structural transformations in the interrelations of cognitive variables.

Both from a design and a substantive viewpoint, a very noteworthy contribution to the understanding of the impact of molar environmental conditions (life histories) on multivariate behavior patterns is the animal work of Denenberg and co-workers (e.g., Denenberg, Karas, Rosenberg, & Schell, 1968; Whimbey & Denenberg, 1967). By applying four different environmental treatments to random samples from a homogeneous group of rats, they were able to "create" heterogeneous groups of adult rats on a total of 23 criterion measures taken at 220 days of age. After establishing that the 16 different programs of life histories had markedly different effects on most of the dependent variables, a factor analysis of the data resulted in a set of factors which, in those authors' opinion, was remarkably similar to that obtained when data from otherwise untreated, heterogeneous groups of adult rats were analyzed. The most exciting feature of these studies is the fact that development of individual differences was under experimental control. Specifically, due to the random assignment of rats to the various life-history conditions and the removal of within-group variance (by use of mean scores), it was possible to conclude that, except for error factors, all individual differences obtained were independent of any contribution from genetic variance.

   c. Short-Term Experimental Evidence. Most of the research summarized
in the preceding sections, being aimed at the explication of long-term ontogenetic
change patterns, was necessarily preexperimental, using natural variations as
antecedent variables. Short-term experimental research into the antecedents of
individual differences can also be relevant for the conceptualization of long-term
ontogeny, but only if it is assumed that it is possible to "simulate" (e.g.,
Baltes & Goulet, 1971) long-term change by short-term change phenomena.
As Anastasi (1970) remarked: "The investigator thus tries to reproduce the
process of trait formation that can be inferred from the observation of age
changes [p. 906]." Although, from a theoretical viewpoint, the question of
homology and/or isomorphy between ontogenetic and short-term, experimentally
produced change is far from being resolved (see also Baer, Chapter 9 in this
volume), one may conclude that the explication of molar ontogeny indeed has
benefited tremendously from research carried out on the assumption that short-
term and long-term changes follow identical, or at least highly similar, behavioral
laws.
   What kind of short-term experimental evidence is available to account for
age-related structural changes in the organizational patterns of intelligence? The
primary strategy of such research would be to design studies which conceive
of ability-type measures as dependent variables and to manipulate treatments
(such as task parameters, practice, reinforcement, etc.) dictated by various models
of learning or development. The effect of such manipulations may then be
examined by comparing structural changes in correlational matrices or factor
patterns. One line of research has examined the structural changes involved
in the relationships between learning performance and intellectual abilities over
successive trials. By and large (e.g., Anastasi, 1970; Dunham, Guilford, &
Hoepfner, 1968; Fredericksen, 1969; Labouvie, Frohring, Baltes, & Goulet,
1973; Roberts, 1968–69), these studies suggest not only that a given performance
(such as a recall performance in a verbal-learning task) is multiply determined,
but also that the factorial composition of a learning performance may change
markedly with increasing trials and/or practice. Such findings are relevant as
they indicate that a "phenotypically" similar performance indeed may be a
reflection of different abilities or processes when different age groups are compared (Lienert & Crott, 1964; Nunnally, Chapter 5 in this volume). In this
case, then, different stages or trials of the learning process would be comparable
to different levels of age or different stages of ontogenetic development.
   From a simulation perspective, there is a second, related research tack, offering
a more genuine examination of ontogenetic integration–differentiation processes,
since it does not imply the operation of a *fixed* set of interrelationships of
the abilities themselves. Following up on early work by Anastasi (1936) and
Woodrow (1939), Fleishman and associates (see Fleishman & Bartlett, 1969,
for a review) examined the effect of general and selective practice on the factorial

composition of various batteries of cognitive and perceptual-motor tasks. Although Corballis's (1965) critical remarks, pointing to the existence of artifactual results due to simplex conditions, appear to preclude any definite conclusion at the present time, the data can be taken as suggesting some authentic changes in factor structures, over trials, as a result of practice. Actually, the fact that the changes appear to be in the direction of increased differentiation with advancing practice prompt the inference that the experimentally produced changes in factor pattern may indeed parallel the kind of structural changes obtained in developmental cross-sectional and longitudinal investigations.

   d. Theoretical Models and Explanatory Attempts.   Remaining to be discussed are the kinds of environmentally oriented explanations and models that have been put forward to elucidate the ontogeny of structural changes in such multiple response systems as that implied by the integration–differentiation hypothesis of intelligence. Aside from very general statements noting that structural changes in ability systems reflect patterns of socialization or patterns of child rearing, etc., the available discussions and attempts at formalization are few (e.g., Anastasi, 1970; Carroll, 1966; Ferguson, 1954, 1956; Horn, 1970; Tryon, 1935; Whiteman, 1964).

   As mentioned earlier, Tryon (1935) was one of the first to conclude that factor analysis as a method does not yield information about the origin of trait organizations, a conclusion which led him to discuss various sources and mechanisms that could be responsible for the clustering of responses and the appearance of factors. One of his three mechanisms concerns the notion of correlated environmental fields. In other words, it is assumed that subjects are exposed to multiple environments which are similar (e.g., high, medium, low) across a multitude of response systems. For example, a generally inferior cultural setting might lack many special environmental fields necessary for the formation of both verbal and arithmetic concepts. Consequently, ontogenetic change sequences should show a fairly high degree of relative stability between and within response clusters.

   A second major approach utilizes the concepts of transfer (Ferguson, 1954, 1956; see also Horn, 1970; Whiteman, 1964) to account for the emergence and maintenance of ability systems. According to Ferguson, the major process operating in the ontogeny of such abilities is transfer (general and specific) with learning being a particular case of transfer. Transfer processes are seen as significant both in the acquisition and subsequent effects of ability systems. It is primarily the amount of positive transfer which is common to prior experiential processes and the nature of the transfer components which are specific to a given task class that define the magnitude of the correlations between abilities. Thus, the emergence and subsequent ontogeny of ability systems are attributed to cumulative effects of preexperimental transfer on the task situations presented at a given point. The effects are not only cumulative, but also differential, since response classes differ as to their mutual (reciprocal) facilitation or inhibition. Of particular interest, are Ferguson's (1954) comments on aspects of differentiation: "We may account for transfer, and for the differentiation of abilities in terms of the learning process itself, which, according to the theory presented here, operates in such a way as to facilitate differentiation [p. 110]."

In the literature, there are a few additional explicit attempts to integrate learning research with ability concepts in order to explicate the processes underlying performance in ability tests and the ontogeny of intelligence patterns. Whiteman (1964), for example, discussed the relationships of intelligence factors to such processes as learning set and Piagetian cognitive operations. With regard to factors, for example, he argued that earlier experience with "learning how to learn" in a variety of related situations, contributes to the establishment of relatively stable individual differences in the strength of learning sets. In a similar vein, Carroll (1966) considered the logical extreme of a learning approach to the development of abilities in a discussion of verbal achievement factors. After enumerating four sources for the co-occurrence of response clustering and the resulting factors (overlap or prerequisite learning, transfer, simultaneous learning of multiple responses, and genetic factors), he hypothesized that whenever one identifies a factor "through factor-analytic procedures, the source of this variance is to be found in differential learning experiences [p. 409]." Moreover, he argued that a demonstration of the impact of differential learning experiences on the appearance of factors could be brought about on an experimental basis: "Indeed, given a series of behaviors, one could arrange a training situation so as to obtain any particular factor structure that one might desire [p. 408]." These suggestions, coming from a noted factor analyst, are most surprising in that they clearly assign factors and factor changes the status of dependent variables which can be brought under environmental control.

V. Organism–Environment Interactions as a Source for Structural Change: A Simulation Experiment

It is hoped that the preceding sections have demonstrated convincingly the need for experimental research aimed at explicating antecedent–consequent relationships in the developmental analysis of multiple response systems. However, the review also pointed out that the details of the interchange processes involved in organism–environment interactions still need to be worked out.

A. Objectives and Design

It would be helpful if we could offer actual data that bear explicitly on the manipulative explication of structural change as a function of organism–

environment interactions. However, whenever such data were not available, a simulation approach has been practiced, if not eagerly accepted, both within and outside psychology. Using a hypothetical simulation as a problem-solving technique, an attempt will now be made to explicate further the ontogeny of integration–differentiation processes in terms of organism–environment interactions involving the cumulative effects of age- and subject-related environmental differentials.

Table 1 shows a flow chart of the simulation experiment. A total of 20 hypothetical subjects (Ss) was included, with each subject having a score on each of six behavioral variables (R). The simulated ontogeny of each of the 20 subjects on six variables proceeded through five phases (A–E).

B. Nature of Simulated Change: Integration–Differentiation

In accordance with the sample case selected, it was decided to focus on processes of integration and differentiation as target changes. Specifically, we settled for simulating a change sequence that involves *integration* first and *differentiation* second. Furthermore, in correspondence with our initial presentation of a factor-analytic change model involving variation of both factor patterns and factor scores on dimensions of invariance and stability, the distinction between *trait* and *state* dimensions was incorporated in the process of differentiation (see Fig. 2). In other words, it is assumed that, following integration, the process of ontogenetic differentiation may result in either trait (invariant patterns, stable factor scores) or state (invariant patterns, fluctuant scores) dimensions. Phases A–C simulate integration, Phases D and E differentiation and the emergence of trait–state dimensions.

C. Nature of Simulated Treatments and Their Effects

We decided to treat the universe of antecedent conditions for the ontogeny of structural change in a similarly simplistic manner. Restricting the level of analysis to molar environmental conditions, we settled for three types of differentials in environmental patterns: (1) *general environmental differences,* (2) *behavior-specific environmental differences,* and (3) *stability versus lability of environmental differences.*

The first environmental condition (general environmental differences) is similar to what is often called cumulative ontogenetic enrichment versus deprivation. The second condition (behavior-specific environmental differences) is an operationalization of Tryon's (1935) concept of correlated environmental fields and also bears some resemblance to Whiteman's (1964) task-specific learning sets and Carroll's (1966) differential learning experiences. The third condition (stability versus lability of environmental differences) is closest to thoughts presented by Bloom (1964), Mischel (1969), and Emmerich (1969), who argued that situational consistency versus lability might be one of the prime antecedents for trait maintenance or long-term predictability.

No attempt is made to specify the nature of the mechanisms mediating the effects of the environmental differences. From an outcome-oriented viewpoint, the effects of the three environmental patterns are represented by means of a simple, *additive growth* model involving increments which reflect the cumulative effects of environmental differentials. Arbitrarily, as described in Tables 2 and 3, the different environmental contingencies were assigned values ranging from 0–5, which were systematically added to the initial performance levels. Note that this simulation is not intended to be a representation of the full scope of variables and principles operating in producing "real" developmental change. Rather, it simulates one set of conditions that may underlie the type of multidimensional changes discussed previously.

The five phases that were simulated, in analogy to developmental sequences, can be thought of as representing developmental conditions which are ordered along the age-continuum in the sense of age-graded environmental changes (see, e.g., Emmerich, 1969). However, it is also possible to conceive of them as being superimposed on the same age interval. Specifically, the five phases (see Table 1) resulted from the following simulation operations.

1. Phase A

Initial Individual Differences. In a first phase, it is assumed that all subjects show random behavior on all six variables. No attempt is made to specify the origin of these initial differences. The simulation *operation* was to assign values ranging from 1–5 randomly to all subjects separately for each of the six variables.

2. Phase B

General Environmental Differences: Short-Term. A second phase consisted of three levels of general environmental enrichment: high, medium, and low. Specifically, this treatment assumes that there are subject-related differences in how supportive or stimulating the environment is with regard to all behaviors considered. The *operation* was to increment all six of a given person's scores by an amount of either 3 (high), 2 (medium), or 1 (low), which was decided randomly. The treatment is general, since the same treatment condition was applied to all six behavioral dimensions for a given subject.

3. Phase C

General Environmental Differences: Long-Term. A third phase was produced to represent long-term effects of the general environmental differentials simulated in Phase B. The *operation* was to assign again increments of 3, 2, or 1 in the same manner and to the same persons as in the previous Phase B. This

TABLE 1

Flow Chart Summarizing Simulation of Multivariate
Change as a Function of Environmental Differentials

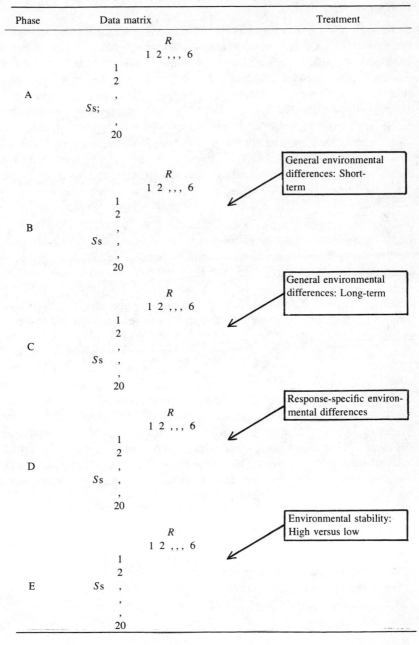

treatment was intended to illustrate the accumulation of effects produced by environmental differentials.

4. Phase D

Behavior-Specific Environmental Differences. The fourth phase consisted of further categorizing the environment as selectively focusing on clusters of behaviors. Arbitrarily, it was decided to form clusters of variables R_1 and R_2, R_3 and R_4, but retain variables R_5 and R_6 as separate response systems. The *operation* was to assign randomly increments of 5, 3, or 1 to subjects on both the variables R_1 and R_2. Independently of R_1–R_2 assignments, increments of 5, 3, or 1 were randomly assigned to both R_3 and R_4. Also independently, increments of the same magnitudes (5, 3, 1) were randomly assigned to variable R_5 and randomly to variable R_6. Values of 5, 3, 1 rather than 3, 2, 1 were chosen to produce the desired effects in one step rather than two.

5. Phase E

Behavior-Specific Environmental Stability: High–Low. The final phase further differentiates the environment into two types. The first is assumed to exhibit a high degree of situational stability in regard to maintaining the developmental product. This implies that the same subjects are always exposed to the same sample of the universe of situations associated with a given behavior pattern. The second type is assumed to exhibit some degree of variation in situational settings, implying that the same subjects are not always exposed to the same subset of the universe of situations, but rather to somewhat different subsets at different occasions. The *operation* was to assign zero increments to a first set of variables, that is, R_3, R_4, and R_6 (high environmental stability). With regard to the second set, R_1 and R_2, on the other hand, subjects were divided into two groups based on their composite scores, and within each of the two groups the subjects' scores were randomly interchanged to indicate switching between adjacent environments. The same procedure was followed for R_5. Note that this operation leaves intact most group-related *inter*individual-differences statistics from Phase D to Phase E (means, variances, within-cluster covariances) and introduces changes related to *intra*individual variability from Phase D to Phase E only.

D. Results

1. Data Analysis

In the normal case, if these were real data, one might first take a look at mean differences and plot separate age gradients. Now, since we know the effects, and since the present study focuses on multivariate aspects of developmental change problems, the presentation will center about the examination of multivariate, structural change with a look at integration–differentiation first and the trait–state differentiation second.

When appropriate, the following computations were performed, separately for each of the phases, to examine processes of integration and differentiation: (1) intercorrelations of variables, (2) principal-axes factor analyses, and (3) varimax rotations. In addition, to illustrate the emergence of trait–state distinctions, (4) factor scores were estimated for Phases D and E and correlated to yield retest stabilities. All factor analyses observed the Kaiser–Guttman criterion of extracting as many factors as there are eigenvalues, in excess of unity, derived from the intact correlation matrix. In addition, Phase D and E solutions, which produced two statistically acceptable factors, were rotated using a varimax routine. The results are presented in Tables 2 and 3.

2. Integration

The process of integration is simulated by Phases A, B, and C. The correlation matrix resulting from analyzing the *Phase A* data is included in Table 2. In line with our "chaos" treatment, the correlation matrix contains coefficients which show a random distribution about zero with an approximately equal number of positive and negative signs (average $r = .05$). In principle, a factoring of this matrix would not produce any stable, underlying structure but, rather, a set of dimensions that account for little variance.

The analysis of *Phase B* data produces a different picture. The treatment of short-term general environmental differences altered the correlation matrix from one having both positive and negative correlations toward one exhibiting a positive manifold, i.e., containing positive correlations only (average $r = .23$). Factoring this matrix resulted in two acceptable factors, the first of which looks (as one would expect when using a principal axes routine on a positive manifold) like a general factor with all variables having positive loadings. Note that the beginning of such a general factor can be seen as the emerging of integration of the six variables considered.

Phase C, involving long-term general environmental differentials, further accentuates this integration process. The correlation matrix shows high positive intercorrelations only, ranging from .47 to .76 with an average of .58. Moreover, the factor solution is further clarified and presents a single, strong general factor. The purity of this solution is quite evident also in the distribution of eigenvalues, which showed the desired sharp drop between the first and all remaining values. Note that this developmental emergence of integration is simulated by consideration of one simple antecedent—individual differences in the general richness of the environments.

TABLE 2

Simulation of Factor Integration (Phases A–C):
Data Matrices, Treatments, and Resulting Individual-Differences Characteristics[a]

Phase	Ss	R_1	R_2	R_3	R_4	R_5	R_6	Treatment and Correlations
	1	1	4	3	1	3	4	Random assignment of
	2	5	1	1	3	3	3	values (1–5) on six
	3	3	3	1	4	3	3	variables (R) to 20
	4	3	2	4	3	3	1	subjects (Ss).
	5	5	3	5	5	2	1	
	6	3	5	5	2	5	3	
	7	5	2	4	3	3	2	
	8	3	4	1	3	2	3	
	9	2	1	4	5	2	3	

								R_1	R_2	R_3	R_4	R_5	R_6
A	10	1	5	5	5	4	1						
	11	4	3	2	5	3	2	R_1 —	−.26	−.11	.02	−.15	−.13
	12	3	1	5	5	2	3	R_2 —		.26	−.08	.49	.09
	13	3	3	4	4	5	4	R_3 —			.25	.19	.20
	14	3	2	4	3	3	5	R_4 —				.10	−.14
	15	4	2	2	2	1	1	R_5 —					.09
	16	1	3	3	4	3	1	R_6 —					
	17	3	2	5	4	2	5						
	18	3	2	2	5	5	1						
	19	5	5	5	4	4	3						
	20	2	5	5	5	4	5						

	1	3	6	5	3	5	6	(a) General environ-
	2	8	4	4	6	6	6	mental differ-
	3	5	5	3	6	5	5	ences: Short-term
	4	4	3	5	4	2	2	(b) Random increments
	5	8	6	8	8	5	4	(1,2,3) on all
	6	4	6	6	3	6	4	six variables.
	7	8	5	7	6	6	5	
	8	6	7	4	6	5	6	
	9	3	2	5	6	3	4	

								R_1	R_2	R_3	R_4	R_5	R_6
B	10	3	7	7	7	6	3						
	11	5	4	3	6	4	3	R_1 —	.09	.15	.38	.26	.13
	12	6	4	8	8	5	6	R_2 —		.28	.17	.56	.10
	13	5	5	6	6	7	6	R_3 —			.38	.26	.17
	14	4	3	5	4	4	6	R_4 —				.37	.05
	15	6	4	4	4	3	3	R_5 —					.14
	16	4	6	6	7	6	4	R_6 —					
	17	5	4	7	6	4	7						
	18	6	5	5	8	8	4						
	19	7	7	7	6	6	5						
	20	3	6	6	6	5	6						

TABLE 2—(*continued*)

Phase		Data matrix						Treatment and Correlations

Phase	Ss	R_1	R_2	R_3	R_4	R_5	R_6
	1	5	8	7	5	7	8
	2	11	7	7	9	9	9
	3	7	7	5	8	7	7
	4	5	4	6	5	5	3
	5	11	9	11	11	8	7
	6	5	7	7	4	7	5
	7	11	8	10	9	9	8
	8	9	10	7	9	8	9
	9	4	3	6	7	4	5
C	10	5	9	9	9	8	5
	11	6	5	4	7	5	4
	12	9	7	11	11	8	9
	13	7	7	8	8	9	8
	14	5	4	6	5	5	7
	15	8	6	6	6	5	5
	16	7	9	9	10	9	7
	17	7	6	9	8	6	9
	18	9	8	8	11	11	7
	19	9	9	9	8	8	7
	20	4	7	7	7	6	7

Treatment and Correlations:

(a) General environmental differences: Long-term
(b) Additional increments (1,2,3) on all six variables

	R_1	R_2	R_3	R_4	R_5	R_6
R_1	—	.51	.53	.68	.53	.54
R_2		—	.57	.55	.76	.47
R_3			—	.65	.58	.49
R_4				—	.69	.49
R_5					—	.54
R_6						—

Factor pattern matrix[b]

Phase	R	FI	FII	h^2
A		Not factor analyzed		
B	R_1	.39	−.29	.24
	R_2	.63	.49	.64
	R_3	.46	−.08	.22
	R_4	.63	−.46	.62
	R_5	.72	.18	.55
	R_6	.20	.00	.04
C	R_1	.76	—	.57
	R_2	.76	—	.57
	R_3	.74	—	.54
	R_4	.82	—	.67
	R_5	.87	—	.75
	R_6	.64	—	.41

[a]Ss = subjects, R = response variable. Treatments refer to sequential operations applied to produce a given phase-specific matrix. For example, Phase-B treatment applied to Phase-A data matrix resulted in Phase-B data matrix.

[b]Coefficients greater than .50 are italicized to indicate salient correlations and loadings. Factor-matrix entries in column headed h^2 are communalities.

TABLE 3

Simulation of Factor Differentiation and Trait-State Emergence (Phases D-E): Data Matrices, Treatments, and Resulting Individual-Differences Characteristics[a]

Phase	Ss	R_1	R_2	R_3	R_4	R_5	R_6	Treatment
	1	8	11	8	6	10	9	(a) Behavior-specific
	2	16	12	8	10	14	10	environmental dif-
	3	10	10	6	9	8	12	ferences
	4	6	5	11†	10	6	8	(b) Random-increments
	5	16	14	16	16	9	10	of 1,3,5 simultane-
	6	6	8	10	7	12	6	ously to $R_{1,2}$ and
	7	16	13	11	10	14	11	independently to both
	8	12	13	12	14	11	12	$R_{3,4}$. Also, independ-
	9	9	8	9	10	7	8	ently to R_5 and R_6.
D	10	8	12	14	14	11	10	
	11	11	10	5	8	6	5	
	12	12	10	12	12	9	12	
	13	8	8	13	13	10	13	
	14	6	5	9	8	8	12	
	15	11	9	9	9	8	10	
	16	12	14	12	13	10	8	
	17	10	9	14	13	11	12	
	18	10	9	11	14	16	12	
	19	14	14	14	13	13	8	
	20	5	8	8	8	9	10	
	1	10	9	8	6	8	9	(a) Behavior-specific
	2	16	12	8	10	10	10	environment stability:
	3	6	5	6	9	8	12	High versus low.
	4	10	10	11	10	10	8	(b) Retain scores on $R_{3,4}$
	5	12	10	16	16	11	10	and R_6. For $R_{1,2}$
	6	8	8	10	7	6	6	subjects were divided
	7	16	13	11	10	16	11	into two groups based
	8	8	12	12	14	9	12	on their composite
	9	9	8	9	10	6	8	scores and, within
E	10	11	9	14	14	11	10	each group, Ss'
	11	14	14	5	8	13	5	scores were randomly
	12	11	10	12	12	14	12	interchanged. The
	13	10	9	13	13	10	13	same procedure for R_5.
	14	8	11	9	8	11	12	
	15	16	14	9	9	8	10	
	16	12	14	12	13	9	8	
	17	5	8	14	13	7	12	
	18	6	8	11	14	12	12	
	19	12	13	14	13	14	8	
	20	6	5	8	8	9	10	

TABLE 3—(*continued*)

Phase		Correlation matrix[b]						Factor pattern matrix[b]			
		R_1	R_2	R_3	R_4	R_5	R_6	R	FI	FII	h^2
	R_1	—	.78	.26	.45	.39	.08	R_1	.81	.13	.68
	R_2		—	.36	.48	.44	−05	R_2	.96	.10	.93
D	R_3			—	.82	.32	.28	R_3	.26	.79	.69
	R_4				—	.32	.38	R_4	.39	.88	.93
	R_5					—	.27	R_5	.41	.27	.24
	R_6						—	R_6	−.01	.43	.19
	R_1	—	.78	−.04	−.03	.45	−.30	R_1	.90	−.17	.84
	R_2		—	.09	.12	.44	−.28	R_2	.89	−.03	.80
E	R_3			—	.82	.20	.28	R_3	.11	.81	.67
	R_4				—	.27	.38	R_4	.15	.97	.97
	R_5					—	.12	R_5	.50	.22	.30
	R_6						—	R_6	−.24	.43	.25

[a]The cross-phase stability coefficients (Phase D and E) are .57 for Factor I, 1.00 for Factor II, and .28 and 1.00 for variables 5 and 6, respectively.

[b]Coefficients greater than .50 are italicized to indicate salient coefficients and loadings. Factor matrix entries in column headed h^2 are communalities.

3. Differentiation

Phases D and E simulate the process of differentiation which, in a factor analytic sense, implies the successive breakdown of a general factor into more narrow group-type dimensions and/or the emergence of a greater variety of factor types as discussed in Section III.

With regard to *Phase D*, on the level of correlations, two aspects are particularly noteworthy. One is that the high positive manifold "developed" from Phase A to Phase C is not continuing, but breaking down. The average correlation in Phase D is .37 as compared with .58 in Phase C. Second, two pairs of variable clusters ($R_1 + R_2$ versus $R_3 + R_4$) develop in conjunction with the response-specific treatment applied. Variables 1 and 2 increase their correlation to .78, and variables 3 and 4 to .82. None of the other correlations is greater than .48.

The effect is also evidenced in the resulting factor pattern. Two factors, rather than one, are necessary to describe the data matrix. Varimax rotation produces a convincing pattern showing a first factor with high loadings (.81, .96) on variables 1 and 2, and a second factor with salient loadings on variables 3 and 4 (.79, .88). None of the remaining loadings is higher than .43, indicating that variables 5 and 6 do not align with the two factors or each other, but remain fairly separate dimensions.

4. Trait versus State

Finally, *Phase E* simulates one way of obtaining a further differentiation of the Phase D pattern by consideration of the distinction between trait and state dimensions. As can be seen from Table 3, this was accomplished by retaining the same correlational relationship between the clusters of variables 1 and 2 (.78) and variables 3 and 4 (.82). Thus, in line with no major changes in the correlational pattern, the varimax rotations could result in highly similar factor patterns for Phases D and E.

However, a clear distinction in the cross-phase stability coefficients for factor scores from Phase D to Phase E resulted. The factor score stability coefficient for Factor I, estimated by the composite of its salient variables (1, 2), on the one hand, is .57, thus exhibiting statelike features. The Factor II scores (variables 3, 4), on the other hand, show perfect stability from Phase D to Phase E $(r = 1.00)$. The same difference (based on raw scores) resulted for the two "specific" variables 5 and 6, with 5 showing only a moderate degree of retest-stability $(r = .28)$ from Phase D to Phase E.

Note that this differentiation into one trait and one state factor was also achieved by simulating aspects of the environment. In the case of the trait product, high environmental stability was used, with all people being exposed continuously to identical ecologies. In the case of the state product, however, low environmental stability was postulated with a fair degree of random "switching" between adjacent environment patterns.

E. Discussion

Note at the outset that this simulation was not intended to be a representation of the full scope of variables and principles operating to produce "real" developmental change sequences. A first set of implications is specific to the study and concerns the question of whether we succeeded in presenting a good environment-based model for integration–differentiation processes. A second set is more general and concerns issues pertaining to advancing the scientific credibility of multiple response-concepts such as factors, by putting them into a framework of antecedent–consequent events and by conceiving of factors as products of historical differences in organism–environment interactions.

Turning to the specific implications first, one may conclude that our simulation of integration and differentiation processes appears fairly convincing in that we were successful in fabricating some sufficient, although not necessary, environmental conditions which lead to the emergence of factor change patterns. Simulation moves us a step beyond descriptive analysis of age-correlated change patterns and shows how multivariate structural changes may be understood as reflecting the operation of relatively simple environmental contingencies inherent in the life history of learning processes. Thus, we were able to render operational some of the abstract (and often vague) proposals by Tryon (1935), Whiteman (1964), Carroll (1966), or Coan (1966) about the mechanisms of factor change patterns by specifying a few, but powerful, assumptions about organism–environment interactions and their effects on multiple response systems. In fact, we feel that the simplicity of the interchanges involved is indeed surprising. Consequently, it is hoped that the simulation study further demonstrates how multivariate individual-differences concepts can be seen as products of historical differences in organism–environment interaction patterns.

Any attempt at simulating "real" phenomena, of course, has various shortcomings. To put our data in perspective, it might be useful to mention a few of them. For example, realize that our simulation of integration and differentiation does not necessarily, point for point, parallel the type of organism-environment interaction patterns as they occur in natural settings. In a similar vein, it was not demonstrated whether our assumptions about environmental differentials and their effects are reasonable from a developmental theory viewpoint. Moreover, the present simulation study did not explore whether other environmental differentials would result in identical or similar changes. Furthermore, we are aware of the fact that the simulation was outcome-oriented, as it did not include parameters involving differential learning processes such as specific or nonspecific transfer. On all counts, however, only additional research that explicitly uses such multivariate, experimental intervention programs is apt to accumulate the necessary evidence to link more directly the simulation results to real developmental phenomena in order to fill the various lacunae in the model presented or to transform it if the data so dictate.

VI. Concluding Commentary

A. Retrospects: Need for Experimental Research

Even now, this inquiry into the status of multiple response constructs, such as factors, may be disappointing to those interested only in rigorous experimentation. Although the increasing refinement of multiple change models is impressive, and the scattered beginning of systematic antecedent–consequent research is promising, there is a conspicuous need for programmatic, experimental research.

Historically, the major deficiency of conventional multivariate research appears to be its cross-sectional focus on the analysis of complex behavior systems at a specific point in time. Such a static approach is inattentive to the analysis of sequential details of the interchange between the environment and the organism. Furthermore, the major lines of research appear to have centered about the conceptualization of "one-sided" (Gewirtz, 1969b, p. 126) networks which involve the specification of multiple consequents without sufficient attempts to link the consequents to a set of corresponding antecedents. Gewirtz (1969b), in another context, is particularly persuasive on this point. Propagating a functional learning approach to the study of development, he criticized existing trait conceptions as "one-sided" and as neglecting the "facets of the S-R interchange" and "the changing conditions of environmental stimulation accompanying development [pp. 194, 195]." In contrast, he proposed the use of a functional learning approach that is explicitly oriented toward constructing two-sided networks and which requires "emphasis upon the sequential details of environment–organism interaction, i.e., stimuli, responses, and their interchanges, [and which] focuses upon the environmental conditions by which child behaviors can be acquired, maintained, extinguished, or otherwise modified. . . [p. 197]."

Whether or not one is willing to accept Gewirtz's specific set of concepts—entrenched, as they are, in an operant framework—is secondary. However, his emphasis on antecedent-process–consequent research appears to be a must for future examinations into the ontogeny of multiple change patterns. In the following sections, an attempt is made to highlight some of the issues that environmentalists may use when conceiving multiple response systems in a framework of antecedent–consequent events.

B. Structuring and Measuring the Environment

The conclusion that the developmental analysis of multivariate constructs should follow a strategy of explicating their empirical referents both with regard to antecedent and consequent conditions raises a host of questions related to the measurement of the environment and age-related changes in environmental patterns. Although Willems (Chapter 10 in this volume) discusses in greater detail the merits of an ecological approach to the study of developmental phenomena, it appears desirable to explore it in the present context of multivariate research.

1. Matching Environmental and Behavioral Analyses

An environmental orientation, of course, is not new to psychology as evidenced, for example, by the widely acclaimed S-R paradigm and the recent resurgence of the ecological and/or environmental tradition (e.g., Barker, 1968;

Bloom, 1964; Sells, 1963; Willems, 1965, Chapter 10 in this volume; Wohlwill, 1970b). What appears to be new in the present context, however, is the growing insight into the need for aligning the assessment and examination of behavioral (R) and environmental (S) systems on conceptually equivalent dimensions.

We suggest that conventional S-R psychology, though explicitly focusing on stimulus aspects of the environment, might not contain the most powerful information for the construction of multivariate change networks. First, its explicit emphasis is on processes and principles (e.g., Gagne, 1968; Goulet, 1970b) and not on a comprehensive assessment of the environment and the organism (see, however, Bijou, Peterson, & Ault, 1968; Gewirtz, 1968, 1969a). Second, the principles developed thus far, due to their largely univariate or bivariate nature, are relatively molecular and might be ill-suited for organizing the ontogeny of molar response systems such as multiple factor patterns.

This critical perspective of classical S-R or R-S psychology should not be taken as suggesting that the approach is not useful, but only as indicating that its scope might not be extended with the same degree of precision to all levels of complexity. In other words, what is emphasized is that a molar approach to the analysis of response systems might be best supplemented by a molar approach to the analysis of environmental and genetic antecedents. Such a position is similar to the one espoused by Gewirtz (1969a, b) for the case of bivariate learning-oriented research in environment-interaction work. In short, our position is that significant advances in theorizing are most probable if an attempt is made to coordinate antecedents, processes, and consequents on conceptually equivalent levels of analysis.

2. Molar Analysis of Age-Correlated Environmental Changes

Bloom (1964), who was one of the first to draw attention to the significance of information about the environment for long-term predictions, emphasized that adequate measures of the environment for long-term predictions are lacking. Aside from relatively global (but unstructured) variations such as social class, educational level of parents, or enrichment and deprivation, the state of the art in assessing the environment is rather crude indeed. This is particularly true for the analysis of multiple aspects of the environment. However, one may hope that various attempts (see, e.g., Beattie, 1970; Dogan and Rokkan, 1969; Duncan, 1968; Lawton, 1970; Schooler, 1970; Sells, 1963) appearing in the literature herald substantial progress in the near future.

In general, we expect the multivariate approach to the study of the environment and environmental change to pattern after the study of individual differences in multiple response systems and to encounter similar drawbacks. First, it will be necessary to search the existing literature for prototheoretical concepts involving a structural system of the universe of environmental variables (e.g., social, physical, psychological, etc.). Second, it will be necessary to explore the feasibility of making operational such concepts as age-graded environments and age-graded socialization patterns oriented toward the analysis of age-correlated environmental fields. With regard to the domain of environmental characteristics of the aged population, for example, Schooler (1970) extracted five multivariate dimensions when structuring the environmental universe of older people in Massachusetts communities (see also Lawton, 1970). In a similar vein, Sells (1963) attempted to develop an outline for a preliminary taxonomy of the total stimulus situation.

From a life-span developmental viewpoint, the most important initial questions will center about accurate description not only of a general model of the environment, but also of age-correlated changes in the environment (e.g., see Beattie, 1970). In particular, in light of the factor change models presented, it may be useful to distinguish between quantitative and structural aspects of environmental change. Moreover, the description of environmental change characteristics may profit from differentiating between various types of environmental dimensions in terms of their location on invariance and stability continua.

Some clusters of environmental variables may exhibit fairly age-invariant patterns (e.g., geography, climate, etc.), other clusters might exhibit partial invariance only and show various degrees of age specifities (e.g., differential socialization patterns shown by age-specific socialization agents such as parents, nursery school teachers, elementary school teachers, college instructors, peers, etc.), whereas a third cluster of environmental conditions (e.g., basic norm systems) may turn out to be relatively invariant, but become increasingly differentiated as age increases. In fact, one assumption of an integration–differentiation–integration model would be that parallel processes should be useful in characterizing the "ontogeny" of the environment and the ontogeny of response systems. In other words, it is the systematic alignment of age-correlated aspects of the environment with the ontogeny of response systems that appears most promising for the explication of developmental change in complex behavior systems.

Similar arguments, of course, would apply to the delineation of the processes mediating complex systems of environmental antecedents to complex systems of responses. It may not be the use of molecular learning units, but the utilization of more molar process concepts that is more powerful in the developmental analysis of multiple response systems. A good example for this suggestion is provided by research in parent–child interactions. Becker (1960, 1964), for example, has presented convincing evidence for linking complex dimension of parental behavior to complex dimension of child behavior, as have Kagan and Moss (1962; see also Longstreth, 1968) for the case of the Fels longitudinal study. The latter study involved the developmental linkage of four dimensions of maternal behavior to five dimensions of child behavior.

Finally, the assessment of the effects of age-correlated environmental fields, similar to efforts aimed at specifying the optimum environment for infancy and childhood, will have significant implications for modification attempts in adulthood and old age (see, e.g., Baltes & Labouvie, 1972). Thus, it is hoped that the molar analysis of organism-environment interactions will lay the groundwork for the planning of life-span education programs aimed at providing not only the young, but also the elderly with the type of environmental input and feedback necessary for maintaining adequate functioning.

CHAPTER **12**

Methodological Problems in Descriptive Developmental Research on Adulthood and Aging[1]

K. WARNER SCHAIE

WEST VIRGINIA UNIVERSITY
MORGANTOWN, WEST VIRGINIA

I. Introduction

Although at about the time of publication of Birren's handbook (1959a), many of us thought that the taxonomic stage of inquiry into adult development had reached the level where experimental work could begin, we have since recognized that much of the literature reported in that work has little to offer to our understanding of aging *within* individuals. This literature merely reports how individuals who differ in chronological age also differ on other dimensions at a given point in time. The few studies that are longitudinal in nature do not help us either, since they contain a host of methodological problems which generally reduce their status to that of biographical accounts of highly selected subgroups over unique time periods. Some of these problems will be considered in this chapter.

In the previous *Life-Span Developmental Psychology* volume (Goulet & Baltes, 1970), an attempt was made to show ways in which more useful information might be obtained by various schemes of reanalysis of the existing literature (Schaie, 1970). By contrast, this chapter is directed to the researcher who is

[1]Preparation of this paper was facilitated by a grant from the National Institute of Child Health and Human Development (HD 04766-02).

about to start a study of change in adult behavior. It will be assumed in this presentation that the prospective investigator has raised a meaningful research question and has defined his independent and dependent variables. The concern here, then, will be with issues of research implementation, which, although implicit in any developmental research problem, will bear special consequences in work with an adult subject population. Questions to be considered will include sampling and generalizability, the utility of representative samples, and the role of alternate hypothetico-deductive models for research implementation in studies of adult development.

Without repeating the detailed presentation of the general developmental model (Schaie, 1965), another tack will be taken at the age differences versus age changes issue, by placing this issue in the context of distinguishing between research questions about within-generation changes and those involving matters of species differentiation. This basic issue will be clarified further by distinguishing the implications for strategy of research efforts involving cohort-specific changes, species-specific changes, and culture-specific changes. Next, some special issues occurring in within-cohort (longitudinal) research designs will be considered, including the effects of sociocultural change, effects of repeated measurement, and changes in factor structure over time. Similarly, between-cohort (cross-sectional) designs will require consideration of comparison within and between cross-sectional studies, prospective and retrospective estimates, as well as the question of whether age-appropriate or cohort-appropriate instruments need to be used to measure one's variables. Finally, some comments will be provided on the hierarchy of priorities to be assigned to the preceding issues to achieve an orderly forward move out of our present methodological dilemmas.

II. Some Questions Related to Sampling and Generalizability

A. What Age Changes Are to Be Studied?

The student of adult behavior has at least three different options for selecting his subject population. These options arise since attrition of samples is inevitable because of the correlation of age with mortality and because there are only rare populations of "captive" adults, in the sense that the researcher can prevent their incidental or purposive removal from further participation in his investigation. The researcher may, therefore, select his sample at the study's inception, to be representative of the population of individuals to which he wishes to generalize, he may consider data only for an intact sample (i.e., those individuals who are members of the residual sample at the study's conclusion), or he may be quite selective in specifying a sample which is appropriate to the variable to be studied, but not necessarily representative with respect to any identifiable population group as such.

1. Aging in Representative Populations

The definition of a "representative sample" is fairly straightforward in a longitudinal study. It implies that random (or stratified) sampling has occurred from a census-type listing of all the members of the population cohort at a specified chronological age within the demographic limitations thought to be reasonable for a given study. Generalization here may be feasible to wider populations dependent upon our knowledge of the demographic characteristics of the sampling base. Note, however, that the representative nature of the sample will hold true only for the first measurement and not thereafter, since sample attrition due to natural causes or experimental artifacts will rarely be random. Two radically different sampling strategies should therefore be advocated, depending on whether the investigator's ojective is to assess age changes within individual organisms or to estimate population parameters of age changes to develop general laws.

In the first instance, in the absence of total control over one's subjects, it will be necessary to conduct collateral studies on the effects of experimental attrition (to be discussed in more detail later) to determine in what manner the sample deviates from its original representative nature at subsequent measurement points. However, it will also be necessary to determine whether the residual sample at subsequent measurement points is still representative of its parent population. In addition, the characteristics of the parent population may change through attrition over time in a systematic manner, but not necessarily in the same manner as the sample drawn from that population. In any repeated measurement study, moreover, a sample ceases to be representative of its parent population as soon as it has been tested once, in the sense that its response characteristics have, of necessity, been modified by the initial assessment in a manner which is not characteristic of the parent population. That is, at subsequent measurement points, it will differ from any other random population sample in that the assessment tools or situation have previously been applied to the longitudinal sample, but to no other.

If the investigator is interested in estimating population parameters without concern for the evaluation of individual age gradients, he should consider the independent random sampling approach to longitudinal study. Specifically, a random sample should be selected from a given cohort at Time 1, and compared at subsequent measurement points with new random samples drawn from the same cohort. Depending on the mobility characteristics of the population base, this approach would require application of a model of sampling either with or without replacement. It is suggested that the latter model is perhaps the only case in which use of a representative sample for the study of developmental questions can be defended at all logically.

It is theoretically possible to obtain a representative sample of the total population at a given point in time in a cross-sectional study. The subsample in such a study for a given age, however, cannot be representative of the total membership of the particular cohort. This can be demonstrated by inspection of actuarial tables, which show that in adult samples, differential attrition occurs for successive cohorts at identical ages. This means that it would be hazardous to argue that a sample of 50-year-olds tested in 1970 is as representative of people born in 1920 as the sample of 40-year-olds is representative of people born in 1930.

To summarize, samples representative of a given cohort at birth will successively become less representative of that cohort because its attrition will not necessarily follow the laws applying to attrition in the population. A cross-sectional sample of a population at one point cannot have generality because rates of cumulative trauma and other factors affecting attrition will change from one generation to the next.

2. Aging in Intact Populations

The major alternative to representative sampling would be the selection of a sample with respect to its stability characteristics, so that one might investigate only those individuals who will survive the duration of a given study. This approach is feasible in terms of criteria such as predictors of longevity if one wishes to study behavior changes in the very old (cf. Platt & Parkes, 1967). However, we do not generally have adequate knowledge of the factors that permit prediction of whether or not a given subject will remain in a study. The study of intact populations is therefore frequently defined either as the retrospective study of a presently available sample, or as the analysis of data restricted to the survivors of a given longitudinal sample. The generality of findings in such a study is impaired again in the first case by the cautions suggested for the representative cross-sectional sample, and in the latter case requires the usual collateral studies regarding the differences between survivors and nonsurvivors.

If population parameters, rather than individual age gradients, are of interest, the further option exists to treat the survivors as a random sample of their population cohort at the final measurement point and to compare their average with the mean for the total sample at the study's initiation. This approach, however, is probably a poor substitute for the independent random sampling approach advocated earlier. Most longitudinal studies will simply be limited by the nature of their sample of survivors, and findings reported therefrom should be carefully identified as being restricted to similar populations.

If the experimenter's objectives are well defined, it may consequently be better to select extreme samples which permit explication of certain relationships albeit for very restricted population bases. When population parameters are to be estimated, however, it seems clear that sequential strategies permitting generalization over several generations will be required, and that stratified sampling should be considered with respect to demographic characteristics which have low correlation with the variables to be investigated, if random or near-random selection with respect to the experimental variables is to be hoped for.

3. Aging in Extreme Instances

There are many cases where the experimenter is not interested in population parameters, but wishes to study how various behaviors express themselves at different developmental stages under idealized or stress conditions. In these instances, one might argue for the desirability rather than the disadvantage of highly biased samples. For example, if one wants to gather data on optimal intellectual function in old age for the purpose of developing retraining programs, it would seem better strategy to work with a sample of the active, intelligent, and intact aged to determine the maximal parameters at which individuals at a given age level can perform.

In contrast to the representative sampling situation, in which as heterogeneous a sample as possible is sought, the extreme sample should be as homogeneous as possible. The special panel or carefully selected volunteer group is therefore a most useful source of subjects. Depending upon the variables to be assessed, careful screening of subjects may be required. If optimal performance levels are to be sought, selection procedures may need to include routines to discourage all but the most highly motivated volunteers. Conversely, if one is interested in defining minimum levels of functioning compatible with survival, institutional populations may be ideal. An explicit example of a study employing the strategy of selecting an extreme sample has been reported by Schaie and Strother (1968c).

Although the question of generality is not at issue with extreme samples, it is still necessary to know the relation of the sample to its parent population. One may need to be concerned about the issue of base rates, that is, the incidence of the extreme subjects in the population, as well as the extent to which the subjects investigated are skewed from the population average. The latter concern is of particular importance when subsequent parametric studies on the entire range of the behavior of interest are contemplated.

Even in extreme samples, the experimenter will face the question of whether he should randomly sample from the class of extreme subjects or whether he should narrowly define his class so as to permit exhaustive study of a finite population. If he uses the random-sampling approach, he will again face the dilemma of whether to base his findings on data restricted to those subjects available at all measurement points or compare the means of his subjects at all points as being representative samples of the parent population. No such dilemma exists if the extreme sample is treated as a finite population. In that case, measures of change must be restricted to the survivors, since it would be absurd to include data on individuals who are no longer members of the changing finite population. By similar reasoning, measures of population status, however, would be based on the total population at each measurement point.

B. Developmental Change versus Development of Pathology

Most developmentalists interested in maturity and old age implicitly accept a model of aging which entails cumulative traumatic experience and loss of function due to pathologic occurrences, which may or may not be causally related to the species-determined biological clock or the mere passage of time. Nevertheless, most sampling plans either ignore such a model or explicitly specify selection criteria which are at best arbitrary conventions. It is commonly specified that no subjects will be selected who suffer from physical disabilities or who are currently under psychiatric care. In view of the fact that the prevalence of physical disability and psychiatric disorder increases systematically with age, such selection would ensure differential representation of successive cohorts in cross-sectional studies and would lead to systematic experimental attrition in longitudinal inquiries. That is, if it were true that decremental developmental changes are exacerbated by physical or emotional trauma, then the changes reported in "normal" populations, defined as previously mentioned, would yield serious underestimates of expected developmental change in samples assessed at age levels with low prevalence of pathology.

A similar objective, that of controlling for the effects of social pathology, is often approached by excluding institutionalized subjects from a study. Again the representativeness of the sample will be impaired since the frequency of institutionalized members of successive cohorts will show a substantial correlation with chronological age if only because of the statutory provisions for handling disabled and aged individuals. Whether or not such exclusion is defensible, will again depend upon the experimenter's principal objective. That is, if population parameters are to be estimated, then the institutionalized population ought to be sampled as well. If not, collateral studies may be in order to determine in what manner institutionalized and noninstitutionalized populations do differ with respect to the variable of interest.

It may, of course, be argued that certain types of physical impairment or institutional restraints may result in the artifactual impairment of psychological functions. The *a priori* assumption, however, that this is indeed the case may be based more on the investigator's hunches than upon empirical data. Indeed, much of the more respectable experimental aging research has been conducted with institutionalized and physically impaired samples. Failure to replicate findings has usually occurred because of specific design flaws rather than the unusual characteristics of the sample employed.

Frequency of pathology increases with age, and cumulative effects of pathology may be noted in all aging individuals. It would seem futile therefore to trace "pathology-free" developmental processes, except in cases where it can be demonstrated that occurrence of a given pathology does *not* correlate with chronological age. In the latter instance, experimental or statistical control of the degree of such pathology is, of course, a must. But otherwise, it is more important to study the prevalence of pathology at different ages in relation to the variables of interest than to search for a nonexistent pathology-free population.

III. Models of Aging and Resulting Research Strategies

If generalizations are to be drawn from studies of adult development, then models of aging must be implicit in the investigator's design and subsequent sampling plan. It would be better if the investigator were to explicate his model while he is still in the design phase rather than to attempt to perform a *post hoc* analysis to determine what kind of model his research design had expressed intuitively. Two different, but equally important issues must be met in the design of any developmental study. First, the investigator must specify the dimension of development which is to be investigated. If he is interested in generalizing over maturational events, he will most likely design a project which investigates age changes within generations. If he is concerned with describing the performance of organisms at different maturational levels at one historic point in time, or with data basic to social policy decisions to be implemented immediately, he will need to look at age differences. However, if he is questioning the stability of behavioral phenomena at given levels of development, or with the effect of treatment variables upon developmental phenomena which are independent of maturational events, he will have to consider a time-lag approach.

The second basic question which should be explicated in any developmental research plan is the nature of the assumed age function. Although it might be attractive to plead ignorance and make no assumption whatsoever, the result of such decision for good research design is clearly unfortunate. Such stance implicitly leads to designs which seek to refute the null hypothesis! A much better approach would seem to be the specification of an experimental hypothesis or alternative hypotheses, with subsequent test of whether or not observed data fit the specified function.

Three different kinds of models for age functions appear to underlie most empirical investigations. The first postulates that once maturity is reached, adult behavior remains stable. The second states that aging in adults is accompanied by decrement phenomena, such that in an irreversible (or unreversed) manner, the old are disadvantaged as compared to the young. The third also implies that there is decrement, but qualifies the "irreversibility" assumption of the second model by introducing the additional condition of cumulative environmental compensation. Each of these models allows further elaboration, since "stability" may involve cycling within a range and decrement functions can have a wide variety of shapes. The question about the nature of the developmental function is equally appropriate whether one investigates age changes, age differences, or time-lags. In the latter two instances, it would, however, be more precise to speak of generation gradients or time of measurement (historical time) gradients, rather than age functions.

A. Stability of Adult Behavior

Stability of adult behavior can occur for a variety of functions which may be of interest to the psychologist. It has previously been pointed out (Schaie, 1970) that the "stability" model is quite reasonable for measures of the crystallized abilities (Cattell, 1963c), where it is assumed that the organism at maturity has acquired all the information available in the environment with respect to the measurement variable, and where there is no reason to suspect that the ratio of new information input to old information obsolescence will seriously deviate from unity. If the information gain–loss ratio is above unity, slight within-generation increment is to be expected, while a gain–loss ratio below unity will create the appearance of a slight decrement function. Secular variations of the gain–loss ratio, moreover, will lead to age functions which appear cyclical in nature.

It should be noted that the "stability" model is suitable also for those few behaviors which are primarily biologically mediated, but whose biological base remains stable from maturity to death. Reversible effects caused by temporary cell or tissue loss and their regeneration would again result in cyclical within-generation functions.

Note further that in the "stability" model, the normal state of the organism is assumed to be stability from maturity to death and that the presence of irreversible changes is incompatible with such a model. To adopt this model, therefore, the investigator must either specify that performance on the variables of interest is uncorrelated with pathology, or he must be prepared to study pathology-free, and consequently unrepresentative samples with respect to chronological age.

It should not be thought that age functions suggested by the stability model are identical or immutable. We have already noted that such functions can imply the maintenance of a constant level from maturity on or the cycling about an optimal level as a function of internal and external events. The function can show changes also in the age at which the asymptotic level is achieved, and in the age level at which performance begins to be correlated with pathology or where pathology-free subjects can no longer be found.

In any event, once the "stability" model is postulated, the investigator is no longer concerned with within-generation age functions or with age differences, since these are specified to be zero for the age range of concern. Instead, one would be concerned with the determination of generational shifts in the asymptotic level attained at maturity and the differentiation of such shifts from the transient cyclical events occurring as a function of time-specific inputs. The cross-sequential method (Schaie, 1965; Schaie & Strother, 1968a) would then become the experimental strategy of choice, as it permits differentiation of cohort and time of measurement effects, given the assumption of zero age differences.

B. *Irreversible Decrement*

If we were to consider the entire life span, we would need to distinguish between developmental functions which are linear or curvilinear, and among the latter those which are concave and those which are J shaped. There are, of course, certain functions that show cumulative decrement from birth on (e.g., number of cells in the central nervous system), but for most variables of interest to the psychologist it is possible to demonstrate a point of peak performance which typically (although not always) occurs in young adulthood. The "irreversible decrement" model, of necessity, assumes that performance is to be charted from that peak point to death. It also assumes, similar to the "stability" model, that the effects of pathology are uncorrelated with the variables of interest, or, conversely to the "stability" model, that the investigator's sample at all age levels contains a representation of pathology characteristic of the general population. The latter assumption is particularly important if it is thought that decrement is to be conceptualized as the result of cumulative pathology.

A further problem with the "irreversible decrement" model, is the need to know the peak point of performance in univariate studies, or the range of peak performances in multivariate studies. However, such peak-performance ages do not remain stable, since they may also be subject to generational shift.

Perhaps the most useful application of the irreversible decrement model is for those variables where performance seems significantly dominated by peripheral sensory functions and psychomotor speed. It may be argued that age functions here are likely to follow a biologically determined pattern which is little influenced by the cyclical events occurring within the life-span of a single organism, even though the function may shift as a consequence of events occurring to the species or any of its subgroups over long periods of time.

Since the irreversible decrement model specifies that age changes will occur as a function of maturational events, regardless of environmental input, it becomes necessary to differentiate the variance which is maturationally determined from that which may be generation specific, that is, level and attainment of peak performance age. The cohort-sequential method has the attributes necessary for this differentiation. However, Wohlwill (1970c) has highlighted the reasons which make this method the least practicable strategy for developmental studies, and it follows that the "irreversible decrement" model is one that can be tested only with considerable difficulty. From a psychological viewpoint moreover, it does not seem probable that environmental input will be of minimal importance.

Cycling effects here, if present, would tend to yield pseudostability functions for high gain–loss ratios and very steep decrement functions where the gain–loss ratio is low.

C. Decrement with Compensation

A more reasonable position than the "irreversible decrement" model may be one which assumes that maturational events require phases of growth and decline which can be approximated by quasi-linear functions for either portion, but where curvilinear alternatives exist which do not require that the peak of performance occur temporally at an early adult stage. Moreover the curvilinear patterns may be explained by environmental compensatory input, which becomes effective during the decrement, but not during the increment phase of a life-span growth gradient. In other words, during the growth phase, environmental input affects observed performance minimally, since the organism has not yet reached its capacity as specified by its biologically determined limits. During the decrement phase, however, biologically determined decrement may be partially compensated by environmental input, at least as observed in complex psychological measures.

The "decrement with compensation" model may be particularly appropriate for measures of fluid intelligence and for many other psychological variables where reaction time is involved. The model is also generally appropriate for variables where age changes during the adult period must be expected, where long-term shifts over generations seem unlikely, but where environmental input should have important cycling effects. For all such variables, it would seem important to differentiate variance due to maturational events from the variance due to transient environmental inputs which might conceal the maturational process. The strategy of choice for such differentiation would generally be the time-sequential method—the most practical of the sequential research strategies—which allows identification of age and time of measurement variance under the assumption of zero generation differences (Schaie, 1965; Schaie & Strother, 1968b).

It should be noted that the last model can be applied to both intact or representative samples, since the presence or absence of age-related pathology is not critical. That is, pathology is assumed to be present due to biologically mediated decrement events, but such pathology may be compensated for by environmental inputs. Depending upon the slope of the underlying maturational gradient, we may expect for this model either that a moderately accelerating decrement gradient will be observed, or that in the extreme case, decrement will be noted just prior to death, that is, when compensatory inputs no longer suffice to stabilize the behavior in question. The latter situation would, of course, be difficult to differentiate from the "stability" model. Indeed, a reasonable design would collect data in such a way that the stability and compensated decrement models could be examined as alternate experimental hypotheses.

D. The General Developmental Model
Restricted to the Period of Adult Development

We must now backtrack to the fundamental question of what it is that the developmentalist wishes to study, with special application to the analysis of the adult phase of the human life cycle. The general developmental model simply holds that the magnitude of a response (as studied by the developmentalist) is determined by the age of the organism, the cohort (generation) to which the organism belongs, and the point in time at which the response is measured. Although the three components of developmental change are theoretically independent, they are empirically confounded in that any two indices will determine the value of the third. Since there are three ways in which three components can combine two at a time, it follows from the general developmental model, that there must be three ways in which empirical data can be collected, each approach resulting in different although related confounds. The three ways in which developmental data can be studied are, of course, the longitudinal, cross-sectional, and time-lag methods (Schaie, 1965). Each approach confounds two components of developmental change. The longitudinal method confounds age and environmental impact between times of measurement, the cross-sectional method confounds age and generation differences, and the time-lag method confounds generation differences and environmental impact between times of measurement.

The general developmental model further calls attention to the fact that the investigator has at his disposal for any particular range of the life span, a "trapezoidal" population, consisting of several generations, available to the investigator over a specified period of time. The investigator therefore has the option to study several cohorts over a specified age range (cohort-sequential method), several cohorts over a specified period of time (cross-sequential method), or several age levels over a specified period of time (time-sequential method). The traditional methods, given the assumption that one of the components has a zero value, by comparison can, of course, yield information only on a single one of the three components. The sequential methods have the advantage that given certain assumptions, they will yield information on two of the three components of developmental change.

Since the age function for any variable would be determined by the combination of functions for the three components of developmental change (taken two at a time), there must be as many as 243 distinct models for any growth function having as few as three observation points, if we allow nine distinguishable gradient slopes (zero, positive, negative, concave, convex, accelerating, decelerating, positive asymptotic, negative asymptotic). All these models will need to be considered for total life-span studies. However, if we define adult development as the period beginning with the attainment of maximal maturation, then matters become considerably simpler. We may immediately neglect all models for the age components of developmental change which specify positive, concave, convex, accelerating, or positive asymptotic slopes, resulting in a reduction to 153 distinct models. If we further assume that for a given variable, environmental input (whether short or long range) is unidirectional, that is, either good or bad, we then find ourselves limited to the manageable number of, at most, 24 alternative component combinations which would explain variation in adult behavior. Explicitly, the stability model would permit 16 combinations of the cohort and time of measurement gradients (zero, positive, accelerating, and positive asymptotic for each). The irreversible decrement model would allow four combinations (negative for age, with either zero, positive, accelerating, or positive asymptotic for the cohort gradient), as would the decrement with compensation model (negative for age, and zero, positive, accelerating, or positive asymptotic for environmental input).

E. Implication of Models for the Selection of Research Strategies

Past descriptive research has frequently collected the wrong data to answer the right question, or even worse collected the right data in ignorance of the questions to be asked appropriately from such data. It may therefore be timely to stress unequivocally that a proper research strategy and design for data collection can be developed only if (a) the specific developmental question is made explicit and (b) the hypothesized shape of the age function is specified. The first constraint is required to know what data are to be collected and should be obvious. The second is less obvious, but must be required if developmental implications are to be inferred from the data. It is argued, then, that descriptive developmental research must utilize a hypothetico-deductive approach, because observational data necessarily confound dimensions of developmental change and do not permit the inductive procedures permissible in the nondevelopmental sciences.

A specific set of recommendations may be deduced from the series of limiting assumptions specified in this chapter. Data-gathering strategies will therefore be classified in terms of their major descriptive appropriateness for each of the questions asked by developmentalists under the assumptions necessary for each of the three major models for adult development.

1. Cohort-Specific Changes

a. Are There Age Changes in General?   This question cannot be answered by any cohort-specific strategy.

b. Are There Age Changes for a Specific Cohort (postdictive)?

(*i*) *Stability model*. We assume that there are no age changes as such, but a *longitudinal* study would yield information on the gain–loss ratio cycling attributable to time of measurement differences.

(*ii*) *Irreversible decrement model*. Since time of measurement differences are here assumed to be zero, the *longitudinal* method would provide the age function for the specific cohort.

(*iii*) *Decrement with compensation model*. *Time-sequential* method to permit differentiation of change due to maturation from that due to specific temporal compensatory inputs.

c. Are There Age Changes for a Specific Cohort (predictive)?

(*i*) *Stability model*. Since no maturational changes are expected, we need the confound of generation and time of measurement differences to predict the future performance of a specific cohort under this assumption. This would involve time-lags and consequently the *cross-sequential* method is needed to sample enough past time-lags to provide realistic estimates.

(*ii*) *Irreversible decrement model*. Here we wish to forecast maturational changes which may differ among generations. The *cohort-sequential* method is therefore required.

(*iii*) *Decrement with compensation*. Performance of a specific cohort at given ages may vary due to changes in environmental input. Estimates must therefore be based on samples at various ages and times of measurement, the *time-sequential* method.

2. Species-Specific Changes

a. Are There Age Changes in General?

(*i*) *Stability model*. No age changes are postulated, but the cross-sectional method would give information about generation differences.

(*ii*) *Irreversible decrement model*. The *cohort-sequential* method would be required to describe both age functions and generation differences therein.

(*iii*) *Decrement with compensation model*. Since compensation has been postulated as trivial with respect to species-specific changes, and generation differences as trivial to the compensation model, the *longitudinal* method should in this case provide an acceptable age function.

b. Do Individuals at Different Ages Require Differential Treatment at the Present Time?

(*i*) *Stability model*. Different treatment would have to be based on the fact of generational differences. These would in the absence of age differences, be directly detected by the *cross-sectional* method.

(*ii*) *Irreversible decrement model.* Present differences could be due to age differences, cohort differences, or both. Since they do not require differentiation to answer this question, the *cross-sectional* method is again appropriate.

(*iii*) *Decrement with compensation model.* This model postulates the absence of generation differences and the *cross-sectional* method is therefore the proper estimate of age differences.

c. Will Social Policies with Respect to Age Require Future Modification? This question is directly concerned with the issue of generation differences. Solutions require the differentiation of age and generation change, using the same designs as provided previously in 2a for the general·question of age changes.

3. Culture-Specific Changes

The basic question here is whether or not individuals at given ages show behavior variations as a function of the time when the behavior is observed. This is generally speaking a question of measuring *time-lag*. The postulated age function model will nevertheless be of importance in planning the data collection if time-lag is to be investigated for more than a single age level.

a. Stability Model. Since no age changes are postulated, a simple *time-lag* design for each of the age levels and points in time of interest will suffice. For more than one age level this is formally equivalent to either cohort- or time-sequential method with intensive sampling at each age level for either cohorts or times of measurement.

b. Irreversible Decrement Model. Here cultural changes in the form of generation differences must be separated from age changes. The *cohort-sequential* method would be most appropriate.

c. Decrement with Compensation Model. In this instance we need to separate the effects of age from those of time of measurement differences, and the *time-sequential* method is the design of choice.

4. What Can the Descriptive Developmental Strategies Tell Us?

At the risk of being unnecessarily redundant this section will be ended by summarizing the questions which can be answered by each of the six alternative methods of data collection.

a. Longitudinal Method. Historical description of age changes in a specific cohort under the assumption of stability (information about gain–loss ratio cycling) or irreversible decrement; detection of species-specific age changes under the assumption of decrement with compensation.

b. Cross-Sectional Method. Detection of species-specific generation differences under the stability assumption; recommendations regarding treatment of individuals at different ages for *immediate* policy decisions under all assumptions; recommendations for long term policy decisions under the stability assumption.

c. Time-Lag Method. Detection of cultural change under the stability assumption.

d. Cohort-Sequential Method. Prediction of specific cohort performance, detection of species-specific age changes and culture-specific changes, and recommendations for long term policy decisions under the irreversible decrement assumption.

e. Time-Sequential Method. Historical account of age changes in a specific cohort, prediction of specific cohort performance, and detection of culture-specific change under the decrement with compensation assumption. This method is also appropriate for information relevant to long term policy recommendation involving both cultural and age changes.

f. Cross-Sequential Method. Prediction of cohort-specific change under the stability assumption. Also appropriate for the separation of culture specific change into cohort and time of measurement components.

IV. Within Cohort (Longitudinal) Studies of Adult Development

We will now consider a number of problems in the implementation of descriptive research on adult development which are particularly relevant to studies concerned with describing or predicting age changes within generations, to which the longitudinal approach or the more general sequential methods are applicable. Most of these problems have conceptual as well as practical implications for research design.

A. Development and Sociocultural Change

Three different types of environmental input must be distinguished. First, there is the input which occurs through the simple act of measurement itself, which may modify the response of the organism whether the experimenter so intends or not. Second, there is the experimental modification, or treatment intervention, programmed or selected by the investigator. Such treatment effects do appear frequently also in purely descriptive research, since we may have selected a population sample which is known to receive a treatment between measurement intervals which differs from that accorded to the parent population. Finally, there is the input unique to a given time period which occurs due to unspecified modifications in the environment over which the researcher has no control or of which he is not cognizant. In all three instances the treatment involved may equally affect organisms of any age, or there may be an age by treatment interaction, i.e., the treatment may affect organisms at one age, but not at another.

The first two sources of treatment variance can be controlled by the traditional method of random assignment of subjects to different treatment or practice conditions (cf. Baltes & Goulet, 1971). No such assignment is possible, however, with respect to the third source, which involves sociocultural change over which the experimenter has no control, illustrating the necessarily quasi-experimental nature (Campbell & Stanley, 1963) of any developmental research design. The dimension of sociocultural change is of paramount importance in descriptive research on aging. It will be particularly bothersome in long-term studies since there is ample evidence that the attitudes of subjects about themselves and the experimental procedures will change, as will the attitudes of the experimenter which may differentially affect the outcome of his procedures.

If the researcher's ingenuity and resources permit, he should consider a mixed model which will permit the study of interactions between age level, experimental treatment effects, and naturalistic treatment effects (the last being attributed to sociocultural change). Such a model, however, requires that all age levels be examined at more than one time and under each of the experimental treatment conditions as well as under control conditions. An empirical example of a design for the differentiation of age, time of measurement, and treatment effects is reported elsewhere for the dimensions of behavioral rigidity (Schaie, 1971).

The investigator conducting descriptive research may be willing to assume that there has been no systematic intervention for which he must control. However, he cannot safely ignore the confounding of the effects of measuring his variables and the general environmental impact in studies of aging. The sequential designs must therefore be used to distinguish between age changes (qua maturational events and/or age specific though environmentally programmed behavior acquisitions) and the temporally unique generalized input from the environment.

If the investigator is interested primarily in population parameters, he may be able to beg the issue of measurement or practice effects by considering the independent random sampling design as the most general form of longitudinal inquiry. Here the investigator would take successive random samples from the same cohort at successive measurement times, testing each subject only once. Specification of sampling either with or without replacement should be made, although it is unlikely that there will be practical consequences of assuming one or the other sampling model. Further complications arise, of course, if individual age changes are to be observed, because a repeated measurement design will then be required.

B. Effects of Repeated Measurement

Despite the many sampling and sample maintenance problems discussed earlier, many investigators of within-generation age changes have preferred to conduct studies which involve the repeated measurement of the same subjects. Whether or not the intent has been to follow individual subjects over time, it has frequently been argued that in circumstances where experimental error is large and changes may be small, variability can be significantly reduced by use of the matched group design of which the longitudinal, repeated-measurement study is an application.

Unless we can assume that there are no sociocultural change effects upon our measurement variables and unless we know that the effect of one measurement upon subsequent measurements is zero, the results of a single-sample repeated-measurement study cannot be interpreted and such a research design, therefore, does not represent a permissible developmental research strategy (see also Schaie, 1972). This prohibition does not apply to the use of repeated measurements in the sequential methods. However, it should be pointed out that the repeated measurement design may be less desirable than the independent random sampling approach for other reasons also. These are (1) lower efficiency, (2) misleading regression effects, (3) design complications in handling effects of practice, and (4) experimental mortality.

1. Comparative Efficiency of Repeated-Measurement Designs

Repeated-measurement designs become efficient only when measures have high reliability or when it is possible to take measures either at many ages or many times of measurement. This follows because, for an equal number of observations, the degrees of freedom available for the error term used to test mean differences will always be less for replicated than for independently derived measurements. The gain in sensitivity must, therefore, exceed the loss caused by testing a smaller number of subjects before the repeated measurement design will begin to pay off.

The preceding statement is not simply a bias in favor of independent random sampling. It can be shown formally that the error term used for the test of significance of cohort differences will be based on the residual variation between subjects which in the cohort-sequential method will have $N - (N/A) - C (A - 1)$ fewer degress of freedom than would an independent random sampling design based on the same number of observations, where N is the number of observations, A the number of age levels, and C the number of cohort levels. Similarly the error term which must be used for testing the significance of cohort differences in the cross-sequential method will have $N - (N/T) - C (T - 1)$ fewer degrees of freedom in the repeated measurement design than in the comparable independent random sampling design. (T stands for time of measurement levels). The error term used to test age and Age × Cohort interaction in the cohort-sequential design will have $N - (N/T)$ fewer degrees of freedom. It should also be noted that the time-sequential method with repeated measurement faces the problem that repeated measurements are not available for the first or last age level, and that between-subjects sums of squares would, therefore, have to be computed upon the means for each subject's scores rather than upon the sums as would customarily be the case. In the latter case, there would be $N - (A + 2)(N/AT)$ fewer degrees of freedom than in the independent random sampling design.

2. Misleading Regression Effects

Orthodox test theory would suggest strong regression effects in any study where the same subjects are measured repeatedly. There has been considerable controversy as to how change should be measured under such circumstances or whether it should be measured at all (Campbell & Stanley, 1963; Cronbach & Furby, 1970). The principal effect of regression consists in the assumed positive correlation between error of measurement and observed score, given that the error scores of subjects on different occasions are uncorrelated. The effect of regression may not be too serious for the estimation of population parameters, but it may lead to an artifactual shrinkage of differences between age levels, cohorts, or times of measurement over long series of repeated observations. The effects of regression seem to be fatal, however, in studies contrasting ability levels. Apparently strong evidence, for example, has been claimed for the proposition that development of intellectual function varies with ability level (e.g., Miles & Miles, 1932; Owens, 1966; Riegel, Riegel, & Meyer, 1967b). However, by using appropriate time reversal procedures, Baltes, Nesselroade, Schaie, and Labouvie (1972) were able to show that the relation of ability level to differences in ontogenetic patterns of adult intelligence—found in a cross-sequential repeated measurement study (Schaie & Strother, 1968a)—occurred due to statistical regression effects. Moreover, in agreement with Lord (1963), it was found that the regression effects were greatest for the least reliable measures. Time-reversal or similar techniques (Campbell & Stanley, 1963) are therefore strongly recommended whenever differences in developmental change as a function of initial performance level are to be investigated.

3. Design Complications in Handling Effects of Practice

It has already been stated that the conventional longitudinal method confounds age, environmental change, and the effects of measurement or practice. The sequential strategies separate the components of developmental change, but in their most straightforward form also confound the effects of practice. A direct estimate of the effect of practice can be obtained from the cohort-sequential repeated measurement design if age changes can be assumed to be zero. Similarly, practice effects can be estimated in the cross-sequential repeated measurement design if time of measurement differences are assumed to be zero. If these assumptions do not hold, then practice will be confounded with either age or time of measurement effects.

It is possible to obtain independent estimates of practice effects under all assumptions, if the investigator is prepared to employ conjointly repeated measurement and independent random sampling designs. These estimates are obtained by examining all levels of the developmental components at two or more levels of practice. Minimal data to assess the effects of measurement or practice involve at least three test occasions for the cross-sequential and time-sequential methods and at least four test occasions for the cohort-sequential method. Tables 1 to 3 provide the necessary sampling plans and generalized analysis of variance models. Note that the estimates of practice effects are based on populations receiving different treatment and not upon within-subject variance. The latter analysis is possible for data collections via the cross-sequential and cohort-sequential methods, but will require even more complex sampling plans. Such designs may be needed when there are specific methodological reasons to estimate within-subject practice effects. In general, however, the design presented here should provide appropriate strategies for accounting for the variance due to measurement effects.

4. Experimental Mortality

Perhaps the most serious limitation of the repeated measurement design is the inevitable nonrandom attrition or what Campbell and Stanley (1963) termed "experimental mortality." It may be profitable to distinguish here between two types of attrition. The first, which may or may not be a function of the experimenter's skill in sample maintenance, involves age differences in experimental mortality due to psychological and/or sociological reasons, for example, attrition caused by lack of interest, active refusal, change of residence, or disappearance. The second type of experimental mortality, over which the experimenter has no influence, involves age differences in sample attrition due to biological causes. Here we would include age-related subject loss due to physical illness and individual differences in longevity. Not all studies need be affected by this problem. However, in all those instances where there is a correlation between attrition and the variable of interest, findings on ontogenetic changes can be markedly affected. The problem seems particularly serious in the area of cognitive function since brighter subjects seem to have greater longevity (e.g., Blum, Jarvik, & Clark, 1970; Jarvik & Falek, 1963; Riegel, Riegel, & Meyer, 1968).

Studies of attrition caused by biological factors typically show that survivors have more positive attributes with respect to interests and attitudes (Riegel, Riegel, & Meyer, 1968; Streib, 1966), but also higher social and educational levels (Rose, 1965; Streib, 1966). Lest it be thought that favorable selection of residual samples in longitudinal study be restricted to biological variables, there is also strong evidence that such favorable selection, at least with respect to intellectual level, occurs due to dropout from all causes (Baltes, Schaie, & Nardi, 1971).

TABLE 1

Sampling Plan and Generalized Analysis of
Variance Model for the Cohort-Sequential Method
Controlled for the Effects of Practice

a. Sampling Plan[a]

Time of test	Samples tested
T_0	Random half of group C_iA_m
T_1	All of C_iA_m; random halves of groups C_iA_n and C_jA_m
T_2	All of C_iA_n; all of C_jA_m; random half of group C_jA_n
T_3	All of C_jA_n

b. Generalized Analysis of Variance Model

Source of variation	Degrees of freedom
Between cohorts (C)	$C - 1$
Between ages (A)	$A - 1$
Between practice levels (P)	$P - 1$
Cohort $\times$ Age	$(C - 1)(A - 1)$
Cohort $\times$ Practice	$(C - 1)(P - 1)$
Age $\times$ Practice	$(A - 1)(P - 1)$
Cohort $\times$ Age $\times$ Practice	$(C - 1)(A - 1)(P - 1)$
Error	$N - (C)(A)(P)$
Total variance	$N - 1$

[a]Scores obtained on the first test for each sample are disregarded. Only the second set of scores for the random halves tested initially and the single set of scores available for the random halves without practice enter into the analysis.

C. Changes in Factor Structure over Time

In addition to the problem that the reliable variance in developmental observations may be obscured by regression effects, we must also be concerned with the change in meaning of the true component of any observed score. The most cautious approach would, of course, consist of relying solely on measures whose factorial structure and stability over time were well known. However, measures of this nature are few and even fewer investigators in the past have paid much attention to the advantage of multivariate approaches to developmental problems (see also Schaie & Marquette, 1972). While the question of equivalence of test instruments is particularly pertinent in species-specific studies which compare generation differences, it is the equivalence of factor structure for the same instrument which is at issue when we consider within-cohort age-related variations

TABLE 2

Sampling Plan and Generalized Analysis of Variance
Model for the Time-Sequential Method
Controlled for the Effects of Practice

a. Sampling Plan[a]

Time of test	Samples tested
T_0	Random halves of samples A_mT_k and A_nT_k
T_1	All of A_mT_k and A_nT_k; random halves of A_mT_1 and A_nT_1
T_2	All of A_mT_1 and A_nT_1

b. Generalized Analysis of Variance Model

Source of variation	Degrees of freedom
Between times (T)	$T - 1$
Between ages (A)	$A - 1$
Between practice levels (P)	$P - 1$
Time × Age	$(T - 1)(A - 1)$
Time × Practice	$(T - 1)(P - 1)$
Age × Practice	$(A - 1)(P - 1)$
Time × Age × Practice	$(T - 1)(A - 1)(P - 1)$
Error	$N - (T)(A)(P)$
Total variance	$N - 1$

[a]Scores obtained on the first test for each sample are disregarded in this analysis. Thus the second set of scores for the random half tested initially and the only set of scores for the random half without practice enter the analysis.

of performance. The issue of equivalence of instruments should be important to the investigator of adult development only in those instances where he wishes to link the behavior of his subjects from childhood to adulthood. In the latter case, equivalence of factor structure within samples over different instruments will also be at issue (e.g., Schaie & Cattell, 1971).

For within-cohort studies, there are three different problems related to the invariance of factor structure which should be considered. These concern the distinction between structural change in the relationship among dimensions and quantitative change in performance level on conceptually identical dimensions (Baltes & Nesselroade, 1970; Cattell, 1969); the question of describing age functions for distinct and ideally orthogonal dimensions (Botwinick, 1967; Reinert, 1970; Schaie, Rosenthal, & Perlman, 1953); and the disentanglement

TABLE 3

Sampling Plan and Generalized Analysis of Variance
Model for the Cross-Sequential Model
Controlled for Effects of Practice

a. Sampling Plan[a]	
Time of test	Samples tested
T_0	Random halves of samples $C_i T_k$ and $C_j T_k$
T_1	All of $C_i T_k$ and $C_j T_k$; random halves of $C_i T_1$ and $C_j T_1$
T_2	All of $C_i T_1$ and $C_j T_1$

b. Generalized Analysis of Variance Model	
Source of variation	Degrees of freedom
Between cohorts (C)	$C - 1$
Between times (T)	$T - 1$
Between practice levels (P)	$P - 1$
Cohort × Time	$(C - 1)(T - 1)$
Cohort × Practice	$(C - 1)(P - 1)$
Time × Practice	$(T - 1)(P - 1)$
Cohort × Time × Practice	$(C - 1)(T - 1)(P - 1)$
Error	$N - (C)(T)(P)$
Total variance	$N - 1$

[a]Scores obtained on the first test for each sample are disregarded. The second set of scores for the random halves tested initially and the only set of scores for the random halves without practice enter the analysis.

of ontogenetic and generation variance on factorially stable dimensions (Nesselroade, Schaie, & Baltes, 1972).

1. Structural Change in Factor Structure

The first problem relates to the possibility that one could have systematic age changes on observables (due to observational artifacts) with concurrent stability of factor scores. That is, we need to know not only whether the factorial structure of a given measurement set remains invariant over different measurement occasions, but also whether there are shifts in factor scores resulting from changes in differential weighting. The question of the invariance of factor structure normally involves the comparison of the correlation patterns among first occasion measures with the correlation patterns for subsequent measurement occasions. Evidence for structural change could take the form of different numbers of factors for different occasions and/or lack of invariance of the factor loading patterns. To protect against the possibility of reporting structural changes as a function of invariance of observational error it is recommended strongly that the zero-order correlation matrices also be compared directly to test the hypothesis that their deviation from one another is no greater than chance (Schaie, 1958). If such a test fails to reject the null hypothesis, it would then be fair to conclude that changes in number of factors or factor loading patterns are chance variations and can be safely ignored.

Rejection of the null hypothesis with respect to equivalence of the zero-order correlation matrices does not necessarily imply the acceptance of the alternate hypothesis of structural change. Before this outcome can be accepted (with the consequent conclusion that results of the study were uninterpretable with respect to quantitative change in performance level), it would be wise to rotate the factor matrices for the different measurement occasions to positions of maximum agreement by means of Meredith's (1964) procedure, with subsequent transformation of the factor pattern to simple structure while maintaining invariance attained by the Meredith rotation (Nesselroade & Cattell, 1970).

2. Quantitative Change in Performance Level

Once the factors which are invariant over time have been identified, it then becomes possible and desirable to estimate factor scores by averaging corresponding first and subsequent occasion weights obtained from the factor pattern loadings (Harman, 1960). However, for a developmental study, it is essential that observed score distributions be standardized jointly over all measurement occasions prior to estimating factor scores. The latter procedure is required in order to permit the appearance of between-occasion mean differences.

The advantage of age functions plotted on the basis of factor scores under those using the observed raw measures should be obvious. We are comparing individuals on idealized variables whose conceptual meaning has been established to be invariant over time. Changes in mean performance level on factor scores can therefore validly be interpreted as change in behavior rather than as possible transformations in the meaning of the measurement variable as is the case when the observed variables are compared over time.

Of interest also will be the assessment of the stability of factor scores. Since the factor scores represent estimates of the reliable components of variance, it may be argued that their magnitude should give an indication of the stability of the behavior rather than of the reliability of the measurement instrument.

3. Ontogenetic and Generation Variance in Factorially Stable Dimensions

The observation of factorial invariance in an adult population can, of course, not be taken as direct evidence of stability over age. Nevertheless it is most likely that both the irreversible decrement model and the decrement with compensation model apply primarily to observable variables which are factorially complex, and whose complexity (i.e., factorial structure) changes over time. The stability model may therefore be most likely to apply to factorially pure and consequently structurally invariant variables. If this latter speculation is correct, then it would follow that the cross-sequential method would be most appropriate for the analysis of factor scores. This method will distinguish between the proportion of variance accounting for mean differences in generational levels and that proportion which is due to temporal variation in the gain–loss ratio represented by the ontogenetic component of variance.

Nesselroade *et al.* (1972) have recently reported an empirical example of this approach for various measures of cognitive behavior. This study clearly demonstrates that significant differences in mean factor scores can be found between generations as well as within generations. But the study also shows—in a design which permits the appropriate comparison—that the proportion of variance within generations (of major interest in longitudinal studies) is quite trivial and for no factor accounts for more than 5% of the total variance. Components of variance due to generational differences, in contrast, account for at least one-third of the total variance and may therefore be assumed to have practical as well as theoretical implications.

V. Between Cohort (Cross-Sectional) Studies of Adult Development

The reader may by now have concluded that in the realm of adult behavior development little is to be gained from a description of age functions as such and that our interest might better be applied to the investigation of cultural change and its impact upon behavior found to occur in adults belonging to different generations at different points in historical time. It is hoped that he will have concluded further that while cross-sectional studies cannot yield age functions, they are admirably useful for investigating intergenerational differences. Both the traditional cross-sectional method and its more general form, the time-sequential method, can be used for this purpose. However, studies of intergenerational differences also have problems. Three issues considered here involve the analysis of differences between successive cross-sectional studies, possible designs involving both prospective and retrospective data, and the question of whether age- or cohort-appropriate measurement devices should be used when we are interested in assessing generation differences.

A. Comparisons within and between Cross-Sectional Studies

If the student of adult development is willing to accept the stability model, he can then utilize the single cross-sectional study to describe differences in behavior between successive generations. This means that much of the psychological literature on age differences can once again become useful if we engage in the massive effort of relabeling tables and graphs by substituting the subjects' year of birth (identifying their cohort membership) for the age designation. That is, whenever we are willing to assume that a variable does not show any significant age changes over the adult period, we can interpret the results of cross-sectional studies as direct descriptions of inter-generational differences. Taken from this point of view it now becomes necessary to conduct a systematic review of the literature, since failure to replicate findings of performance level for given ages is no longer critical. What we are looking for now would be the replicability of findings for given cohorts.

However, what happens in the event that the assumption of stability of adult behavior were false? Surprisingly, no serious consequences would result in those instances where cross-sectional data are appropriate in the first place. Since cross-sectional data would normally be applied only to problems requiring judgment about population differences at the present point in time, it would not really be crucial if one of the components of the observed difference between successive cohorts were due to change in maturational level. However, the failure of the stability assumption would be quite critical when the cross-sectional model is used to detect generation differences for the purpose of long-range forward planning.

Studies directed toward generating data for forward planning assume, of course, that intergenerational differences detected at the present time are likely to shift. If the reader will recall our analysis of the principal models accounting for adult development, he will note that this assumption is most compatible with the decrement with compensation model. We want to know to what extent the shift in environmental input affects performance level at different ages. The comparisons provided by the time-sequential method do indeed provide the necessary information and permit isolation of the components of variance due to change in maturational level from those due to change in environmental input, and from the shift in intergenerational differences which would be represented by the interaction term. If we replicate a cross-sectional study over several measurement occasions, we will find that age differences which are observed at one measurement point and which are actually generation differences will tend to disappear when averaged over many measurement points. But if such age differences are indeed differences in maturational level, then they will remain, no matter how many replications are taken. Environmental input will be assessed by comparing the difference between measurement occasions over many age-generational levels, and it becomes possible after a few replications to plot projected trends which may be useful for long range predictions.

It should be noted, though, that comparison of cross-sectional studies based on independent samples can yield information on the stability of performance levels within generations only under the assumption of the stability model.

To draw meaningful conclusions under other models would require replication of the same cross-sectional study by drawing successive, independent samples covering the same age range from the same parent population.

B. Comparison by Means of Prospective and Retrospective Estimates

Although the one-shot cross-sectional approach has been faulted *ad nauseam*, it remains obviously attractive to the researcher (such as the graduate student) who has only limited time to complete a given project. Serious attention has therefore been given to the possibility of generating data covering the adult life span by obtaining retrospective or prospective information over many points of the respondents' experience, but collected at one point in time (e.g., Bell, 1960; Lehr, 1967; Yarrow, Campbell, & Burton, 1970). Leaving aside the serious questions with respect to the reliability and validity of information thus gathered, it should be noted that such studies suffer from the general problems of the longitudinal repeated measurement model, although in an asymmetric fashion. That is, in the retrospective report of behavior, each earlier episode reported will be affected by the report of more recent episodes as well as the present condition of the respondent. Conversely, in prospective reports, each later projected episode will be affected by reports about earlier episodes. Whether or not the sequential methods are applicable to the study of retrospective and prospective data remains to be investigated. One major problem here would be the necessity of comparing cohorts with relatively unequal representation of past and future life intervals at comparable age levels. An attempt at utilizing such models has been made by Back and Bourgue (1970) in a study of life satisfaction.

While there are difficulties in using prospective and retrospective methods for the study of actual behavior, these methods seem to be quite suitable for the consideration of perceived age and cultural changes. This area, which has received considerable recent interest, is bound to expand further if Neugarten (1969) was correct in her assertion that role perception associated with age level is indeed one of the most important determinants of ontogenetic change. Since role perception of any age level must be viewed from a constant point in historical time, the cross-sectional approach is quite appropriate here, and the time-sequential method could be used to test the stability of such role perceptions. (See also Ahammer & Baltes, 1970; Bekker & Taylor, 1966; Britton & Britton, 1969.)

C. Age-Appropriate versus Cohort-Appropriate Test Instruments

Whenever comparisons are to be made between cohorts we must concern ourselves with the question of whether or not test instruments are equally appropriate for members of different cohorts. This issue has been studied for some time with respect to tests thought appropriate for different age levels. For example, forms suitable at different ages have been developed for the Wechsler Intelligence Tests and for the factored series of personality tests developed by Cattell and his associates. The fact that a given test is or is not appropriate for a given age level does not, however, assure us that it will continue to be appropriate for that age level. Because of changes in the content of the culture, many tests may become inappropriate for a given age level. In this sense, it is conceivable that the original Wechsler–Bellevue may be a more valid test for older adults than is its more recent revision. That revision may now be discriminating against 20-year-olds because the cohort appropriateness of its content has shifted.

Perhaps the most serious work bearing on the issue of cohort appropriateness of test material, crucial for adequate comparison of the membership of different generations, is currently being conducted at Syracuse University.[2] Monge and his associates classified words in terms of their entry into the accepted vocabulary as demonstrated by appropriate dictionary search. They were able to show that the cohort word familiarity gradient could be readily manipulated for slang items and other words depending upon the entry of the term into active vocabulary. Thus, while 20- and 30-year-olds performed significantly better on items entering the language after 1960, it was found that 40- to 60-year-olds performed significantly better on items entering the language in the late 1920s. It appears then that differences in verbal performance between cohorts typically reported from cross-sectional studies could well be artifacts related to the cohort appropriateness of the test instruments used.

VI. Some Comments on Research Priorities in the Study of Adult Development

This discussion of methodological issues in descriptive research on adult development was prefaced by saying that the time was not yet ripe for laboratory manipulative investigation because we need to take another look at what is to be manipulated. This does not mean, however, that we should ignore the possibilities offered by experiments of nature nor that we should revert to an aimless search for evidence which differentiates the behavior of the old from that of the young. It is suggested, instead, that high priority be given to a hypothetico-deductive approach which specifies the kind of models according to which adult development is expected to occur and then assemble data which could support or discredit such models. This means that we should not reject the use of cross-sectional approaches out of hand, but rather, by means of suitable replication, test the generalizations possible for such data. It is further suggested that studies of extreme groups should be encouraged because they

[2]R. F. Monge, personal communication, 1971.

are likely to yield quicker payoff in terms of developmental laws regarding adult development than is the search for representative data which may often be irrelevant or impossible to obtain. Where population estimates are sought, again it would seem appropriate to give much thought to the purpose for which data are to be collected. Finally, it is argued that the emphasis for students of adult development, at least for psychological variables, must be directed toward intergenerational differences and cultural change as being more meaningful parameters than chronological age.

CHAPTER 13

The Interfaces of Acquisition:
Models and Methods for
Studying the Active, Developing Organism[1]

L. R. GOULET

UNIVERSITY OF ILLINOIS
URBANA-CHAMPAIGN, ILLINOIS

I. Introduction

It is perhaps appropriate to state at the outset that contemporary research identified with the study of learning presents something of a paradox when evaluated in the context of historical approaches.[2] For example, we now know that very little new information is actually acquired in a learning experiment since subjects usually have the basic requisites of task mastery already available in their repertoire of habits and skills. Not so contradictory is the fact that changes in performance with practice reflect not only the acquisition and/or "strengthening" of a specified behavior or set of behaviors but, just as important, the inhibition of alternate or competing behaviors or response tendencies which are negatively correlated with task mastery. In other words learning *not* to respond in a particular fashion is likely just as responsible for performance

---

[1]Helpful comments by Hayne W. Reese are gratefully acknowledged.

[2]"Historical approaches" refer, in general, to the era dominated by classic learning theories. Also, in agreement with Mandler (1967), the period circa 1950 marks the emergence of research problems and strategies which continue today.

changes with practice as the two mechanisms which are most commonly identified with the phenomenon of learning; i.e., the acquisition of a specific habit or skill, and the selection or use of an appropriate skill or strategy available in the subject's behavioral repertoire.

Contemporary experiments, for the most part, focus on "what" is learned when practice is provided and little emphasis is placed on the design of critical experiments relating to "how" learning occurs. The current focus of research on learning processes is oriented to the transfer of what has been learned to new problems and tasks rather than to the number of trials, amount of time, or number of errors to criterion in the solution of a single task. Finally, a basic assumption of contemporary studies is that performance on any task requires not just a single mechanism, but a series of higher-order habits and skills (e.g., Gagne, 1968; Grant, 1964; Kausler, 1970; Mandler, 1967; Melton, 1964; Postman, 1969; Underwood, 1964b).

I do not imply that contemporary research is divorced from, or unrelated to the research precipitated by classic theories such as those of Hull, Tolman, and Guthrie. As one example, the notion that learning involves the strengthening of habits is still with us, although in modified form (e.g., Kausler, 1970; Underwood, 1964b). Nevertheless, as Mandler (1967) and Kausler (1970) have adequately documented, current research emphasizes the acquisition and use of complex, higher-order skills in performance, while deemphasizing the role of rote processes. In making the same distinction, Spence (1963), in the classic tradition, argued for the study of the basic processes of conditioning in young adults in a manner which obfuscated the effects of complex, cognitive processes. In this example, we see another commonality in classic and contemporary research, namely the admission of the role of (and possible interaction between) cognitive and rote processes in human performance.

The evident time lag in the study of the effects of cognitive factors in learning performance has an interesting parallel in developmental research. That is, the research related to learning and acquisition phenomena seems to have "developed" in much the same way that current developmental theories suggest that children develop. Developmental changes in the behavior of young children, for example, are often described as a shift away from a mode of responding characterized by rote, animal-like processes to processes best identified as cognitive, mediational, or symbolic (e.g., Kendler and Kendler, 1962; Kuenne, 1946; White, 1965). Furthermore, experimental approaches to the study of these phenomena have appeared essentially during the same time interval in the literature of human experimental psychology (e.g., Mandler, 1967) and developmental psychology.

There is no intent here to attribute a cause-effect relation to the similar current emphases in the literature of experimental psychology and of experimental-developmental psychology. The research in both disciplines changed in the 1950's as the emphasis gradually shifted from the study of the animal to the human organism. The most likely reason for these changes, however, was the availability of research methods which permitted the learning theorists to study complex processes without the necessity of conducting "complex" experiments. As Mandler (1967) has noted, just this issue formed the basis of earlier (i.e., pre-1950) theoretical controversies between the proponents of the Gestalt position and the learning theory models based on conditioning principles.

This paper emphasizes the developmental analysis of higher-order skills which affect performance in learning tasks. The assumptions made are interrelated and are perhaps best identified now. These assumptions are:

1. Developmental changes in behavior are attributable, in large part, to differences in the availability and/or use of higher-order habits and skills.

2. Complex skills used in learning, thinking, problem solving, etc., are (or least can be) acquired and are accessible to experimental scrutiny.

3. The higher-order skills which govern performance may be grouped into two broad classes; i.e., *enactive* skills which are *positively* correlated with task mastery and *inhibitory* skills which are *negatively* correlated with task mastery. By this distinction I mean to differentiate between those skills which subjects use directly in the solution of a learning task; e.g., the use of mnemonics or mediational mechanisms in learning, and those skills which permit subjects to inhibit inappropriate response tendencies, strategies, or habits which interfere with efficient performance.

In the following sections of this chapter, selected theories and hypotheses related to development and aging are explored with regard to their reliance on these two types of skills in explaining age changes in behavior. In addition, alternate research designs are presented which permit the experimental study of age-related differences in higher-order skills. Finally, a theoretical proposition is offered which suggests that life-span changes in learning, memory, and forgetting are attibutable to the differential rate at which *enactive* and *inhibitory* skills are acquired in the natural environment.

II.   Developmental Processes and the Specificity of Habits and Skills

The habits and skills which are available in a child's repertoire or are acquired as a result of practice vary both with the amount and type of prior or preexperimental experience and with the type of task on which the subject is practiced. These issues are discussed in detail later in the paper. However, these habits and skills vary on another dimension; i.e., the range of situations to which they may be applied or transferred once they are acquired. Specific habits or specific transfer factors, on the one hand, are relevant to or transfer only to tasks which share the same, or have similar components or stimuli (Goulet,

1970b; Postman, 1969). On the other hand, nonspecific transfer factors refer
to higher-order skills which, once acquired, affect the manner in which the
subject attempts to learn the task (Postman, 1969). Moreover, and an important
issue for the study of developmental processes, subjects acquire both nonspecific
and specific habits and skills when any task is mastered. As an example, the
mastery of a simple two-choice object-discrimination task leaves the subject
with information regarding the objects to be discriminated (specific transfer)
and at least partial information relevant to strategies of discrimination learning.

The distinctions between specific and nonspecific transfer factors are not new.
As one instance, theories of learning may be differentiated along the specificity–nonspecificity dimension. For example, the Hull–Spence theory (e.g., Hull,
1943; Spence, 1936) was predicated on and relevant only to the acquisition
and transfer (or generalization) of specific habits (Goulet, 1970b). On the opposite
pole, Harlow's (1959) error factor or ''learning set'' theory is most appropriately
identified with the acquisition of nonspecific skills (Goulet, 1970b).

More important for present purposes, major theories or hypotheses related
to developmental phenomena may be examined from the specificity–nonspecificity viewpoint. Clear examples of this point can be drawn from
the literature relating to the development of mediational processes in young
children. In one domain, Kuenne (1946), Alberts and Ehrenfreund (1951), Stevenson and Bitterman (1955), Reese (1962a) and many others have used the two-
stimulus or middle-sized transposition problem to study the transition from
absolute to relational responding in young children. The Kendlers (e.g., Kendler
& Kendler, 1962) and again many others (see Shepp & Turrisi, 1966; Slamecka,
1968; and Wolff, 1967 for reviews) have used one variation or another of
the reversal-shift paradigm to study the developmental transition from a single-
stage, incremental, habit-governed learning mechanism to a multi-stage mediational process. In both examples, the developmental phenomenon of interest
is the apparent shift in children away from a reliance on specific habits to
higher-order nonspecific habits or skills governing transfer to new tasks.

The preceding discussion has oversimplified the nature and number of issues
surrounding the literature relating to the development of mediational processes.
Nevertheless, the issues we have stressed exemplify four major problems of
considerable theoretical interest in the study of the ontogenesis of learning skills
and abilities.

A. Acquisition and What is Learned

The first issue relates to the developmental changes in what children learn
or, alternatively, the identification of the skills children use in acquisition. Take
the following example of a concept-sorting problem where children are presented

a successive series of "animal" and "vegetable" pictures with the task requiring a distinct sorting response for the pictures within each concept. Children can "acquire" or use at least five different mechanisms or components during acquisition (Bozinou, 1971).

(a) Children can acquire a set of distinct rote habits; i.e., they can acquire a specific sorting response for each of the stimuli involved in the task.

(b) Children can "learn-how-to-learn" a discrimination-sorting problem; or, in Harlow's (1959) terms, they can acquire a "discrimination learning set."

(c) Children can learn that stimuli *in the list* which share the same superordinate or representational response are sorted in the same manner.

(d) Children can learn or deduce that all "animal" pictures (even those not contained in the list) share the same sorting response, with all "vegetable" pictures sharing the alternate response.

(e) Children can deduce that tasks of this nature have a conceptual or mediational solution which can be used as the basis for sorting.

The first of the components is a "pure" example of a specific habit, and the second component is nonspecific. The last three components are also nonspecific, but their acquisition and/or use in this or similar tasks is contingent on the prior availability of the specific associations between the instances of the concept and the superordinate category name.

It is apparent, first, that performance on a task of this nature may be determined by one or a number of these components, and second, that one of the tasks of the developmental psychologist is to identify the set of components which govern children's learning and cognitive performance.

B. The Acquisition of Higher-Order Habits and Skills

A second problem, and one which currently occupies the attention of a large number of developmental psychologists, concerns whether children whose behavior is governed by specific habits can acquire and use higher-order cognitive skills. There are three excellent examples of this problem in the research literature.

The first relates to the distinction between "mediation deficiency" (Reese, 1962b) and "production deficiency" (Flavell, Beach, & Chinsky, 1966) in young children. The weight of experimental evidence now seems to suggest that young children can be trained in the use of higher-order conceptual skills. Here we have the evidence provided by Flavell and others (e.g., Flavell, 1970) that children heretofore characterized by an inability to use mediators and mnemonics (mediation deficiency) can use them if provided at least short periods of training in their use. For example, Keeney, Cannizzo, and Flavell (1967) and Kingsley and Hagen (1969) have found that training in verbal rehearsal leads to both the enhancement of recall and the subsequent use of rehearsal in similar tasks. Moeley, Olson, Halwes, and Flavell (1969) have also successfully trained children in the use of conceptual mediators, such training enhancing both recall and conceptual clustering, the latter a measure of the degree to which the children used the concept names to mediate recall.

Another excellent example of the contemporary interest in the training of conceptual skills is provided by the now-long list of "Piagetian training studies" (see Brainerd & Allen, 1971; and Sigel & Hooper, 1968 for reviews). These studies, for the most part, have attempted to induce conservation behavior in "nonconservers" through the provision of a circumscribed set of experiences deemed to be relevant to or prerequisites for responding appropriately on a conservation task. Again, the weight of evidence favors the conclusion that the skills necessary for conservation can be acquired (e.g., Gelman, 1969; Mehler & Bever, 1967; Sigel, Roeper, & Hooper, 1966).

The third set of studies can be drawn from the literature related to transposition. As mentioned previously, young children are best characterized as responding in an absolute rather than a relational fashion on two-stimulus or middle-sized transposition problems (e.g., Alberts & Ehrenfreund, 1951; Kuenne, 1946). One of the explanations for these findings is that young children lack the verbal concept of "larger than" (or "smaller than") necessary for relational responding in two-stimulus transposition studies (e.g., Kuenne, 1946) or that the children lack the concept of "middle size" (Reese, 1962a) necessary for responding relationally in the middle-size transposition task. Another explanation, suggested by Caron (1966), among others, is that the critical mediator in transposition is attentional rather than verbal.

The nature of the mechanisms governing choice behavior, whether verbal or attentional, is not of central concern here. However, without belaboring the issue, there are now several studies which have unequivocally demonstrated that young children trained to respond in a relational fashion, do transpose (Beaty & Weir, 1966; Caron, 1966; Gonzalez & Ross, 1958; Johnson & Zara, 1960; Yeh, 1970). The lone exception here are the results provided by Zeiler (1967). These findings have been obtained even for children who apparently were without the concept of "middle-size" (Caron, 1966).

The logical conclusion to be drawn from these studies is that the apparent absence of higher-order skills in young children is subject to modification through specific and directed training in the use of such skills. In fact, effects have been found even when the training is not so specific (Dornbush & Winnick, 1966; House & Zeaman, 1960; Jeffrey & Cohen, 1965). These types of data acquire more importance when they are evaluated in the context of developmental theories which suggest that the course of development is characterized by a series of distinct, unmodifiable, and qualitative stages (Piaget & Inhelder, 1969).

C. Necessary and Sufficient Skills for Learning

The third major issue of concern relates to the skills necessary or sufficient for the behavioral man:festation of complex, cognitive behavior. These issues have appeared in a variety of different contexts in the developmental literature, but relate generally to the question of whether developmental changes in behavior are best described by the acquisition of new (enactive) skills, the inhibition of habits or skills which are no longer appropriate, or some combination of the two.

As a simple example, the apparent developmental transition from absolute to relational responding on transposition tasks may be a function of the acquisition of the skills appropriate for relational learning (enactive skills), the inhibition of the tendency or habit to respond in an absolute fashion (inhibitory skills), or both. Here there is empirical evidence that young children can be taught to respond in either an absolute or relational fashion on tests of transposition (Yeh, 1970).

This issue has interesting implications for developmental research. For example, training children who respond relationally to respond in an absolute fashion actually involves the reinstatement of a "developmentally-prior" response tendency[3] whereas the training of "absolute responders" in the skills necessary for relational responding refers most directly to the notion of "developmental acceleration" (Graham et al., 1964; Yeh, 1970).

The course of cognitive development as Piaget describes it, has also been cast in the form of the acquisition–inhibition dichotomy. Sigel, Roeper, and Hooper (1966), for example, have successfully induced conservation in children through informal training designed to establish the component skills (i.e., addition–substraction, reversibility, etc.) considered necessary for the manifestation of this behavior. Smedslund (1961a), in contrast, has suggested that conservation can best be induced through training which leads to the inhibition of the tendency to attend to competing perceptual cues. Other research related to the inducing of conservation through training (e.g., Gelman, 1969) has also been predicated on this notion.

The research related to the training of mediational and mnemonic behaviors (e.g., Flavell, 1970a) has focused exclusively on the training conditions which facilitate cognitive performance by either establishing or enhancing the availability of appropriate cognitive skills. It should be noted, however, that available theoretical conceptions relating to the developmental transition from rote to mediational responding place differential emphasis on the role of inhibitory

---

[3]Training a relational responder to respond absolutely probably does not involve the reinstatement of rote responding; absolute responses in these subjects are probably mediated rather than rote. Nevertheless, the task requirements (responding absolutely) do reinstate a developmentally prior form of behavior.

and facilitative factors in this process. For example, both White (1965) and Kendler and Kendler (1962) suggest that children below the age of 5 solve problems according to a set of processes that are associative and rote in nature and that the developmental transition is characterized by the emergence of a cognitive level of functioning. As such, both White and Kendler and Kendler entertain a stage conception of development whereby the appearance of the cognitive functions signals the general inhibition of associative processes.

Nevertheless, White, and Kendler and Kendler apparently place differential emphasis on the role of inhibitory factors during this period. For example, Kendler and Kendler have explained the differences in performance on reversal and nonreversal shifts of pre-5 and post-5-year-old children to differences in the use of mediational mechanisms, whereas White (1965) has stressed the age differences in the capacity to inhibit earlier-learned responses. As is apparent, Kendler and Kendler stress the facilitative effects on performance resulting from the use of mediational mechanisms for post-5-year-old children. White has stressed the interfering effects resulting from mechanisms akin to associative interference for pre-5-year-old children to account for the same types of data. However, they share the conception that the behavior of children below the age of 5 is strongly affected by specific transfer factors; i.e., associative interference, etc.

The subtle differences between the conceptions of White and Kendler and Kendler provide alternate explanations of the performance differences observed on reversal and half-reversal shifts for young, but "mediating" children. And, fortunately, these theoretical differences can be put to experimental test. As an example, the logical extension of White's (1965) hypothesis would imply that the provision of training to assist the children in inhibiting interfering factors from prior learning (such as those present on a half-reversal shift) should reduce the performance differences observed on reversal and half-reversal shifts. Alternatively, the logical extension of the Kendlers' hypotheses would imply that training in the use of mediational skills will enhance the performance differences observed on reversal and half-reversal shifts. It is possible, of course, that both conceptions are true, but these issues do warrant experimental investigation.

The differences between the theoretical conceptions of White and Kendler and Kendler also bring into question the methodological adequacy of performance comparisons on reversal and half-reversal shift tasks. As Kendler and Kendler (1962) have implied, these paradigms were designed to permit the experimental test as to whether the behavior of young children is governed by a specific habit or "single-unit" mechanism or by mediational or symbolic mechanisms. Performance comparisons between the paradigms will permit these inferences if and only if other confounding factors are not present. Slamecka (1968), Wolff (1967), and Goulet (1971) have noted some of the potential sources of confounding and alternative theoretical explanations of the performance differences in reversal and half-reversal shifts. However, the present emphasis on the training of higher-order skills highlights the fact that practice on the two paradigms may result in the acquisition of distinctly different types of complex, nonspecific skills. That is, the practice on the reversal-shift paradigm may be assumed to enhance the child's ability to use mediational or symbolic cues in learning. This is a likely possibility since both the training and transfer task in this paradigm involve the use of a consistent response for each attribute within a specified dimension or conceptual category.

The half-reversal shift, however, requires children to inhibit the use of a mediational cue for responding, a task which certainly requires a qualitatively different type of conceptual skill. The training and transfer tasks conforming to a half-reversal shift also involve inconsistent and incompatible higher-order skills, another possible reason for the superior performance observed on a reversal shift.

III. Higher-Order Skills and Life-Span Processes

Prior sections of the paper have emphasized the discussion of data and theoretical propositions which relate to developmental changes in the behavior of young children. There are, however, parallel types of issues which have permeated the literature related to aging phenomena. The issues have arisen, for the most part, in the context of studying the processes of learning, transfer of training, and forgetting. The hypothesis guiding most of this research is that forgetting increases with age after middle adulthood and the explanation most often provided is that the aged are more "interference prone" than their younger adult counterparts (e.g., Jerome, 1959).

It is immediately apparent that identical theoretical questions underlie the investigation of the interference proneness hypothesis in the aged and the study of the development of higher-order skills in children. First, we have the question as to the "modifiability" of interference proneness. The second, and somewhat related question concerns the manner in which interference manifests its effects over the age continuum.

One difference, however, does differentiate the research concerned with development through young adulthood and research identified with the study of aging phenomena. The studies with children reported here have been concerned with the acquisition and development of both enactive and inhibitory skills, but the study of age changes which occur after young adulthood have been primarily concerned with the latter. In other words, the very nature of the interference proneness hypothesis suggests that the behavior of aged adults is governed by inhibitory mechanisms. It will be recalled that similar propositions have been offered to account for the learning performance of pre-five-year-old children (e.g., Kendler & Kendler, 1962; Kuenne, 1946; White, 1965).

There is also evidence that age and the rate of mastering learning problems are correlated through the entire life span, albeit negatively from early childhood through young adulthood, and positively from middle adulthood on (Arenberg, 1967; Bromley, 1958; Canestrari, 1963, 1968; Inglis, Ankus, & Sykes, 1968; Jensen & Rohwer, 1965). Kausler (1970) and Goulet (1970a) have each noted that the apparent curvilinear relation between age and rate of learning over the life span likely reflects the differential role of mediational or mnemonic factors in learning by samples representing different points along the life span. These observations have major import for the study of age-sensitive processes related to learning and also highlight distinctions of a qualitative nature including questions as to what is learned and how learning occurs, as well as bearing directly on developmental hypotheses associated with both ends of the age spectrum.

For example, Kausler (1970) has recognized the broad distinction between rote versus mediated associative learning, the latter having reference to acquisition processes mediated by verbal or visual mnemonic devices employed by the subject. There is increasing evidence that both acquisition and retention are markedly facilitated in young adult subjects when mnemonic devices are used (e.g., Adams, 1967; Adams & Montague, 1967; Bugelski, 1968). Such findings can also be generalized to children (e.g., Jensen & Rohwer, 1965; Milgram, 1967; Reese, 1965). There is also increasing evidence that the spontaneous, unprompted use of mnemonic devices in acquisition increases with age in children (e.g., Flavell, 1970a; Flavell et al., 1966) and then declines after middle adulthood (e.g., Canestrari, 1968; Grimm, 1970; Hulicka & Grossman, 1967; Hulicka, Sterns, & Grossman, 1967). Such findings, in themselves, provide a first approximation to explaining any retention deficit in either the young or the elderly if the assumption is made that mediated habits are "protected" from interfering activities, are more resistant to interference from competing habits, or are simply better learned than those acquired rotely (Kausler, 1970).

As a direct implication of the preceding discussion, the provision of instructions to mediate or to use mnemonic aids in learning to subjects before (and during) acquisition for samples varying in age is perhaps appropriate in most studies involving the age variable. Such a procedure should assist in equating both the degree and type of learning for the samples involved in developmental studies (Hulicka & Grossman, 1967; Jensen & Rohwer, 1965). Without such instructions, learning or retention deficits demonstrated in the young or the elderly may be artifactual due to the different proportions of subjects in each age sample who spontaneously employ mnemonic aids in learning or retention, or may reflect actual age changes in retention.

In this context, Kausler (1970) has suggested that the attempted use of mediational devices by subjects who do not use them effectively or who use them in inappropriate situations should increase the magnitude of interference (and thus retroactive inhibition) relative to rotely-learned tasks. He suggested that children generally within the age range from six to eight fall into this category, since it is the period characterized by the initial occurrences of spontaneous mediational activity.

Such an hypothesis when carried to its logical extreme, implies that spontaneous or induced mediational activity will facilitate both acquisition and simple retention, but will increase the magnitude of forgetting for subjects who cannot inhibit inappropriate mediational activity. The degree to which such an hypothesis is appropriate for the aged remains unexplored. However, it is important to note that the demonstration of facilitative effects of mnemonic prompting on acquisition for the elderly (Hulicka & Grossman, 1967) does not imply that the relationship holds for retention functions as well.

The developmental research concerned with transfer of training and retention has been predicated on the notion that both the very young (e.g., White, 1965) and the elderly are "interference prone" (e.g., Jerome, 1959). Variations of the "interference proneness" hypothesis have also been invoked in other contexts to explain, for example, acquisition and transfer deficits in children younger than 5 (White, 1965), and learning, mediational, and retention deficits in the retarded (e.g., Lipman, 1963), in schizophrenics (e.g., Lang & Buss, 1965; Mednick, 1958), and in high-anxious subjects (e.g., Eysenck, 1963; Spence, 1958). However, these hypotheses have all been proposed, albeit not directly, in the context of specific transfer mechanisms (e.g., see Goulet, 1968a, 1968b, 1968c). It is, however, important to explore this hypothesis from the viewpoint of nonspecific transfer mechanisms, and the interactive influences of specific and nonspecific transfer in determining the performance of samples varying in age.

As a direct example of the potential influence of nonspecific transfer mechanisms on retention, Underwood and Schulz (1960) have suggested the presence of a selector mechanism whereby young adult subjects adopt a response set or disposition to limit themselves to the repertoire of required responses when exposed to learning materials. Subsequent recall of these materials thus may be assumed to be a function either of the degree to which the response set was established or utilized in acquisition, the subject's success in reestablishing this response set during the period of recall, or both. In the context of research on aging, retention deficits in elderly populations may have their locus in the acquisition process per se or during the retrieval or recall phase. And, in the context of life-span changes in retention, the relative effects of these factors may be different for children and the aged; i.e., any retention deficit may be localized primarily in acquisition for young children (through lack of differentiation) and in the retrieval phase for the aged.

Retention, and indeed the magnitude of interference reflected in transfer of training and retroactive inhibition, has also been shown to be a function of the type of prior practice to which young adult subjects have been exposed. For example, Postman (1964) and Keppel and Postman (1966) have found that the magnitude of negative transfer manifested when subjects are exposed to the A–B, A–C transfer paradigm was decreased when subjects were provided prior practice with this paradigm. Similarly, Postman (1969) has demonstrated that retroactive inhibition observed with this paradigm is markedly reduced when practice relevant to this paradigm (except with different lists) is provided. In effect, Postman suggested that subjects acquire certain paradigm-specific skills in learning (in this case, skills to circumvent retroactive inhibition) which can be generalized to later experimental situations which require these skills. Furthermore, Postman (1969) suggested that since retroactive inhibition is rapidly reduced by relevant experience, retroactive interference of the type described by the A–B, A–C paradigm may play a limited role in forgetting which occurs *outside* the laboratory. In other words, subjects motivated to retain old habits may readily adopt strategies which lead to the circumvention of retroactive inhibition and thus "permit the steady accumulation of the products of learning [p. 293]."

The implications of results such as these for developmental and/or aging research are clear. For example, young children may not have acquired these higher-order rules or strategies (inhibitory skills) to circumvent the interference manifested in negative transfer and retroactive inhibition, but such rules or strategies may actually dominate the behavior of the aged. This proposition is developed fully in the next section of the paper. However, it is clear that the previous discussion implies that "interference proneness" has a different meaning for the young and for the aged. On a simple level, the susceptibility to the interfering effects of prior learning, i.e., associative interference (White, 1965), in the very young may be attributable to the relative lack of higher-order inhibitory skills which permit these children to inhibit the interfering effects of competing, specific transfer factors. In the aged, however, apparent susceptibility to interference is assumed to reflect generalized (or overgeneralized) tendencies to inhibit the effects of prior learning, whether acquired in the laboratory or in the natural environment.

IV. The Development of Enactive and Inhibitory Skills over the Life Span

Figure 1 presents hypothetical functions which trace the development of enactive and inhibitory skills over the life span. As mentioned previously, enactive skills relate to the repertoire of higher-order skills which individuals acquire and use in learning, memory, etc. As an example, the ability to generate mediators or mnemonic devices useful in learning or problem solving falls in this category. And, as an inclusive description, enactive skills refer to the pool of skills which subjects have found to be positively correlated with task mastery. To call enactive skills "dispositions to respond" or "problem-solving strategies" is likely correct in most instances.

Inhibitory skills, in contrast, are conceived here to relate generally to the ability to inhibit either (a) strategies of problem solving which are inappropriate for the task at hand or (b) specific transfer factors which are responsible for associative interference.

The hypothetical growth function for enactive skills (see Fig. 1) was generated making the assumption of an increase through middle adulthood, an assumption similar to that used by Riegel (1966) in accounting for life-span changes in verbal behavior and language facility. This assumption is also consonant with most developmental theories (e.g., Gagne, 1968; Kendler, Kendler, & Marken, 1969; Piaget & Inhelder, 1969).

A similar assumption was made in generating the function for inhibitory skills. However, additional assumptions are that inhibitory skills are developed later than enactive skills, but, nevertheless, are the dominant influences on behavior and performance beginning in middle adulthood. The suggestion that inhibitory skills "lag behind" enactive skills is predicated on the simple notion that skills in inhibition can be acquired only after there are other skills to be inhibited and from Mandler's (1954, 1967) suggestions that the acquisition of a "set" to eliminate inappropriate responses occurs only after the attainment of criterion performance on a specified task. This assumption is also consistent with the hypotheses expressed by Kausler (1970) in his attempt to explain life-span changes in retention. A final assumption made in developing the present model is that performance is a joint function of the relative influences of enactive and inhibitory skills.

With these stated assumptions, it is appropriate to examine the model as to its consistency with available data and existing theories. For expository purposes, the life span is divided into five sections, the period preceding age 5, the period between the ages of 5 and 12, the period from the age of 12 through young adulthood, from young adulthood to middle adulthood, and from middle adulthood to the point of natural death.

As Fig. 1 implies, the early periods of life (e.g., chronological age (CA) < 5) mark the initial development of both enactive and inhibitory skills. Thus, the children within this period may be assumed to be deficient in the use of mediational (i.e., enactive) skills in acquisition (e.g., Kendler & Kendler, 1962; Kuenne, 1946; Reese, 1962b; White, 1965), their behavior rather being determined by rote processes (e.g., Gagne, 1968; Kendler & Kendler, 1962; Kuenne, 1946; White, 1965). In addition, the relative lack of inhibitory skills suggests a susceptibility to associative interference (White, 1965), a tendency for response perseveration (Goulet & Goodwin, 1970; Weir, 1964), and a lack of response inhibition (Mednick & Lehtinen, 1957; White, 1965).

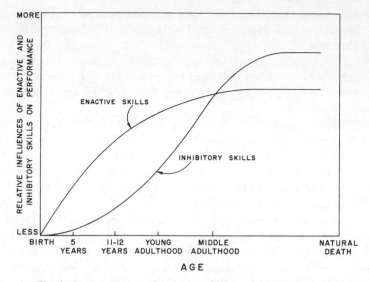

Fig. 1. The hypothetical development of enactive and inhibitory skills.

The period around the age of 5 marks the initial occurrences of spontaneous mediational activity (e.g., Flavell, 1970a; Flavell *et al.,* 1966; Kendler & Kendler, 1962; Kuenne, 1946; Reese, 1962b) and strategies of problem solving (Goulet & Goodwin, 1970; Weir, 1964) but is, nevertheless, a period marked by an inability to inhibit, change, or modify a strategy once implemented (e.g., Goulet & Goodwin, 1970; Kausler, 1970; Weir, 1964), and a period characterized by the inefficient use of associative strategies (e.g., Davis, 1966; Goulet, 1968c; Palermo, 1962).

The period from adolescence through young adulthood has been seen as one in which children "test" and reject inefficient problem-solving strategies, and one where mediational or mnemonic skills are used in appropriate (and not in inappropriate) situations (e.g., Kausler, 1970), and as a period where subjects effectively use a "selector mechanism" as a means to limit themselves to a repertoire of required responses in learning tasks (e.g., Kausler, 1970; Postman, 1969; Underwood & Schulz, 1960).

As in most domains in developmental psychology, theoretical speculation becomes more "hazy" as one extrapolates from data beyond young adulthood. Nevertheless, this is attempted here as a means to integrate the data associated with aging with those from younger populations. The major assumption made is that inhibitory skills exert major influences on performance. It is interesting to note, however, that there is not one whit of evidence to suggest that the decline in learning efficiency after middle adulthood is attributable to the "forgetting'' of enactive skills. There is, on the other hand, evidence that the behavior of the aged is characterized by response inhibition (Botwinick, 1967, 1970; Braun & Geiselhart, 1959; Kimble & Pennypacker, 1963). Furthermore, if the assumption is made that such inhibition generalizes across a broad class of skills, the apparent lack of mediational or mnemonic activity in the aged can be explained. This analysis suggests that the decline in learning efficiency in the aged, and indeed, more rapid forgetting, is attributable to the inhibition of enactive (e.g., mediational) skills and habits rather than the inability of aged subjects to use such skills in learning and memory.

A number of additional comments related to life-span changes in behavior warrant mentioning in the present context. First, it should be emphasized that Fig. 1 was constructed making the assumptions that enactive and inhibitory skills are acquired through the life span and no assumption of their decline in old age is intended or implied. Nevertheless, the model does imply that overt performance will be related in a curvilinear fashion to age because of the relative influences of enactive and inhibitory skills in the young and the aged.

Second, an assumption implicit in Fig. 1 and stated explicitly throughout the paper is that enactive and inhibitory skills are acquired. As such, they are also subject to experimental manipulation and to modification through training. Third, enactive and inhibitory skills, as discussed in this chapter, refer to general classes of skills and there is no intention to suggest that each class is governed by unitary mechanisms or processes. Nevertheless, it is suggested that particular and specifiable enactive and inhibitory skills are subject to experimental analysis through appropriate training designed to lead to the acquisition of the skill of interest (e.g., Goulet, 1970a, 1970b; Postman, 1969). A logical conclusion which follows from these assumptions is that subjects vary on selected enactive and inhibitory skills as a result of differential training, and that the acquisition or development of these skills can be accelerated through massed (i.e., time-compressed) training or practice. The methodological implications of these suggestions are discussed in the next section.

V. Methodological Implications for Developmental Research

The prior discussion has emphasized the theoretical implications which follow from developmental studies related to the acquisition, transfer, and training of higher-order skills. There are, however, major methodological implications of this work. Figure 2 provides a convenient mnemonic for the illustration and explication of these implications.

In this example, the performance of two age groups is compared across each of a series of tasks designed to provide training in the acquisition of a particular,

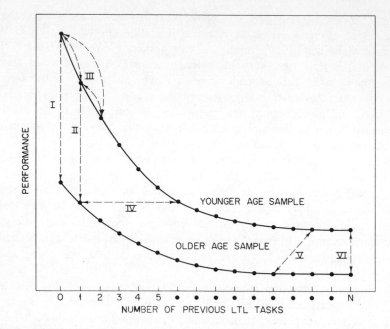

Fig. 2. Alternate research designs for the study of developmental processes. [Adapted from Goulet (1972) with permission of the Gerontological Society.]

nonspecific skill (here designated as learning-to-learn, LTL). The functions are hypothetical and were constructed making the assumptions that:

(1) The provision of practice on multiple problems leads to the acquisition of the nonspecific skill (an assumption that is adequately documented in the present paper).
(2) Rate of acquisition of the skill varies with age.
(3) Performance differences remain among age groups even after learning-to-learn has reached an asymptote (an assumption which has not been empirically tested).

The assumptions made in (2) and (3) are not necessary for present purposes.

Figure 2 illustrates six research designs which may be used in the study of developmental phenomena. In each of the designs the subjects are compared on the treatment of interest after learning a specified number of prior tasks (from none to many) designed to lead to the acquisition of a specified nonspecific skill. Design I exemplifies a conventional study in which the subjects are compared on the treatment of interest without prior experimental exposure to the nature of the task, the stimulus materials, etc. Age differences observed with the use of this design may be attributable to differential transfer of preexperimentally acquired specific transfer factors, enactive or inhibitory skills, differential comprehension of the requirements necessary for learning the task, transient motivational characteristics related to the apprehension of the "experiment" or experimenter, differences in the rate or degree to which the subjects adopt the appropriate set to learn (whether attentional, postural, etc.), differences in entering subject strategies (e.g., Goulet & Goodwin, 1970; Jeffrey & Cohen, 1965; Weir, 1964), or to a host of other variables.

In Design II, comparisons are made after the provision of a minimum of practice (e.g., the acquisition of one prior task) to familiarize the subject with the nature and requirements of the task and experimental situation, etc. As may be seen, the use of this design eliminates a number of the factors which may influence or determine the magnitude of the age differences in performance.

With Design III, the major focus is on the interaction of the experimental treatments with amount of prior practice on the successive tasks. A number of recent studies exemplify the use of this design in its most simple form. For example, many Piagetian training studies compare the performance of two groups of subjects (one group trained and the other not trained) on tests of conservation (e.g., Smedslund, 1961b). As another example, Keeney, Cannizzo, and Flavell (1967) compared the performance of children in a serial recall task before and after they were provided a short period of training in verbal rehearsal activities.

With Design IV, the purpose for training is to equate the subjects in the respective age groups on a particular nonspecific skill. This means, of course, that the slowest-learning subjects would be provided more learning-to-learn practice on the tasks than the faster-learning subjects. In other words, the transfer of the nonspecific skill would be equated among the age groups, but the amount of experimental practice provided would vary for the groups. This use of this design is particularly important in transfer, memory, or retention studies where differences in rate or degree of learning among the age groups may confound the developmental comparison of interest (Goulet, 1968c, 1970a).

In Design V, age comparisons on the treatment of interest are made at the point in practice where the subjects have reached their respective asymptotes with regard to the skill in question. Here, the age groups may vary both as to the amount of experimental practice provided and the rate at which the transfer task of experimental interest is learned. However, the groups are equated in the sense that both have been trained to their respective asymptotes on the skills necessary for acquiring the task. Design VI is similar to Design V since the age groups are compared after the asymptote of learning-to-learn has been reached. However, in this instance, the amount of experimental practice provided is also equated for all age groups.

It is emphasized that one or a combination of the six research designs can be incorporated into a single experiment. For example, the requirements for

Designs I, II, and III are met if subjects are provided differing amounts of practice (from none to some) prior to being administered the treatment of interest, and if age or another developmental variable is incorporated into the experiment. The adoption of such a design strategy permits, at the same time, the assessment of the reliability of the developmental phenomenon of interest, besides providing evidence about the nature of the variables (whether transient or persistent) interacting with age.

The suggestion here is that Designs IV, V, and VI are the most powerful for purposes of identifying and explaining developmental differences in behavior. Their use provides the opportunity to equate subjects on experiental factors which influence age-related differences in behavior, to equate subjects varying in age on one higher-order skill in order to assess the interaction with other such skills, and to study the acquisition of higher-order skills themselves. And, as Postman (1969) has suggested "experimental findings encourage the view that such concepts as learning strategies and rule-governed behavior need not be invoked in an ad hoc fashion but can be brought under experimental control by the systematic manipulation of the conditions of practice [p. 296]."

CHAPTER 14

Cognitive Assessment across the Life-Span: Methodological Implications of the Organismic Approach[1]

FRANK H. HOOPER

UNIVERSITY OF WISCONSIN
MADISON, WISCONSIN

I. Introduction

The study of cognitive processes, whereby an organism attains an awareness of and knowledge about external objects, the self, and the salient self–object relationships provides the essential continuity between the preexperimental era of epistemological philosophy and the modern concern (and preoccupation) with experimental analyses and manipulation of complex processes. The current popularity of cognition is shown in a perusal of two current volumes dealing with developmental psychology (Mussen, 1960, 1970) which present a wide range of content-specific domains, e.g., sensory processes and perception, learning, problem-solving and thinking, concept development, language and psycholinguistics, standardized ability assessment, creativity, and educational implications, all under the rubric of cognitive development. In the context of Koch's (1964) articulate comment on neo-neobehaviorism's return of the repressed ". . . *to a concern with empirical problem areas long bypassed or only glancingly*

[1]The author wishes to thank Irving E. Sigel, William R. Looft, and Jane A. Goldman for their comments on earlier drafts of this chapter.

acknowledged because of their subjectivistic 'odor' [p. 19]," one may well wonder which psychological investigators are *not* concerned with cognitive functioning? Acknowledging, then, the current major emphasis in psychology upon cognitive matters, we may examine the special conceptual and methodological problems germane to the life-span study of cognitive development.

The first point that can be made, since there are so may subareas or content domains subsumed under cognition, is that it naturally follows that there exist a wide variety of specific methodological domains, e.g., psycholinguistics, learning, problem solving, standardized ability assessment, etc., each with its own general evaluation and particular technical considerations. Aside from the fact that the blatant over-usage of the term cognition leads to confusion and nonjustifiable generalizations, a primary contention of the present paper is that the major determinant of methodological problem specification, assessment strategies, and associated instrumentation is *not* the substantive interests of the particular investigator, but rather the type of developmental model or world view (Reese & Overton, 1970) that he accepts as potentially valid and generalizable to life-span applications. From this view, the adopted conceptual-theoretical model of man's relationship to his surrounding milieu presents an obvious operational constraint upon the particular definition of cognitive functioning, and the general conception of developmental change, which will be acceptable to any student of human development. It therefore follows that the problems of life-span research design and methodology (cf., Birren, 1959b; Goulet & Baltes, 1970; Inhelder & Matalon, 1960; Kessen, 1960; Wohlwill, 1970a, b) are indissociably linked to developmental models and related conceptual issues (e.g., Beilin, 1969, 1971a, Kessen, 1962; Langer, 1969; Nagel, 1957; Piaget, 1960; Reese & Overton, 1970; Van den Daele, 1969; Werner, 1957; Zigler, 1963).

Although a number of developmental models, e.g., classical or neo-Freudian psychoanalytic, Hullian, Skinnerian, social learning, maturational–ethological, systems theory, and psychometric approaches, could be compared in terms of methodological implications for cognitive analysis, probably the most distinctive contrasts concern the organismic versus the various neobehavioristic theoretical systems (Kaplan, 1967; Reese & Overton, 1970). While rapprochement and synthesis between these viewpoints may conceivably be an eventual outcome (e.g., the work of Berlyne 1960, 1965, 1966), the present status of these positions generates rather distinct research perspectives. The present paper will explore the implications of the organismic model of human development for considerations of life-span methodology.

II. The Organismic View of Developmental Change

The organismic orientation to cognitive development, as exemplified in the work of Werner and Piaget, presents a relativistic interactional view of man's progressive ability to acquire knowledge concerning the world in which he lives. This "constructive rationalism" (Beilin, 1971a), while recognizing the formally similar roles of the traditional content domains of perception, learning, and cognition in adaptive behavior, places greater emphasis on the fundamental distinctions which underlie these modes of human functioning. Thus Piaget and Inhelder (1969) distinguished between the role of exercise and experiential factors based upon:

> (a) physical experience, which consists of acting upon objects in order to abstract their properties (for example, comparing two weights independently of volume); and (b) logico-mathematical experience, which consists of acting upon objects with a view to learning the result of the coordination of actions (for example, when a child of five or six discovers empirically that the sum of a group of objects is independent of their spatial disposition or the order in which they are counted) [p. 155].

They reserved the latter area for primary emphasis as an exemplar of cognitive functioning. Perceptual functioning, although presenting certain parallel developmental patterns, is assigned a distinctively subordinate status in the Piagetian system in view of the degree of equilibration and range of application which perceptual processes demonstrate. Werner's theory also distinguishes among the motoric, the perceptual, and the contemplative forms of cognitive development. In contrasting reflex reactions *to* stimuli and sensorimotor action *upon* signaled things with knowledge *about* objects, only the final category is seen as a definitive case of symbol formation and utilization (Werner & Kaplan, 1963). Distinctions such as these must be borne in mind when the organismic orientation toward qualitative analysis is considered.

The designation of exactly what constitutes a valid developmental change in cognitive functioning for the organismic theorists largely defines and constrains the degree of impact this orientation may have upon life-span developmental psychology. The term *developmental* is reserved

> . . . for changes which are not merely irreversible, or which yield only a greater numerical complexity; those changes must in addition eventuate in modes of organization not previously manifested in the history of the developing system, such that the system acquires an increased capacity for self-regulation, a larger measure of relative independence from environmental fluctuations.
> . . . The connotation of development thus involves two essential components: the notion of a system possessing a definite structure and a definite set of pre-existing capacities; and the notion of a sequential set of changes in the system, yielding relatively permanent but novel increments not only in its structure but in its modes of operation as well [Nagel, 1957, pp. 16–17].

From this definition it may be seen that (in contrast to learning models)

> . . . developmental psychology . . . is concerned with the changes in the form or organization of responses over time as contrasted with the change in the strength or accuracy

of the response. . . . Thus, the developmentalist focuses upon structural changes in a response, changes which cannot be defined simply in terms of changes which occur within single trials or stimulus presentations [Zigler, 1963, p. 345].

Behavioristic views, in contrast to the orientation emphasized in the present paper, assume that cognitive processes are fundamentally similar (identical?) at all points on the life-span, at least following the emergence of language. Thus, the child's thought represents only a less complex and quantitatively reduced form of the mature adult's (Beilin, 1971b).

Wohlwill (1970a) has recently presented a delimitation of true developmental behavior phenomena which excludes age-correlated changes which are explicitly associated with situationally specific experiences as *necessary* determinants. Valid developmental changes in cognition (or in any behavioral domain) are accepted "only to the extent that we are dealing with behavioral variables for which the general course of development (considered in terms of direction, form, sequence, etc.) remains invariant over a broad range of particular environmental conditions or circumstances, as well as genetic characteristics [Wohlwill, 1970a, p. 52]." As will be seen, this general disavowal of stimulus, situation, and instructional specificity may raise serious methodological problems for a life-span assessment program and serves to question the potential relevance of training-enrichment research as a source of meaningful information germane to long-range developmental analysis.

It is clear from the preceding statements that the prototypical cognitive behavior, for the organismic theorist, differs markedly from the traditional neobehavioristic concept-elicitation research.[2] In discussing the distinction between these latter forms of concept acquisition and Piagetian cognitive "processes," Beilin (1971a) has commented:

In regard to this, it is necessary to distinguish between two types of novelty—species novelty and individual novelty. In the development of intelligence or cognition, novelty, in the sense of developing new processes or mechanisms of thought (e.g., induction), is likely to be a very rare event in the history of the species. Such novelty is to be accounted for by the same propositions that explain the evolution of the species and the emergence of novel species qualities, namely, theories of genetic coding, natural selection, mutation, etc. Novelty in individual cognition can be thought of in two senses. When novelty occurs as the rare event in which a process change occurs, then it is explicable in the same evolutionary terms as indicated above [p. 90].

Of course these cognitive process domains coincide with the fundamental categories of space, time, relationality, and causality, which link neo-Kantian philosophy to the modern genetic epistemology of Piaget. (See Campbell, in

[2]This assumes, of course, some consensual acceptance of what denotes a "concept" for the neobehavioristic viewpoints. Judging from Flavell's recent overview, a commonly accepted definition of concept formation-elicitation is not currently available (Flavell, 1970b, pp. 983–991).

press, for an overview of the attempts to provide an evolutionary interpretation for Kantian epistemology.)

III. Qualitative Analysis

Following from this view of what defines cognition and what denotes a developmental change, the major concern of a life-span Piagetian orientation naturally becomes *qualitative* analysis. In Piagetian theory, two aspects are fixed or invariant across the life-span: the functional constants of organization and adaptation (the assimilation-accommodation dyad). Theoretically juxtaposed between these components and the ever variant (indeterminant?) environmental inputs or aliments, is the organism's structure. It is this structural component which alters from birth to maturity and which presents the subject focus (and defining characteristics) for the qualitative changes which inevitably lead to "stage" designations within organismic theory. The integral role which the mandatory stage construct plays in Piaget's system presents the major conceptual and methodological issues for life-span cognitive assessment.

The use of stage designations (and the related extensive discussions) probably rivals in current popularity the use of the label of cognitive processes. In this instance, we may conclude that, although psychologists are using stages more and more, they appear to be enjoying them less and less. It should be noted that we are distinguishing the theoretically "weaker" uses of the stage term (the stage designations of Bijou and Baer, 1965, or Gagnés', 1968, hierarchial learning model, for example) from the fundamentally "strong" use of stages by Piaget and his associates (see Goulet, 1970, for a contrary view as to this incompatibility). The defining characteristics of a developmental stage for Piaget include hierarchization, integration, consolidation, structuring, and equilibration (Pinard & Laurendeau, 1969).[3] Three of these characteristics, hierarchization, integration, and structuring, follow directly from the definition of developmental change (Nagel, 1957) given previously, which specifies cumulative, relatively permanent, sequential, and novel behavior alterations as the essential focus of developmental investigations.

Hierarchization refers to the well-known postulate of stage invariance or transitivity of progression throughout the developmental sequence. Later stages or levels can never precede the earlier acquisitions; i.e., in the sequence of stages, A–B–C–D, all individuals demonstate C capabilities after Stage B and prior to Stage D. Integration is a closely related concept which specifies that subsequent stages or levels "transform" earlier stage behaviors into new structural entities. Prior stages are not simply replaced, but rather become subordinated and sub-

---

[3]Descriptions of Piagetian stage criteria may be found in Beilin (1969), Inhelder (1956, 1962), and Piaget (1955, 1960).

sumed within the higher level functioning. This implies that later stage-related behavioral manifestations cannot be exhaustively predicted or causally linked from information specific to earlier modes of responding although the converse relationship may hold.

Structuring, in the present context,

> concerns the actual organization of the intellectual behaviors characteristic of a particular level of functioning. According to this criterion, the typical actions or operations of a given level are not simply juxtaposed one with another in an additive fashion, but are organically interconnected by ties of implication and reciprocal dependence that unite and group them into total structures—Piaget's *structures d'ensemble* [Pinard & Laurendeau, 1969, p. 136].

This characteristic underlies the prediction of within-stage correspondence or convergence (Wohlwill, 1963), and its singular relationship to the assumption of logical operations has recently been stated:

> If, in the first place, any given operation has the profundity and generality which Piaget's theory ascribes to it, then its acquisition should be manifested by the child's sudden ability to solve any and all cognitive tasks to which it is applicable. In other words, the picture ought to be one of pronounced developmental concurrence across this ensemble of tasks—either consistent success or consistent failure, depending upon whether the child has or has not yet acquired the underlying operation. If, in the second place, these highly general operations are also bound together into structures (with these structures in turn tightly interlinked), then one would likewise expect developmental synchronisms across operations. As soon as a child can master any task requiring one operation, therefore, he should be able to master any other task requiring any other operation, whether it belongs to the same group or not. To the extent that developmental reality fails to accord with this ideal picture, that is, it presents numerous asynchronisms within and between operations, to that extent would such key Piagetian expressions as "stage", "operation", and "structure" become imprecise and even misleading [Flavell, 1970b, pp. 1037–1038].

In the qualitative analyses of cognitive functioning which follow from this utilization of a stage construct, the *age* of acquisition becomes theoretically (and empirically?) irrelevant (Wohlwill, 1970a). All that concerns the developmental observer is the *order* in which conceptually related behaviors emerge and the degree of within-stage generality or convergence found across representative task settings. It is essential, of course, that these various behaviors be conceptually interrelated (logically interrelated in the majority of the interesting Piagetian cases) in addition to any temporal considerations. Thus, the fact that a mastery of differential calculus conventionally follows the mastery of reading-comprehension skills, which in turn usually follows the emergence of meaningful vocalizations in normative development, while presenting an order of acquisition which is universally "valid" for Western societies, does not convey any useful information concerning the dependence of later cognitive capabilities upon previous achievements (see Wohlwill, 1970c, for similar examples). In contrast, a sequence of conceptually linked abilities, or behavioral acquisitions, which has a congruent empirical counterpart in normative developmental data, may notably enhance our understanding of the genesis of the respective component behaviors. In the general case of an ordinal developmental progression, the task response dimensions must be conceptually and operationally *independent* of age changes across the life-span (Wohlwill, 1970c). Among the many candidates for this type of analysis, one would likely include the general categories of logical reasoning emphasized by Piaget and his associates.

IV. Research Related to the Stage Construct

There exists a considerable body of research literature which has focused upon the sequential relationship requirements of the Piagetian concept domains (cf. Hooper, Goldman, Storck, & Burke, 1971). It should be noted that the majority of these endeavors have investigated behaviors *within* a general period of development (e.g., the six substages of the sensory-motor period or the substages of classification skill acquisition within the concrete operations period) rather than a behavioral analysis across the major stages of human development (see Nassefat, 1963, for a notable exception). Although a few longitudinal studies of logical operations functioning have been carried out (Almy, Chittenden, & Miller, 1967; Deal, 1969; Skard, Inhelder, Noelting, & Murphy, 1960; Wohlwill, Fusaro, & Devoe, 1969), almost all of this research has employed conventional cross-sectional assessment strategies (including applications of special scaling techniques) and shares the potential theoretical (Baltes, 1968; Schaie, 1965) and empirical (Baltes & Reinert, 1969; Schaie & Strother, 1968b,c; Riegel, Riegel, & Meyer, 1967a) shortcomings of these designs. Scalogram approaches or related correlational strategies have been applied to the cognitive domains of quantity concepts (Davol, Chittenden, Plante, & Tuzik, 1967; McRoy, 1967; Papalia & Hooper, 1971; Schwartz & Scholnick, 1970; Uzgiris, 1964); spatial concepts (Laurendeau & Pinard, 1970), number concepts (Dodwell, 1961; Mannix, 1960; Wohlwill, 1960), classification abilities (Kofsky, 1966), causal reasoning (Laurendeau & Pinard, 1962), as well as a series of concrete and formal operations tasks (Goldschmid & Bentler, 1968; Nassefat, 1963; Siegelman & Block, 1969). Specific examples of the type of conceptual linkage presently under consideration would include the role of coordinated visual–motoric exploration as a precursor of infant object permanence concepts (Schofield & Uzgiris, 1969), the earlier acquisition of distance conservation as compared to the ability to deal with the spatial coordinate concepts of horizontality – verticality (Ford, 1970; Piaget & Inhelder, 1956; Piaget, Inhelder, & Szeminska, 1960; Shantz & Smock, 1966; Vandeventer, 1968), the number concept analysis of Wohlwill (1960), the classification concept analysis of Kofsky (1966), the developmental priority of conservation skills as compared to content similar transitivity abilities (Kooistra, 1963; Lovell & Ogilvie, 1961; Smedslund, 1959, 1961a, 1963, 1964), the relationship of serial ordering abilities to skills in inferential transitivity (Braine, 1959; Murray & Youniss, 1968), and the general sequence of geometric concept development, topological to projective and Euclidian (Dodwell, 1963; Lovell, Healy, & Rowland, 1962). The concrete operations period within-stage sequential patterns found for the substance–weight–volume quantity concepts and length–area–volume measurement cases (the volume concepts may, perhaps, belong more properly in the formal operations period) may also represent a conceptual linkage, i.e., the well-known horizontal décalage, but the logical interrelationships, beyond the number of salient dimensions involved, remain to be elucidated.

The research of Dodwell (1962), Shantz (1967), and Smedslund (1963) raises a number of critical methodological issues relevant to the specification of exact degrees of within-stage correspondence to be expected from Piagetian theory. It also brings into question the problem of general task or situational specificity which may be involved in an operational assessment of Piagetian task performance.

While it may be possible to acknowledge Wohlwill's (1970a) definitional ideal of situational nonspecificity for valid developmental events, operational assessment of any configuration of conceptually related task behaviors must consider the general methodological issues concerned with instructional sets, stimulus settings, item difficulties, internal consistency, retest reliability, etc. These issues appear to be particularly troublesome in any evaluation of the within-stage correspondence questions. In essence, the problem becomes a matter of specifying exactly what levels of interrelationship must be attained (certainly not only in terms of correlations significantly different from zero-order levels), in view of the measurement error to be expected, which will substantiate the stage construct. This would involve construct validity approaches in which the resulting proportions of variability attributable to method distinctions should be relatively minor compared to the proportions representing trait or ability communality (Campbell & Fisk, 1959).

The few studies which have attacked this question have not found clearcut support for the within-stage correlate of Piagetian theory (e.g., the concrete operations period task relationship investigations of Dodwell, 1960, 1962; Lunzer, 1960; MacKay, Fraser, & Ross, 1970; Nassefat, 1963; Shantz, 1967; Smedslund, 1964; and Siegleman & Block, 1969). The nine logico-symbolic groupings from which all reasoning in middle childhood are said to derive (Flavell, 1963) have not, as yet, produced a unitary or cohesive configuration of cognitive acquisitions (indeed, many of the empirical findings concerning the developmental sequences or linkages cited earlier represent fundamental evidence against the convergence postulate). This is true even if we restrict our consideration to a single cognitive domain—egocentrism—where a number of tasks putatively assessing the same underlying ability (albeit in distinctly different task formats) were not found to be significantly interrelated (Shantz, 1968).

The major confounding feature of these research attempts concerns the various acquisition and consolidation phases *within* a particular cognitive stage. Recent discussions of the conceptual linkage and convergence-correspondence corollaries of the stage construct have distinguished between the degrees of intra- and interindividual variability found at the initial and final phases of a stage as contrasted with the higher levels to be expected at the transitional or intermediate phases (Flavell, 1970a, b; Flavell & Wohlwill, 1969; Pinard & Laurendeau, 1969; Turiel, 1969). It is somewhat ironic that the more fundamentally interesting and important aspects of stage-oriented theory, i.e., the stabilization interval within a general level or period and the critical transition points between certain stages, also present the greatest methodological assessment difficulties. It is precisely at these developmental intervals that the concepts of sequential linkage and convergence assume major value in contributing to our comprehension of the underlying acquisition processes. The most promising recent viewpoints have adopted probablistic models of the stage-dependent acquisition process. Thus, Turiel (1969) distinguished between the contentive versus the structural aspects of moral development, Looft (in press) suggested a similar distinction for the egocentrism domain, while Flavell and Wohlwill (1969) have proposed a model which contrasts the competence (structural) and performance aspects of age-related behavioral change. Each of these alternatives demands explicit and precise diagnosis of the various conceptual acquisition possibilities (e.g., Task A may be the genetic precursor to Task B; Task B may substitute for, or subsume the earlier appearing task A; or each task may develop under the auspices of another mediating factor thus yielding synchronous emergence) before the exact temporal relationships may be ascertained. In this context the normative acquisition age-points do assume obvious importance. For example, it is difficult to imagine any definitive conclusions regarding the relationship of inferential transitivity abilities to other logical cognitive achievements if there is little consensual agreement as to what "defines" the behavior in question (i.e., the recent logical transitivity controversy between Braine, 1959, 1962, 1964, and Smedslund, 1963, 1965; see also Gruen, 1966).

Although the notable presence of response variability at stage transition intervals has led investigators such as Turiel (1969) to view a "mixture" of stage-related responses as a necessary aspect of development through successive structures, it is clear that we lack essential information concerning the dimensional reliability and homogeneity of our operational indices of cognitive development. One would generally expect that the measures of each conceptual ability domain should prove to be relatively unidimensional in nature prior to any consideration of a determination of functional (synchronous, parallel, or sequential) relationship among different variables over the life span (Wohlwill, 1970c). These issues become particularly salient when we consider the discontinuity assumptions or qualitative distinctions generally associated with stage designations. How may we deal realistically with across-stage developmental comparability issues, for example, if we are not capable of exhaustively describing the major defining characteristics of a particular substage within the overall ontogenetic series? Application of correlational assessment strategies and related multivariate analytic techniques appears to offer a potential route to resolving these problems (Baltes & Nesselroade, 1970; Nesselroade, 1970). Insofar as the Piagetian task formats are concerned, cluster analysis (Dodwell, 1963), discriminant function analysis (Orpet & Meyers, 1970), monotonicity analysis (Bentler, 1969), as well as conventional factor analysis (Berzonsky, 1971; Vernon, 1965) may offer a means to evaluate the degree of dimensional homogeneity present within a given stage or level of cognitive development.

Flavell's (1971) analysis of alternatives to the present stage sequence and correspondence assumptions is particularly noteworthy. Flavell pointed out that the child's task performances which represent Stage X behavior develop *gradually* rather than *abruptly*. Typically, task-specific behavior reaches "functional maturity" during a stage following the one in which it first develops.

> The fact that the acquisition period of a stage-specific item appears to constitute an extended temporal interval rather than a temporal point renders ambiguous the notion of developmental synchrony or concurrence. . . . Two conclusions were drawn with respect to interitem concurrence, after having restricted the term to mean only the synchronous emergence (i.e., synchronous *initial* development) of two or more items. First, items from the same stage may often emerge in an invariant or near-invariant sequence rather than concurrently, although important methodological problems cloud the research evidence on this point. Second, a stage theory such as Piaget's does not in any event logically require or predict anything but a very loose sort of item concurrence at most, and research attempts at establishing strict concurrences have been accordingly misguided in rationale [pp. 450–451].

V. Implications for Future Research

In view of these generalizations, we may well ask what direction should guide our subsequent research endeavors. If it is recognized that our ultimate goal is a comprehensive understanding (with the implications of accurate prediction and associated control) of the functional relationships underlying normative cognitive development, then certain implications are evident. At present, we know very little about the major factors and variables which, in the routine life experiences of humans, determine the course of cognitive growth. An understanding of these factors clearly requires an ecological analysis concerning the spontaneous activities of children in natural situations. Ideally, these ecological analyses should be conducted within longitudinal assessment designs with appropriate sampling and measurement control features. It may be noted that of the great number of secondary Piagetian studies, a paucity have utilized longitudinal measurement designs. Acknowledging the well-known procedural and economic difficulties associated with longitudinal assessment designs, the relatively brief duration of the notable cognitive changes associated with middle childhood makes this lack of relevant information even more obvious. Any longitudinal assessment of intellectual functioning should also include explicit consideration of the many *non*cognitive aspects of human development such as personality factors, socialization influences, peer group interactions, etc. The literature on cognitive development, has, to a great extent, ignored the affective dimensions of intellectual development and has thus revealed a distinctly sterile and unrealistic overall picture. Children do not demonstrate cognitive growth in an affective vacuum!

It follows from much of the preceding discussion that a critical problem area remains essentially unsolved, the design and validation of methodologically adequate assessment indices or instrumentation to permit an operational evaluation of life-span cognitive processes. The primary guiding criterion in these endeavors must be the provision of functionally comparable, and relevant tasks for the various age intervals under consideration. A composite array of task formats which assess analogous functional capabilities for young children, as well as mature and aged adults, will certainly constitute a notable achievement. In view of this goal, it is important to recall the well-recognized (and often disregarded) distinction between similarities in absolute performance levels and possible differences in the underlying process mechanisms which may generate these performances at markedly disparate age intervals. As Werner (1937), in contrasting these "process" and "achievement" aspects, has stated:

> A fundamental issue is involved. Does the genesis of "learning", "abstraction", "reasoning", or whatever term one chooses to use, mean the development of a unitary function? Or does it mean the history of an accomplishment achieved by process-patterns which are quite different at different levels? It is correct, if development is interpreted according to the first assumption, to take the degree of accomplishment as the objective measure of the genetic stage of the unitary function in question. If it is admitted, following a growing tendency among psychologists, that the latter assumption is more tenable, the conclusion must be drawn that mental development, or training, does not consist so much of a quantitative increase in accomplishment, one based on a unitary function, as of a reorganization of processes conditioned either by the introduction of a new function, or by a change of dominance of function in a given process-pattern [p. 353].

This orientation offers the possibility that the comparable performances of widely differing age groups (young children and aged adults, for example) may be based upon qualitatively different underlying processes. Aside from the implications for the well-established, standardized ability-testing literature, this approach suggests the possible utilization of task formats which provide for alternative solution strategies or process employment. Examples of task settings which permit the use of problem-solving strategies differentially related to developmental levels are offered by Wapner (1969). A notable developmental shift in the cognitive mechanisms used in serial learning tasks was observed by Kempler (1964) and formally similar strategy distinctions were found in the word-context meaning research of Werner and Kaplan (1952) for children from 6 to 13 years of age. Classification or categorization tasks, which—by the nature of the stimulus material and instructional sets employed—permit a number of appropriate response types, have shown marked differences between younger subjects and adults.

A major issue remains, even assuming that a number of functionally analogous tasks with comparable cognitive requirements and motivational attractiveness, and with appropriate item difficulty adjustments (absence of performance ceiling effects) are available (possible candidates for the age intervals beyond infancy might include the traditional discrimination learning settings, standardized tests such as the *Raven Progressive Matrices*, the measures of egocentrism and social communication employed by Cowan, 1967, and Looft and Charles, 1971, in addition to the Piagetian concrete and formal operations tasks). The observation of performance similarities or differences on specific cognitive measures for various age groups across the life-span provides little information as to the *interrelation* of ability domains. Although the average performance characteristics for a particular ability measure may be similar for differing age intervals, the relationship of these achievements to other cognitive areas may differ considerably (Hooper, Papalia, & Fitzgerald, 1971). In addition, the experimentally derived manipulations which relate specified attributes of age changes to particular independent variables at one interval in the life-span may not be found for all chronological time segments. It is possible, for example, that the role of demographic factors, sensory capacities, the degree of initial learning, and general training or enrichment programs, will differ depending upon the criterial tasks and age interval comparisons in question. In general we must be aware of the possibility that the process of decline following maturity may be mediated by process mechanisms rather different from those which underlie development from birth to adulthood. As Turiel (1969) has stated, "the conditions causing regressive change may not be the same as those causing progressive change [p. 113]."

Another consideration concerns the use of age simulation strategies in lieu of conventional concurrent or longitudinal assessment designs. These short-term manipulations, e.g., retrospective and prospective observation strategies, may be extremely valuable approaches insofar as they are applicable to the problems of task comparability and functional relevance across the life-span. A recent description of the potential role of these alternatives (Baltes & Goulet, 1971; see also Baltes & Nesselroade, this volume) makes brief reference to the employment of Werner's (1957) "microgenetic" techniques for analysis of developmental processes with mature subjects. As the research with perceptual functioning (Pollack & Chaplin, 1963), language development (Flavell & Draguns, 1957), and symbolic processes (Werner & Kaplan, 1963) has clearly indicated, the microgenetic approach offers a valuable complementary addition to conventional developmental analysis. The major consideration in the present context concerns, of course, the *validity* of these research approaches. All "economical" alternatives (including the Baltes and Goulet, 1971, suggestions) may share potential shortcomings in validity. These issues will never be completely and exhaustively resolved until actual comparative analyses are undertaken, e.g., a longitudinal study of subjects from early infancy to adolescence to be compared with later microgenetic analyses of the same subjects following maturity.

VI. The Role of Training-Intervention Research

Experimental or naturalistically based intervention research probably represents the area of greatest potential convergence and complementary contribution for the organismic and neobehavioristic approaches. Although they are frequently overstated, the role of environmentally derived behavior alterations are certainly assigned differential status and importance in these orientations. Fundamentally, from the neobehavioristic viewpoint, experiential variables (the quality, duration, and intensity of training or general environmental encounters) should operate (a) to determine (permit control of) cognitive developmental progressions, (b) to govern extinction of these developmental acquisitions, and (c) to govern the potential reacquisition of these criterion behaviors following decline during senescence, assuming the usual maturational and neurophysiological constraints are met. The great majority of the experimental attempts to induce or accelerate Piagetian concept attainment (Beilin, 1971b; Brainerd & Allen, 1971; Flavell, 1970b; Goulet, 1970b; Sigel & Hooper, 1968) follow directly from these suppositions.

The organismic theorists, in contrast, view the role of general life experiences and specific instructional programs in the various cognitive domains rather differently (for example, see the distinctions of Piaget and Inhelder, 1969, and the definitional considerations of Wohlwill, 1970a, cited earlier). The interactionist basis of this position demands an equal emphasis upon structural considerations as well as environmentally derived inputs in any evaluation of training endeavors. In this view, although current cognitive structure is partially determined by past life encounters, the overriding consideration is the contemporaneous alignment of present structural capacity and the demands of the instructional program. Thus, equal emphasis is accorded to the individual's cognitive status, the amount and type of training to be utilized, and the conceptual structure of the cognitive content area involved (Piaget, 1970a). Far from denying the fundamental importance of experiential factors, the organismic viewpoint considers these factors as interacting with maturational variables. Thus it is stated:

> . . . we see that maturation consists essentially of opening up new possibilities and thus constitutes a necessary but not in itself a sufficient condition for the appearance of certain behavior patterns. The possibilities thus opened up also need to be fulfilled, and for this to occur, the maturation must be reinforced by functional exercise and a *minimum* of experience [Piaget & Inhelder, 1969, p. 154].

As Goulet (1970b) made clear, when age *alone* is the independent variable, maturation and experience are inextricably confounded. Thus, retrospective analyses of the relative contribution of maturational and experiential determinants must be replaced by prospective analyses of developmental phenomena, e.g., remedial or compensatory enrichment experiences for younger subjects, the effects of which may be compared to the normative performances of older children. The overall meaning and relevance of this research approach should be viewed as contributing to an understanding of developmental functions, i.e., "the form or mode of the relationship between an individual's age and the changes occuring in his responses on some specified dimension of behavior over the course of his life [Wohlwill, 1970c, p. 151]."

It should be noted that a potentially paradoxical situation may exist for the organismic theorist who accepts as a definition of valid developmental change Wohlwill's (1970a) criterion of situational independence; for this leads to a general disavowal of the relevance of the effects of specific experience, practice, or learning within the individual's reinforcement history. The issue here probably reduces to the manner in which situationally specific experience is defined. It is undoubtedly true that the traditional short-term "laboratory" version of the training study offers a very poor approximation to natural experience situations such as found in the typical family, classroom, or neighborhood settings (Wohlwill, 1966, 1970c). Nonetheless, it is clear that the general intervention–enrichment design offers the only viable approach (in the human organism) to studying the interactive influences of genetic-maturational and experiential factors on developmental events and functions.

Theoretically based training designs may provide additional information pertinent to the stage construct analyses discussed previously. For the cases of predicted sequential linkage, training on the conceptually prerequisite task should (theoretically) influence subsequent performance on the later appearing task domain. In the cases of concept areas for which specific substages are postulated, training on advanced levels of the hypothesized sequence for subjects who demonstrate only lower level capabilities may be used as an experimental test of the stage invariance corollary. Note here that in order to reject the stage invariance assumption, the experimental subjects must demonstrate the higher order skills without a concomittant ability to deal with the intermediate stage-related task requirements. This criterion has seldom been systematically evaluated in the experimental attempts to induce or "accelerate" Piagetian concept attainments. Turiel (1969; see also Rest, Turiel, & Kohlberg, 1969) has presented an interesting application of training strategies within the context of stage-dependent moral development. In applying training sessions focused at varying points above and below the specific stage location of an individual subject, it was found that the most marked behavioral changes resulted from training at a stage locus one interval above or below the subject's pretraining status. Training efficiency was optimal when directed at the next highest adjacent stage in the developmental series.

The question of within-stage convergence or correspondence may also be profitably investigated by the use of transfer of training designs. If this stage postulate is valid, training on one component of a conceptually integrated stage structure, (e.g., the logical groupings of the middle childhood period) should show evidence of nonspecific transfer to other component abilities representative of the same stage structure. Perhaps the best examples of this approach as applied to concrete operations functioning is the work of Beilin (1965) and Laurendeau and her associates (Carbonneau, 1965; Fournier, 1965, as cited in Pinard & Laurendeau, 1969). In these efforts the degree of task interrelationship is evaluated before and after training, in addition to the analysis of conceptually derived posttraining generalization. An overview of the studies which have applied this criterion of nonspecific transfer to training yields a decidedly mixed picture, i.e., an absence of positive transfer effects by Beilin (1965), Beilin and Franklin (1962), Hooper (1972), Murray (1968), Peters (1970), and Smedslund (1959); contrasted with positive nonspecific transfer effects by Bearison (1969), Gelman (1969), Kingsley and Hall (1967), Rothenberg and Orost (1969), Shantz and Sigel (1967), and Sigel, Roeper, and Hooper (1966).

If we examine the distinctions between the successful versus the nonsuccessful far-transfer cases, an interesting dichotomy emerges. All six of the studies (cited above) which failed to find nonspecific or far-transfer utilized a *single*, relatively unitary training procedure for any particular experimental treatment condition. In contrast, the six studies which showed significant far-transfer employed *multiple* training strategies for any treatment group. Thus, Bearison (1969) trained children on the comparison and numeration (counting) of discrete units within the liquid quantity conservation format, Gelman (1969) trained on number and length conservation, Kingsley and Hall (1967) trained on weight and length conservation, Rothenberg and Orost (1969) employed a wide variety of number conservation instructional techniques in combination, and Shantz and Sigel (1967) as well as Sigel, Roeper, and Hooper (1966), focused upon a number of related logical operations skills including multiple labeling, multiplicative classification, and relationality concepts. As Beilin (1971b) has made clear, although these multiple training approaches produce far-transfer, they fail to provide information as to the relative contributions of particular aspects or components of the overall training program. In brief, we do not know *what* it was that primarily influenced the subjects' new behavioral acquisitions.

Nonetheless, these multiple strategy studies appear to be notably effective insofar as nonspecific transfer is concerned. These results imply that training approaches which emphasize the provision of maximally structured, focused learning experiences (task specific) may not be the most effective means of facilitating cognitive growth. Wohlwill (1970d) has suggested a theoretical lattice model of experiential input which distinguishes between specific instruction, which leads to vertical transfer, and more general, nonspecific training, which leads to more broadly based, horizontal transfer. It is the latter, horizontal transfer, which appears to be involved in the present descriptions of within-stage far-transfer. A related interpretation of these results would involve learning sets or "learning to learn" phenomena (Harlow, 1949, 1959). It appears that the provision of a variety of instructional settings or a series of experiences with differing task formats is ideally suited to the developmental capacities of the typical preoperational child. Most importantly, these variegated experiences lead to across-task generalization (a defining characteristic of Learning to Learn research) as represented by the present nonspecific far-transfer criterion. These learning set considerations are in general accord with a great deal of the research on concept or complex skills learning (see Goulet, 1970b, for a theoretical overview) and complement the suggestion of multiple, simultaneous training on more than one logical operations component as optimal for potential cognitive reorganization (Pinard & Laurendeau, 1969). The use of multiple-training strategies in experimental formats probably offers a closer approximation to the generalized life experiences found in typical natural settings or as revealed in longitudinal ecological analysis (Wohlwill, 1966, 1970d). In discussing the relevance of the learning set research, Wohlwill (1970d) has stated:

> The work on the development of learning sets is of particular interest, since it may provide a clue to the questions of what it is that the older children possess that permits such broadly-based transfer, and how they came by it. One way of putting it is that they have acquired the ability to formulate rules for dealing with the stimulus input that operate for any particular set of stimuli, providing certain structural invariants are exemplified in them. This way of putting it brings the problem of the formation of learning sets rather close to the formation of concrete operations, notably the conservations. Indeed, though the two types of problems have yet to be investigated correlatively in the same children, the close link between them is suggested not only by the fact that discrimination-learning set formation appears to reach a peak toward the end of the concrete-operations

period, but also by the demonstrated relationship to general intelligence, rather than chronological age (Harter, 1965) [pp. 21–22].

The most efficacious training approach may well be a program which combines enrichment experiences on a number of related conceptual task settings theoretically linked to the same developmental stage. Following a suggestion by Pinard and Laurendeau (1969), for example, it may be potentially effective to combine seriation and classification enrichment experiences into a unified instructional program format. These experiences may then be compared to training which focuses upon seriation or classification concepts exclusively. A training program utilizing these components for children in the 3 to 5 year age-range is currently in progress at the University of Wisconsin preschool laboratory. The training assessment focus of this investigation includes near-transfer to the training-specific task settings, intermediate-transfer to the complementary logical task format (for the seriation only, and classification only treatment conditions), and far-transfer to various conservation tasks.

A major question which bears upon any training program designed to influence cognitive functioning concerns the stability of the experimentally induced behavioral achievements (Piaget, 1964). It is obvious that the experimentally mediated response changes should evidence stability over time, resistance to countersuggestion or nonconfirmatory information, etc., comparable to that displayed by nontreatment control subjects of appropriate developmental levels. Smedslund's (1961b) often-cited study of extinction responses by experimental as compared to "natural" weight conservers is an appropriate example. In this instance greater numbers of subjects who were given experimental training in weight conservation showed nonconservation responses in a contrived test setting as compared to a group of conserving but nontrained controls (it may be noted that the response patterns of the seven natural conservers who *did* extinguish are certainly of equal interest to the developmental observer; see Hall and Simpson, 1968; Kingsley & Hall, 1967; Smedslund, 1968; Smith, 1968). Notwithstanding the obvious experimental weaknesses insofar as the adequacy of the type and duration of the extinction procedures used in Smedslund's research (cf. Watson, 1968), additional studies employing this type of training criterion are necessary.

Of more general interest to the present considerations are Wohlwill's (1970a) recommendations concerning long-range stability measures following experimental manipulations. In formal parallel to conventional longitudinal assessment (the problems of repeated measurement are germane to both cases) these designs must include evaluation across the entire age-span over which the variable is undergoing alteration. This requires extensive follow-up assessments (across generations?) of experimental and control groups in deprivation or enrichment studies. This would be particularly true of an application of training research designs to a potential resolution of the nature–nurture controversy. A recent version of this "elderly" argument poses the question of whether universally equivalent life experiences (Wohlwill, 1966) or species specific genetic preprogramming (Beilin, 1969) best "explains" the uniform cognitive development of human organisms from widely varying sociocultural backgrounds insofar as Piagetian conceptual functioning is concerned. Systematic utilization of training programs based upon experimental transfer paradigms (Goulet, 1970b) provide the best opportunity for evaluating these alternatives.

The most compelling rationale for including training–enrichment research as an integral aspect of life-span developmental analysis is, of course, the opportunity it provides for experimentally manipulating the normative developmental progression or regression patterns.

> The objective of such interventions, which augment those that normally occur in spontaneous development, is not so much the actual acceleration of the development of a particular concept, as though it were a matter of inducing the subjects to pass rapidly through the normal stages. It rather consists in seeking out and analyzing the factors responsible for any such eventual accelerations, thus furnishing the essential elements of solution to the theoretical and practical problems involved in understanding spontaneous intellectual development and the rational application of this knowledge to educational purposes [Pinard & Laurendeau, 1969, pp. 155–156].

Thus, training research provides the natural liaison between the organismic emphasis upon descriptive developmental analysis and the antecedent–consequent research paradigm so vigorously defended by the neobehaviorists.

References

Abelson, R. P. Simulation of social behavior. In G. Lindzey & E. Aronson (Eds.), *The handbook of social psychology*. Vol. II. Reading, Massachusetts: Addison-Wesley, 1968. Pp. 274–356.

Adams, J. A. *Human memory*. New York: McGraw-Hill, 1967.

Adams, J. A., & Montague, W. E. Retroactive inhibition and natural language mediation. *Journal of Verbal Learning and Verbal Behavior*, 1967, **6**, 528–535.

Aebli, H. *Didactique psychologique: Application à la didactique de la psychologie de Jean Piaget*. Neuchatel: Delachaux et Niestel, 1951. (*Psychologische Didaktik*. Stuttgart: Klett, 1962.)

Aebli, H. Ein Beitrag zur Frage der genetischen Kontinuität in der kognitiven Entwicklung des Kindes, illustriert am Beispiel des Zeitbegriffes. In H. Heckhausen (Ed.), *Bericht über den 24. Kongress der Deutschen Gesellschaft für Psychologie in Wien*. 1964. Goettingen: Hogrefe, 1965. Pp. 100–125.

Ahammer, I. M., & Baltes, P. B. Desirability judgments of adolescents, adults, and older people: Self vs. hetero-perceptions. Paper presented at the meeting of the American Psychological Association, Miami, September 1970.

Alberts, E., & Ehrenfreund, D. Transposition in children as a function of age. *Journal of Experimental Psychology*, 1951, **41**, 30–38.

Almy, M., Chittenden, E., & Miller, P. *Young children's thinking: Studies of some aspects of Piaget's theory*. New York: Columbia Teacher's College Press, 1967.

American College Dictionary. New York: Random House, 1958.

American Psychological Association. Ethical standards for psychologists. *American Psychologist*, 1963, **18**, 56–60.

Anandalakshmy, S., & Grinder, R. E. Conceptual emphasis in the history of developmental psychology: Evolutionary theory, teleology, and the nature-nurture issue. *Child Development*, 1970, **41**, 1113–1123.

Anastasi, A. The influence of specific experience upon mental organization. *Genetic Psychology Monographs*, 1936, **18**, 245–355.

Anastasi, A. *Differential psychology*. New York: Macmillan, 1958. (a)

Anastasi, A. Heredity, environment, and the question "How?" *Psychological Review*, 1958, **65**, 197–208 (b)

Anastasi, A. On the formation of psychological traits. *American Psychologist*, 1970, **25**, 899–910.

Anderson, R. B. W. On the comparability of meaningful stimuli in cross-cultural research. *Sociometry*, 1967, **30**, 127–136.

317

Apostel, L. Toward a formal study of models in the non-formal sciences. *Synthese,* 1960, **12,** 125–161.

Arenberg, D. Regression analysis of verbal learning on adult age at two anticipation intervals. *Journal of Gerontology,* 1967, **22,** 411–414.

Asch, S. E. Forming impressions of personality. *Journal of Abnormal and Social Psychology,* 1946, **41,** 258–290.

Back, K. W., & Bourgue, L. B. Life graphs: Aging and cohort effects. *Journal of Gerontology,* 1970, **25,** 249–255.

Baer, D. M. An age-irrelevant concept of development. *Merrill-Palmer Quarterly of Behavior and Development,* 1970, **16,** 238–246.

Baer, D. M., Peterson, R. F., & Sherman, J. A. The development of imitation by reinforcing behavioral similarity to a model. *Journal of the Experimental Analysis of Behavior,* 1967, **10,** 405–416.

Baer, D. M., & Sherman, J. A. Behavior modification: Clinical and educational applications. In H. W. Reese & L. P. Lipsitt (Eds.), *Experimental child psychology.* New York: Academic Press, 1970. Pp. 643–672.

Baer, D. M., & Wolf, M. M. The reinforcement contingency in preschool and remedial education. In R. D. Hess & R. M. Bear (Eds.), *Early education: Current theory, research, and practice.* Chicago: Aldine, 1968. Pp. 119–129.

Bailey, J. S., Wolf, M. M., & Phillips, E. L. Home-based reinforcement and the modification of predelinquents' classroom behavior. *Journal of Applied Behavior Analysis,* 1970, **3,** 223–233.

Baird, L. L. Big school, small school: A critical examination of the hypothesis. *Journal of Educational Psychology,* 1969, **60,** 253–260.

Bakan, D. *On method: Toward a reconstruction of psychological investigation.* San Francisco: Jossey-Bass, 1967.

Balinsky, B. An analysis of the mental factors of various age groups from nine to sixty. *Genetic Psychology Monographs,* 1941, **23,** 191–234.

Baltes, P. B. Longitudinal and cross-sectional sequences in the study of age and generation effects. *Human Development,* 1968, **11,** 145–171.

Baltes, P. B., Baltes, M. M., & Reinert, G. The relationship between time of measurement and age in cognitive development of children: An application of cross-sectional sequences. *Human Development,* 1970, **13,** 258–268.

Baltes, P. B., Eyferth, K., & Schaie, K. W. Intra- and inter-cultural factor structures of social desirability ratings by American and German college students. *Multivariate Behavioral Research,* 1969, **4,** 67–78.

Baltes, P. B., and Goulet, L. R. Status and issues of a life-span developmental psychology. In L. R. Goulet & P. B. Baltes (Eds.), *Life-span developmental psychology: Research and theory.* New York: Academic Press, 1970. Pp. 3–21.

Baltes, P. B., & Goulet, L. R. Exploration of developmental variables by manipulation and simulation of age differences in behavior. *Human Development,* 1971, **14,** 149–170.

Baltes, P. B., & Labouvie, G. V. Adult development of intellectual performance: Description, explanation, modification. In C. Eisdorfer & P. L. Lawton (Eds.), *APA Task Force on Aging,* Washington: American Psychological Association, 1972.

Baltes, P. B., & Nesselroade, J. R. Multivariate longitudinal and cross-sectional sequences for analyzing generational change: A methodological note. *Developmental Psychology,* 1970, **2,** 163–168.

Baltes, P. B., Nesselroade, J. R., Schaie, K. W., & Labouvie, E. W. On the dilemma of regression effects in examining ability level related differentials in ontogenetic patterns of adult intelligence. *Developmental Psychology,* 1972, **6,** 72–84.

Baltes, P. B., & Reinert, G. Cohort effects in cognitive development of children as revealed by cross-sectional sequences. *Developmental Psychology,* 1969, **1,** 169–177.

Baltes, P. B., Schaie, K. W., & Nardi, A. H. Age and experimental mortality in a seven-year longitudinal study of cognitive behavior. *Developmental Psychology*, 1971, **5**, 18–26.

Bandura, A. *Principles of behavior modification*. New York: Holt, 1969.

Barker, R. G. Observation of behavior: Ecological approaches. *Journal of Mt. Sinai Hospital*, 1964, **31**, 268–284.

Barker, R. G. Explorations in ecological psychology. *American Psychologist*, 1965, **20**, 1–14.

Barker, R. G. *Ecological psychology: Concepts and methods for studying the environment of human behavior*. Stanford, California: Stanford University Press, 1968.

Barker, R. G. Wanted: An eco-behavioral science. In E. P. Willems & H. L. Raush (Eds.), *Naturalistic viewpoints in psychological research*. New York: Holt, 1969. Pp. 31–43.

Barker, R. G., & Gump, P. V. *Big school, small school*. Stanford, California: Stanford University Press, 1964.

Bateson, P. P. G. An effect of imprinting on the perceptual development of domestic chicks. *Nature*, 1964, **202**, 421–422. (a)

Bateson, P. P. G. Effect of similarity between rearing and testing conditions on chicks' following and avoidance responses. *Journal of Comparative and Physiological Psychology*, 1964, **57**, 100–103. (b)

Bateson, P. P. G. Relation between conspicuousness of stimuli and their effectiveness in the imprinting situation. *Journal of Comparative and Physiological Psychology*, 1964, **58**, 407–411. (c)

Bateson, P. P. G. The characteristics and context of imprinting. *Biological Reviews*, 1966, **41**, 177–220.

Bayiey, N. Development of mental abilities. In P. H. Mussen (Ed.), *Carmichael's manual of child psychology*. New York: Wiley, 1970. Pp. 1163–1209.

Beament, J. W. L. (Ed.) *Models and analogues in biology*. Cambridge: Cambridge University Press, 1960.

Bearison, D. Role of measurement operations in the acquisition of conservation. *Developmental Psychology*, 1969, **1**, 653–660.

Beattie, W. M. The design of supportive environments for the life-span. *Gerontologist*, 1970, **10**, 190–193.

Beaty, W. E., & Weir, M. W. Children's performance on the intermediate-size problem as a function of two different training procedures. *Journal of Experimental Child Psychology*, 1966, **4**, 332–340.

Becker, W. C. The relationship of factors in parental ratings of self and each other to the behavior of kindergarten children as rated by mothers, fathers and teachers. *Journal of Consulting Psychology*, 1960, **24**, 507–527.

Becker, W. C. Consequences of different kinds of parental discipline. In M. L. Hoffman & L. W. Hoffman (Eds.), *Review of child development research*. Vol. 1. New York: Russell Sage, 1964. Pp. 169–208.

Beilin, H. Learning and operational convergence in logical thought development. *Journal of Experimental Child Psychology*, 1965, **2**, 317–339.

Beilin, H. Developmental stages and developmental processes. Paper presented at the Invitational Conference on Ordinal Scales of Cognitive Development, Monterey, California, February 1969.

Beilin, H. Developmental stages and developmental processes. In D. R. Green, M. P. Ford, & G. P. Flamer (Eds.), *Measurement and Piaget*. New York: McGraw-Hill, 1971 Pp. 172–189. (a)

Beilin, H. The training and acquisition of logical operations. In M. R. Rosskopf, L. P. Steffe, & S. Taback (Eds.), *Piagetian cognitive-development research and mathematical education*. Washington: National Council of Teachers of Mathematics, 1971. Pp. 81–124. (b)

Beilin, H. On the development of physical concepts. In T. Mischel (Ed.), *Cognitive development and epistemology*. New York: Academic Press, 1971. (c)

Beilin, H., & Franklin, D. C. Logical operations in area and length measurement; age and training effects. *Child Development*. 1962, **33**, 607–618.

Bekker, L. D., & Taylor, C. Attitudes toward the aged in a multi-generational sample. *Journal of Gerontology*, 1966, **21**, 115–118.

Bell, R. Q. Retrospective and prospective views of early personality development. *Merrill-Palmer Quarterly of Behavior and Development*, 1960, **6**, 131–144.

Benedict, R. *Patterns of culture*. Boston: Houghton, 1934.

Bentler, P. M. Measurement of common factor change. Paper presented at the meeting of the Society for Psychophysiological Research, Denver, Colorado, October 1966.

Bentler, P. M. Monotonicity analysis: An alternative to factor test analysis. Paper presented at the Conference on Ordinal Scales of Development, Monterey, California, February 1969.

Bentler, P. M. A comparison of monotonicity analysis with factor analysis. *Educational and Psychological Measurement*, 1970, **30**, 241–250. (a)

Bentler, P. M. A regression model for factor analysis. *Proceedings of 78th Annual Convention, American Psychological Association*, 1970, **5**, 109–110. (b)

Bentler, P. M. Clustran, a program for oblique transformation. *Behavioral Science*, 1971, **16**, 183–185. (a)

Bentler, P. M. An implicit metric for ordinal scales: Implications for assessment of cognitive growth. In D. R. Green, M. P. Ford, & G. B. Flamer (Eds.) *Measurement and Piaget*. New York: McGraw-Hill, 1971. Pp. 34–63. (b)

Bentler, P. M. Monotonicity analysis: An alternative to linear factor and test analysis. In D. R. Green, M. P. Ford, & G. B. Flamer (Eds.), *Measurement and Piaget*. New York McGraw-Hill, 1971. Pp. 220–244. (c)

Bentler, P. M. A lower-bound method for the dimension-free measurement of internal consistency. *Social Science Research*, 1972, **1**, No. 4.

Berlyne, D. E. Les équivalences psychologiques et les notions quantitatives. In D. E. Berlyne & J. Piaget (Eds.), *Théorie du comportement et opérations. Etudes d'épistemologie génétique*. Vol. 12. Paris: Presses Université France, 1960. Pp. 1–76.

Berlyne, D. E. *Structure and direction in thinking*. New York: Wiley, 1965.

Berlyne, D. E. Discussion: The delimitation of cognitive development. In H. W. Stevenson (Ed.), The concept of development. *Monographs of the Society for Research in Child Development*, 1966, **31** (5, Whole No. 107), 71–81.

Berrien, F. K. Cross-cultural equivalence of personality measures. *Journal of Social Psychology*, 1968, **75**, 3–9.

Berry, J. W. On cross-cultural comparability. *International Journal of Psychology*, 1969, **4**, 119–128.

Berstecher, D. *Zur Theorie und Technik des internationalen Vergleichs*. Stuttgart: Klett, 1970.

Bertalanffy, L. von. Comments on Professor Piaget's paper. In J. M. Tanner & B. Inhelder (Eds.), *Discussion on child development*. Vol. 4. New York: International University Press, 1960. Pp. 69–76.

Bertalanffy, L. von. *General system theory*. New York: George Braziller, 1968.

Berzonsky, M. D. Interdependence of Inhelder and Piaget's model of logical thinking. *Developmental Psychology*, 1971, **4**, 469–479.

Bijou, S. W., & Baer, D. M. *Child development*. Vol. 1. *A systematic and empirical theory*. New York: Appleton, 1961.

Bijou, S. W., & Baer, D. M. Some methodological contributions from a functional analysis of child development. In L. P. Lipsitt & C. C. Spiker (Eds.), *Advances in child development and behavior*. Vol. 1. New York: Academic Press, 1963. Pp. 197–231.

Bijou, S. W., & Baer, D. M. *Child Development*. Vol. 2. New York: Appleton, 1965.

Bijou, S. W., Peterson, R. F., & Ault, M. H. A method to integrate descriptive and experimental field studies at the level of data and empirical concepts. *Journal of Applied Behavior Analysis*, 1968, **1**, 175–191.

Birren, J. E. (Ed.) *Handbook of aging and the individual: Psychological and biological aspects*. Chicago: University of Chicago Press, 1959. (a)

Birren, J. E. Principles of research on aging. In J. E. Birren (Ed.), *Handbook of aging and the individual: Psychological and biological aspects*. Chicago: University of Chicago Press, 1959. Pp. 3–42. (b)

Bjarväll, A. The critical period and the interval between hatching and exodus in mallard ducklings. *Behaviour*, 1967, **28**, 141–148.

Bjarväll, A. The hatching and nest-exodus behaviour of mallards. *Wildfowl*, 1968, **19**, 70–80.

Black M. *Models and metaphors*. Ithaca, New York: Cornell University Press, 1962.

Bloom, B. S. *Stability and change in human characteristics*. New York: Wiley, 1964.

Blum, J. E., Jarvik, L. F., & Clark, E. T. Rate of change on selective tests of intelligence: A twenty-year longitudinal study of aging. *Journal of Gerontology*, 1970, **25**, 171–176.

Boesch, E. E. Psychologische Theorie des sozialen Wandels. In H. Besters & E. E. Boesch (Eds.), *Entwicklungspolitik: Handbuch und Lexikon*. Stuttgart, Berlin: Kreuz-Verlag, Mainz: Matthias Grünewald Verlag, 1966. Pp. 335–416.

Boesch, E. E., & Eckensberger, L. H. Methodische Probleme des interkulturellen Vergleichs. In C. F. Gräumann (Ed.), *Handbuch der Psychologie in 12 Bänden*. Vol. 7, 1. *Sozialpsychologie: Theorien und Methoden*. Göttingen: Hogrefe, 1969. Pp. 515–560.

Botwinick, J. *Cognitive processes in maturity and old age*. New York: Springer, 1967.

Botwinick, J. Learning in children and aged adults. In L. R. Goulet & P. B. Baltes (Eds.), *Life-span developmental psychology: Research and theory*. New York: Academic Press, 1970. Pp. 258–284.

Boulding, K. E. Dare we take the social sciences seriously? *American Psychologist*, 1967, **22**, 879–887.

Boulding, K. E. Ecology and environment. *Trans-action*, 1970, **7**, No. 5, 38–44.

Box, G. E. P., & Jenkins, G. M. *Time series analysis–forcasting and control*. San Francisco: Holden-Day, 1970.

Box, G. E. P., & Tiao, G. C. A change in level of a non-stationary time series. *Biometrika*, 1965, **52**, 181–192.

Bozinou, E. Conceptual mediation in the discrimination learning of young children: A component analysis. Unpublished doctoral dissertation, University of Ilinois, 1971.

Braine, M. D. S. The ontogeny of certain logical operations: Piaget's formulation examined by nonverbal methods. *Psychological Monographs*, 1959, **73** (4, Whole No. 475).

Braine, M. D. S. Piaget on reasoning: A methodological critique and alternative proposals. In W. Kessen & C. Kuhlman (Eds.), Thought in the young child. *Monographs of the Society for Research in Child Development*, 1962, **27** (2, Whole No. 83).

Braine, M. D. S. Development of a grasp of transitivity of length: A reply to Smedslund. *Child Development*, 1964, **35**, 799–810.

Brainerd, C. J., & Allen, T. W. Experimental inductions of the conservation of "first-order" quantiative invariants. *Psychological Bulletin*, 1971, **75**, 128–144.

Braithwaite, R. B. *Scientific explanation*. New York: Harper, 1953.

Braithwaite, R. B. Models in empirical science. In E. Nagel, P. Suppes, & A. Tarski (Eds.), *Logic, methodology, and philosophy of science*. Stanford: Stanford University Press, 1962.

Brandt, R. M. *Studying behavior in natural settings*. New York: Holt, in press.

Braun, H. W., & Geiselhart, R. Age differences in the acquisition and extinction of the conditioned eyelid response. *Journal of Experimental Psychology*, 1959, **57**, 386–388.

Breland, K., & Breland, M. *Animal behavior*. New York: Macmillan, 1966.

Brim, O. G. Socialization through the life cycle. In O. G. Brim & S. Wheeler (Eds.), *Socialization after childhood*. New York: Wiley, 1966. Pp. 1–49.

Brislin, R. W. Back-translation for cross-cultural research. *Journal of Cross-cultural Psychology*, 1970, **1**, 185–216.

Britton, J. O., & Britton, J. H. Discrimination of age by preschool children. *Journal of Gerontology,* 1969, **24**, 457–460.

Bromley, D. B. Some effects of age on short-term learning and remembering. *Journal of Gerontology,* 1958, **13**, 398–406.

Brown, L. A critical period in the learning of motionless stimulus properties in chicks. *Animal Behaviour,* 1964, **12**, 353–361.

Bruner, J. S. The course of cognitive growth. *American Psychologist,* 1964, **19**, 1–15.

Bruner, J. S. *Toward a theory of instruction.* Cambridge, Massachusetts: Harvard University Press, 1966.

Brunswik, E. *Perception and the representative design of psychological experiments.* Berkeley: University of California Press, 1956.

Buech, B. U., & Schaie, K. W. Generational vs. ontogentic components of change: A second follow-up. Paper presented in symposium on Intellectual Development in Adulthood and Old Age, at the meeting of the American Psychological Association, Washington, D. C., September 1971.

Bugelski, B. R. Images as mediators in one-trial paired-associate learning. II. Self-timing in successive lists. *Journal of Experimental Psychology,* 1968, **77**, 328–334.

Bunge, M. *Causality: The place of the causal principle in modern science.* New York: World Publishing Co., 1963.

Burghardt, G. M., & Hess, E. H. Food imprinting in the snapping turtle, Chelydra serpentina. *Science,* 1966, **151**, 108–109.

Burt, C. L. The differentiation of intellectual abilities. *British Journal of Educational Psychology,* 1954, **24**, 76–90.

Burt, C. L. Heredity and environment. *Bulletin of the British Psychological Society,* 1971, **24**, 9–15.

Calhoun, J. B. Ecological factors in the development of behavioral anomalies. In J. Zubin & H. F. Hunt (Eds.), *Comparative psychopathology.* New York: Grune & Stratton, 1967. Pp. 1–51.

Campbell, D. T. The mutual methodological relevance of anthropology and psychology. In F. L. K. Hsu (Ed.), *Psychological anthropology: Approaches to culture and personality.* Homewood, Ilinois: Dorsey Press, 1961. Pp. 333–352.

Campbell, D. T. Reforms as experiments. *American Psychologist,* 1969, **24**, 409–429.

Campbell, D. T. Evolutionary epistemology. In P. A. Schilpp (Eds.), *The philosophy of Karl R. Popper: The library of living philosophers.* La Salle, Illinois: Open Court, in press.

Campbell, D. T., Brislin, R. W., Steward, V. M., & Werner, O. Back-translation and other translation techniques for cross-cultural research. *International Journal of Psychology,* 1971, in press.

Campbell, D. T., & Fiske, D. W. Convergent and discriminant validation by the multitrait-multimethod matrix. *Psychological Bulletin,* 1959, **56**, 81–105.

Campbell, D. T., & Stanley, J. C. Experimental and quasi-experimental designs for research on teaching. In N. L. Gage (Ed.), *Handbook of research on teaching.* Chicago: Rand McNally, 1963. Pp. 171–246.

Campbell, D. T., & Stanley, J. C. *Experimental and quasi-experimental designs for research.* Chicago: Rand McNally, 1966.

Canestrari, R. E. Paced and self-paced learning in young and elderly adults. *Journal of Gerontology,* 1963, **18**, 165–168.

Canestrari, R. E., Jr. Age changes in acquisition. In G. A. Talland (Ed.), *Human aging and behavior.* New York: Academic Press, 1968. Pp. 169–188.

Carbonneau, M. *Apprentissage de la notion de conservation des surfaces.* Thèse de licence inédite, Université Montreal, 1965.

Caron, A. J. Far transposition of intermediate size in preverbal children. *Journal of Experimental Child Psychology,* 1966, **3**, 296–311.

Carroll, J. B. Factors of verbal achievement. In A. Anastasi (Ed.), *Testing problems in perspective*. Washington, D. C.: American Council on Education, 1966.

Cassirer, E. *The philosophy of the enlightenment*. Boston: Beacon Press, 1951.

Cattell, R. B. *The description and measurement of personality*. New York: Harcourt, 1946.

Cattell, R. B. The dimensions of culture patterns by factorization of national characters. *Journal of Abnormal and Social Psychology*, 1949, **44**, 443–469.

Cattell, R. B. *Factor analysis*. New York: Harper, 1952. (a)

Cattell, R. B. The three basic factor-analytic research designs—their interrelations and derivations. *Psychological Bulletin*, 1952, **49**, 499–520. (b)

Cattell, R. B. A quantitative analysis of the change in the culture patterns of Great Britain 1837–1937 by P-technique, *Acta Psychologia*, 1953, **9**, 99–121. (a)

Cattell, R. B. Research designs in psychological genetics with special reference to the multiple variance method. *American Journal of Human Genetics*, 1953, **5**, 76–93. (b)

Cattell, R. B. *Personality and motivation structure and measurement*. New York: World Book, 1957.

Cattell, R. B. The dynamic calculus: A system of concepts derived from objective motivation measurement. In G. Lindzey (Ed.), *Assessment of human motives*. New York: Holt, 1958.

Cattell, R. B. The multiple abstract variance analysis equations and solutions: For nature-nurture research on continuous variables. *Psychological Review*, 1960, **67**, 353–372.

Cattell, R. B. The interaction of hereditary and environmental influences. *British Journal of Statistical Psychology*, 1963, **16**, 191–210. (a)

Cattell, R. B. The structuring of change by P-technique and incremental R-technique. In C. W. Harris (Ed.), *Problems in measuring change*. Madison, Wisconsin: University of Wisconsin Press, 1963. Pp. 167–198. (b)

Cattell, R. B. Theory of fluid and crystallized intelligence: A critical experiment. *Journal of Educational Psychology*, 1963, **54**, 1–22. (c)

Cattell, R. B. *Personality and social psychology: Collected papers*. San Diego, California: R. R. Knapp, 1964.

Cattell, R. B. The definition and measurement of national morale and morality. *Journal of Social Psychology*, 1965, **67**, 77–96. (a)

Cattell, R. B. Methodological and conceptual advances in evaluating hereditary and environmental influences and their interaction. In S. G. Vandenberg (Ed.), *Methods and goals in human behavior genetics*. New York: Academic Press, 1965. (b)

Cattell, R. B. *The scientific analysis of personality*. London: Penguin, 1965. (c)

Cattell, R. B. Guest editorial: Multivariate behavioral research and the integrative challenge. *Multivariate Behavioral Research*, 1966, **1**, 4–23. (a)

Cattell, R. B. (Ed.) *Handbook of multivariate experimental psychology*. Chicago: Rand McNally, 1966. (b)

Cattell, R. B. Patterns of change: Measurement in relation to state-dimension, trait change, lability, and process concepts. In R. B. Cattell (Ed.), *Handbook of multivariate experimental psychology*. Chicago: Rand McNally, 1966. Pp. 355–402. (c)

Cattell, R. B. Comparing factor trait and state scores across ages and cultures. *Journal of Gerontology*, 1969, **24**, 348–360.

Cattell, R. B. The isopodic and equipotent principles for comparing factor scores across different populations. *British Journal of Mathematical and Statistical Psychology*, 1970, **23**, 23–41. (a)

Cattell, R. B. Separating endogenous, exogenous, ecogenic, and epogenic component curves in developmental data. *Developmental Psychology*, 1970, **3**, 151–162. (b)

Cattell, R. B. Structured learning theory. *Advanced Laboratory Publication No. 13*. Champaign, Illinois: Laboratory of Personality and Group Analysis, 1970. (c)

Cattell, R. B. *Abilities: Their structure, growth and action*. Boston: Houghton, 1971.

Cattell, R. B. Real base, true zero factor analysis. *Multivariate Behavioral Research Monographs,* 1972, No. 72-1.

Cattell, R. B., Blewett, D. B., & Beloff, J. R. The inheritance of personality. A multiple variance analysis determination of approximate nature-nurture ratios for primary personality factors in Q-data. *American Journal of Human Genetics,* 1955, **7**, 122–146.

Cattell, R. B., Bruel, H., & Hartman, H. P. An attempt at more refined definition of the cultural dimensions of syntality in modern nations. *American Sociological Review,* 1952, **17**, 408–421.

Cattell, R. B., & DeYoung, G. E. Confactor rotation, some solutions to the central problem of resolution in structured psychology, 1972 (in preparation).

Cattell, R. B., & Kawash, G. F. Test of a theory of ergs and sentiments as dynamics states: By a dR analysis of ninety objective motivation measures. (in press).

Cattell, R. B., & Nesselroade, J. R. *Human behavior genetics: Concepts and methods.* (in press).

Cattell, R. B., Stice, G. F., & Kristy, N. F. A first approximation to nature-nurture ratios for eleven primary personality factors in objective tests. *Journal of Abnormal and Social Psychology,* 1957, **54**, 143–159.

Chapanis, A. Men, machines, and models. *American Psychologist,* 1961, **16**, 113–131.

Chapanis, A. The relevance of laboratory studies to practical situations. *Ergonomics,* 1967, **10**, 557–577.

Charles, D. C. Historical antecedents of life-span developmental psychology. In L. R. Goulet & P. B. Baltes (Eds.), *Life-span developmental psychology: Research and theory.* New York: Academic Press, 1970. Pp. 23–52.

Child, I. L. Personality in culture. In E. F. Borgatta & W. W. Lambert (Eds.), *Handbook of personality theory and research.* Chicago: Rand McNally, 1968. Pp. 82–145.

Chomsky, N. *Language and mind.* New York: Harcourt, 1968.

Clark, R. D., III, & Willems, E. P. Where is the risky shift? Dependence on instructions. *Journal of Personality and Social Psychology,* 1969, **13**, 215–221.

Coan, R. W. Child personality and developmental psychology. In R. B. Cattell (Ed.), *Handbook of multivariate experimental psychology.* Chicago: Rand McNally, 1966. Pp. 732–752.

Coffield, K. E. Research methodology: A possible reconciliation. *American Psychologist,* 1970, **25**, 511–516.

Cohen, H. L., Filipczak, J., & Bis, J. A study of contingencies applicable to special education: CASE I. In R. Ulrich, T. Stachnik, & J. Mabry (Eds.), *Control of human behavior.* Vol. II. Glenview: Scott, Foresman, 1970. Ph. 51–69.

Cooley, W. W., & Lohnes, P. R. *Multivariate data analysis.* New York: Wiley, 1971.

Corballis, M. C. Practice and the simplex. *Psychological Review,* 1965, **72**, 399–406.

Corballis, M. C., & Traub, R. E. Longitudinal factor analysis. *Psychometrika,* 1970, **35**, 79–93.

Cowan, P. A. The link between cognitive structure and social structure in two-child verbal interaction. Paper presented at the meeting of the Society for Research in Child Development, New York, March 1967.

Craik, K. H. Environmental psychology. In *New directions in psychology–IV.* New York: Holt, 1970. Pp. 1–121.

Cronbach, L. J. The two disciplines of scientific psychology. *American Psychologist,* 1957, **12**, 671–684.

Cronbach, L. J. Year-to-year correlations of mental tests: A review of the Hofstaetter analysis. *Child Development,* 1967, **38**, 283–289.

Cronbach, L. J. *Essentials of psychological testing.* (3rd ed.) New York: Harper, 1970.

Cronbach, L. J. & Furby, L. How should we measure "change"—or should we? *Psychological Bulletin,* 1970, **74**, 68–80.

Darling, F. F. The ecological approach to the social sciences. In P. Shepard & D. McKinley (Eds.), *The subversive science: Essays toward an ecology of man.* Boston: Houghton, 1969. Pp. 316–327.

Davies, D. F. Mortality and morbidity statistics. I. Limitations of approaches to rates of aging. *Journal of Gerontology,* 1954, **9**, 186–195.

Davis, C. M. Development of the probability concept in children. *Child Development,* 1965, **36**, 779–788.

Davis, J. A. The campus as a frog pond: An application of the theory of relative deprivation to career decisions of college men. *American Journal of Sociology,* 1966, **72**, 17–31.

Davis, J. K. Mediated generalization and interference across five grade levels. *Psychonomic Science,* 1966, **6**, 273–274.

Davol, S. H., Chittenden, E. A., Plante, M. L., & Tuzik, J. A. Conservation of continuous quantity investigated as a scalable developmental concept. *Merrill-Palmer Quarterly of Behavior and Development,* 1967, **13**, 191–200.

Dawe, H. C. The influence of size of kindergarten group upon performance. *Child Development,* 1934, **5**, 295–303.

Dawson, J. L. M. Cultural and physiological influences upon spatial perceptual processes in West-Africa. Part I. *International Journal of Psychology,* 1967, **2**, 115–128. (a)

Dawson, J. L. M. Cultural and physiological influences upon spatial perceptual processes in West-Africa. Part II. *International Journal of Psychology,* 1967, **2**, 171–185. (b)

Deal, T. Longitudinal case study analysis of the development of conservation of numbers and certain sub-skills. Paper presented at the meeting of the Society for Research in Child Development, Santa Monica, California, March 1969.

Denenberg, V. H., Karas, G. G., Rosenberg, F. M., & Schell, S. F. Programming life histories: An experimental design and initial results. *Developmental Psychophysiology,* 1968, **1**, 3–9.

Denenberg, V. H., & Whimbey, A. E. Experimental programming of life histories: Toward an experimental science of individual differences. *Developmental Psychophysiology,* 1968, **1**, 55–59.

Digman, J. M. Interaction and non-linearity in multivariate experiment. In R. B. Cattell (Ed.), *Handbook of multivariate experimental psychology.* Chicago: Rand McNally, 1966. Pp. 459–475.

Dodwell, P. C. Children's understanding of number and related concepts. *Canadian Journal of Psychology,* 1960, **14**, 191–205.

Dodwell, P. C. Children's understanding of number concepts: Characteristics of an individual and of a group test. *Canadian Journal of Psychology,* 1961, **15**, 29–36.

Dodwell, P. C. Relation between the understanding of the logic of classes and of cardinal number in children. *Canadian Journal of Psychology,* 1962, **16**, 152–160.

Dodwell, P. C. Children's understanding of spatial concepts. *Canadian Journal of Psychology,* 1963, **17**, 141–161.

Dogan, M., & Rokkan, S. (Eds.) *Quantitative ecological analysis in the social sciences.* Cambridge, Massachusetts: MIT Press, 1969.

Dornbush, R. L., & Winnick, W. A. The relative effectiveness of stereometric and pattern stimuli in discrimination learning. *Psychonomic Science,* 1966, **5**, 301–302.

Driver, H. E. Statistics in anthropology. *American Anthropologist,* 1953, **55**, 41–59.

Driver, H. E., & Schuessler, K. F. Factor analysis of ethnographic data. *American Anthropologist,* 1957, **59**, 655–663.

Dubois, P. H. *Multivariate correlational analysis.* New York: Harper, 1957.

Ducket, E. S. Carolingian portraits. Ann Arbor, Mchigan: University of Michigan Press, 1962.

Duijker, H. C. J. Comparative research in social science with special reference for attitudinal research. *International Social Science Bulletin,* 1955, **7**, 555–566.

Duncan, L. E., Jr. Ecology and aging. *Gerontologist,* 1968, **8**, 80–83.

Dunham, J. L., Guilford, J. P., & Hoepfner, R. Multivariate approaches to discovering the intellectual components of concept learning. *Psychological Review,* 1968, **75**, 206–221.

Dwyer, P. S. The determination of the factor loadings of a given test from the known factor loadings of other tests. *Psychometrika,* 1937, **2**, 173–178.

Eckensberger, L. H. Unterrichtsproblemean technisch-gewerblichen Ausbildungsstätten in Entwicklungsländern. Stuttgart: Klett, 1968.

Eckensberger, L. H. *Methodenprobleme der kulturvergleichenden Psychologie.* Saarbrücken: Verlag der SSIP-Schriften, 1970.

Edwards, A. L. *Experimental design in psychological research.* New York: Holt, 1960.

Emmerich, W. Personality development and concepts of structure. *Child Development,* 1968, **39**, 671–690.

Emmerich, W. Models of continuity and change in development. Paper presented in symposium on Behavioral Continuity and Change with Development at the meeting of the Society for Research in Child Development, Santa Monica, California, March 1969.

Erikson, E. *Childhood and society.* New York: Norton, 1950.

Erikson, E. *Young man Luther.* New York: Norton, 1958.

Erikson, E. *Identity, youth and crisis.* New York: Norton, 1968.

Ervin, S. M. Language and TAT content in bilinguals. *Journal of Abnormal and Social Psychology,* 1964, **68**, 500–507.

Evans, G. T. Factor analytical treatment of growth data. *Multivariate Behavioral Research,* 1967, **2**, 109–134.

Evans, S. H. & Anastasio, E. J. Misuse of analysis of covariance when treatment effect and covariate are confounded. *Psychological Bulletin,* 1968, **69**, 225–234.

Eysenck, H. J. The biological basis of personality. *Nature,* 1963, **199**, 1031–1034.

Eysenck, H. J. *The biological basis of personality.* Springfield, Illinois: Thomas, 1967.

Ferguson, G. A. On learning and human ability. *Canadian Journal of Psychology,* 1954, **8**, 95–112.

Ferguson, G. A. On transfer and the abilities of man. *Canadian Journal of Psychology,* 1956, **10**, 121–131.

Ferré, F. Mapping the logic of models in science and theology. *Christian Scholar,* 1963, **46** (Spring), 9–39.

Feyerabend, P. K. How to be a good empiricist—a plea for tolerance in matters epistemological. In P. H. Nidditch (Ed.), *The philosophy of science.* New York: Oxford University Press, 1968. Pp. 1–12.

Fischer, G. H. (Ed.) *Psychologische Testtheorie.* Psychologisches Kolloquium Bd. V. Bern: Huber, 1968.

Fischer, G. H. A further note on estimation in Rasch's measurement model with two categories of answers. Unpublished Research Bulletin No. 3 of the Psychological Institute of the University of Vienna, November 1970.

Fischer, G. H., & Scheiblechner, H. H. Two simple methods for asymptotically unbiased estimation in Rasch's measurement model with two categories of answers. Unpublished Research Bulletin No. 1 of the Psychological Institute of the University of Vienna, February 1970.

Flavell, J. H. *The developmental psychology of Jean Piaget.* Princeton, New Jersey: Van Nostrand-Reinhold, 1963.

Flavell, J. H. Concept development. In P. Mussen (Ed.), *Carmichael's manual of child psychology.* New York: Wiley, 1970. Pp. 983–1059. (a)

Flavell, J. H. Developmental studies of mediated memory. In H. W. Reese & L. P. Lipsitt (Eds.), *Advances in child development and behavior.* Vol. 5. New York: Academic Press, 1970. Pp. 181–211. (b)

Flavell, J. H. Stage-related properties of cognitive development. *Journal of Cognitive Psychology,* 1971, **2**, 421–453.

Flavell, J. H., Beach, D. H., & Chinsky, J. M. Spontaneous verbal rehearsal in a memory task as a function of age. *Child Development*, 1966, **37**, 283–299.

Flavell, J. H., & Draguns, J. A microgenetic approach to perception and thought. *Psychological Bulletin*, 1957, **54**, 197–217.

Flavell, J. H., & Wohlwill, J. F. Formal and functional aspects of cognitive development. In D. Elkind & J. H. Flavell (Eds.), *Studies in cognitive development: Essays in honor of Jean Piaget*. New York: Oxford University Press, 1969. Pp. 67–120.

Fleishman, E. A., & Bartlett, C. J. Human abilities. *Annual Review of Psychology*, 1969, **20**, 349–380.

Fodor, J. *Psychological explanation: An introduction to the philosophy of psychology*. New York: Random House, 1968.

Ford, L. H., Jr. Predictive versus perceptual responses to Piaget's waterline task and their relation to distance conservation. *Child Development*, 1970, **41**, 193–204.

Fournier, E. *Généralisation intranotionnelle et internotionnelle d'un apprentissage empirique de la notion de conservation des surfaces*. Thèse de licence inédite, Université de Montréal, 1965.

Frederiksen, C. H. Abilities, transfer, and information retrieval in verbal learning. *Multivariate Behavioral Research Monographs*, 1969 (No. 2).

Frijda, N., & Jahoda, G. On the scope and methods of cross-cultural research. *International Journal of Psychology*, 1966, **1**, 109–127.

Fruchter, B. Manipulative and hypothesis testing factor-analytic experimental designs. In R. B. Cattell (Ed.), *Handbook of multivariate experimental psychology*. Chicago: Rand McNally, 1966. Pp. 330–354.

Fuller, J. L., & Thompson, W. R. *Behavior genetics*. New York: Wiley, 1960.

Furth, H. G. *Piaget for teachers*. Englewood Cliffs: Prentice Hall, 1970.

Gagné, R. M. Contributions of learning to human development. *Psychological Review*, 1968, **75**, 177–191.

Garrett, H. E. A developmental theory of intelligence. *American Psychologist*, 1946, **1**, 372–378.

Gelman, R. Conservation acquisition: A problem of learning to attend to relevant attributes. *Journal of Experimental Child Psychology*, 1969, **7**, 167–187.

Gewirtz, J. L. On designing the functional environment of the child to facilitate behavioral development. In L. L. Dittman (Ed.), *Early child care: The new perspectives*. New York: Atherton Press, 1968. Pp. 169–213.

Gewirtz, J. L. Levels of conceptual analysis in environment-infant interaction research. *Merrill-Palmer Quarterly of Behavior and Development*, 1969, **15**, 7–47. (a)

Gewirtz, J. L. Mechanisms of social learning: Some roles of stimulation and behavior in early human development. In D. A. Goslin (Ed.), *Handbook of socialization theory and research*. Chicago: Rand McNally, 1969. Pp. 57–212. (b)

Gibb, C. A. Changes in the culture pattern of Australia, 1906–1946, as determined by *P*-techniques. *Journal of Social Psychology*, 1956, **43**, 225–238.

Giorgi, A. Psychology: A human science. *Social Research*, 1969, **36**, 412–432.

Goldschmid, M. L., & Bentler, P. M. The dimensions and measurement of conservation. *Child Development*, 1968, **39**, 787–802.

Goldsmith, W. *Comparative functionalism*. Berkeley: University of California Press, 1966.

Gollin, E. A developmental approach to learning and cognition. In L. P. Lipsitt & C. C. Spiker (Eds.), *Advances in child development and behavior*. Vol. 2. New York: Academic Press, 1965. Pp. 159–187.

Gonzalez, R. C., & Ross, S. The basis of solution by preverbal children of the intermediate-size problem. *American Journal of Psychology*, 1958, **71**, 742–746.

Goodnow, J. Problems in research on culture and thought. In D. Elkind & J. H. Flavell (Eds.), *Studies in cognitive development*. New York: Oxford University Press, 1969. Pp. 439–462.

Gordon, L. V. Comments on "cross-cultural equivalence" of personality measures. *Journal of Social Psychology*, 1968, **75**, 11–19.

Gordon, L. V., & Kikuchi, A. American personality tests in cross-cultural research. A caution. *Journal of Social Psychology*, 1966, **69**, 179–183.

Gottlieb, G. Developmental age as a baseline for determination of the critical period in imprinting. *Journal of Comparative and Physiological Psychology*, 1961, **54**, 422–427.

Gottlieb, G. The facilitatory effect of the parental exodus call on the following response of ducklings: One test of the self-stimulation hypothesis. *American Zoologist*, 1963, **3**, 518. (Abstract) (a)

Gottlieb, G. Following-response initiation in ducklings: Age and sensory stimulation. *Science*, 1963, **140**, 399–400. (b)

Gottlieb, G. "Imprinting" in nature. *Science*, 1963, **139**, 497–498. (c)

Gottlieb, G. A naturalistic study of imprinting in wood ducklings (*Aix sponsa*). *Journal of Comparative and Physiological Psychology*, 1963, **56**, 86–91. (d)

Gottlieb, G. Refrigerating eggs prior to incubation as a way of reducing error in calculating developmental age in imprinting experiments. *Animal Behaviour*, 1963, **11**, 290–292. (e)

Gottlieb, G. Components of recognition in ducks. *Natural History*, 1965, **25** (February), 12–19. (a)

Gottlieb, G. Imprinting in relation to parental and species identification by avian neonates. *Journal of Comparative and Physiological Psychology*, 1965, **59**, 345–356. (b)

Gottlieb, G. Prenatal auditory sensitivity in chickens and ducks. *Science*, 1965, **147**, 1596–1598. (c)

Gottlieb, G. Species identification by avian neonates: Contributory effect of perinatal auditory stimulation. *Animal Behaviour*, 1966, **14**, 282–290.

Goulet, L. R. Anxiety (drive) and verbal learning: Implications for research and some methodological considerations. *Psychological Bulletin*, 1968, **69**, 235–237. (a)

Goulet, L. R. Verbal learning and memory research with retardates: An attempt to assess developmental trends. In N. R. Ellis (Ed.), *International review of research in mental retardation*. Vol. 3. New York: Academic Press, 1968. Pp. 97–134. (b)

Goulet, L. R. Verbal learning in children: Implications for developmental research. *Psychological Bulletin*, 1968, **69**, 359–376. (c)

Goulet, L. R. Interference in retention. Paper presented in symposium on Memory and Thinking at the meeting of the American Psychological Association, Miami Beach, September 1970. (a)

Goulet, L. R. Training, transfer, and the development of complex behavior. *Human Development*. 1970, **13**, 213–240. (b)

Goulet, L. R. Basic issues in reversal-shift behavior: A reply to Kendler and Kendler. *Psychological Bulletin*, 1971, **75**, 286–289.

Goulet, L. R. New directions for research on aging and retention. *Journal of Gerontology*, 1972, in press.

Goulet, L. R., & Baltes, P. B. (Eds.) *Life-span developmental psychology: Theory and research*. New York: Academic Press, 1970.

Goulet, L. R., & Goodwin, K. S. Development and choice behavior in probabilistic and problem-solving tasks. In H. W. Reese & L. P. Lipsitt (Eds.), *Advances in child development and behavior*. Vol. 5. New York: Academic Press, 1970. Pp. 213–254.

Graham, F. K., Ernhart, C. B., Craft, M., & Berman, P. W. Learning of relative and absolute size concepts in preschool children. *Journal of Experimental Child Psychology*, 1964, **1**, 26–36.

Grant, D. A. Analysis of variance tests in the analysis and comparison of curves. *Psychological Bulletin*, 1956, **53**, 141–154.

Grant, D. A. Classical and operant conditioning. In A. W. Melton (Ed.), *Categories of human learning*. New York: Academic Press, 1964. Pp. 3–31.

Greenfield, P. M. On culture and conservation. In J. S. Bruner, R. R. Olver, & P. M. Greenfield (Eds.), *Studies in cognitive growth.* New York: Wiley, 1966. Pp. 225–256.

Gregory, R. L. On physical model explanations in psychology. *British Journal of Philosophical Science,* 1953, **4**, 192–197.

Grimm, B. A developmental study of interference in paired-associated learning. Unpublished Master's Thesis, West Virginia University, 1970.

Grinder, R. E. *A history of genetic psychology.* New York: Wiley, 1967.

Gruen, G. E. Note on conservation: Methodological and definitional considerations. *Child Development,* 1966, **37**, 977–983.

Gruvaeus, G. T. A general approach to procrustes pattern rotation. *Psychometrika,* 1970, **35**, 493–505.

Guess, D., Sailor, W., Rutherford, G., & Baer, D. M. An experimental analysis of linguistic development: The productive use of the plural morpheme. *Journal of Applied Behavior Analysis,* 1968, **1**, 297–306.

Gulliksen, H. Methods of determining equivalence of measures. *Psychological Bulletin,* 1968, **70**, 534–544.

Gump, P. V. Persons, settings, and larger contexts. In B. P. Indik & F. K. Berrien (Eds.), *People, groups, and organizations.* New York: Teachers College Press, 1968. Pp. 223–249.

Gump, P. V. Intra-setting analysis: The third grade classroom as a special but illustrative case. In E. P. Willems & H. L. Raush (Eds.), *Naturalistic viewpoints in psychological research.* New York: Holt, 1969. Pp. 200–220.

Gump, P. V., & Friesen, W. V. Satisfactions derived from nonclass settings. In R. G. Barker & P. V. Gump, *Big school, small school.* Stanford, California: Stanford University Press, 1964. Pp. 94–114.

Gutmann, D. On cross-cultural studies as a naturalistic approach in psychology. *Human Development,* 1967, **10**, 187–198.

Guttman, L. A. A basis for scaling qualitative data. *American Sociological Review,* 1944, **9**, 139–150.

Hall, J., & Williams, M. S. A comparison of decision-making performances in established and ad hoc groups. *Journal of Personality and Social Psychology,* 1966, **3**, 214–222.

Hall, R. V., Lund, D., & Jackson, D. Effects of teacher attention on study behavior. *Journal of Applied Behavior Analysis,* 1968, **1**, 1–12.

Hall, V. C. & Simpson, G. J. Factors influencing extinction of weight conservation. *Merrill-Palmer Quarterly of Behavior and Development,* 1968, **14**, 197–210.

Hamlyn, D. W. The psychology of perception. London: Routledge & Kegan Paul, 1957.

Haney, J. H., & Hooper, F. H. A developmental comparison of social class and verbal ability influences on Piagetian tasks. Preprint, submitted to *Child Development,* 1971.

Hannan, E. J. *Time series analysis.* London: Methuen, 1960.

Hardin, G. The cybernetics of competition: A biologist's view of society. In P. Shepard & D. McKinley (Eds.), *The subversive science: Essays toward an ecology of man.* Boston: Houghton, 1969. Pp. 275–296.

Harlow, H. F. The formation of learning sets. *Psychology Review,* 1949, **56**, 51–65.

Harlow, H. F. Learning set and error factor theory. In S. Koch (Ed.), *Psychology: A study of a science.* Vol. 2. *General szstematic formulations, learning, and special processes.* New York: McGraw-Hill, 1959. Pp. 492–537.

Harman, H. H. *Modern factor analysis.* Chicago: University of Chicago Press, 1960.

Harris, C. W. Canonical factor models for the description of change. In C. W. Harris (Ed.) *Problems in measuring change.* Madison, Wisconsin: University of Wisconsin Press, 1963. Pp. 138–155.

Harris, C. W. (Ed.). *Problems in measuring change.* Madison, Wisconsin: University of Wisconsin Press, 1963.

Harris, C. W. On factors and factor scores. *Psychometrika,* 1967, **32**, 363–379.

Harter, S. Discrimination learning set in children as a function of IQ and MA. *Journal of Experimental Child Psychology,* 1965, **2**, 31–43.

Hastings, P. K. The Roper Public Opinion Research Center. *International Social Science Journal,* 1964, **16**, 90–100.

Hay, D. *The medieval centuries.* London: Methuen, 1964.

Heckhausen, H. *The anatomy of achievement motivation.* New York: Academic Press, 1967.

Heisenberg, W. *Philosophic problems of nuclear science.* New York: Pantheon, 1952.

Hess, E. H. Effects of meprobamate on imprinting in waterfowl. *Annals of the New York Academy of Sciences,* 1957, **67**, 724–733.

Hess, E. H. Imprinting. *Science,* 1959, **130**, 133–141. (a)

Hess, E. H. The relationship between imprinting and motivation. In M. R. Jones (Ed.), *Nebraska symposium on motivation.* Lincoln, Nebraska: University of Nebraska Press, 1959. Pp. 51–65. (b)

Hess, E. H. Imprinting and the "critical period" concept. In E. L. Bliss (Ed.), *Roots of behavior.* New York: Harper, 1962. Pp. 254–263.

Hess, E. H. Imprinting in birds. *Science,* 1964, **146**, 1128–1139.

Hess, E. H. Ethology and developmental psychology. In P. H. Mussen (Ed.), *Carmichael's manual of child psychology.* (3rd ed.), Vol. 1. New York: Wiley, 1970. Pp. 1–38.

Hess, E. H. Incubation duration and hatching synchronism in mallard ducks. 1971, in preparation. (a)

Hess, E. H. The natural history of imprinting. *Annals of the New York Academy of Sciences,* 1971, in press. (b)

Hesse, M. *Models and analogies in science.* Notre Dame, Indiana: University of Notre Dame Press, 1966.

Hirsch, J. *Behavior-genetic analysis.* New York: McGraw-Hill, 1967.

Hirsch, J. Behavior-genetic analysis and its biosocial consequences. In R. Cancro (Ed.), *Intelligence: Genetic and environmental influences.* New York: Grune & Stratton, 1971.

Hofstaetter, P. R. A factorial study of culture patterns in the U.S. *Journal of Psychology,* 1951, **32**, 99–113.

Hofstaetter, P. R. *Sozialpsychologie.* Berlin: de Gruyter, 1956.

Holtzman, W. H. Cross-cultural research on personality development. *Human Development,* 1965, **8**, 65–86.

Holtzman, W. H., Diaz-Guerrero, R., Swartz, J. D., & Tapia, L. L. Cross-cultural longitudinal research on child development: Studies of American and Mexican schoolchildren. In J. P. Hill (Ed.), *Minnesota symposia on child psychology.* Vol. 2. Minneapolis: University of Minnesota Press, 1969. Pp. 125–159.

Holzkamp, K. Wissenschaftstheoretische Voraussetzungen kritisch-emanzipatorischer Psychologie: Teil I. *Zeitschrift für Sozialpsychologie,* 1970, **1**, 5–21.

Honzik, M. Environmental correlates of mental growth: Prediction from the family setting at 21 months. *Child Development,* 1967, **38**, 337–364.

Hooper, F. H. The Appalachian child's intellectual capabilities—deprivation or diversity? *Journal of Negro Education,* 1969, **38**, 224–235.

Hooper, F. H. An evaluation of logical operations instruction in the preschool. In R. K. Parker (Ed.), *The Preschool in Action: Exploring early childhood programs.* Boston: Allyn & Bacon, 1972. Pp. 134–186.

Hooper, F. H., Fitzgerald, J., & Papalia, D. Piagetian theory and the aging process: Extensions and speculations. *Aging and Human Development,* 1971, **2**, 3–20.

Hooper, F. H., Goldman, J. A., Storck, P. A., & Burke, A. M. Stage sequence and correspondence in Piagetian theory: A review of the middle-childhood period. *Research Relating to Children,* Bulletin 28, Summer 1971. Urbana, Illinois: Educational Resources Information Center.

Horn, J. L. Fluid and crystallized intelligence: A factor analytic and developmental study of structure among primary mental abilities. Unpublished doctoral dissertation, University of Illinois, 1965.

Horn, J. L. Motivation and dynamic calculus concepts from multivariate experiment. In R. B. Cattell (Ed.), *Handbook of multivariate experimental psychology*. Chicago: Rand McNally, 1966. Pp. 553–561.

Horn, J. L. Organization of abilities and the development of intelligence. *Psychological Review*, 1968, **75**, 242–259.

Horn, J. L. Factor analysis with variables of different metric. *Educational and Psychological Measurement*, 1969, **29**, 753–762.

Horn, J. L. Organization of data on life-span development of human abilities. In L. R. Goulet & P. B. Baltes (Eds.), *Life-span developmental psychology: Research and theory*. New York: Academic Press, 1970. Pp. 424–466.

Horn, J. L., & Cattell, R. B. Refinement and test of the theory of fluid and crystallized general intelligences. *Journal of Educational Psychology*, 1966, **57**, 253–270.

Horn, J. L., & Cattell, R. B. Age differences in fluid and crystallized intelligence. *Acta Psychologica*, 1967, **26**, 103–129.

Horn, J. L., & Little, K. B. Isolating change and invariance in patterns of behavior. *Multivariate Behavioral Research*, 1966, **1**, 219–228.

Horst, P. *Factor analysis of data matrices*. New York: Holt, 1965.

House, B. J., & Zeaman, D. Transfer of a discrimination from objects to patterns. *Journal of Experimental Psychology*, 1960, **59**, 298–302.

Hudson, B. B., Barakat, M. K., & LaForge, R. Problems and methods in cross-cultural research. *Journal of Social Issues*, 1959, **15**, 5–19.

Hulicka, I. M., & Grossman, J. L. Age-group comparisons for the use of mediators in paired-associate learning. *Journal of Gerontology*, 1967, **22**, 46–51.

Hulicka, I. M., Sterns, H., & Grossman, J. L. Age-group comparisons of paired associate learning as a function of paced and self-paced association and response times. *Journal of Gerontology*, 1967, **22**, 274–280.

Hull, C. L. *Principles of behavior*. New York: Appleton, 1943.

Hull, C. L. *A behavior system*. New Haven: Yale University Press, 1952.

Hunt, J. McV. *Intelligence and experience*. New York: Ronald Press, 1961.

Hutten, L. H. The role of models in physics. *British Journal of Philosophical Science*, 1954, **4**, 284–301.

Indik, B. P. Some effects of organization size on member attitudes and behavior. *Human Relations*, 1963, **16**, 369–384.

Indik, B. P. Organization size and member participation: Some empirical tests of alternative explanations. *Human Relations*, 1965, **18**, 339–350

Ingham, G. K. *Size of industrial organization and worker behaviour*. Cambridge: Cambridge University Press, 1970.

Inglis, J., Ankus, M. N., & Sykes, D. H. Age-related differences in learning and short-term memory from childhood to the senium. *Human Development*, 1968, **11**, 42–52.

Inhelder, B. Criteria of the stages of mental development. In J. M. Tanner & B. Inhelder (Eds.), *Discussions on child development*. Vol. I. The Proceedings of the First Meeting of the World Health Organization Study Group on the Psychological Development of the Child. New York: International University Press, 1956. Pp. 75–86.

Inhelder, B. Some aspects of Piaget's genetic approach to cognition. In W. Kessen & C. Kuhlman (Eds.), *Thought in the young child*. Monographs of the Society for Research in Child Development, 1962, **27** (2), 19–34.

Inhelder, B., & Matalon, B. The study of problem solving and thinking. In P. Mussen (Ed.), *Handbook of research methods in child development*. New York: Wiley, 1960. Pp. 421–455.

Inhelder, B., & Sinclair, H. Learning cognitive structures. In P. Mussen, J. Langer, & M. Covington (Eds.), *Trends and issues in developmental psychology*. New York: Holt, 1969. Pp. 2–22.

Irvine, S. H. Gibt es kulturunabhängige Tests?—Faktorielle Untersuchungen des Progressiven Matrizentests von Raven in mehreren afrikanischen Kulturen. In K. Ingenkamp & T. Marsolek (Eds.), *Möglichkeiten und Grenzen der Testanweisung in der Schule*. Paedagog. Zentrum. Veroeffentl. Reihe C: Berichte Bd. 15. Weinheim: Beltz, 1968. Pp. 417–436.

Irvine, S. H. Factor analysis of African abilities and attainments: Constructs across cultures. *Psychological Bulletin*, 1969, **71**, 20–32.

Irvine, S. H. Affect and construct—A cross-cultural check on theories of intelligence. *Journal of Social Psychology*, 1970, **80**, 23–30.

Jacobi, J. S. *The psychology of C. G. Jung*. (6th ed.) New Haven: Yale University Press, 1962.

Jahoda, G. Child animism: A critical survey of cross-cultural research. *Journal of Social Psychology*, 1958, **47**, 197–212. (a)

Jahoda, G. Child animism: II. A study in western Africa. *Journal of Social Psychology*, 1958, **47**, 241–248. (b)

Jakobovits, L. A. Comparative psycholinguistics in the study of culture. *International Journal of Psychology*, 1966, **1**, 15–38.

Jarvik, L. F., & Falek, A. Intellectual stability and survival in the aged. *Journal of Gerontology*, 1963, **18**, 173–176.

Jeffrey, W. E., & Cohen, L. B. Response tendencies of children in a two-choice situation. *Journal of Experimental Child Psychology*, 1965, **2**, 248–254.

Jensen, A. R. How much can we boost IQ and scholastic achievement? *Harvard Educational Review*, 1969, **39**, 1–123.

Jensen, A. R., & Rohwer, W. D., Jr. Syntactical mediation of serial and paired-associate learning as a function of age. *Child Development*, 1965, **36**, 601–608.

Jerome, E. A. Age and learning: Experimental studies. In J. E. Birren (Ed.), *Handbook of aging and the individual*. Chicago: University of Chicago Press, 1959. Pp. 655–699.

Jessor, R. The problem of reductionism in psychology. *Psychological Review*, 1958, **65**, 170–178.

Jinks, J. L. & Fulker, D. W. Comparison of the biometrical genetical, MAVA, and classical approaches to the analysis of human behavior. *Psychological Bulletin*, 1970, **73**, 311–349.

Johnson, R. C., & Zara, R. C. Relational learning in young children. *Journal of Comparative and Physiological Psychology*, 1960, **53**, 594–597.

Kagan, J. On the need for relativism. *American Psychologist*, 1967, **22**, 131–142.

Kagan, J., & Moss, H. A. *Birth to maturity: A study in psychological development*. New York: Wiley, 1962.

Kallina, H. Das Unbehagen in der Faktorenanalyse. *Psychologische Beiträge*, 1967, **10**, 81–86.

Kapferer, C. The use of sample surveys by OECD. *International Social Science Journal*, 1964, **16**, 63–69.

Kaplan, A. *The conduct of inquiry*. San Francisco: Chandler, 1964.

Kaplan, B. The study of language in psychiatry. The comparative developmental approach and its application to symbolization and language in psychopathology. In S. Arieti (Ed.), *American handbook of psychiatry*. Vol. 3. New York: Basic Books, 1966. Pp. 659–688.

Kaplan, B. Meditations on genesis. *Human Development*, 1967, **10**, 65–87.

Kausler, D. H. Retention-forgetting as a nomological network for developmental research. In L. R. Goulet & P. B. Baltes (Eds.), *Life-span developmental psychology: Research and theory*. New York: Academic Press, 1970. Pp. 305–353.

Kavanau, J. L. Behavior: Confinement, adaptation, and compulsory regimes in laboratory studies. *Science*, 1964, **143**, 490.

Kavanau, J. L. Behavior of captive white-footed mice. In E. P. Willems & H. L. Raush (Eds.), *Naturalistic viewpoints in psychological research*. New York: Holt, 1969. Pp. 221–270.

Keeney, T. J., Cannizzo, S. R., & Flavell, J. H. Spontaneous and induced verbal rehearsal in a recall task. *Child Development*, 1967, **38**, 953–966.

Kelley, H. H. The warm-cold variable in first impressions of persons. In H. Proshansky & B. Seidenberg (Eds.), *Basic studies in social psychology*. New York: Holt, 1965. Pp. 65–71.

Kempler, B. Developmental level and serial learning. Unpublished doctoral dissertation, Clark University, 1964.

Kendler, H. H. & Kendler, T. S. Vertical and horizontal processes in human concept formation. *Psychological Review,* 1962, **69**, 1–18.

Kendler, H. H., & Kendler, T. S. Developmental processes in discrimination learning. *Human Development,* 1970, **13**, 65–89.

Kendler, H. H., Kendler, T. S., & Marken, R. Developmental analysis of reversal and half-reversal shifts. *Developmental Psychology,* 1969, **1**, 318–326.

Keppel, G., & Postman, L. Studies of learning to learn: III. Conditions of improvement in successive transfer tasks. *Journal of Verbal Learning and Verbal Behavior,* 1966, **5**, 260–267.

Keppel, G., Postman, L., & Zavortink, B. Studies of learning to learn. VIII. The influence of massive amounts of training upon the learning and retention of paired-associate lists. *Journal of Verbal Learning and Verbal Behavior,* 1968, **7**, 790–796.

Kerlinger, F. N. *Foundations of behavioral research: Educational and psychological inquiry.* New York: Holt, 1964.

Kessel, F. The philosophy of science as proclaimed and science as practiced: Identity or dualism? *American Psychologist,* 1969, **24**, 999–1006.

Kessen, W. Research design in the study of developmental problems. In P. H. Mussen (Ed.), *Handbook of research methods in child development.* New York: Wiley, 1960. Pp. 36–70.

Kessen, W. Stages and structure in the study of children. *Monographs of the Society for Research in Child Development,* 1962, **27** (2, Whole No. 103), 65–86.

Kessen, W. Questions for a theory of cognitive development. In H. W. Stevenson (Ed.), The concept of development. *Monographs of the Society for Research in Child Development,* 1966, **31** (5, Whole No. 107). Pp. 55–70.

Kessen, W. Comparative personality research. In E. F. Borgatta & W. W. Lambert (Eds.), *Handbook of personality theory and research.* Chicago: Rand McNally, 1968. Pp. 365–410.

Kimble, G. A., & Pennypacker, H. S. Eyelid conditioning in young and aged subjects. *Journal of Genetic Psychology,* 1963, **103**, 283–289.

King, J. A. Ecological psychology: An approach to motivation. In W. J. Arnold & M. M. Page (Eds.), *Nebraska symposium on motivation.* Lincoln, Nebraska: University of Nebraska Press, 1970. Pp. 1–33.

Kingsley, P. R., & Hagen, J. W. Induced versus spontaneous rehearsal in short-term memory in nursery school children. *Developmental Psychology,* 1969, **1**, 40–46.

Kingsley, R. C., and Hall, V. C. Training conservation through the use of learning sets. *Child Development,* 1967, **38**, 1111–1126.

Klingensmith, S. Z. Child animism: What a child means by alive. *Child Development,* 1953, **24**, 51–61.

Klopfer, P. H. Behavioral aspects of habitat selection: The role of early experience. *Wilson Bulletin,* 1963, **75**, 15–22.

Koch, S. Psychology and emerging conceptions of knowledge as unitary. In T. W. Wann (Ed.), *Behaviorism and phenomenology.* Chicago: University of Chicago Press, 1964. Pp. 1–45.

Kofsky, E. Developmental scalogram analysis of classificatory behavior. *Child Development,* 1966, **37**, 191–204.

Kooistra, W. Developmental trends in the attainment of conservation, transitivity, and relativity in thinking of children: A replication and extension of Piaget's ontogenetic formulation. Unpublished doctoral dissertation, Wayne State University, 1963.

Kristof, W. Die beste orthogonale Transformation zur gegenseitigen Überprüfung zweier Faktorenmatrizen. *Diagnostica,* 1964, **10**, 87–90.

Kristof, W. Orthogonal inter-battery factor analysis. *Psychometrika,* 1967, **32**, 199–228.

Kroeber, A. L., & Kluckhohn, C. *Culture: A critical review of concepts and definitions.* Harvard University Peabody Museum of American Archeology and Ethnology Papers, Vol. 47, No. 1. Cambridge, Massachusetts: The Museum, (Republished: New York: Vintage Books, 1963).

Krug, R. E. Some suggested approaches for test development and measurement. *Personnel Psychology,* 1966, **19,** 24–35.

Krug, S. E. An examination of experimentally induced changes in ergic tension level. Unpublished doctoral dissertation, University of Illinois, 1971.

Kuenne, M. R. Experimental investigation of the relation of language to transposition behavior in young children. *Journal of Experimental Psychology,* 1946, **36,** 471–490.

Kuhn, T. S. *The structure of scientific revolutions.* Chicago: University of Chicago Press, 1962.

Labouvie, G. V., Frohring, W., Baltes, P. B., & Goulet, L. R. The differential validity of a recall task at various stages of learning and as a function of two experimental conditions. *Journal of Educational Psychology,* 1973, in press.

Lachman, R. The model in theory construction. *Psychological Review,* 1960, **67,** 113–129.

Lambert, W. E. Measurement of the linguistic dominance of bilinguals. *Journal of Abnormal and Social Psychology,* 1955, **50,** 197–200.

Lambert, W. E., Havelka, J., & Crosby, G. The influence of language-acquisition contexts on bilingualism. *Journal of Abnormal and Social Psychology,* 1958, **56,** 239–244.

Lang, P. J., & Buss, A. H. Psychological deficit in schizophrenia: II. Interference and activation. *Journal of Abnormal Psychology,* 1965, **70,** 77–106.

Langer, J. *Theories of development.* New York: Holt, 1969.

Langer, J. Werner's theory of development. In P. H. Mussen (Ed.), *Carmichael's manual of child psychology.* New York: Wiley, 1970. Pp. 733–771.

Latané, B., & Darley, J. M. *The unresponsive bystander: Why doesn't he help?* New York: Appleton, 1970.

Laurence, M. W. Age differences in performance and subjective organization in the free-recall learning of pictorial material. *Canadian Journal of Psychology,* 1966, **20,** 388–399.

Laurendeau, M., & Pinard, A. *Causal thinking in the child.* New York: International Universities Press, 1962.

Laurendeau, M., & Pinard, A. *The development of the concept of space in the child.* New York: International Universities Press, 1970.

Lawton, M. P. Assessment, integration, and environments for older people. *Gerontologist,* 1970, **10,** 38–46.

Leach, E. R. The comparative method in anthropology. In D. L. Sills (Ed.), *International encyclopedia of the social sciences.* Vol. 1. New York: McMillian, 1968. Pp. 339–345.

LeCompte, W. F. The taxonomy of the treatment environment. Paper presented at the American Congress of Rehabilitation Medicine, New York, August 1970.

LeCompte, W. F., & Willems, E. P. Ecological analysis of a hospital: Location dependencies in the behavior of staff and patients. In J. Archea & C. Eastman (Eds.), *EDRA-2: Proceedings of the 2nd Annual Environmental Design Research Association Conference.* Pittsburgh: Carnegie Press, 1970. Pp. 236–245.

Lehr, U. Attitudes towards the future in old age. *Human Development,* 1967, **10,** 230–238.

Lenin, V. I. *Philosophical notebook.* (*Collected works,* Vol. 29.) New York: International Publishers, 1929.

Lent, J. R. Mimosa Cottage: Experiment in hope. *Psychology Today,* 1968, **June,** 57–58.

Lent, J. R., & Childress, D. A demonstration program for intensive training of institutionalized mentally retarded girls. Progress Report: 5-year summary, 1965-1970. Parsons, Kansas 67357: Bureau of Child Research, Parsons State Hospital and Training Center, 1970.

Lent, J. R., LeBlanc, J., & Spradlin, J.E. Designing a rehabilitative culture for moderately retarded adolescent girls. In R. Ulrich, T. Stachnik, & J. Mabry (Eds.), *Control of human behavior.* Vol. II. Glenview: Scott, Foresman, 1970. Pp. 121–135.

Levin, J. Three-mode factor analysis. *Psychological Bulletin,* 1965, **64,** 442–452.

LeVine, R. A. Towards a psychology of populations: The cross-cultural study of personality. *Human*

Development, 1966, **9**, 30–46.

LeVine, R. A. Culture, personality, and socialization: An evolutionary view. In D. A. Goslin (Ed.), *Handbook of socialization theory and research.* Chicago: Rand McNally, 1969. Pp. 503–541.

LeVine, R. A. Cross-cultural study in child psychology. In P. H. Mussen (Ed.), *Carmichael's manual of child psychology.* Vol. II. New York: Wiley, 1970. Pp. 559–612.

Lewis, C., & DeYoung, G. E. A distance minimizing least squares procedure. (in press).

Lienert, G. A. *Testaufbau und Testanalyse.* Zeinheim: Beltz, 1967.

Lienert, G. A. & Crott, H. W. Studies on the factor structure of intelligence in children, adolescents and adults. *Vita Humana,* 1964, **7**, 147–163.

Lipman, R. S. Learning: Verbal, perceptual motor and classical conditioning. In N. R. Ellis (Ed.), *Handbook of mental deficiency.* New York: McGraw-Hill, 1963. Pp. 391–423.

Lockard, R. B. Reflections on the fall of comparative psychology: Is there a message for us all? *American Psychologist,* 1971, **26**, 168–179.

Loehlin, J. C. An heredity-environment analysis of personality inventory data. In S. G. Vandenberg (Ed.), *Methods and goals in human behavior genetics.* New York: Academic Press, 1965. (a)

Loehlin, J. C. Some methodological problems in Cattell's multiple abstract variance analysis. *Psychological Review,* 1965, **72**, 156–161. (b)

Loehlin, J. C. & V,andenberg, S. G. Genetic and environmental components in the covariation of cognitive abilities: An additive model. In S. G. Vandenberg (Ed.), *Progress in human behavior genetics.* Baltimore: Johns Hopkins Press, 1968.

Loevinger, J. A systematic approach to the construction and evaluation of tests of ability. *Psychological Monographs,* 1947, **61** (Whole No. 285).

Longstreth, L. *Psychological development of the child.* New York: Ronald Press, 1968.

Looft, W. R. The psychology of more. *American Psychologist,* 1971, **26**, 561–565.

Looft, W. R. Egocentrism and social interaction across the life-span. *Psychological Bulletin,* 1972, **78**, 73–92.

Looft, W. R., & Charles, D. C. Egocentrism and social interaction in young and old adults. *Aging and Human Development,* 1971, **2**, 21–28.

Lord, F. M. Elementary models for measuring change. In C. W. Harris (Ed.), *Problems in measuring change.* Madison: University of Wisconsin Press, 1963.

Lord, F. M., & Novick, M. R. *Statistical theories of mental test scores.* Reading, Massachusetts: Addison-Wesley, 1968.

Lovaas, O. I. A behavior therapy approach to the treatment of childhood schizophrenia. In J. P. Hill (Ed.), *Minnesota symposium on child psychology.* Vol. I. Minneapolis: University of Minnesota Press, 1967. Pp. 108–159.

Lovaas, O. I., & Simmons, J. Q. Manipulation of self-destruction in three retarded children. *Journal of Applied Behavior Analysis,* 1969, **2**, 143–157.

Lovell, K., Healey, D., & Rowland, A. D. Growth of some geometrical concepts. *Child Development,* 1962, **33**, 751–767.

Lovell, K., & Ogilivie, E. A study of the conservation of weight in the junior school child. *British Journal of Educational Psychology,* 1961, **31**, 138–144.

Lunzer, E. A. Some points of Piagetian theory in the light of experimental criticism. *Journal of Child Psychology and Psychiatry,* 1960, **1**, 191–202.

Lynd, S. Historical past and extential present. In T. N. Guinsburg (Ed.), *The dimensions of history.* Chicago: Rand McNally, 1971. Pp. 73–79.

MacKay, C. K., Fraser, J., & Ross, I. Matrices, three by three: Classification and seriation. *Child Development,* 1970, **41**, 787–798.

Mandelbaum, D. G. Cultural anthropology. In D. L. Sills (Ed.), *International encyclopedia of the social sciences.* Vol. 1. New York: MacMillan, 1968. Pp. 313–319.

Mandler, G. Response factors in human learning. *Psychological Review,* 1954, **61**, 235–244.

Mandler, G. Verbal learning. In G. Mandler, P. Mussen, N. Kogan, & M. A. Wallach (Eds.), *New directions in psychology III.* New York: Holt, 1967. Pp. 3–50.

Mann, R. A. The behavior-therapeutic use of contingency contracting to control adult behavior problems: Weight control. Unpublished doctoral dissertation, Department of Human Development, University of Kansas, 1971.

Mannix, J. B. The number concepts of a group of E. S. N. children. *British Journal of Educational Psychology,* 1960, **30**, 180–181.

Marsh, R. M. *Comparative sociology: A codification of cross-societal analysis.* New York: Harcourt, 1967.

Marx, K. *Capital, a critical analysis of capitalistic production.* Moscow: Foreign Languages Publishing House, 1954.

Matson, F. *The broken image.* New York: George Braziller, 1964.

McCall, R. B. The use of multivariate procedures in developmental psychology. In P. H. Mussen (Ed.), *Carmichael's manual of child psychology.* New York: Wiley, 1970. Pp. 1366–1377.

McClearn, G. E. Genetic influences on behavior and development. In P. H. Mussen (Ed.), *Carmichael's manual of child psychology.* New York: Wiley, 1970. Pp. 39–76.

McDonald, R. P. Three common factor models for groups of variables. *Psychometrika,* 1970, **35**, 111–128.

McEwen, W. J. Forms and problems of validation in social anthropology. *Current Anthropology,* 1963, **4**, 155–183.

McGuire, W. J. Theory-oriented reseach in natural settings: The best of both worlds for social psychology. In M. Sherif & C. W. Sherif (Eds.), *Interdisciplinary relationships in the social sciences.* Chicago: Aldine, 1969. Pp. 21–51.

McLaughlin, G. H. Psycho-logic: A possible alternative to Piaget's formulation. *British Journal of Educational Psychology,* 1963, **33**, 61–67.

McNemar, Q. *Psychological statistics.* New York: Wiley, 1962.

McRoy, J. J. A study of the development of the concept of quantity by scalogram analysis. *Dissertation Abstracts,* 1967, **28**, 1231–1232.

Mednick, S. A. A learning theory approach to research in schizophrenia. *Psychological Bulletin,* 1958, **55**, 316–327.

Mednick, S. A., & Lehtinen, L. E. Stimulus generalization as a function of age in children. *Journal of Experimental Psychology,* 1957, **53**, 180–183.

Mehler, J., & Bever, T. J. Cognitive capacity of very young children. *Science,* 1967, **158**, 141–142.

Melton, A. W. (Ed.) *Categories of human learning.* New York: Academic Press, 1964.

Menzel, E. W., Jr. Naturalistic and experimental approaches to primate behavior. In E. P. Willems & H. L. Raush (Eds.), *Naturalistic viewpoints in psychological research.* New York: Holt, 1969. Pp. 78–121.

Meredith, W. Rotation to achieve factorial invariance. *Psychometrika,* 1964, **29**, 187–206.

Merleau-Ponty, M. *The structure of behavior.* Boston: Beacon Press, 1963.

Meyer, W. J., & Bendig, A. W. A longitudinal study of the Primary Mental Abilities Test. *Journal of Educational Psychology,* 1961, **52**, 50–60.

Miles, C. C. & Miles, W. R. The correlation of intelligence scores and chronological age from early to later maturity. *American Journal of Psychology,* 1932, **44**, 44–78.

Milgram, N. A. Verbal context versus visual compound in paired-associate learning by children. *Journal of Experimental Child Psychology,* 1967, **5**, 597–603.

Milgram, S. The experience of living in cities. *Science,* 1970, **167**, 1461–1468.

Mischel, W. Continuity and change in personality. *American Psychologist,* 1969, **24**, 1012–1018.

Mitchell, J. C. On quantification in social anthropology. In A. L. Epstein (Ed.), *The craft of social anthropology.* London: Tavistock, 1967. Pp. 17–45.

Mitchell, R. E. The Survey Research Center, University of California, Berkeley. *International Social Science Journal,* 1964, **16,** 86–89.

Mitchell, R. E. Information storage and retrieval. Part I: Information services. In D. L. Sills (Ed.), *International encyclopedia of the social sciences.* Vol. 7. New York: MacMillan, 1968. Pp. 304–314.

Moede, W. Die Richtlinien der Leitungspsychologie. *Industrielle Psychotechnologie,* 1927, **4,** 193–209.

Moley, B. E., Olson, F. A., Halwes, T. G., & Flavell, J. H. Production deficiency in young children's clustered recall. *Developmental Psychology,* 1969, **1,** 26–34.

Moltz, H. Imprinting: Empirical bases and theoretical significance. *Psychological Bulletin,* 1960, **57,** 291–314.

Moltz, H. Imprinting: An epigenetic approach. *Psychological Review,* 1963, **70,** 123–138.

Monge, R. F. Experimental tests from the Syracuse Adult Development Study. Personal Communication 1971.

Morris, G. S. The final cause as principle of cognition and principle in nature. (Reprinted from *Journal of the Transactions of the Victoria Institute or Philosophical Society of Great Britain*). London: Robert Hardwicke, 1875.

Moscati, S. *Ancient Semitic civilizations.* London: Elek, 1957.

Mumford, L. *The myth of the machine.* Vol. II. New York: Harcourt, 1970.

Murdoch, W., & Connell, J. All about ecology. *The Center Magazine,* 1970, **3,** No. 1, 56–63.

Murdock, G. P. *Ethnographic atlas.* Pittsburgh: University of Pittsburgh Press, 1967.

Murdock, G. P., Ford, C. S., Hudson, A. E., Kennedy, R., Simmons, L. W., & Whiting, J. W. M. *Outline of cultural materials.* New Haven: HRAF Press, 1950.

Murray, F. B. Cognitive conflict and reversibility training in the acquisition of length conservation. *Journal of Educational Psychology,* 1968, **59,** 82–87.

Murray, J. P., & Youniss, J. Achievement of inferential transitivity and its relation to serial ordering. *Child Development,* 1968, **39,** 1259–1268.

Mussen, P. H. (Ed.) *Handbook of research methods in child development.* New York: Wiley, 1960.

Mussen, P. H. (Ed.) *Carmichael's manual of child psychology.* (3rd ed.) New York: Wiley, 1970.

Nadel, S. F. *The foundation of social anthropology.* London: Cohen & West, 1951.

Nagel, E. Determinism and development. In D. B. Harris (Ed.), *The concept of development.* Minneapolis: University of Minnesota Press, 1957. Pp. 15–24.

Naroll, R. Two solutions to Galton's problem. *Philosophy of Science,* 1961, **28,** 15–39.

Naroll, R. On ethnic unit classification. *Current Anthropology,* 1964, **5,** 282–312. (a)

Naroll, R. A fifth solution to Galton's problem. *American Anthropologist,* 1964, **66,** 863–867. (b)

Nassefat, M. *Etude quantitative sur l'évolution des opérations intellectuelles.* Neuchatel: Delachaux & Niestlé, 1963.

Neill, A. S. *Summerhill: A radical approach to child rearing.* New York: Hart, 1960.

Nesselroade, J. R. A comparison of cross-product and differential R-factoring regarding cross study stability of change patterns. Unpublished doctoral dissertation, University of Illinois, 1967. (a)

Nesselroade, J. R. A model for psychological states, moods, and role sets. Paper presented at the conference on Modern Personality Theory, University of Illinois, November 1967. (b)

Nesselroade, J. R. Application of multivariate strategies to problems of measuring and structuring long-term change. In L. R. Goulet & P. B. Baltes (Eds.), *Life-span developmental psychology: Theory and research.* New York: Academic Press, 1970. Pp. 193–207.

Nesselroade, J. R. Note on the "longitudinal factor analysis" model. *Psychometrika,* 1972, **37,** 187–191.

Nesselroade, J. R. Faktorenanalyse von Kreuzprodukten zur Beschreibung von Veränderungs-phänomenen (change). *Zeitschrift für Experimentelle und Angewandte Psychologie,* 1973, in press.

Nesselroade, J. R., & Baltes, P. B. On a dilemma of comparative factor analysis: A study of factor matching based on random data. *Educational and Psychological Measurement,* 1970, **30,** 935–948.

Nesselroade, J. R., Baltes, P. B., & Labouvie, E. W. Evaluating factor invariance in oblique space: Baseline data generated from random numbers. *Multivariate Behavioral Research,* 1971, **6,** 233–241.

Nesselroade, J. R., & Bartsch, T. W. Multivariate experimental perspectives on the construct validity of the trait-state distinction. In R. B. Cattell & R. M. Dreger (Eds.), *Handbook of modern personality study.* 1973, in press.

Nesselroade, J. R., & Cattell, R. B. Examination of short-term invariance and stability of personality factor structure. Unpublished manuscript, West Virginia University, 1970.

Nesselroade, J. R., Schaie, K. W., & Baltes, P. B. Ontogenetic and generational components of structural and quantitative change in adult cognitive behavior. *Journal of Gerontology,* 1972, **27,** 222–228.

Nestle, W. *Vom Mythos zum Lagos.* Stuttgart: Kröner, 1940.

Neugarten, B. L. (Ed.) *Middle age and aging.* Chicago: University of Chicago Press, 1968.

Neugarten, B. L. Continuities and discontinuities of psychological issues into adult life. *Human Development,* 1969, **12,** 121–130.

Nichols, R. C. The national merit twin study. In S. G. Vandenberg (Ed.), *Methods and goals in human behavior genetics.* New York: Academic Press, 1965. Pp. 231–242.

Nietzsche, F. W. *Die Geburt der Tragödie.* Stuttgart: Kröner, 1872. (*The birth of tragedy.* New York: Doubleday, 1956).

Nunnally, J. C. *Psychometric theory.* New York: McGraw-Hill, 1967.

Orpet, R. E., & Meyers, C. E. Discriminant function analysis of conservation stage by structure of intellect and conceptual style variables. Paper presented at the meeting of the American Psychological Association, Miami, Florida, September 1970.

Osgood, C. E. The cross-cultural generality of visual-verbal synthetic tendencies. *Behavioral Sciences,* 1960, **5,** 146–169.

Osgood, C. E. Semantic differential technique in the comparative study of cultures. *American Anthropologist,* 1964, **66,** Suppl., 171–200.

Osgood, C. E. Cross-cultural comparability in attitude measurement via multilingual semantic differentials. In I. D. Steiner, & M. Fishbein (Eds.), *Current studies in social psychology.* New York: Holt, 1965. Pp. 95–107.

Osgood, C. E. On the strategy of cross-cultural research into subjective culture. *Social Science Information,* 1967, VI, **1,** 5–37.

Osgood, C. E. Toward a wedding of insufficiencies. In T. R. Dixon & D. L. Horton (Eds.), *Verbal behavior and general behavior theory.* Englewood Cliffs, New Jersey: Prentice-Hall, 1968. Pp. 495–519.

Osgood, C. E., Suci, G. J., & Tannenbaum, P. H. *The measurement of meaning.* Urbana: University of Illinois Press, 1957.

Overall, J. E. Note on the scientific status of factors. *Psychological Bulletin,* 1964, **61,** 270–276.

Overton, W. F. Piaget's theory of intellectual development and progressive education. In J. R. Squire (Ed.), *A new look at progressive education.* Washington: Association for Supervision and Curriculum Development, 1972. Pp. 88–105.

Owens, W. A. Age and mental ability: A second adult follow-up. *Journal of Educational Psychology,* 1966, **57,** 311–325.

Palermo, D. S. Mediated association in a paired-associate transfer task. *Journal of Experimental Psychology,* 1962, **64,** 234–238.

Pap, A. *Elements of analytic philosophy.* New York: Macmillan, 1949.

Papalia, D., & Hooper, F. H. A developmental comparison of identity and equivalence conservations. Paper presented at the meeting of the Eastern Psychological Association, New York, April 1971.

Payne, T. R. *S. L. Rubinstein and the philosophical foundation of Soviet psychology*. New York: Humanities Press, 1968.

Pepper, S. C. *World hypotheses*. Berkeley, California: University of California Press, 1942.

Peters, D. L. Verbal mediators and cue discrimination in the transition from nonconservation to conservation of number. *Child Development*, 1970, **41**, 707–722.

Peters, R. S. *The concept of motivation*. New York: Humanities Press, 1958.

Peters, R. S. (Ed.) *Brett's history of psychology*. Cambridge, Massachusetts: MIT Press, 1962.

Phillips, E. L. Achievement Place: Token reinforcement procedures in a home-style rehabilitation setting for "pre-delinquent" boys. *Journal of Applied Behavior Analysis*, 1969, **1**, 213–223.

Piaget, J. *Introduction a l'epistemologie genetique*. (3 Vols.) Paris: Presses Universitaires de France, 1950.

Piaget, J. Les stades du développement intellectuel de l'enfant et de l'adolescent. In P. Osterrieth et al. (Eds.), *Le problème des stades en psychologie de l'enfant*. Paris: Presses Universitaires de France, 1955. Pp. 33–42.

Piaget, J. *Psychologie der Intelligenz*. Zürich: Rascher, 1958.

Piaget, J. The general problems of the psychobiological development of the child. In J. M. Tanner & B. Inhelder (Eds.), *Discussions on child development: Proceedings of the World Health Organization study group on the psychobiological development of the child*. Vol. IV. New York: International Universities Press, 1960. Pp. 3–27.

Piaget, J. Three lectures. In R. E. Ripple & V. N. Rockcastle (Eds.), *Piaget rediscovered*. Ithaca, New York: Cornell University Press, 1964. Pp. 6–48.

Piaget, J. *Six psychological studies*. New York: Random House, 1967.

Piaget, J. Piaget's theory. In P. H. Mussen (Ed.), *Carmichael's manual of child psychology*. New York: Wiley, 1970. Pp. 703–732. (a)

Piaget, J. *Structuralism*. New York: Basic Books, 1970. (b)

Piaget, J., & Inhelder, B. *The child's conception of space*. London: Routledge & Kegan Paul, 1956.

Piaget, J., & Inhelder, B. *The psychology of the child*. New York: Basic Books, 1969.

Piaget, J., Inhelder, B., & Szeminska, A. *The child's conception of geometry*. New York: Basic Books, 1960.

Pinard, A., & Laurendeau, M. "Stage" in Piaget's cognitive-developmental theory: Exegesis of a concept. In D. Elkind & J. H. Flavell (Eds.), *Studies in cognitive development: Essays in honor of Jean Piaget*. New York: Oxford University Press, 1969. Pp. 121–170.

Pirenne, H. *Mohammed and Charlemagne*. New York: Norton, 1939.

Platt, L., & Parkes, A. S. *Social and genetic influences on life and death*. New York: Plenum Press, 1967.

Pollack, R. H. & Chaplin, M. R. Perceptual behavior: The necessity for a developmental approach to its study. *Acta Psychologica*, 1963, **21**, 371–376.

Postman, L. Studies of learning to learn II: Changes in transfer as a function of method of practice and class of verbal materials. *Journal of Verbal Learning and Verbal Behavior*, 1964, **3**, 437–449.

Postman, L. Experimental analysis of learning to learn. In G. H. Bower and J. T. Spence (Eds.), *The psychology of learning and motivation*. Vol. 3. New York: Academic Press, 1969. Pp. 241–297.

Postman, L., & Tolman, E. C. Brunswik's probabilistic functionalism. In S. Koch, (Ed.), *Psychology: A study of a science*. Vol. 1. New York: McGraw-Hill, 1959. Pp. 502–564.

Powell, H. A. An analysis of present day social structure in the Trobriand Islands. Unpublished doctoral dissertation, University of London, 1957.

Price-Williams, D. R. A. A study concerning concepts of conservation of quantity among primitive children. *Acta Psychologica*, 1961, **18**, 297–305.

Price-Williams, D. R. A. Abstract and concrete modes of classification in a primitive society. *British Journal of Educational Psychology,* 1962, **32**, 50–61.

Proshansky, H. M., Ittelson, W. H., & Rivlin, L. G. (Eds.) *Environmental psychology.* New York: Holt, 1970.

Przeworski, A., & Teune, H. Equivalence in cross-national research. *Public Opinion Quarterly,* 1966, **30**, 551–568.

Ramsay, A. O., & Hess, E. H. A laboratory approach to the study of imprinting. *Wilson Bulletin,* 1954, **66**, 196–206.

Rao, C. R. Some statistical methods for comparison of growth curves. *Biometrics,* 1958, **14**, 1–17.

Rasch, G. *Probabilistic models for some intelligence and attainment tests.* Kopenhagen: Nielson & Lydiche, 1960.

Rasch, G. An item-analysis which takes individual differences into account. *British Journal of Mathematical and Statistical Psychology,* 1966, **19**, 49–57.

Rashevsky, N. Is the concept of an organism as a machine a useful one? *Scientific Monthly,* 1955, **80**, 31–35.

Reese, H. W. The distance effect in transposition in the intermediate size problem. *Journal of Comparative and Physiological Psychology,* 1962, **55**, 528–531. (a)

Reese, H. W. Verbal mediation as a function of age level. Psychological Bulletin, 1962, **59**, 502–509. (b)

Reese, H. W. Imagery in paired-associate learning. *Journal of Experimental Child Psychology,* 1965, **2**, 290–296.

Reese, H. W., & Overton, W. F. Models of development and theories of development. In L. R. Goulet & P. B. Baltes (Eds.), *Life-span developmental psychology: Theory and research.* New York: Academic Press, 1970. Pp. 115–145.

Reinert, G. Comparative factor analytic studies of intelligence throughout the human life span. In L. R. Goulet & P. B. Baltes (Eds.), *Life-span developmental psychology: Research and theory.* New York: Academic Press, 1970. Pp. 467–484.

Rest, J., Turiel, E., & Kohlberg, L. Relations between level of moral judgment and preference and comprehension of the moral judgment of others. *Journal of Personality,* 1969, **37**, 225–252.

Riegel, K. F. Age and cultural differences as determinants of word associations: Suggestions for their analysis. *Psychological Reports,* 1965, **16**, 75–78.

Riegel, K. F. Development of language: Suggestions for a verbal fallout model. *Human Development,* 1966, **9**, 97–120.

Riegel, K. F. History as a nomothetic science: Some generalization from theories and research in developmental psychology. *Journal of Social Issues,* 1969, **25**, 99–127.

Riegel, K. F. The language acquisition process: A reinterpretation of selected research findings. In L. R. Goulet & P. B. Baltes (Eds.), *Life-span developmental psychology: Research and theory.* New York: Academic Press, 1970. Pp. 351–399. (a)

Riegel, K. F. Relational interpretation of the language acquisition process. In G. B. Flores d'Arcais & W. J. M. Levelt (Eds.), *Advances in psycholinguistics.* Amsterdam: North-Holland Publ., 1970. Pp. 224–236. (b)

Riegel, K. F. The influence of economic and political ideology upon the development of developmental psychology. *Psychological Bulletin,* 1972 (in press). (a)

Riegel, K. F. Time and change in the development of the individual and society. In J. Gewirtz (Ed.), (untitled). New York: Academic Press, 1972 (in press). (b)

Riegel, K. F., & Riegel, R. M. Development, drop, and death. Unpublished manuscript. Department of Psychology, University of Michigan, 1971.

Riegel, K. R., Riegel, R. M., & Meyer, G. Socio-psychological factors of aging: A cohort-sequential analysis. *Human Development,* 1967, **10**, 27–56. (a)

Riegel, K. F., Riegel, R. M., & Meyer, G. A study of the drop-out rates in longitudinal research on aging and the prediction of death. *Journal of Personality and Social Psychology,* 1967, **4**, 342–348. (b)

Riegel, K. F., Riegel, R. M., & Meyer, G. The prediction of retest resisters in research on aging. *Journal of Gerontology,* 1968, **23**, 370–374.

Riley, M. W., Foner, A., Hess, B., & Toby, M. L. Socialization for the middle and later years. In D. A. Goslin (Ed.), *Handbook of socialization theory and research.* Chicago: Rand McNally, 1969. Pp. 951–982.

Risley, T. R. The effects and side effects of punishing the autistic behaviors of a deviant child. *Journal of Applied Behavior Analysis,* 1968, **1**, 21–35.

Risley, T. R. & Baer, D. M. Operant conditioning: "Develop" is a transitive, active verb. In B. Calwell & H. Ricciuti (Eds.), *Review of child development research.* Vol. III. *Social influence and social action.* In press.

Risley, T. R., & Wolf, M. M. Establishing functional speech in echolalic children. *Behaviour Research and Therapy,* 1967, **5**, 73–88.

Roberts, D. M. Abilities and learning: A brief review and discussion of empirical studies. *Journal of School Psychology,* 1968-69, **7**, 12–21.

Rodgers, D. Behavior genetics and overparticularization: An historical perspective. In J. N. Spuhler (Ed.), *Genetic diversity and human behavior.* Chicago: Aldine, 1967. Pp. 47–59.

Rokkan, S. Archives for secondary analysis of sample survey data: An early inquiry into the prospects for Western Europe. *International Social Science Journal,* 1964, 16, 49–62.

Rose, C. L. Representativeness of volunteer subjects in a longitudinal aging study. *Human Development,* 1965, **8**, 152–156.

Rosenbleuth, A., & Wiener, N. The role of models in science. *Philosophy of Science,* 1954, **12**, 316–321.

Ross, W. D. *Aristotle.* Cleveland: World Publishing Co., 1959.

Rothenberg, B., & Orost, J. The training of conservation of number in young children. *Child Development,* 1969, **40**, 707–726.

Rummel, R. J. *Applied factor analysis.* Evanston, Illinois: Northwestern University Press, 1970.

Russell, B. On the notion of cause, with applications to the free-will problem. In H. Feigl & M. Brodbeck (Eds.), *Readings in the philosophy of science.* New York: Appleton, 1953. Pp. 387–408.

Rychlak, J. *A philosophy of science for personality theory.* Boston: Houghton, 1968.

Ryder, N. B. The cohort as a concept in the study of social changes. *American Sociological Review,* 1965, **30**, 843–861.

Sapolsky, A. Effect of interpersonal relationships upon verbal conditioning. *Journal of Abnormal and Social Psychology,* 1960, **60**, 241–246.

Schaie, K. W. Tests of hypotheses about differences between two intercorrelation matrices. *Journal of Experimental Education,* 1958, **26**, 241–245.

Schaie, K. W. A general model for the study of developmental problems. *Psychological Bulletin,* 1965, **64**, 92–107.

Schaie, K. W. A reinterpretation of age related changes in cognitive structure and functioning. In L. R. Goulet & P. B. Baltes (Eds.), *Life-span developmental psychology: Research and theory.* New York: Academic Press, 1970. Pp. 485–507.

Schaie, K. W. Cultural change and repeated assessment in the study of the adult personality. Paper presented in symposium on Personality Assessment of the Aged at the meeting of the American Psychological Association, Washington, D. C., September 1971.

Schaie, K. W. Can the longitudinal method be applied to the psychological study of human development? In F. Z. Monks, W. W. Hartup, & J. DeWit (Eds.), *Determinants of behavioral development.* New York: Academic Press, 1972. In press.

Schaie, K. W., & Cattell, R. B. Upper and lower boundary alignment of personality factors measured by the Child Personality Questionnaire. Unpublished manuscript. West Virginia University, 1971.

Schaie, K. W., & Marquette, B. W. Personality in maturity and old age. In R. M. Dreger (Ed.), *Multivariate personality research: Contributions to the understanding of personality in honor of R. B. Cattell*. Baton Rouge, Louisiana: Claitor, 1972.

Schaie, K. W., Rosenthal, F., & Perlman, R. M. Differential mental deterioration of factorially "pure" functions in later maturity. *Journal of Gerontology*, 1953, **8**, 191–196.

Schaie, K. W., & Strother, C. R. Cognitive and personality variables in college graduates of advanced age. In G. A. Talland (Eds.), *Human aging and behavior: Recent advances in research and theory*. New York: Academic Press, 1968. Pp. 281–308. (a)

Schaie, K. W., & Strother, C. R. A cross-sectionel study of age changes in cognitive behavior. *Psychological Bulletin*, 1968, **70**, 671–680. (b)

Schaie, K. W., & Strother, C. R. The effects of time and cohort differences on the interpretation of age changes in cognitive behavior. *Multivariate Behavioral Research*, 1968, **3**, 259–294. (c)

Scheiblechner, H. Eine parameterfreie Modelkontrolle des eindimensionalen probabilistischen Messmodells von Rasch. Unpublished Research Paper of the Psychological Institute of the University of Vienna, January 1970.

Scheuch, E. K. Society as context in cross-cultural comparisons. *Social Science Information*, 1967, VI, **5**, 7–23.

Scheuch, E. K., & Bruening, I. The Zentralarchiv of the University of Cologne. *International Social Science Journal*, 1964, **16**, 77–85.

Schmid, J., & Leiman, J. M. The development of hierarchical factor solutions. *Psychometrika*, 1957, **22**, 53–61.

Schofield, L., & Uzgiris, I. C. Examining behavior and the development of the concept of object. Paper presented at the meeting of the society for Research in child Development, Santa Monica, California, March 1969.

Schon, D. *The displacement of concepts*. London: Tavistock Publications, 1963.

Schooler, K. K. Effect of environment on morale. *Gerontologist*, 1970, **10**, 194–197.

Schumaker, J., & Sherman, J. A. Training generative verb usage by imitation and reinforcement procedures. *Journal of Applied Behavior Analysis*, 1970, **3**, 273–287.

Schwartz, M. M., & Scholnick, E. K. Analysis of logical and perceptual components of conservation of discontinuous quantity. *Child Development*, 1970, **41**, 695–705.

Scott, W. A., & Wertheimer, M. *Introduction to psychological research*. New York: Wiley, 1962.

Sears, P. B. The inexorable problem of space. In P. Shepard & D. McKinley (Eds.), *The subversive science: Essays toward an ecology of man*. Boston: Houghton Mifflin, 1969. Pp. 77–93.

Sears, R. R. Transcultural variables and conceptual equivalence. In B. Kaplan (Ed.), *Studying personality cross-culturally*. New York: Harper, 1961. Pp. 445–455.

Seeger, R. J. Beyond operationalism. *Scientific Monthly*, 1954, **79**, 226–227.

Segall, M. H., Campbell, D. T., & Herskovits, M. Cultural differences in the perception of geometric illusions. *Science*, 1963, **139**, 769–771.

Sells, S. B. Dimensions of stimulus situations which account for behavior variance. In S. B. Sells (Ed.), *Stimulus determinants of behavior*. New York: Ronald Press, 1963. Pp. 3–15.

Sells, S. B. Ecology and the science of psychology. In E. P. Willems & H. L. Raush (Eds.), *Naturalistic viewpoints in psychological research*. New York: Holt, 1969. Pp. 1–30.

Shantz, C., A developmental study of Piaget's theory of logical multiplication. *Merrill-Palmer Quarterly of Behavior and Development*, 1967, **13**, 121–137.

Shantz, C. Egocentrism in children: Its generality and correlates. Unpublished manuscript, Merrll-Palmer Institute, 1968.

Shantz, C., & Sigel, I. E. *Logical operations and concepts of conservation in children: A training study*. (Final Report, Grant No. OEG-3-6-068463-1645) Washington, D. C.: U. S. Office of Education, 1967.

Shantz, C. & Smock, C. Development of distance conservation and the spatial coordinate system.

Child Development, 1966, **37**, 943–948.

Shepp, B. E., & Turrisi, F. D. Learning and transfer of mediating responses in discriminative learning. In N. R. Ellis (Ed.), *International review of research in mental retardation.* Vol. 2. New York: Academic Press, 1966. Pp. 86–120.

Siegelmann, E., & Block, J. Two parallel scalable sets of Piagetian tasks. *Child Development,* 1969, **40**, 951–956.

Sigel, I. E., Anderson, L. M., & Shapiro, H. Categorization behavior of lower- and middle-class Negro preschool children: Differences in dealing with representation of familiar objects. *Journal of Negro Education,* 1966, **35**, 218–229.

Sigel, I. E., & Hooper, F. H. *Logical thinking in children: Research based on Piaget's theory.* New York: Holt, 1968.

Sigel, I. E., Roeper, A., & Hooper, F. H. A training procedure for acquisition of Piaget's conservation of quantity: A pilot study and its replication. *British Journal of Educational Psychology,* 1966, **36**, 301–311.

Sixtl, F. Faktoreninvarianz und Faktoreninterpretation. *Psychologische Beiträge,* 1967, **10**, 99–111.

Sixtl, F. Kritik an der theoretischen Konzeption der Leistungstests: Die faktische Inkonsistenz der Testtheorie. In K. Ingenkamp & T. Marsolek (Eds.), *Möglichkeiten und Grenzen der Testanweisung in der Schule.* Paedagog. Zentr. Veroeffentl. Reihe C: Berichte Bd. 15. Weinheim: Beltz, 1968. Pp. 467–476.

Sixtl, F., & Fittkau, B. Critical issues in comparing factorial structures. Unpublished manuscript, Department of Psychology, University of Saar, Germany, 1968.

Skard, A. G., Inhelder, B., Noelting, G., Murphy, L. B., & Thomae, H. Longitudinal research in personality development. In H. David & J. C. Brengelmann (Eds.), *Perspectives in personality research.* London: Crosby Lockwood & Son, 1960. Pp. 247–269.

Skinner, B. F. Experimental psychology. In W. Dennis (Ed.), *Current trends in psychology.* Pittsburgh: University of Pittsburgh Press, 1947. Pp. 16–49.

Skinner, B. F. *Walden two.* New York: Macmillan, 1948.

Slamecka, N. J. A methodological analysis of shift paradigms in human discrimination learning. *Psychological Bulletin,* 1968, **69**, 423–438.

Sluckin, W. *Imprinting and early learning.* London: Methuen, 1964.

Smedslund, J. Apprentissage des notions de la conservation et de la transitivité du poids. L'apprentissage des structures logiques. *Etudes d'epistemologié génétique,* 1959, **IX**, 85–124.

Smedslund, J. The acquisition of conservation of substance and weight in children: II. External reinforcement of conservation of weight and of the operations of addition and subtraction. *Scandinavian Journal of Psychology,* 1961, **2**, 71–84. (a)

Smedslund, J. The acquisition of conservation of substance and weight in children: III. Extinction of conservation of weight acquired "normally" and by means of empirical controls on a balance scale. *Scandinavian Journal of Psychology,* 1961, **2**, 85–87. (b)

Smedslund, J. Development of concrete transitivity of length in children. *Child Development,* 1963, **34**, 389–405.

Smedslund, J. Concrete reasoning: A study of intellectual development. *Monographs of the Society for Research in Child Development,* 1964, **29** (2, Whole No. 93).

Smedslund, J. The development of transitivity of length: A comment on Braine's reply. *Child Development,* 1965, **35**, 577–580.

Smedslund, J. Conservation and resistance to extinction: A comment on Hall and Simpson's article. *Merrill-Palmer Quarterly of Behavior and Development,* 1968, **14**, 211–214.

Smith, F. V. *Attachment of the young.* Imprinting and other developments. Edinburgh: Oliver & Boyd, 1969.

Smith, I. The effects of training procedures upon the acquisition of conservation of weight. *Child Development,* 1968, **39**, 515–526.

Smith, M. B. Anthropology and psychology. In J. Gillin (Ed.), *For a science of social man: Convergences in anthropology, psychology, and sociology.* New York: MacMillan, 1954. Pp. 32–66.

Smith, N. W. Some background considerations to the development of Greek psychology. Unpublished manuscript, Department of Psychology, State University of New York, Plattsburgh, 1970.

Spada, H. F. Intelligenztheorie und Intelligenzmessung. *Psychologische Beiträge*, 1970, **12**, 84–96.

Spence, K. W. The nature of discrimination learning in animals. *Psychological Review*, 1963, **43**, 427–449.

Spence, K. W. A theory of emotionally based drive (D) and its relation to performance in simple learning situations. *American Psychologist*, 1958, **13**, 131–141.

Spence, K. W. Cognitive factors in the extinction of the conditioned eyelid response in humans. *Science*, 1963, **140**, 1224–1225.

Spence, K. W. Anxiety level and performance in eyelid conditioning. *Psychological Bulletin*, 1964, **61**, 129–139.

Spengler, O. *Der Untergang des Abendlandes*. München: Beck, 1918–1922. (*The decline of the West*. New York: Knopf, 1946).

Spiker, C. C. The hypothesis of stimulus interaction and an explanation of stimulus compounding. In L. P. Lipsitt & C. C. Spiker (Eds.), *Advances in child development and behavior*. Vol. 1. New York: Academic Press, 1963. Pp. 233–264.

Staats, A. *Child learning, intelligence, and personality: Principles of a behavioral interaction approach*. New York: Harper, 1971.

Stalin, J. *Marxism and linguistics*. New York: International Publishers, 1951.

Staub, E. A child in distress: The influence of age and number of witnesses on children's attempts to help. *Journal of Personality and Social Psychology*, 1970, **14**, 130–140.

Stavrianos, B. K. Research methods in cultural anthropology in relation to scientific criteria. *Psychological Review*, 1950, **57**, 334–344.

Steinhagen, K. Untersuchung zur Veränderung von faktoriellen Intelligenzstrukturen im Erwachsenenalter. *Diagnostica*, 1970, **16**, 149–164.

Stene, I. Einführung in Raschs Theorie der psychologischen Messung. In G. H. Fischer (Ed.), *Psychologische Testtheorie*, Bern: Huber, 1960. Pp. 229–268.

Stevenson, H. W., & Bitterman, M. E. The distance effect in the transposition of intermediate size by children. *American Journal of Psychology*, 1955, **68**, 274–279.

Streib, G. F. Participants and drop-outs in a longitudinal study. *Journal of Gerontology*, 1966, **21**, 200–201.

Strodtbeck, F. L. Considerations of meta-method in cross-cultural studies. In A. K. Romney & R. G. D'Andrade (Eds.), Transcultural studies in cognition. *American Anthropologist*, 1964, **66**, Special Publ., 223–229.

Sutton-Smith, B. Developmental laws and the experimentalist's ontology. *Merrill-Palmer Quarterly of Behavior and Development*, 1970, **16**, 253–260.

Sweney, A. B., & Cattell, R. B. Dynamic factors in twelve year old children as revealed in measures of integrated motivation. *Journal of Clinical Psychology*, 1961, **17**, 360–369.

Taylor, C. *The explanation of behavior*. New York: Humanities Press, 1964.

Terhune, K. W. An examination of some contributing demographic variables in a cross-national study. *Journal of Social Psychology*, 1963, **59**, 209–219.

Textor, R. B. *A cross-cultural summary*. New Haven: HRAF Press, 1967.

Thiessen, D., & Rodgers, D. Behavior genetics as the study of mechanism-specific behavior. In J. N. Spuhler (Ed.), *Genetic diversity and human behavior*. Chicago: Aldine, 1967. Pp. 61–73.

Thompson, W. R. Multivariate experiment in behavior genetics. In R. B. Cattell (Ed.), *Handbook of multivariate experimental psychology*. Chicago: Rand McNally, 1966.

Thompson, W. R., & Grusec, J. Studies of early experience. In P. H. Mussen (Ed.), *Carmichael's manual of child psychology*. New York: Wiley, 1970. Pp. 565–701.

Thurstone, L. L., & Thurstone, T. G. Factorial studies of intelligence. *Psychometric Monographs*, 1941, **No. 2**.

Tolman, E. C. A theoretical analysis of the relation between sociology and psychology. *Journal of Abnormal and Social Psychology,* 1952, **47**, 291–298.

Toulmin, S. *The philosophy of science: An introduction.* London: Hutchinson University Library, 1962.

Tryon, R. C. A theory of psychological components—an alternative to "mathematical factors." *Psychological Review,* 1935, **42**, 425–454.

Tucker, L. R. An inter-battery method of factor analysis. *Psychometrika,* 1958, **23**, 111–136.

Tucker, L. R. Learning theory and multivariate experiment: Illustration by determination of generalized learning curves. In R. B. Cattell (Ed.), *Handbook of multivariate experimental psychology.* Chicago: Rand McNally, 1966. Pp. 476–501. (a)

Tucker, L. R. Some mathematical notes on three-mode factor analysis. *Psychometrika,* 1966, **31**, 279–311. (b)

Turiel, E. Developmental processes in the child's moral thinking. In P. H. Mussen, J. Langer, & M. Covington (Eds.), *Trends and issues in developmental psychology.* New York: Holt, 1969. Pp. 92–133.

Turner, M. *Psychology and the philosophy of science.* New York: Appleton, 1968.

Tylor, E. B. On a method of investigating the development of institutions: Applied to laws of marriage and descent. *Journal of the Anthropological Institute of Great Britain and Ireland,* 1889, **18**, 245–272.

Underwood, B. J. Degree of learning and the measurement of forgetting. *Journal of Verbal Learning and Verbal Behavior,* 1964, **3**, 112–129. (a)

Underwood, B. J. The representativeness of rote verbal learning. In A. W. Melton (Ed.), *Categories of human learning.* New York: Academic Press, 1964. Pp. 48–78. (b)

Underwood, B. J., & Schulz, R. W. *Meaningfulness and verbal learning.* Philadelphia: Lippincott, 1960.

Uzgiris, I. Stuational generality of conservation. *Child Development,* 1964, **35**, 831–842.

Vandenberg, S. G. The hereditary abilities study: Hereditary components in a psychological test battery. *American Journal of Human Genetics,* 1962, **14**, 220–237.

Vandenberg, S. G. Multivariate analysis of twin differences. In S. G. Vandenberg (Ed.), *Methods and goals in human behavior genetics.* New York: Academic Press, 1965.

Vandenberg, S. G. Human behavior genetics: Present status and suggestions for future research. *Merrill-Palmer Quarterly of Behavior and Development,* 1969, **15**, 120–154.

Van den Daele, L. D. Qualitative models in developmental analysis. *Developmental Psychology,* 1969, **1**, 303–310.

Vandeventer, M. Development of distance conservation and the spatial coordinate system reconsidered. *Research Bulletin,* Princeton, New Jersey: Educational Testing Service, 1968.

Vernon, P. E. Environmental handicaps and intellectual development. *British Journal of Educational Psychology,* 1965, **35**, Part II, 13–22.

Vernon, P. E. Practice and coaching effects in intelligence tests. *Education Forum,* 1954, **18**.

Vince, M. A. Social facilitation of hatching in the bobwhite quail. *Animal Behaviour,* 1964, **12**, 531–534.

Vince, M. A. Artificial acceleration of hatching in quail embryos. *Animal Behaviour,* 1966, **14**, 39–394. (a)

Vince, M. A. Potential stimulation produced by avian embryos. *Animal Behaviour,* 1966, **14**, 34–40.(b)

Vince, M. A. The effect of rate of stimulation on hatching time in the Japanese quail. *British Poultry Science,* 1968, **9**, 87–91. (a)

Vince, M. A. Retardation as a factor in the sychronization of hatching. *Animal Behaviour,* 1968, **16**, 332–335. (b)

Vince, M. A., & Cheng, R. The retardation of hatching in Japanese Quail. *Animal Behaviour,* 1970, **18**, 210–214.

Vineberg, S. E. The environment as a network of judgments regarding staff roles. Paper presented at the American Congress of Rehabilitation Medicine, New York, August 1970.

Vineberg, S. E., & Levine, A. J. The network of perceptions and judgments regarding staff roles. Paper presented at the meeting of the American Psychological Association, Washington, D. C., September 1969.

Vineberg, S. E., & Willems, E. P. Observation and analysis of patient behavior in the rehabilitation hospital. *Archives of Physical Medicine and Rehabilitation,* 1971, **52**, 8–14.

Vygotskii, L. S. II. The problems of cultural development of the child. *Journal of Genetic Psychology,* 1929, **36**, 415–534.

Vygotskii, L. S. *Thought and language.* Cambridge, Massachusetts: MIT Press, 1962.

Wahrstrom, M., & Boersma, F. J. The influence of test-wiseness upon achievement. *Educational and Psychological Measurement,* 1968, **28**, 413–420.

Wapner, S. Organismic-developmental theory: Some applications to cognition. In P. H. Mussen, J. Langer, & M. Covington (Eds.), *Trends and issues in developmental psychology.* New York: Holt, 1969. Pp. 38–67.

Watson, J. B. *Behavior: An introduction to comparative psychology.* New York: Holt, 1914.

Watson, J. S. Conservation: An S-R analysis. In I. E. Sigel & F. H. Hooper (Eds.), *Logical thinking in children: Research based on Piaget's theory.* New York: Holt, 1968. Pp. 447–459.

Webb, E. J., Campbell, D. T., Schwartz, R. D., & Sechrest, L. *Unobtrusive measures.* Chicago: Rand McNally, 1966.

Wechsler, D. *The measurement of adult intelligence.* (3rd ed.) Baltimore: Williams & Wilkins, 1944.

Weinert, F. Über den Einfluss kurzzeitiger Lernprozesse auf die Denkleistungen von Kindern. In F. Merz (Ed.), *Bericht über den 25. Kongress der Deutschen Gesellschaft für Psychologie in Münster,* 1966. Göttingen: Hogrefe, 1967. Pp. 395–400.

Weir, M. W. Developmental changes n problem-solving strategies. *Psychological Review,* 1964, **71**, 473–490.

Werner, H. Process and achivement—A basic problem of education and developmental psychology. *Harvard Educational Review,* 1937, **7**, 353–368.

Werner, H. *Einführung in die Entwicklungspsychologie.* Leipzig: Barth, 1926. (*Comparative psychology of mental development.* New York: Follett, 1948.

Werner, H. *Comparative psychology of mental development.* New York: International Universities Press, 1948.

Werner, H. The concept of development from a nomparative and organismic point of giew. In D. B. Harris (Ed.), *The concept of development.* Minneapolis: University of Minnesota Press, 1957. Pp. 125–148.

Werner, H. *Einführung in die Entwicklungspsychologie.* München: Barth, 1959.

Werner, H., & Kaplan, B. The acquisition of word meanings: A developmental study. *Monographs of the Society for Research in Child Development,* 1952, **15**, 190–200.

Werner, H., & Kaplan, B. *Symbol formation.* New York: Wiley, 1963.

Wheeler, A. J., & Sulzer, B. Operant training and generalization of a verb response form in a speech-deficient child. *Journal of Applied Behavior Analysis,* 1970, **3**, 139–147.

Whimbey, A. E., & Denenberg, V. H. Experimental programming of life histories: The factor structure underlying experimentally created individual differences. *Behaviour,* 1967, **28**, 296–314.

White, B. L. *Human infants: Experience and psychological development.* Englewood Cliffs, New Jersey: Prentice-Hall, 1971.

White, S. H. Evidence for a hierarchical arrangement of learning processes. In T. P. Lipsitt & C. C. Spiker (Eds.), *Advances in child development and behavior.* Vol. 2. New York: Academic Press, 1965. Pp. 187–220.

White, S. H. The learning theory approach. In P. H. Mussen (ed.), *Carmichael's manual of child psychology*. New York: Wiley, 1970. Pp. 657–703.

Whiteman, M. Intelligence and learning. *Merrill-Palmer Quarterly of Behavior and Development*, 1964, **10**, 298–309.

Whiting, J. W. M. The cross-cultural method. In G. Lindzey (Ed.), *Handbook of social psychology*. Vol. I: *Theory and method*. Reading, Massachusetts: Addison-Wesley, 1954. Pp. 523–531.

Whiting, J. W. M. Methods and problems in cross-cultural research. In G. Lindzey & E. Aronson (Eds.), *The Handbook of social psychology*. Vol. II. Reading, Massachusetts: Addison-Wesley, 1968. Pp. 693–728.

Whitney, G., McClearn, G. E., & DeFries, J. C. Heritability of alcohol preference in laboratory mice and rats. *Journal of Heredity*, 1970, **61**, 4.

Wicker, A. W. Undermanning, performances, and students' subjective experiences in behavior settings of large and small high schools. *Journal of Personality and Social Psychology*, 1968, **10**, 255–261.

Wicker, A. W. Cognitive complexity, school size, and participation in school behavior settings: A test of the frequency of interaction hypothesis. *Journal of Educational Psychology*, 1969, **60**, 200–203.

Wicker, A. W., & Mehler, A. Assimilation of new members in a large and a small church. *Journal of Applied Psychology*, 1971, **55**, 151–56.

Willems, E. P. Review of research. In R. G. Barker & P. V. Gump, *Big school, small school*. Stanford, California: Stanford University Press, 1964. Pp. 29–37.

Willems, E. P. An ecological orientation in psychology. *Merrill-Palmer Quarterly of Behavior and Development*, 1965, **11**, 317–343.

Willems, E. P. Architecture and psychology: Beyond the honeymoon. *Architecture at Rice*, 1967, **No. 22** (Whole No.). (a)

Willems, E. P. Sense of obligation to high school activities as related to school size and marginality of student. *Child Development*, 1967, **38**, 1247–1260. (b)

Willems, E. P. Toward an explicit rationale for naturalistic research methods. *Human Development*, 1967, **10**, 138–154. (c)

Willems, E. P. Planning a rationale for naturalistic research. In E. P. Willems & H. L. Raush (Eds.), *Naturalistic viewpoints in psychological research*. New York: Holt, 1969. Pp. 44–71.

Willems, E. P. The interface of the hospital environment and patient behavior. Paper presented at the American Congress of Rehabilitation Medicine, New York, August 1970.

Willems, E. P., & Raush, H. L. (Eds.) *Naturalistic viewpoints in psychological research*. New York: Holt, 1969.

Winer, B. J. *Statistical principles in experimental design*. New York: McGraw-Hill, 1962.

Winkel, G. H. The nervous affair between behavior scientists and designers. *Psychology Today*, 1970, **3**, No. 10, 31–35, 74.

Wiseman, S., & Wrigley, J. The comparative effects of coaching and practice on the results of verbal intelligence tests. *British Journal of Psychology*, 1953, **44**, 83–94.

Wohlwill, J. F. A study of the development of the number concept by scalogram analysis. *Journal of Genetic Psychology*, 1960, **97**, 345–377.

Wohlwill, J. F. Piaget's system as a source of empirical research. *Merrill-Palmer Quarterly of Behavior and Development*, 1963, **9**, 253–262.

Wohlwill, J. F. Vers une réformulation du rôle de l'expérience dans le développement cogitif. In J. B. Grize & B. Inhelder (Eds.), *Psychologie et epistemologie génétiques: Thèmes Piagétiens*. Paris: Dunod, 1966. Pp. 211–222.

Wohlwill, J. F. The age variable in psychological research. *Psychological Review*, 1970, **77**, 49–64. (a)

Wohlwill, J. F. The emerging discipline of environmental psychology. *American Psychologist*, 1970, **25**, 303–312. (b)

Wohlwill, J. F. Methodology and research strategy in the study of developmental change. In L. R. Goulet & P. B. Baltes (Eds.), *Life-span developmental psychology: Research and theory.* New York: Academic Press, 1970. Pp. 149–191. (c)

Wohlwill, J. F. The place of structured experience in early cognitive development. *Interchange,* 1970, **1**, 13–27. (d)

Wohlwill, J. F. Correlational methods in the study of developmental change. Unpublished manuscript, Pennsylvania State University, 1971.

Wohlwill, J. F., Fusaro, L., & Devoe, S. Measurement, seriation and conservation: A longitudinal analysis of their interrelationship. Paper presented at the meeting of the Society for Research in Child Development, Santa Monica, California, March 1969.

Wolf, M. M., Giles, D., & Hall, R. V. Experiments with token reinforcement in a remedial classroom. *Behavior Research and Therapy,* 1968, **6**, 51–64.

Wolf, M. M., Risley, T. R., & Mees, H. Application of operant conditioning procedures to the behavior problems of an autistic child. *Behaviour Research and Therapy,* 1964, **1**, 305–312.

Wolff, J. L. Concept-shift and discrimination reversal learning in humans. *Psychological Bulletin,* 1967, **68**, 369–408.

Woodrow, H. Factors in improvement with practice. *Journal of Psychology,* 1939, **7**, 55–70.

Wright, H. F. *Recording and analyzing child behavior.* New York: Harper, 1967.

Wright, H. F. *Children's behavior in communities differing in size.* (5 volumes) Lawrence, Kansas: University of Kansas Press, 1969–1970.

Wundt, W. *Probleme der Völkerpsychologie.* Leipzig: Wiegandt, 1911.

Wyatt, F. The reconstruction of the individual and collective past. In R. W. White (Ed.), *The study of lives: Essays on personality in honor of Henry A. Murray.* New York: Atherton Press, 1963.

Yarrow, M. R., Campbell, J. D., & Burton, R. V. Recollections of childhood: A study of the retrospective method. *Monographs of the Society for Research in Child Development,* 1970, **35** (5, Whole No. 138).

Yeatman, S., & Hirsch, J. Review of D. Rosenthal and S. Kety (Eds.), *The transmission of schizophrenia. Psychiatry,* 1971, **34**, 103–105.

Yeh, J. C. W. Transposition and transfer of absolute responding as functions of learning-set training and stimulus similarity. *Journal of Experimental Child Psychology,* 1970, **10**, 57–66.

Zeiler, M. D. Stimulus definition and choice. In L. P. Lipsitt & C. C. Siker (Eds.), *Advances in child development and behavior.* Vol. 3. New York: Academic Press, 1967. Pp. 125–156.

Zigler, E. Metatheoretical issues in developmental psychology. In M. Marx (Ed.), *Theories in contemporary psychology.* New York: MacMillan, 1963. Pp. 341–369.

Zimbardo, P. G. Physical integration and social segregation of northern Negro college students (1953, 1963, and 1965). Paper presented at the meeting of the Eastern Psychological Association, New York, April 1966.

Author Index

Numbers in italics refer to the pages on which the complete references are listed.

Subject Index

357